ADVANCE PRAISE FOR

AN Educational Psychology
of Methods IN Multicultural Education

"This is a fantastic book that covers the many aspects of today's multicultural education in a pluralistic society. Its content collectively opens the eye of prospective educators and students to gain so much knowledge in social and cultural domains that enhance teaching and learning to better prepare academic instructors for dealing with cultural diversity in the classroom."

Jonas Vangay, Ed.D, PDSO/Director of the International Students Services,
Professor in Cultural Anthropology and Hmong Language,
Merced Community College, California

"This new book is an excellent addition to our essential and expanding compendium of literature on diversity, and I believe all students of critical pedagogy will welcome Vang's contribution and perspective. This…adds to our understanding of the elements of teaching and learning within multicultural communities."

Peter McLaren, Professor, Graduate School of Education, UCLA

"Christopher Vang has put together a brilliantly lucid, splendidly readable, and intellectually synthesized multicultural book that addresses major issues in the teaching and learning circle involving students of diverse backgrounds. This book shows teachers the methods of teaching to reach out to all students and explains the psycho-social environment which both students and teachers are sharing each and every day. I am pleased to recommend this book to all credential students in preparing prospective educators to work with children in the diverse classroom."

Tony Vang, Associate Professor of Teacher Education and Literacy and Early
Education/Hmong BCLAD Coordinator, California State University, Fresno and an elected
member of School Board of Education for Fresno Unified School District

D1558731

AN Educational Psychology
of Methods IN Multicultural
Education

Educational
PSYCHOLOGY

Critical Pedagogical Perspectives

Greg S. Goodman, *General Editor*

Vol. 6

PETER LANG
New York • Washington, D.C./Baltimore • Bern
Frankfurt • Berlin • Brussels • Vienna • Oxford

CHRISTOPHER THAO VANG

AN Educational Psychology *of* Methods IN Multicultural Education

PETER LANG
New York • Washington, D.C./Baltimore • Bern
Frankfurt • Berlin • Brussels • Vienna • Oxford

Library of Congress Cataloging-in-Publication Data

Vang, Christopher T.
An educational psychology of methods in multicultural education / Christopher T. Vang.
p. cm. — (Educational psychology: critical pedagogical perspectives; vol. 6.)
Includes bibliographical references and index.
1. Multicultural education. 2. Educational psychology. I. Title.
LC1099.V36   370.11701'9—dc22   2009048253
ISBN 978-1-4331-0791-7 (hardcover)
ISBN 978-1-4331-0790-0 (paperback)
ISSN 1943-8109

Bibliographic information published by **Die Deutsche Nationalbibliothek**.
Die Deutsche Nationalbibliothek lists this publication in the "Deutsche
Nationalbibliografie"; detailed bibliographic data is available
on the Internet at http://dnb.d-nb.de/.

The paper in this book meets the guidelines for permanence and durability
of the Committee on Production Guidelines for Book Longevity
of the Council of Library Resources.

Contents

PART TWO: THE STUDENT DIVERSITY DOMAIN

Tables and Figures

Figure

Foreword

In the wide and diverse world of writing about multiculturalism, there are many voices seeking our ears, attention, empathy, and humanistic understanding of cultural diversity in today's pluralistic society. What makes this book so appealing to prospective and current multicultural educators is the way it is carefully crafted to help both students and teachers learn, share, understand, and live the values and benefits of multicultural education. Christopher Vang presents multicultural perspectives through a broad array of lenses. His work of synthesis makes this book a brilliantly lucid, splendidly readable, admirably impressive, and most fascinating study of multicultural education.

Vang knows deeply and intimately how diverse students would feel about learning from teachers of similarly broad backgrounds and how teachers would feel about teaching students who do not possess singularly White, middle-class values. In this book, the emphasis upon both the psychosocial and the educational psychology dimensions helps educators understand the feeling tone of teaching and learning by revealing comprehensive pedagogical applications, instructional approaches, and sociocultural paradigms that are responsive to today's multicultural education settings.

Certainly, the field of multicultural education has been fortunate to have some significant and widely renowned stars like Sleeter, Nieto, West, Said, the Lees, the Banks, and McLaren, just to credit a scant few. But from within the Hmong and Southeast Asian community, there have been few scholars equal to the caliber of Christopher Vang. Representing the experience of Southeast Asians, and especially for the Hmong community, Vang offers a new, vibrant, and articulate voice supporting the educational needs of this unique group of diverse students.

The Hmong are special for many reasons. Their nomadic history traces roots to ancient China, and possibly before that in Southern Mongolia. The history of this people is scant because the Chinese denied them their rights to maintain written language, freedom, social justice, equal opportunity, and sociopolitical advancement in order to suppress their growth and development as a people. Given the great expanse of time, perhaps as far back as 2000 BC, it is inconceivable to think of the experiences these people had to endure as the lack of a written history has kept many historians unaware of this people's past. Conveyed almost exclusively through an oral and pictorial history, the Hmong story is only now being revealed in academic and curricular settings.

In the past 50 years, the Hmong have been re-developing their written language, and their culture reflects a diverse amalgam of several dialects (White, Blue, Green, etc.) corresponding to family clans and local Laotian origins. Despite this diversity within the Hmong culture, the Hmong share a common bond with the United States military, the State Department, and especially with the Central Intelligence Agency (CIA). The fact that the Hmong were allies of the United States in the Vietnam War, known as the Secret War's Special Guerrillas Unit (SGU) in Laos, and that they suffered huge losses in support of American troops to rescue American downed pilots in the jungle of Laos, Americans owe the Hmong a great debt and gratitude. In partial re-payment for that support, approximately 60,000 Hmong were brought to the U.S. to be spared political execution, persecution, imprisonment, and extermination by the communist genocide of Cambodians and Laotians after America's departure from Southeast Asia in 1975.

Christopher Vang is one of the thousands of children of Hmong refugees who immigrated to America in the past 35 years through the Hmong refugee resettlement in the Western nations. Speaking only Hmong, Chris lived with his parents and attended American public schools. As he grew, he learned English, and he observed the opportunities available to those pursuing higher education. Vang's intellectual curiosity has been rewarding for both his family and himself. Christopher Vang is currently one of a select few Hmong who have earned a doctorate in higher education.

Vang's true talent is in his ability to describe other Southeast Asians and the Hmong people and to identify their needs to our public school educators. His presentation of the educational psychology of the Southeast Asian students is a boon for any educator eager to explore the uniquely conflicted situation that first-, second-, and third-generation Hmong students experience. Vang knows firsthand experiences of what works with these students, and he carefully describes the teaching methodology best situated for successful relationship building and educational outcomes. This insight has wide applicability for any multicultural educator.

I am proud to introduce Christopher Vang's scholarship achievements as represented by this insightful and well-researched collection. As a long time friend of education and of using the learning process to promote social justice, Vang offers the reader considerable insight through grounded knowledge in issues related to critical pedagogy, psychosocial dimension, instructional strategy, and sociocultural paradigm. Vang's gift is his sensitive voice for the acceptance and engagement of all diverse people in today's pluralistic and multicultural settings.

Therefore, I am honored to recommend his book to all prospective and current educators who are working with children of diverse backgrounds in the public school system. The practical information in this book will benefit both teachers and students in the learning circle.

Dr. Greg S. Goodman
Assistant Professor
Clarion University of Pennsylvania

Preface

As the planet evolves, the multiracial force of mankind is emerging into a new universe, encompassing cultural diversity from all countries of the world. This book, *An Educational Psychology of Methods in Multicultural Education*, was written to help prospective educators address socio-cultural questions, ideas, issues, and curiosities they encounter in multicultural education. This book was designed to appeal to all educators and is based on the premise that the United States of America is a multilingual and multicultural nation made up of people of culturally, economically, religiously, and linguistically diverse backgrounds. Differences in race, ethnicity, culture, religion, social class, and socio-economic status call for comprehensive multicultural education—not only for students, but also for teachers. Today's pre-service and in-service educators—teachers, administrators, parents, and teacher candidates—need to understand how students of various cultures feel, learn, understand, and behave in elementary and secondary schools as well as how these students adjust and adapt to the mainstream society in the communities where they live. The information in this book will lead educators in exploring the socio-cultural issues of cultural diversity and multiculturalism.

What Is Educational Psychology?

Educational psychology invests great interests in learning, knowing, and understanding the applications of scientific methods involving teaching and learning to the study of the behaviors of people in instructional settings. In this book, educational psychology focuses on how teachers and learners feel about the complexities of teaching and learning in a multicultural setting where cultural diversity plays a big role in how teachers teach and how students learn.

What Is in This Book for Educators?

This book is designed for everybody. Here is why: Multicultural education theorists and researchers advocate for *all* students, maintaining that cultural diversity enriches the nation and that educators who learn, understand, and know the underlying psychological issues of multicultural education have a better understanding of *all* people. Understanding differences in race, ethnicity, religion, class, socioeconomic status, language, culture, values, customs, and traditions enables teachers to elevate the socialization process to obtain a higher level of acceptance and respect for *all* people. Multicultural education employs different paradigms and frameworks to promote social justice and seek opportunities, restructuring, changes, and approaches that minimize negative impacts related to diversity in the education of all students. At the same time, multicultural curricula aim for fair practices to maximize educational opportunities, career possibilities, and equal access to quality public education for all.

The U.S. has nearly 300 million people, and the number of diverse people from different cultures and indigenous groups is projected to increase in the next few decades. Consider languages, for example. In 2006 the National Education Association reported that approximately 425 dialects other than English are spoken by elementary and secondary students in American public schools. Multicultural education experts and researchers predict that diverse cultural groups will grow at different rates over the next two decades. According to Manning and Baruth (2009) and Banks (2008), the Hispanic student population will outnumber the student population of African Americans and European Americans because of high birth rates and cultural preservation. If the trends continue, Hispanics student will soon be the majority, and the descendants of European Americans and African Americans will be the minority. Similarly, the Asian-American student population is increasing dramatically. Recent influxes of immigrants and refugees from Southeast Asian nations—Laos, Thailand, Cambodia, and Vietnam—will add more racially heterogeneous ingredients to the cultural diversity of America.

Moreover, Arab-American students have begun to show a noticeable increase in number in recent years. In California's public schools, growing numbers of these students enrolled in K-12 classrooms present challenges for school teachers and administrators. Students from India who speak Punjabi, Hindi, or Urdu also bring rich cultural heritages into the school culture; however, these groups of students need more teachers who share their ancestries and cultural backgrounds. As with Hmong, Cambodian, Laotian, and Vietnamese students, the presence of Arab-American students and students from non-European cultures demonstrates that public schools need to grow their own teachers to help these students; otherwise, students of color may be subject to lip service, capricious teaching, cosmetic education, surface-level assessment, and impoverished curricula.

Scholars of multicultural education, such as Banks (2008) and Dillon (2006), have reported that the number of students of color has already exceeded the number of mainstream American students in six states: California, Hawaii, Louisiana, Mississippi, New Mexico, and Texas. Banks further noted that the proportion of students of color in American schools doubled in the 30 years between 1973 and 2004, from 22% to 43%. Banks also observed that ethnic, racial, cultural, and religious diversity is increasing in all segments of American life, including communities, K-12 schools, colleges, and universities.

Today's Challenges and Their Implications

Undoubtedly, cultural diversity poses serious challenges, complexities, opportunities, and perhaps, cross-cultural obstacles for today's educators. However, people working with students of color need to move away from the "melting pot" concept proposed in the 1950s and 1960s because it does not accurately depict the socialization of the diverse population in the U.S. currently. In fact, according to experts in multicultural education, this futile concept has been replaced with the notion of cultural pluralism. Banks (2008) referred to this replacement as a paradigm shift. De Villar (1994) noted that this paradigm shift requires a new socio-academic framework.

People have difficulty letting go of their cultural heritages when living in the U.S. and becoming Americanized. Societal assimilation is unnecessary and has negative consequences. People of diverse backgrounds can adopt the values of the mainstream society and live the American dream while maintaining their cultures and traditions. Hmong Americans, for example, embrace a socialization process they call *accommodation*—acculturation without assimilation. This process enables them to preserve their cultural heritage. In other words, Hmong Americans have learned to accept American values—those of middle-class European Americans—while maintaining their own, thus building cross-cultural competency in schools, communities, and workplaces.

Today, people see the U.S. as a multilingual and multicultural nation with a heterogeneous mixture of cultural characteristics, much like a salad bowl. All kinds of unique cultures are displayed, like the colors of the rainbow. In this salad bowl, American society is open to change, provides opportunity, and offers a high standard of living.

Critics of diversity and of multicultural education might view the differences among people as negatives that need to be eradicated through assimilation and enculturation, as in the melting pot model. This way of thinking is narrow-minded. Cultural diversity has enriched the fabric of U.S. society in so many ways that one cannot imagine the country without the richness and strengths of its different peoples. Of course, this fact cannot erase racism, discrimination, bigotry, prejudice, stereotyping, and hatred from the minds of people who are ethnically, religiously, and racially encapsulated (Banks, 2008). But experts in multicultural education feel that celebrating cultural diversity brings unity, understanding, sensitivity, awareness, compassion, and empathy. When different voices come together, society is the better.

Recognizing and celebrating differences are only the first steps toward enriching society through formal understanding and schooling. This author agrees with Manning and Baruth (2009) and Banks (2008) that consistent, significant, comprehensive, and deliberate efforts are needed to promote a total-school approach to the delivery of instruction in multicultural education for all students in the 21st century.

All educational institutions should foster positive attitudes toward multicultural education. Educators can play a vital role in teaching students of color and mainstream American students how to demonstrate acceptance, appreciation, and respect for all cultures. To develop effective curricula that reflect sensitivity to cultural diversity, public schools need to move beyond present academic boundaries that focus on Anglo-centric curricula. Most importantly, public schools should avoid hidden and null curricula since their hegemonic principles are culturally and academically detrimental to the education of all students.

Multiculturalism is undeniable today. Look at our sports, politics, schools, restaurants, neighborhoods, religious denominations, and communities. Each of us is one of many. However, we still have homogeneous communities as well as heterogeneous communities. Each cultural group has its own niche in which it keeps its culture and traditions alive. But by far, people are moving away from xenophobic attitudes and embracing multicultural attitudes, moving eventually to pluralism.

The big question in education is: How are teachers feeling about dealing and working with students of diverse abilities and needs? How do teachers feel about teaching students of color who do not possess middle-class American values? How do teachers feel about their inability to speak different languages? How do teachers feel about themselves and their ability to set students up for either success or failure? Another important question is: How do children of color feel about being in the classroom with teachers with whom they are barely able to communicate? These are some tough questions, but they are part of professional psychological profiling.

The goal of this book is to promote fair multicultural education for all students by presenting and illustrating the psycho-social dimensions of the socio-cultural issues related to educational foundations and conceptualizations, the socialization process, curricula, teaching methodologies, and communication with diverse parents. I hope the contents of this book will serve as a guiding light that leads prospective educators through the steps of devising cultural models of acceptance, appreciation, and respect for students from different cultural backgrounds, including European Americans, Hispanic Americans, Native Americans, African Americans, Arab Americans, Asian Americans, and Southeast Asian Americans.

My Reason for Writing This Book

I am passionate about this topic because of my experiences teaching college courses in multicultural and multilingual education in a multiple-subject credential program. I want future educators to have comprehensive knowledge of the seven major cultural groups in the American public schools today as well as skills for teaching them. Cultural diversity is still relatively new to many pre-service and in-service professionals even though they are entering the teaching profession to become classroom teachers in a pluralistic society. Their feelings about cultural diversity are very important as those feelings will play a significant role in how they perceive students with language and cultural barriers to learning. For instance, many student teachers from the Midwest do not live in diverse communities. These individuals may lack firsthand contact experiences, an understanding of multicultural education, cross-cultural competencies, psycho-social information, and background knowledge of specific cultures. Yet they will more likely than not be called upon to teach students who are culturally different from themselves. Meeting the academic needs of all students can be tremendously difficult because teaching students with diverse abilities and diverse needs is always a challenging task.

This book presents various components of multicultural education programs and curricula that are responsive to the academic needs of all students. The goal of this book is to expand the psycho-social horizons of educators and to make sure that the school curricula, instructional strategies, methodologies, materials, settings, personnel, and academic practices reflect the diversity of multilingualism and multiculturalism.

Significance of All Cultural Groups

Each culture is unique and special and has its own way of expressing its cultural characteristics. Describing every culture in America is literally possible, but time and space do not permit. This book focuses on the seven major groups—European Americans, Hispanic Americans, Native Americans, African Americans, Arab Americans, Asian Americans, and Southeast Asian Americans. Each major group contains subgroups and thus intra-cultural diversity. Multicultural education experts and researchers agree that these groups have the highest number of children in today's schools and that their numbers will continue to increase. By writing about these groups, my intention is to promote greater understanding of cultural diversity and, at the same time, motivate educators to study and explore the cultural dynamics and characteristics of other cultures. For instance, teachers in schools with Punjabi students need to understand the culture and traditions of these people, who may speak one or more of three different dialects—Punjabi, Hindi, or Urdu.

Limitations of This Book

I realize that in limiting discussion to the seven major cultural groups and their subgroups, some groups are not represented. In addition, all cultural background information presented may not truly portray the actual heritages of a specific group. Some discussions may risk provoking generalizations, stereotyping, and negative connotations. Even though the information in this book is based on current research from experts in the field of multicultural education, the assumptions of each cultural group may not be accurately explained as the research was limited to available ethnographic data. Therefore, I encourage you to consider that one of the best ways to validate this information regarding cultural characteristics of children of color is to engage in in-depth study and/or firsthand experience, such as ethnographic observations and documentation. Check with experts on specific cultures to clarify and enhance your knowledge of any specific cultural issues.

Keep in mind that multicultural issues are sensitive, and any inappropriate misapplication of cultural information could result in undesired consequences.

How This Book Is Organized

This book contains five parts organized into 14 chapters. Each part presents a different domain with a variety of topical issues. Part One has three chapters and introduces broad topics related to the concepts of multilingual and multicultural education and the psycho-social dimensions of cultural diversity. Part Two has seven chapters and reviews the cultural characteristics of each ethnic group, giving a comprehensive overview of the group's cultural characteristics. Part Three has one chapter and discusses topical issues related to the characteristics of at-risk students. Part Four has two chapters and focuses on topical issues related to curricula and approaches in response to the goals of multicultural education. Finally, Part Five has one chapter that explores meaningful means of communication between schools and parents.

Acknowledgments

This book could not have been written without the expertise of Dr. Greg Goodman. Dr. Goodman is the instrumental editor for this book. The author of this book is indebted to Dr. Goodman for his invaluable contributions and scholarship as well as his kindness, friendship, and mentoring.

Special appreciation goes to Mr. Christopher Myers, the Manager of Marketing for Peter Lang Publishing. His encouragement has made this book possible and given the author the momentum to complete it.

A Personal Note

This book is based on my experience teaching multicultural and multilingual education courses in a multiple-subject credential program. It reflects my passion for teaching college courses—Methods in Multilingual Education, Foundations of Education in a Diverse Society, Health and Science Methodologies, and Classroom Management and Professional Practices. My professional development guided me in creating the conceptual framework for this book.

In addition, my observations, firsthand experience, and personal multilingual and multicultural background inspired me to put my thoughts into a book that will help educators because I understand the inadequacies of our educational system in providing and advocating for the needs of students of diverse cultural backgrounds. This book will not be the last one I write about issues related to the psycho-social dimensions of multicultural education; this is what I love to do.

PART ONE

THE MULTICULTURAL EDUCATION DOMAIN

Chapter One

The Psycho-Social Dimensions of Multicultural Education

> If civilization is to survive, we must cultivate the science
> of human relationship, the ability of all people, of all kinds,
> to live together, in the same world at peace.
> —President Franklin D. Roosevelt

Overview

The educational climate has changed dramatically, and the change calls for comprehensive multicultural academic programs that reflect pluralistic understanding and acceptance, respect, and tolerance for all children of any group. Because ethnic, racial, cultural, religious, language, political, and sexual diversity is increasing, American schools are now facing tremendous pressure and tough challenges in fulfilling their mandate to teach all students, including students of color. America is an open society that embraces all races, cultures, traditions, religions, and classes. However, the American educational system has been slow to adequately address the socio-cultural issues of diversity. Perhaps the time to engage in academic discourse regarding multicultural and multilingual education is now, and that is the focus of this chapter.

Global Perspectives on Multicultural and Multilingual Education

Historically, multilingual and multicultural education began in the ancient world and has continued into modern times. Societal bilingualism has always played an important role in the civilization of mankind. Merchants, for example, had to speak two or more languages in order to do business or trade goods with tribal villagers. Hmong, for example, are members of a preliterate society, but most older Hmong are bilingual. In the 21st century, very few nations are monolingual or mono-cultural. In the past, religious, political, territorial, and tribal consolidations as well as dominations resulted in the addition of one or more languages to a society's means of communication (Lessow-Hurley, 2000).

Because schooling was limited in the ancient world, bilingualism does not appear to have been an academic matter. Rather, it was a normative societal value necessary for facilitating mutual understanding cross-culturally among diverse linguistic groups. Moreover, in olden days, the scarcity of written materials encouraged people to learn languages other than the language spoken in the home in order to access whatever written information was available (Lessow-Hurley, 2000). Consider, for example, the fact that old religious manuscripts were written only in Hebrew and Greek. Religious scholars compiled the Old and New Testaments from 39 ancient manuscripts written in Hebrew and 27 written in Greek. To translate these manuscripts into other languages, scholars had to be multilingual or at least bilingual.

Many nations around the world still offer courses in foreign languages in their public schools. English, for example, is taught in many countries, and it is perhaps the most popular and widely used language in the 21st century as indicated in Table 1.1. However, English is ranked as the world's fourth most commonly spoken language, with Mandarin the first, followed by Hindi as second, and Spanish as third.

Furthermore, in California, besides CLAD and BCLAD teaching credentials, California's Commission on Teaching Credentials (CCTC) offers foreign language teaching credentials for many languages, such as Hmong, Lao, Cambodian, Punjabi, Farsi, French, Italian, German, Russian, Spanish, Vietnamese, Tagalog, Portuguese, Chinese, and others.

What Is Multilingual Education?

Various definitions have been offered for multilingual education. Scholars in the field of bilingual and multicultural education apply the concepts of bilingualism differently, and they would disagree on the acceptance of a single definition. However, for the purpose of this discussion, we will define multilingual education as the use of two or more languages as media in the instructional process for helping students, especially students of color, learn in the classroom setting.

Multilingual education includes the academic ability or speaking ability to function with the use of two or more languages in the process of learning and communicating. Bear in mind that individual levels of fluency and competency in two or more languages could be different, depending on the length of exposure to the languages and the conditions under which the language was acquired or learned. Hmong, for example, have two distinct dialects—

White Hmong and Blue Hmong—and Hmong students are generally able to speak one dialect fluently but may not understand the other dialect. Also, having the ability to speak Hmong dialects does not mean that a person is competent in writing those dialects.

Table 1.1. Native and Academic Languages of Selected Countries

Country	Native Language	Academic Language	Samples of Foreign Languages in Schools
Canada	English or French	English and French	French, English, Russian, German, Italian, Spanish, and Latin
China	Mandarin or Cantonese	Mandarin or Cantonese	English, French, Russian, German, Italian, and Spanish.
France	French	French	English, British, German, Russian, Italian, Spanish, and Latin.
India	Hindi or Punjabi	Hindi or Punjabi and English	English, French, Spanish, German, Russian, and Chinese
Laos	Lao	Lao and French	English, French, Chinese, German, Russian, Italian, and Spanish.
United States	English	English	English, French, German, Russian, Italian, Latin, and Spanish.

Multilingual education should be practical and useful, an integral part of instruction in the multicultural classroom. Teachers with a Bilingual Cross-cultural Language in Academic Development (BCLAD) credential use a primary and a second or third language to provide students of color with primary language support during the instructional process. Monolingual teachers may lack this multilingual approach; however, schools with large numbers of English learners usually hire bilingual instructional aides (BIA) or other paraprofessionals to meet part of the instructional needs in the class, referring to the process as *one teaches and one drifts*.

What Is Multicultural Education?

Multicultural education was widely practiced in past centuries and started emerging in America in the mid-1900s. It has continued to be emphasized to the present day. Banks (1988) brilliantly described the historical evolution of multicultural education in the U.S. as occurring in five distinct phases:

1. Phase I, monotonic studies, focused on the black civil rights movement. It advocated for equitable representation related to the needs of African American children and communities.
2. Phase II, multiethnic studies, emphasized the broader need to include other cultural groups in the study of minority experiences.
3. Phase III, multiethnic education, focused on the insufficiency of education to meet the challenges of cultural diversity and demanded educational reform to accommodate societal changes brought about by wars, immigration, the civil rights movement, discrimination, racism, and the presence of diverse languages and religions.
4. Phase IV, multicultural education, focused on a universal approach to understanding cultural diversity through broader perspectives instead of maintaining a limited emphasis on racial and ethnic minorities.
5. Phase V, the institutionalized process, focused on strategies, applications, school curricular efforts, and other reforms that include the teaching of multicultural education in schools.

Ovando, Combs, and Collier (2006) described multicultural education as a concept, idea, reform, movement, process, and affirmation of cultural pluralism that forms the basis of teaching and learning on the foundation of ideals, values, and beliefs that are democratic.

As with multilingual education, multicultural education has been defined in various ways. At the heart of every definition is a broad emphasis on the academic and social interactions of race, ethnicity, class, culture, religion, gender, language, and socioeconomic diversity of students. Multicultural education stresses educational reform, movement, restructuring, inclusion, and public policy that address multifaceted aspects of cultural diversity in order to provide all students with equal opportunities in the total school environment. Most importantly, multicultural education plays a vital role in advocating for social justice.

Roles of Multicultural Education

Banks (2008) described the beauty of multicultural education as follows:

> [Multicultural education is] an educational reform movement whose major goal is to restructure curricula and educational institutions so that students from diverse social-class, racial, and ethnic groups—as well as both gender groups—will experience equal educational opportunities. Multicultural education consists of three major components: (1) an educational reform movement whose aim is to create equal educational opportunities for all students; (2) an ideology whose aim is to actualize

American democratic ideals, such as equality, justice, and human rights; and (3) a process that never ends because there will always be a discrepancy between democratic ideals and school and societal practices. (p. 135)

Without doubt, discussion of multicultural education produces misconceptions and a great deal of socio-cultural confusion. Proponents view it as a necessity; opponents see it as a handicap. Many feel strongly that the American educational system cannot function well either academically or culturally without including the cultural ingredients of multicultural applications that address inequality, prejudice, and cultural diversity in public schools.

Proponents ask: Who is responsible to educate all American children enrolling in grades K-12 about different cultures? Who can help children understand the differences in race, ethnicities, classes, cultures, religions, and socioeconomic status? Who can differentiate instruction so as to include all students with diverse learning styles, diverse needs, and diverse abilities in the learning process? These questions are not new; they express the daily struggles of every responsible educator.

Pre-service and in-service educators need to think outside the Anglo-centric curriculum when teaching in a pluralistic society. The number of students of color is increasing in nearly every community throughout the United States. Most schools and classrooms have students from at least three different cultural groups. European Americans, Hispanic Americans, and African Americans are the three populations most prominent in many schools. Public policies, such as those embodied in the federal No Child Left Behind Act of 2001 and California Senate Bill 2042, require that new and current teachers devise academic standards, sensible instructional strategies, and purposeful adaptations that will assist English learners learn the English language and mathematical skills. These policies are not requests from parents, children, or community organizations. In fact, these are legal mandates that are required by federal laws, landmark decisions, state legislation, and education codes.

Theoretical Principles

The definitions of multicultural education describe its principles and purposes; however, they do not capture all its goals. Banks (2008) suggested, "A key goal of multicultural education is to help individuals gain greater self-understanding by viewing themselves from the perspective of other cultures.... [This] assumes that with acquaintance and understanding, respect may follow" (p. 2). When respect is present, acceptance of cultural diversity is natural.

Multicultural education has a purpose beyond acquisition of academic knowledge; it is a societal platform as well as an educational philosophy that aims at teaching all people to recognize, accept, respect, promote, and appreciate differences in culture, ethnicity, social class, sexual orientation, religion, special needs, and gender and at the same time to advocate on behalf of the marginalized, the powerless, the voiceless, and the oppressed for social justice, fairness, equity, and democracy. It also seeks to instill in educators, during their professional development, a sense of personal responsibility and a civic commitment to work toward democratic ideals.

Despite some opposition to multicultural education, the United States is now a multilingual and multicultural nation with many linguistic groups, and its various cultural groups have enriched the nation in many ways. Multicultural education has as a goal making sure that advocacy for equality is not an option. So far, educators who have embraced multicultural education have made impressive strides in addressing the needs of and advocating for all students, and these advances have benefited both the macro culture and the many micro cultures that exist in America (Banks, 2008). However, to be even more successful, the multicultural education movement requires new understandings, rethinking of old paradigms and practices, and new approaches in the classroom. It also needs the support of parents, teachers, administrators, policy makers, and the community at large in implementing consistent and systematic total-school approaches.

Fundamental Approaches

An important goal of multicultural education is the elimination of surface level assessments, broken promises, lip service, cosmetic education, and mere talk about cultural diversity. Multicultural education must consist of more than celebrating holidays, giving information, holding cross-cultural trainings, and using on-call interpreters when needed. In fact, intense intentionality is needed to provide quality, effective multicultural education for students and teachers.

As Banks (2008) and Manning and Baruth (2009) suggested, educators can promote appreciation of cultural diversity by doing one or more of the following:

1. Use appropriate multicultural education curricular materials with all students, materials that reflect the cultural backgrounds of the students in the classroom.

2. Have multicultural materials evaluated by experts in the field to make sure they are appropriate for students' age, grade level, development of primary and second language, and gender.
3. Use multicultural materials that enhance and promote self-esteem, positive self-concept, and self-pride to promote learning and understanding among diverse groups of students.
4. Focus multicultural teaching on the development of knowledge, skills, and critical thinking through the process of learning and acquisition of skills.
5. In multicultural education curricular efforts, include authentic and multi-dimensional approaches to foster understanding of racial, ethnic, class, religion, gender, and language differences as well as cultural diversity.
6. Select curricular materials that meet and align with content-obligatory objectives rather than content-compatibility objectives.
7. Design multicultural lesson plans and instruction according to the length of time the students have been living in the U.S. or have been otherwise exposed to the English language.
8. Base teaching modalities on the results of formal assessments of primary and second-language proficiency.
9. Provide primary language support to accompany instruction in the second language when necessary.
10. Ensure access to equal and high quality instruction for all students.

Conceptual Context

Teachers who lack the foundations of multicultural education might have negative feelings about teaching in a pluralistic society and could rely heavily on Western methodologies. However, it is crucial for today's teachers to know and understand the basic concepts of multicultural education. Perhaps the concepts are not completely new; they may simply require relearning to recognize as well as accept the diverse fabric of American culture.

The first concept is that educators in a diverse society must understand the differences in race, ethnicity, culture, religion, class, language, and socioeconomic status that exist among people and the impact of those differences on teaching and learning. This concept is extremely important in a pluralistic society. Socio-cultural discourse must be a part of professional development if teachers are to understand the complexity of cultural diversity. For instance, many university programs require that teachers take multicultural education classes as part of their credential requirements to broaden their views toward culturally diverse student populations. Moreover, some teacher preparation programs require academic experience with a target culture.

The second concept is that social injustice should be eliminated—oppression, marginalization, powerlessness, exploitation, hegemony, prejudice, baggage, bias, inequality, and racial discrimination. Multicultural education targets cultural groups that are subject to blatant unequal treatment. In some cases, multicultural education is portrayed as a concern only for and of minorities. In fact, multicultural education is concerned with quality education for all students, but that goal cannot be attained without special consideration for those students who experience barriers to quality education. For instance, states often require that new teachers learn how to address the special needs of English language learners and students with other specific needs.

The third concept is that every student has constitutional rights—civil rights, human rights, rights to equal opportunities—that require that an equitable system is in place that enables all students to access the total school curriculum so they can acquire meaningful social and academic skills needed for success in life. The American educational system and education policies regarding quotas that address the needs of students of color is inadequate in many areas. However, improvements have been made in some areas. For instance, new elementary teachers are expected to take four methodology courses: math, language arts, social studies, and science. In these courses, teachers learn different techniques for delivering teaching modalities such as ELD, SDAIE, TESOL, and ESL in order to meet the needs of students of color.

The fourth concept is that public policy and education policy should advocate for multicultural curricula that teach students historical events, facts, and cultural characteristics that reflect cultural diversity. For instance, the No Child Left Behind Act requires that schools devise academic standards that measure student learning outcomes regarding cultural diversity and that schools recruit teachers of cultural backgrounds that reflect the cultural diversity of the student body.

The fifth concept is that social empowerment improves human civility and reciprocity in a pluralistic society. Good human behavior, adequate understanding of cultural diversity, racial tolerance, and cross-cultural competency bring a higher level of acceptance and respect among cultural groups. Social empowerment can be achieved by integrating into the social studies curriculum activities related to social events important in various cultures, such as New Year festivals and special holidays. Such activities help students learn about, understand, respect, and accept aspects of other cultures and traditions.

The Multicultural Curriculum

The goals of multicultural education are achievable and measurable through the use of a multicultural curriculum. Gollnick and Chinn (2009) described a good multicultural curriculum as one that incorporates the histories, experiences, traditions, and cultures of students in the classroom and supports and celebrates diversity in the broadest sense.

At present, not all schools utilize a multicultural curriculum. Some schools are extremely skeptical about offering a multicultural curriculum and others claim they lack the resources to implement such a curriculum, including materials, teachers, and money. Some schools follow a multicultural curriculum, but they use instructional strategies that are inconsistent with the goals of the curriculum or are capricious. Goals for implementing multicultural education vary, depending on a school's culture, environment, personnel, commitment, and program design. Regardless of the hindrances, comprehensive multicultural curricula are needed in American schools to address differences in race, ethnicity, class, religion, language, gender, and socioeconomic status and the occurrence of prejudice, bias, stereotyping, injustice, inequity, and discrimination.

Setting targeted goals for a multicultural curriculum would help teachers understand its value and how it should be used. Experts and scholars in multicultural education suggest educators consider the following goals for a curriculum that is effective for all students:

1. A multicultural curriculum should be viewed as a positive, a strength, not as a negative or a weakness. It provides opportunities for students to experience, learn, understand, promote, and accommodate other cultures as well as their own.
2. A multicultural curriculum should be used to educate all students regardless of cultural background. All students, rich or poor, bilingual or monolingual, of majority or minority status, need to recognize cultural differences and understand cultural diversity.
3. A multicultural curriculum helps minimize cultural baggage—biases, prejudices, perceptions, values, backgrounds, beliefs, customs, stereotypes, racism, and discrimination. Cross-cultural teaching and learning help educators and students develop attitudes of acceptance and respect of cultural diversity.

4. A multicultural curriculum should be implemented throughout the school as part of the total-school effort to address both majority and minority needs and expectations and to promote understanding, acceptance, and respect among all cultural groups.

5. A multicultural curriculum must provide all students with equal opportunities to succeed academically. Culturally diverse minority students tend to lose their competitiveness when confronted with language barriers, cultural barriers, and odd or different learning styles. They may also lack middle-class characteristics associated with success in academic tasks. These factors often contribute to minority students faring poorly in school and having a high rate of school dropout.

6. A multicultural curriculum should provide a learning climate that reflects the cultural diversity of the students in order to increase awareness of race, ethnic, class, gender, religious, socioeconomic, sexual orientation, lifestyle, and language diversity.

7. A multicultural curriculum should promote cross-cultural understanding and good cross-cultural relationships by downplaying the negative attitudes and mindsets of bias, prejudice, racism, stereotyping, sexism, classism, inferiority, superiority, and discrimination

8. A multicultural curriculum should help students improve their self-concepts, self-understanding, and self-consciousness by enabling them to view themselves from the cultural perspectives, or through the cultural lenses, of other people.

9. A multicultural curriculum should help students acquire academic knowledge and social skills that empower them to deal with cultural differences and function in the mainstream culture.

10. A multicultural curriculum should help students cope with their internal feelings and thus reduce and heal any pain suffered from the past to the present time.

11. A multicultural curriculum should enable educators to not only teach, but also model acceptance and respect for all. Even though the learning process could be mentally dramatic during children's formative years, responsible multicultural education should play a key role in reducing myths, misconceptions, and misperceptions in learners' minds.

12. A multicultural curriculum opens students' eyes to cultural alternatives, helping them gain global perspectives on different cultures.

Furthermore, a modern multicultural curriculum should also focus on how teachers teach and how students learn in the classroom, which is critical pedagogy. Keep in mind that focusing on cultural diversity alone in a curriculum is not sufficient to help students of color learn and excel academically. Teachers can pay too much attention to students' cultural values that they give too little attention to their academic struggles and barriers. Most importantly, to help language minority students enhance their language skills needed for academic tasks, teachers ought to think about the internal feelings that students may have while learning and processing the information given to them in the classroom. Sometimes, it is not just the way teachers teach that matters; it is both how the teachers are feeling about teaching and how students are feeling about learning that really matter. Table 1.2 illustrates some basic multicultural approaches that teachers can use to enhance student learning.

Table 1.2. Basic Multicultural Approaches

Approach	Examples of Activities
Text representation	Allowing students to retell their stories in oral or written form.
Schema building	Using graphic organizers to compare or contrast concepts and show interconnectedness, such as mapping or idea web.
Bridging	Engaging prior knowledge or personal experience as a starting point for learning new concepts before tapping into lesson plan objective.
Metacognitive development	Allowing students to engage in thinking process to think about ways to solve problems or to find answers to questions.
Modeling	Showing students how to do something by giving them step-by-step directions.
Contextualization	Embedding language in different contexts by using manipulatives, regalia, visual aids, pictures, gestures, maps, diagrams, or idea web.

The purpose of multicultural approaches is to help students develop two kinds of language: basic interpersonal communication skills (BICS) and cognitive academic language proficiency (CALP). If students do not learn both kinds of language, the multicultural approaches merely result in superficial teaching and learning. Consider, for example, a high school ESL teacher who once told the students in his ESL class that all they needed was to learn 500 specific English words that would enable them to survive in America because learning any additional English would be quite difficult for most of them. How do language minority students feel about this kind of hegemonic academic curriculum? Some may believe that all they need is to learn 500 words. Others might feel discouraged and disheartened to hear such a thing from their teacher.

Keep in mind that multicultural curriculum is not about making language minority students feel good about who they are; it is about how to transit their learning experience from one level to the next academically, and how to help them transform from being newcomers to becoming experienced learners. For instance, rather than keeping language minority students in an ESL class for a long period of time, the multicultural curriculum should be used as a transitional process to mainstream them periodically; otherwise, these students would fail to develop CALP needed for regular course of studies. Moreover, a large number of English language learners would only retain a superficial knowledge of most academic subject because they lack the opportunity to experience real academic learning and challenges in classes that require critical thinking and analysis.

Understanding Myths, Misconceptions, and Misperceptions

Many people have strong feelings about multicultural education, and the subject has ignited a psychological warfare between proponents and opponents. Citizenship education is a tough sell in some parts of today's pluralistic society. Critics feel that use of a multicultural curriculum puts too much emphasis on bilingualism and cultural education. Their objections may stem from xenophobia, the melting pot model, racism, stereotyping, bias, culture shock, or an ethno-centric approach toward cultural diversity.

Of course, anyone looking for examples of inconsistent results of multicultural education can find some. Bilingual education, for example, started more than 30 years ago, but most American schools still have serious problems implementing bilingual education consistently in an academic curriculum that addresses the needs of students of color. Bilingual education is often implemented very differently from the way the program was intended to be operated. Proponents of multicultural education call this difference *espoused policy* versus *policy in use*.

In order to see that education on cultural diversity does not pose a threat to equal treatment and equal education of all students, educators should pay close attention to the students they do *not* serve as the result of cultural and language barriers. Multicultural education benefits all if the design is based on academic content geared to helping students learn, understand, and appreciate differences in race, ethnicity, class, religion, socioeconomic status, language, and gender.

Multicultural education faces dire challenges in schools because people have failed to overcome myths, misconceptions, and misperceptions about the practice.

Is Multicultural Education Only for "Others"?

The idea that multicultural education is of benefit only for "others," for minorities, is a single-sided view of the issue from the dominant culture. Some critics view multicultural education as an entitlement program for specific groups of people—people of color, people who are marginalized, the oppressed, minorities, and the underprivileged. The fact is that all people need this education to function civilly and effectively in America. The notion that multicultural education is for "others" must be dispelled. Actually, most cross-cultural trainings are designed for upper-class and middle-class Americans who may lack cultural sensitivity, awareness, understanding, and appreciation. On the other hand, members of most cultural groups do not receive training on the dominant culture, especially the White culture, or on American culture in general.

Regardless, this author defines multicultural education broadly and does not believe that multicultural education should be only for people who need to understand cultural diversity. The dimensions of multicultural education are framed to educate and empower all people to become sensitive, understanding, knowledgeable, appreciative, loving, caring, altruistic, benevolent, and compassionate citizens in a pluralistic society.

Is Multicultural Education Opposed to Western Views?

In some sense, multicultural education may appear to be in opposition to Western views on public policy because it advocates for inclusiveness, equality, justice, and democracy. However, according to Banks (2008), most proponents of multicultural education are Western, and multicultural education has been orchestrated by Westerners to address the issues of cultural diversity. Moreover, the misconception that multicultural education distorts, minimizes, or attempts to displace Western civilization is false. After all, most school textbooks are written by Westerners. Most importantly, educators should know that the multicultural education movement originated in the West in the mid-1900s, during the civil rights movement. Its framers sought to influence public policy and education policy to deal with issues of equality, freedom, social justice, segregation, and discrimination with the ultimate aim of improving the realization of democratic ideals.

Does Multicultural Education Divide People?

The question of whether multicultural education divides people springs from misguided misinformation. Birkel (2000) and Manning and Baruth (2009) explained that multicultural education often has been misunderstood and referred to as a program on race relations, as an affirmative action tool, as a vehicle of the civil rights movement, as an entitlement program, as an anti-assimilation ideology, and as a means to undercut unity. However, none of this is true; multicultural education is not divisive.

On the contrary, it promotes unity, cooperation, empowerment, and cross-cultural competency. People in America are uniquely diverse, and their differences in race, ethnicity, culture, class, religion, socioeconomic status, gender, and language may pose challenges and discomfort for some.

However, cultural groups continue to suffer incidents of racism, prejudice, injustice, and discrimination. At one time, Western countries were understandably considered to be racist. Birmingham, Alabama, for example, was called Bombingham during the fight against racial discrimination in the 1960s. In fact, multicultural education has helped reduce racial discrimination and prejudice by actively promoting acceptance and appreciation of diversity.

Banks (2008) asserted that multicultural education is designed to unify rather than divide a nation. Multicultural education supports the notion of "one out of many"—*e pluribus unum*. But Banks cautioned that America is deeply divided along racial, gender, sexual orientation, and class lines, and that social stratification is the most pernicious of the dividing lines.

Is Multicultural Education Debatable?

Multicultural education is a social movement as well as an educational philosophy. As with any social movement, the push for multicultural education has sometimes triggered political debate over the restructuring and reformulating of the academic canon. Discussion of implementing multicultural education has also increased racial and ethnic tension in some areas. The struggles are similar to the ways the actions of *Viva La Raza*, a movement to preserve the Latino race, spark heated debate in the educational community as well as in the political arena. However, without a doubt, multicultural education has played a vital role in promoting citizenship education that has improved social justice and advocated for equal opportunity for all.

Does Multicultural Education Divide Instruction?

Some critics claim that use of a multicultural curriculum hinders the education of mainstream American students. These critics might feel that all students should learn from the same Anglo-centric curriculum regardless of cultural background. However, if teachers lack an understanding of cultural diversity, do not know how to teach the children in their classrooms, and do not understand how those children learn, the education of all the students in their classrooms is hindered. Moreover, students of color should not be subjected to different instructional modalities; teachers should use one modality for all students. Research shows that the factor that influences student learning the most is the quality of the teacher; in other words, effective teaching is about how to teach, not what to teach. Another important factor is the quality of instruction, not the language of instruction.

Is Multicultural Education Designed for Legal Segregation?

The criticism that multicultural education encourages segregation is not entirely true, but the way the multicultural curriculum is used in some schools appears to be divisive. Instead of grouping diverse students together, teachers sometimes use homogeneous grouping to segregate students of specific cultures. The risk here is that schools put too much emphasis on students' cultures rather than on their education.

Is Multicultural Education Responsible for Low Academic Achievement?

Multicultural education does not result in low academic achievement because most standardized testing instruments are either norm-referenced or criterion-referenced. Test results are compared to results from a sample group, which may or may not have the same or similar academic and cultural characteristics as the tested group. In fact, norm-referenced testing is based on a normal curve. Both types of instruments appear to have construct bias when they are used to measure students of color. Test makers are mostly European Americans, and they design tests based on Anglo-centric, or middle-class, values. Moreover, most schools use measurement-driven curricula to drill students on testing strategies. In other words, students of color receive inadequate instructional services to help them perform well on tests. However, schools expect these students to do well on the tests even though they have been subjected to ineffective instruction.

Furthermore, this author supports the argument made by Banks (2008) that schools often use a cultural deprivation paradigm to measure the academic outcomes of students of color. Use of this paradigm blames the students for their academic failure. Instead, schools should use a cultural difference paradigm, which places much of the responsibility for any gap in academic achievement on the school.

Another way to help educators understand student achievement is to examine the distinction between standards and standardization. Sleeter (2005) described standards as measures that provide a quality approach to helping students reach high levels of academic achievement and standardization as an ineffective approach to instruction that focuses on low levels of knowledge and skills easily measured by norm-referenced tests.

Is the Multicultural Education Approach Effective?

For the most part, if a multicultural curriculum is used appropriately, all students benefit. The instructional methodologies employed in most multicultural education curricula—English Language Development (ELD), Specially Designed Academic Instruction in English (SDAIE), and Teaching English to Speakers of other Language (TESOL), for example—are effective and appropriate for all learners. On the other hand, direct instruction is effective in responding to time constraints and the lack of creative teaching, but it leaves students of color with limited English proficiency out of the engagement process. A multicultural curriculum prefers eclectic methods of teaching that engage all students regardless of cultural and linguistic background or ability.

Is Multicultural Education Teacher-Centered?

Direct instruction is teacher-centered instruction. In some senses, the multicultural education approach emphasizes specific teaching techniques for targeting specific groups of students. Hmong students, for example, learn English, math, social studies, and science more effectively with a specific teaching scheme designed by Hmong BCLAD teachers because that scheme uses primary language support. In most cases, the multicultural approach is student-centered because teachers prescribe instructional strategies based on the students' levels of comprehension in the English language.

Is Multicultural Education Appropriate for All Subject Matter?

Multicultural education is absolutely appropriate for any and all subject matter! Methods in multicultural education are appropriate across all subject areas. Manning and Baruth (2009) pointed out that multicultural education is interdisciplinary as an integral part of all curricular areas and should be administered across all subject areas.

For language arts, teachers can use scaffolding and reciprocal techniques to engage English language learners in a variety of ways. For social science, teachers can use prior experiences or embedded skills to engage students of color in activities related to their personal lives and cultural events. Regarding math, most students of color, even those with limited English language skills, can learn because learning math initially does not require a high level of language skills. Also, teachers can use the parts-to-whole approach to help students learn the process. In science, teachers can use hands-on and minds-on activities to introduce science concepts related to personal experiences, such as cooking, cleaning, farming, gardening, grooming, animals, and plants, before going into the more complex science concepts involved in biology, chemistry, physics, and botany.

Is Multicultural Education a Legal Necessity?

The struggle for educational equality for all students has been ongoing for some time. The multicultural education movement started in the mid-1900s and forerunners were present in America even earlier. In 1896, in the case of *Plessy v. Ferguson*, the Court ruled that the Civil Rights Act of 1875 was unconstitutional, and the judges approved "separate but equal" facilities. Later laws and court rulings overturned this decision and instead protected human rights, equal opportunity, and justice for all. These legislative and judicial actions eventually led to school desegregation. In 1954, in the case of *Brown v. Topeka Board of Education*, the Court ruled in favor of desegregation of Blacks and Whites. A few years later, in 1957, the Commission on Civil Rights was created to investigate complaints of alleged discrimination in violation of human rights.

The Civil Rights Act of 1964 forbade schools that received federal monies from discriminating on the basis of race, color, creed, or national origin.

In other words, it mandated that schools protect minority groups. In 1968, Title VII of the Elementary and Secondary Education Act (ESEA), together with the Bilingual Education Act (BEA), assisted American schools in providing services to needy and at-risk students. In 1974, in the case of *Lau v. Nichols*, the Court ruled that according to Title VI of the Civil Rights Act of 1964, children must receive equal access to public education regardless of their ability or lack of ability to speak English. In 1975, a national report titled *A Better Chance to Learn: Bilingual, Bicultural Education* issued by the U.S. Commission on Civil Rights recommended that schools provide equal opportunity for language-minority students. In 1994, Public Law 103-382, the Improving America's Schools Act of 1994, reauthorized the ESEA of 1965 along with Title VII, renamed Bilingual Education Language Enhancement and Language Acquisition Programs.

Most recently, the No Child Left Behind Act of 2001 mandated that schools develop sound academic standards to address the academic gap between mainstream American students and students of color and formulate testing strategies to measure reading and mathematics skills of students in grades 3 through 8 annually.

At the state level, California, for example, passed Senate Bill 2042 that revamped the state's teacher preparation programs to include Teacher Performance Expectations (TPE) and Teacher Performance Assessments (TPA). TPE has thirteen standards. Standard 7 requires that teacher candidates learn how to teach, monitor, and assess English language learners. TPA requires prospective teachers to master four main tasks. Measurement of mastery for each task is conducted with at least four different case scenarios. For Task 1, for example, Case Scenario 3 requires teacher candidates to design lesson plan adaptations for English learners. Furthermore, Task 1 Case Scenario 4 requires teacher candidates to design a lesson plan to respond to the adaptation needs of a student with special needs.

Should Teachers Become Knowledgeable About Multicultural Education?

Absolutely! Today's teachers need a repertoire of psycho-social skills for a variety of applications. Equipping themselves with the knowledge and skills that will enable them to overcome the challenges and complexities from culturally diverse students is critically important. Knowledgeable educators are teachers without borders who can deal with both cultural diversity and different learning styles. Teachers who avail themselves of multicultural education programs at the professional level can remove long-held cultural biases and stereotypes. To be inclusive, competent, and effective teachers in a pluralistic society, educators must possess knowledge (factual information), skills (appropriate applications), and attitudes (ways to respond to the needs of students) that foster learning for all students.

Toward that end, prospective educators should look at the statements given in Table 1.3 and determine whether they believe each is true or false. The purpose of this exercise is to generate thought-provoking discussion and engage prospective teachers in constructive multicultural discourse to help them gain insights into the reasons multicultural approaches are necessary for dealing with today's academic needs and the educational issues of a pluralistic society. Regardless of the answers, the discussion should enlighten students about multicultural education and why many language-minority students lag behind in school. The one-model-fits-all is not the only way to educate children. The results of this exercise should open students up to realize some of the complexities involved in teaching and learning.

Table 1.3. Statements About Multicultural Education

True	False	Statement
_____	_____	Cultural differences are apparent in how students learn, think, interact, communicate, and socialize in school.
_____	_____	Discontinuity between home and school culture has little effect on academic achievement and school success.
_____	_____	Parental goals and attitudes toward school programs, teaching, and learning have little effect on academic achievement and school success of students.
_____	_____	Culturally diverse students may have learning styles at odds or incompatible with those of other students in the traditional U.S. school.
_____	_____	All children of all races should learn about the beliefs, values, traditions, and contributions of other people in society.

Summing Up

This chapter presented an overview of the psycho-social dimensions of multicultural education that have to do with the way people feel, think, learn, and understand cultural diversity in today's schools. The issues discussed in this section were selected to provide a broad base for the study of multicultural education to help prospective educators as well as students explore the dynamics of diversity in order to understand their school environments and set them free from their own cultural boundaries. The author hopes that this foundation will equip readers with democratic perspectives and guide them through the process of acquiring the positive attitudes, the knowledge, and the skills needed to become productive and responsible educators while participating in civic action in the pursuit of social justice, equality, and democracy.

Chapter Two

The Dimensions of Student Diversity

> Rather than deny that we are racist, we need to learn how to look at
> our racism and see through it…by examining how racism is reflected
> in our actions, we can transform ourselves and our schools.
> —Franklin L. Jones

Overview

Today's elementary and secondary schools are flooded with students of diverse backgrounds, cultural traits, needs, abilities, and learning styles. Culture and language diversity place tremendous stress on teachers because each culture brings its own beliefs, values, customs, traditions, needs, and demands to the classroom. The school culture is thus tremendously diverse culturally, and teachers need to provide a multicultural curriculum that is responsive to the educational needs of all students.

This discussion is organized in three parts. The first part of this chapter examines factors associated with diversity in general to help educators understand the dimensions of cultural diversity—race, ethnicity, gender, sexual orientation, socioeconomic status, language, cultural identity, and exceptionalities. The second part focuses on specific challenges caused by differences among people in these dimensions—racism, prejudice, White privilege, stereotypes, cultural bias, ethnocentrism, and the achievement gap. The third part presents three multicultural paradigms—the cultural deprivation model, the cultural mismatch model, and the cultural difference model.

Student Diversity in Public Schools

Of the 55 million students in K-12 schools in 2006, the National Education Association (NEA) reported that Whites made up the largest student group (62%), followed by Blacks (17%), Hispanics (16%), Asians or Pacific Islanders (4%), and American Indians or Alaska Natives (1%). The NEA further reported that the number of English language learners had increased by nearly 65% in the 13 years since 1993. In some schools, classroom teachers who had not previously seen such diversity are now asking for assistance in curricular areas as well as multicultural resources to address the opportunities and challenges that student diversity brings to the schools. Currently, approximately 5.2 million ELLs or LEP students are enrolled in the public school system; 1 in 10 children is not fluent in English. Menken and Look (2000) noted that limited English proficient students make up the fastest growing student group in the American educational system; their number has increased 104% in the last 10 years.

Like some other states, California has a very diverse student population. Of the 6 million students in California's K-12 schools in 2004, 31.9% were White, 8% were Black, 11% were Asian or Pacific Islander, 45.2% were Hispanic, and 0.8% were American Indian or Alaska Native. Moreover, 47.9% of students were economically disadvantaged, 24.9% were English language learners, 10.6% were students with disabilities, and 2.5% were migrant students. As mentioned previously, California is home to 1.5 million LEP students and 1 million FEP students. To help prospective educators understand the dimensions of student diversity, Table 2.1 shows how some of the demographic characteristics of California students compare with national figures.

Table 2.1. California and National Student Demographics

Characteristic	California	Nation
White	31.9%	58.0%
Black	8.0%	16.9%
Asian/Pacific Islander	11.0%	4.4%
Hispanic	45.2%	19.5%
American Indian/Alaska Native	0.8%	1.2%
Economically disadvantaged	47.9%	36.7%
English language learners	24.9%	7.8%
Students with disabilities	10.6%	12.8%
Migrant students	2.5%	0.6%
LEP students	1.5 million	5.2 million

Note: Data from the National Education Association, 2006, and California Department of Education, 2005-2006. Some numbers are rounded.

As the figures in Table 2.1 indicate, there is no doubt that student diversity is growing. The increase in the diversity of learning abilities and needs bring even more complex challenges as well as opportunities to the classroom.

What Is Cultural Diversity?

Diversity literally means *difference*. The term *cultural diversity* refers to differences in culture, race, ethnicity, language, class, religion, gender, and socioeconomic status. Today, educators use the term to refer to differences between students of color and mainstream American students. Common designations for different groups are low-income students, economically disadvantaged students, language minority students, English language learners (EL), limited English-proficient students (LEP), fluent English-proficient students (FEP), students with special needs (SSN), exceptional students, majority students, and minority students.

Figure 2.1 shows that the student is connected to home, the school, the community, and the nation. When students encounter conflicts between the values, practices, and expectations of the different environments, they become confused. The values they learn in school may not necessarily be the same as the values in their home or their community. Students have difficulty when there is a discontinuity between home and school, incongruence between school and community, or a mismatch between community and the nation. Perhaps, multicultural education could be the common thread weaving all four spheres together.

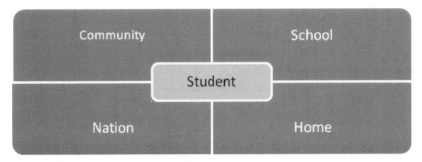

Figure 2.1. Environment of the student

What Is Culture?

Culture has complex connotations. It can be defined and expressed in different ways. Manning and Baruth (2009) described culture as comprised of values, language, religion, ideals, artistic expressions, social relationships, thinking patterns, and behaviors. Gollnick and Chinn (2009) explained that culture is the social transmission of life—thinking, believing, feeling, and acting—within a group of people. De Melendez and Beck (2010) defined culture simply as the way of life of a social group. Similarly, Ovando et al. (2006) asserted that culture is a deep and multilayered interplay with language, values, beliefs, and behaviors pervading life situations and undergoing modifications. In sum, culture is the norm of life that encompasses the core of all aspects of living situations of a particular group.

Today, our understanding of culture is quite sophisticated, and we recognize that culture is applied differently in different aspects of life. Lessow-Hurley (2000) observed that culture is dynamic and creative; it is learned and shared. Culture may be expressed overtly or covertly. For instance, designs in clothing, decoration, and housing; time orientation and spatial orientation; and values are all expressions of culture.

Two terms associated with culture are biculturalism and cultural capital. Bicultural refers to the ability to function in two cultures, perhaps including speaking a different or second language. Cultural capital refers to the socioeconomic status of an individual who is equipped with wealth, assets, and advantages.

What Is Race?

Race is one of the most misunderstood and misleading identifications in a pluralistic society. Educators should not rush to judge or assume knowledge of a person's race based on facial characteristics or other aspects of physical appearance because color of skin and other physical traits do not necessarily correctly identify a person's race. Race refers to the inherent biological makeup that characterizes one group of people as compared to other groups. Keep in mind that people within a race can have a wide range of traits, behaviors, attitudes, and values; therefore, racial information should be defined carefully and respectfully. In multicultural education, race, in most cases, is identified by the physical characteristics of a group of people who have a somewhat similar genetic history, share a common language, and share the same cultural heritage (de Melendez & Beck, 2010).

What Is Ethnicity?

Ethnicity is a broad concept that denotes biological or social membership in a group of people based on that group's national origin, the national origin of one's ancestors, racial identity, culture, traditions, language, and social interests. Manning and Baruth (2009) defined ethnicity as denoting a person's national origin, religion, race, and any combination of these features. The "social interests" component of ethnicity refers to the organization of community, the physical attributes of the people, and cultural events shared within the group to honor its way of life.

Educators should be cautious about equating students' ethnicities with their racial identities. Different ethnicities may be found within one race. For example, Hmong is considered a race, but within the Hmong race are different family clans and tribal groups with different dialects and heritages. Manning and Baruth (2009) noted that strong ethnic identification should include sharing, accepting, practicing, and respecting group values, beliefs, thinking patterns, behaviors, communication styles, dialects, languages, and cultural characteristics.

What Is Gender?

Gender is identification according to the characteristics of femininity and masculinity determined by biological characteristics, culture, thoughts, feelings, behaviors, communication, attitudes, family roles, and responsibilities that help identify a person as either male or female (Gollnick & Chinn, 2009; Manning & Baruth, 2009).

Gender inequality is prevalent in today's schools. Educators should minimize gender inequality by using gender-appropriate curricula that meet the needs of both sexes. Furthermore, each culture has distinct issues regarding gender equality. Arab Americans, for example, tend to favor male children over female children. Similarly, parents from India prefer to see the birth of a son over that of a daughter. Right now in China, Chinese parents face a difficult decision when considering whether to have a child. Because government policy allows only one child per couple, most parents prefer a son who will preserve the family in accordance with their beliefs in filial piety and the kinship system.

Manning and Baruth (2009) reported that, in school, female students tend to choose fewer mathematics and science courses than do male students. However, female students seem to work better with groups than male students. Legally, educators need to be cautious about the exclusionary activities and curricular designs that bar female or male students from participating and thus create gender discriminatory learning environments.

Keep in mind that minority students of diverse cultures may have different attitudes toward the curriculum used in the classroom. Traditional Hispanic and Hmong students, for example, have a natural tendency to be reserved, quiet, and timid in class because of the cultural roles and responsibilities they are taught at home. Educators should use the multicultural approach of cooperative learning to help these students become involved in group activities so they can express their thoughts and feelings.

What Is Sexual Orientation?

Sexual orientation refers to an individual's sexual attraction to persons of the same or opposite sex or both sexes (Gollnick & Chinn, 2009). Some of the terms for various orientations used today are gay, lesbian, bisexual, straight, transsexual, transvestite, and heterosexual. Talking about students' sexuality remains one of the most sensitive areas in education. Many parents do not approve of sex education or discussions of family planning or parenthood in the classroom. It is critical that multicultural education include all students no matter what their sexual orientation; however, educators question when schools should provide educational experiences that address and clarify differences in sexual orientation. No doubt secondary students need to have some kind of formal education about human sexuality, but schools face challenges designing curricula to educate all students about sexual orientation if the community does not support such efforts.

Without doubt, gay and lesbian students have been treated differently and unequally in school. The number of cases of discrimination involving these types of students is increasing across the nation. Gays and lesbians have been subjected to humiliation, insults, harassment, and use of sexual epithets. Once these students are identified, their needs are often downplayed, ignored, or denied by the schools.

To minimize the negative impact of differences in sexual orientation, Manning and Baruth (2009) suggested that schools and educators do as follows:

1. Provide factual and educational information about youth sexuality.
2. Abandon the myth that discussing homosexuality will cause adolescents to grow up to be gay or lesbian.
3. Promote and protect the human and civil rights of all students in the classroom.

4. Encourage and support the hiring of gay and lesbian educators who can provide healthy role models.

Educators have the responsibility to educate all students without condition and regardless of their sexual orientation. Educators should always protect the interests of all students by not disclosing students' sexual orientations in a manner that will cause them irreparable damage.

What Is Socioeconomic Status (SES)?

As indicated earlier, 36.7% of the nation's students are economically disadvantaged as compared to 47.9% of students in California. Socioeconomic status refers to the composite of family economic status, or personal success, on the basis of professional occupation, educational attainment, income, wealth, power, and recognition. Socioeconomic status is also measured by a family's status, social class, and contribution to the community. Typically, social standing and economic level are directly related. In today's American school system, rich people generally receive a quality education and poor people receive a basic, survival education.

Generally, people tend to believe that affluent students fare better than minority students in all academic areas, without considering individual differences, because they live better and have access to resources. On the other hand, minority children who live at or below the poverty level have more health problems and lack health insurance. In other words, minority children live in poor inner-city areas where overcrowded and underperforming schools are all that are available. Schools located in upper-middle-class neighborhoods seem to have better facilities, more resources, better programs, and higher quality teaching staffs.

Socioeconomic disparities continue to divide minority groups and dominant groups in various ways. Social stratification is seen in family income, college degrees, profession, occupation, wealth, social status, power, recognition, and location of residence. Manning and Baruth (2009) pointed out that over half of Hispanics, African Americans, and American Indians are poor and near poor as compared to 26% of Whites and 33% of Asian Americans and Pacific Islanders.

Family status plays an important role in determining socioeconomic status. According to Manning and Baruth (2009) and Newman and Ralston (2006), approximately 29 million children of diverse backgrounds receive free lunch each day in school. Of this number, two-thirds come from female-headed households.

Social class refers to the stratification of families into four categories—upper class, middle class, low class, and underclass. Children of different social classes behave, think, act, relate, respond, and understand their environments differently. Affluent students, for example, may have difficulty understanding the needs of English language learners who are from a lower class. Because today's classrooms contain children from both lower and upper socioeconomic strata, educators should bear in mind that all children deserve the same academic benefits and the same opportunities as well as the same quality of instruction.

Underclass children are the most unrecognized individuals in school. These are children of homeless families and dysfunctional families, children from families with substance abuse or incarcerated parents, and children in the foster care system. A large number of these children live in foster homes or with relatives other than their parents, often with grandparents. However, keep in mind that across all social classes, there are commonalities and all children can share, learn, understand, and grow through the socialization process.

When considering socioeconomic status, educators must realize that social class alone does not determine or accurately indicate children's motivation to break out of their family's status quo. Sometimes, educators overlook children of lower classes because they assume that the children's situations limit their possibilities in life. In other words, teachers may think lower-SES students lack ambition to work hard to improve their educational standing or their lives. For example, studies indicate that many high schools help Hmong students accumulate only enough units to graduate, determining that the students are not college bound (Goldstein, 1985). In fact, however, most Hmong students are, by culture, reserved students who work very hard to get their education, and many earn college degrees.

Health status plays another key role in the academic success of minority students. Even if minority Americans have a higher prevalence of health problems such as diabetes, obesity, and hypertension, it is unfair to attempt to predict the health conditions of children of any cultural group. Minority children of low and under classes receive tremendous benefits from healthcare programs provided by the state and federal government. Upper-class families consider these benefits inadequate, just enough for survival; but for the economically disadvantaged, these benefits are lifesavers.

What Is Language?

In 2006, the National Education Association (NEA) reported that 425 dialects or primary languages are spoken in U.S. K-12 schools. Language diversity poses a very difficult challenge for schools today since most educators are not trained and ready to handle the needs of diverse students who speak different dialects. Language refers to the way people communicate, share, understand, and convey information through verbal, oral, written, gesture, or codes form. Gollnick and Chinn (2009) defined language as a written or spoken human speech system that enables people to communicate and share with one another their thoughts and ideas. For some, language is a complex and dynamic system designed by mankind with conventional symbols applied in various modes for communication and thought (American Speech-Language-Hearing Association, 1983; Lessow-Hurley, 2000).

Lessow-Hurley described language from four different perspectives— linguistics, or the structural aspects of language; psycholinguistics, or the relationship of language and the mind; neurolinguistics, or the relationship of language and the brain; and sociolinguistics, or how language works and is used in society. Lessow-Hurley listed five subsystems of language: phonology or sound system, morphology or root system, syntax or structural system, semantics or meaning system, and pragmatics or the system of using language in social context.

Furthermore, Lessow-Hurley explained that language attitudes and language varieties play different roles in society today. Language attitudes have to do with the ways people use language and the ways they view, accept, respect, and understand it. Language varieties have to do with the quality of applications: standard form, dialect, register, and slang.

Despite the complexities of language, Manning and Baruth (2009) observed that the number of diverse students with diverse languages has increased exponentially in today's schools. Between 1992 and 2002, the number of English language learners increased 72%. In 2002, approximately 4 million students who speak a language other than English enrolled in the nation's K-12 schools. Interestingly, most of these students resided in California, Texas, New York, Florida, and Illinois (Perkins-Cough, 2007, as cited in Manning & Baruth, 2009).

No doubt language diversity has been the most difficult challenge facing the nation's educational system. It is unclear whether language diversity has anything to do with the socio-academic movement, or the achievement gap, between affluent students and minority students. In some states, over the last 2 decades, policy makers wanted to eliminate bilingual education programs designed to help English learners. California, for example, passed Proposition 227 in 1998, requiring English-only instruction for all students in grades K-12. In other words, the state eliminated the bilingual education program. However, in 2006, a 5-year study conducted by the American Institute of Research (AIR) reported that the passage of Proposition 227 had not led to significant improvement in English skills in ELLs. The report concluded that academic success is based on the quality of instruction, not the language of instruction.

What Is Cultural Identity?

Culturally diverse students can face tremendous pressure in developing and forming cultural identities for themselves because the classroom has so many different cultures, traditions, customs, and values from which to learn. Students of color sometimes take drastic measure to imitate unacceptable behaviors that are opposite of those traditional in their culture. Most importantly, cultural identity should include the self-image, self-esteem, and self-worth students bring with them to schools.

Manning and Baruth (2009) explained that identity is the sense of place within the world, meaning that people attach themselves to the broader context of daily life. Banks (2008) described identity as multiple, changing, overlapping, and contextual rather than fixed and static. In other words, people have some kind of attachment to the race, culture, language, traditions, values, customs, and beliefs of the community of which they are a part.

Cultural identity involves the numerous cultural and cross-cultural elements of a group that influence or help form a person's individuality (de Melendez & Beck, 2010). As Banks (2008) explained, students might develop several identities or characteristics at once because they feel a need to fit in multiple places while learning to adapt to the cultural norms of the community. However, educators have a big role: they help facilitate positive identity formation within the community of the classroom. Within the larger cultural community there is room for individual and cultural differences and perceptions. Assuming all students of one culture to be alike could mislead teachers into forming a false cultural identity for all.

Individual students may have cultural baggage that affects how they develop, accept, change, and form their cultural identities. Educators need to model cross-cultural sensitivity in order to help students understand their individual personalities and their attitudes toward their peers of other cultural backgrounds. They need to be aware of positive and negative situations that may arise during the process of instilling self-acceptance and positive self-concepts in their students.

Keep in mind that minority students can experience acceptance and rejection of other cultures simultaneously. They may reject cultural elements from the dominant culture as undesirable or inappropriate. In some situations, minority students suffer unexpected adverse effects when replacing their cultural beliefs and characteristics with new values, behaviors, attitudes, and styles.

Multicultural educators can encourage minority students to maintain and preserve their cultural identities without making drastic changes that could jeopardize their self-concept and affiliations in the community. Teachers can encourage, for example, the display of respect, a positive attitude that fosters acceptance of different cultural identities. Valuing differences in language, race, ethnicity, class, socioeconomic status, and religion is a powerful first step in understanding and validating students' perceptions about being unique and accepted.

As Manning and Baruth (2009) explained, educators need to design teaching-learning experiences in the classroom in such a way that minority students can believe in themselves and realize that they do not have to change their cultural identities or adopt the dominant culture in order to experience school success. However, helping culturally diverse students form their cultural identities through a formalized process requires time and energy. Educators could prescribe regular curricular activities that allow students to experience cross-cultural interaction and socialization, such as cooperative learning, group activities, and group projects.

Who Are Students with Exceptionalities?

Educators should not be confused about the distinction between students with exceptionalities and students with language barriers. Language deficiency and lack of proficiency in English are not considered learning disabilities. The term *exceptionalities* is used of students with special needs. Exceptional students have one or more learning disabilities—mental retardation; hearing, speech or language impairment; visual impairment; emotional difficulties; orthopedic issues; autism; traumatic brain injury; other health impairments; and specific learning disabilities (Manning & Baruth, 2009). Moreover, as noted in Table 2.1, 12.8% of the nation's students have some kind of learning disabilities as compared with 10.6% in California. McNamara (2007) explained that the term *learning disabilities* refer to a wide range of academic deficits found in the student population and it does not denote cultural or linguistic deficiencies.

The widely used definition for learning disabilities presented by Kirk (1962, as cited in McNamara, 2007) is as follows:

> A learning disability refers to retardation, disorder, or delayed development in one or more of the processes of speech, language, reading, writing, arithmetic, or other school subjects resulting from a psychological handicap caused by a possible cerebral dysfunction and/or emotional or behavioral disturbance. It is not the result of mental retardation, sensory deprivation, or cultural and instructional factors.

Furthermore, McNamara listed 10 of the most common characteristics of students classified as having a learning disability: (a) hyperactivity; (b) perception impairments; (c) emotional lability; (d) general coordination deficits; (e) disorders of attention, short attention span, distractibility preservation; (f) impulsivity; (g) disorders of memory and thinking; (h) specific learning disabilities—reading, arithmetic, writing, spelling; (i) disorders of speech and learning, and (j) equivocal neurological signs and EEG irregularities.

In addition to giving attention to students with exceptionalities, educators should be aware of students who are gifted and talented because they are often neglected, unidentified, unrecognized, and ignored in regular classrooms (Manning & Baruth, 2009). As shown in Table 2.2, the profiles of gifted and talented students are culturally diverse; however, Native American/Alaska Native children are underrepresented. According to Gollnick and Chinn (2009), gifted and talented students are individuals with very high intelligence or who possess unusual gifts and talents in the arts. They need specially designed educational programs or curricula in order to reach their full potential.

Table 2.2. Ethnic Distribution of Students in Gifted and Talented Programs

Ethnicity	Percentage
White	74
Black	8
Hispanic	10
Asian or Pacific Islander	7
American Indian or Alaska Native	1

Note. Data from the National Education Association, 2006.

Ryan and Cooper (2001) pointed out that gifted children usually have high intellectual ability, and talented children have creative or artistic abilities. Gifted and talented children give evidence of potential for high achievement or performance in academic, creative, artistic, or leadership areas. As with all other children, gifted and talented students have specific strengths and weaknesses. Manning and Baruth (2009) observed that these students are exceptionally diverse and sometimes appear as antisocial, creative, high achieving, divergent thinkers, and perfectionists; they may have attention-deficit disorders, dyslexia, or other complex disorders. They also need to learn how to form personal identities, deal with independence, explore romantic relationships, and develop warm and loving interpersonal relationships. They need to identify and develop their personal values, attitudes, personalities, and belief systems. Some students with exceptionalities who are culturally diverse from the mainstream face very complex issues, limitations, and challenges.

The presence of multiple intelligences in the classroom may be challenging for some teachers. For instance, an athlete who has great physical abilities in sports may lack the mental capacity to perform well in school, or a learner who is a math genius may not have the auditory capacity to learn music. Moreover, Asian American students, for example, are generally good in math, but they may lack the cognates needed to perform in areas that require language skills. In some cases, gifted and talented students may encounter serious relationship problems because they are self-centered, look down on less intelligent classmates, or have poor communication and interpersonal skills. For instance, an intelligent individual who has a short attention span would have a difficult time teaching culturally diverse students who may need extra time to perform a given task or respond to a question.

What Is Racism?

Traditionally, racism refers to prejudice directed at people of color because of their ethnic and racial identity. Manning and Baruth (2009) defined racism as the domination of one social, racial, or ethnic group by another. They implied that racism is an ideological system used to justify the discrimination of some racial groups against others.

Today, people face a different kind of racism. It is a subtle form of prejudice in which people—educators, professionals, students, parents, and leaders—appear not to harbor prejudice on the surface, but in reality, they do hold prejudicial attitudes toward other races, ethnicities, and groups. In other words, modern racism is covert prejudice. Educators should pay close attention to their actions, behaviors, attitudes, and body language while working with a culturally diverse student population because modern racism is quite prevalent and harmful.

Racism is not an innate characteristic, but rather a learned attitude. Students often develop prejudicial attitudes in the homes and the communities where they live. Racism, with its misunderstandings or lack of information, creates bias. Educators should design appropriate curricular activities and implement them in such a way as to reduce racial tensions, ignorance, and bigotry. Keep in mind that racial issues are emotionally sensitive, and before broaching the subject, educators need to make sure their students are ready to discuss it; otherwise, school could be viewed as a breeding ground for racism. Having said that, regardless of what educators intend to do, the subtle evil of racism will never disappear or be eliminated (Manning & Baruth, 2009).

What Is Prejudice?

As with racism, prejudice is contagious and harmful. Prejudice is any unjustified negative attitudes or expressions toward a group of people solely on the basis of their membership in a group different from that of the prejudiced. De Melendez and Beck (2010) defined prejudice as a social perspective and a negative attitude not supported by facts or evidence, but rather held on the basis of ideas and stereotypes about an individual or group. Multicultural education aims at reducing prejudice in school in order to provide all students with equal opportunity, equity of instruction, and social empowerment.

Without dealing with racism and prejudice, educators would have a tough time bringing social justice into the classroom environment. Educators should offer meaningful, appropriate teaching-learning experiences with multicultural materials to counter the presence of prejudice and reduce the impact of cultural intolerance.

What Is White Privilege?

In a multilingual and multicultural nation, every race has certain privileges, advantages, and disadvantages as well as guilty feelings. However, in America, White privilege has been viewed by multilingual and multicultural people as an unearned asset, favorable treatment, or benefits given only to those who possess "whiteness" or White cultural characteristics. Experts define White privilege as a combination of exclusive standards and opinions that are

supported by Whites in a way that continually reinforces social distance between groups on the basis of power, access, advantage, majority status, control, choice, autonomy, authority, possessions, wealth, opportunity,
materialistic acquisition, connection, access, preferential treatment, entitlement, and social standing (Hays & Chang, 2003; Manning & Baruth, 2009).

White privilege carries with it the disadvantage of guilt feelings. Some
Whites who feel they do not benefit from their whiteness claim to be victims
of unequal treatment because they are judged to be responsible for having
illegitimate advantages over other racial groups. In some cases, feelings of
guilt validate the perception of favored social position involuntarily given by
other racial groups. Moreover, guilt could be either negative or positive, depending on an individual's social status. Some Whites see themselves as superior to people in other groups and disregard others' attitudes toward them.
Ironically, others see themselves as oppressors because they are illegiti-
mately favored, and, at the same time, their status penalizes people in other
groups for no legitimate reason (Manning & Baruth, 2009).

The concept of White privilege has different impacts on cultural groups.
Not long ago, a teacher shared this story with her college class: "As a Hispanic daughter, my father told me to act, do, behave, and talk like Whites if I
want to overcome racism and prejudice in life. And I did." Some Hmong
Americans also encourage their offspring to copy White counterparts as
much as possible in order to assimilate and saturate the "White culture" to
take part in White privilege.

However, minorities still suffer an incredible amount of prejudice and
racial inequality even when they successfully change their behaviors and attitudes to blend in. Everyone should have a sense of pride in who they are, but
sometimes people abandon their cultural identity and assume a new one for
socio-political reasons.

For example, Hmong Americans often shed their native names and take
American names when becoming naturalized U.S. citizens because they want
to be recognized as "real Americans" on paper. They have strong feelings
that the American label is important to Whites and having a non-Hmong
name makes it is easy for Whites to accept them when they are seeking employment opportunities. However, in their Hmong community, these individuals continue to use their Hmong names to maintain recognition,
acceptance, and respect in that community.

What perceptive educators need to do to help all students in a pluralistic
society understand White privilege is provide social studies curricula that
engage students in cooperative activities that enable them to learn about one
another's cultures and feelings. It is important for educators to include dis-

cussion of White privilege and identity. Here is why: In most classrooms, minority students are asked to share their cultural identities, characteristics, values, traditions, and differences with mainstream American students, but rarely does anyone share with the minority students about White identity or White privilege. Minority students have a difficult time understanding the "American culture" if no one shares with them what it is all about. As many experts have pointed out, educators should design curricula that allow all students the opportunity to explore, discover, examine, and study their own racial, cultural, ethnic, linguistic, and religious backgrounds and let them share with other students in such a way that all benefit (Abrams & Gibson, 2007; Manning & Baruth, 2009). Educators should at least attempt to dispel attitudes that would lead students to develop animosity toward poor and minority groups (McLaren, 1998).

Educators should keep in mind that White privilege is somewhat prevalent and alive in some areas of today's society, and in others, Whiteness could be invisible because of socioeconomic disparities, racial discrimination, and social segregation.

What Are Stereotypes?

De Melendez and Beck (2010) described a stereotype as an oversimplified generalization about a particular group, race, culture, or sex that usually carries a derogatory implication. Similarly, Manning and Baruth (2009) defined *stereotype* as an attitude toward a person or cultural group characterizing or describing an entire group, race, gender, or religion. Manning and Baruth further observed that these descriptions have negative and positive consequences as a result of a generalized mental picture, judgment, and misperceptions about a person or the whole group.

Gollnick and Chinn (2009) explained that a stereotype is an exaggerated and usually biased view of a group. Generally, stereotype refers to a person's belief, judgment, perception, or attitude that generalizes the association of a whole group of people with certain traits or characteristics. Keep in mind that cultural stereotypes are contagious and evil. Some people have a false consensus bias toward other people, believing that most people who share their cultural characteristics share their stereotypes. Typically, biased people develop some kind of stereotype threat on the basis of their conscious or unconscious reinforcement of stereotypic attitudes, behaviors, feelings, and prevailing norms.

Despite all this, educators should bear in mind that no one is free of cultural biases or stereotypes. To help all students learn, know, and understand the dangers of stereotypes, educators should recognize their own cultural biases; students imitate what they see adults do. Because cultural stereotypes could lead students toward other damaging cultural attitudes and behaviors such as prejudice, racism, and discrimination, educators should implement multicultural curricula that allow students to experience differences in race, ethnicity, class, religion, language, culture, and socioeconomic status.

Cultural stereotypes are developed from learned experiences; they are not innate traits or characteristics. In other words, no one is born as a stereotypic individual. Also, educators should understand that children have misperceptions and misconceptions about other cultures because they lack the truth and they imitate others. Teachers must help students recognize and clarify their personal stereotypes and biases toward other people. The goal of multicultural education is to create a positive and inclusive learning community that benefits all.

What Is Cultural Bias?

Cultural bias is vividly present today in the school and elsewhere in the community because of the presence of so many different cultures, traditions, religions, classes, races, ethnicities, and levels of socioeconomic status. Cultural bias refers to the favoritism of one specific cultural group over others. Ovando et al. (2006) described cultural bias as bias in favor of the cultural majority group and against minority groups. Whether cultural bias is covert or overt, it impairs educators' professional ability to work well with all students while working with students from different racial groups and diverse backgrounds. Cultural bias can be deliberate or unintentional, depending on an individual's attitudes, beliefs, and perceptions toward cultural diversity.

One subtle form of cultural bias is attitudinal bias. Attitudinal bias refers to the practices of favoring one particular language or dialect over others. In America, people speak English differently in different geographic regions; there are southern accents, Midwestern accents, and New England accents, for example. Similarly, British and Australian accents are distinctly different, but they are understandable to anyone who speaks English. Hmong have two distinct dialects—White Hmong and Blue Hmong. Most people prefer to use White Hmong in public communication because it has a simpler written form than Blue Hmong. As a result, some Blue Hmong professionals voluntarily switch their dialect to White Hmong when giving a public speech or teaching a class. Such professionals do not exhibit attitudinal bias; they are adapting to the community norm.

What Is Ethnocentrism?

America is a multilingual and multicultural nation, and culture influences the way people behave, talk, feel, think, believe, and communicate. Some people take cultural identity and pride to an extreme, assuming an ethnocentric view. Ethnocentrism is the belief that one culture is superior to others (Gollnick & Chinn, 2010; Manning & Baruth, 2009; Ovando et al., 2006). Ethnocentrism is the tendency of individuals or groups to regard their own ethnic group, nation, religion, culture, gender, class, language, and/or socioeconomic status as being more accurate, suitable, acceptable, civilized, or in some other way superior to all others.

On the contrary, people should realize that some elements of their culture they regard as natural, correct, and perhaps superior may be viewed by others as shocking, odd, inferior, primitive, and barbaric. For instance, in some cultures in America, people eat certain foods to preserve their cultural heritage; however, eating raccoon, bear, and 'possum dishes could be regarded as very odd, perhaps even repugnant, to Americans who are unfamiliar with the culture that enjoys these foods.

To keep ethnocentrism from the classroom, educators should provide multicultural curricula that helps children understand their misperceptions of different cultures. Curricular activities should include appropriate cross-cultural exercises, empowerment, positive responses, encouragement, adaptations, understanding, and sensitivity because some children may have deep-seated beliefs, attitudes, feelings, grudges, and misperceptions about other cultures. Removing these ingrained and embedded attitudes may be challenging and difficult, but positive modeling and guidance will minimize the impact of ethnocentrism. And keep in mind that cultural reservations and hesitations are likely to persist until students are comfortable enough to change, respect, and accept cultural diversity. One reason it is so important for educators to work to overcome these challenges is the presence of an achievement gap.

What Is the Achievement Gap?

The achievement gap is a difference in academic attainment between students of color and mainstream students. It is determined by aggregate data of composite scores on standardized tests. Despite any claims to the contrary, the gap is either stable or widening, depending on the source of the data analysis. Some data seem to indicate the gap is narrow; however, quantifying the actual achievement gap between minority students and majority students remains elusive because of measurement complexities that generate controversial interpretations and misrepresentations.

Banks (2008) reported that the No Child Left Behind Act of 2001 requires school districts to compile test scores for all students and to disaggregate academic achievement data based on certain criteria in order to determine if the gap is closing or widening. Those criteria are income, race, ethnicity, disability, and limited English proficiency. Lessow-Hurley (2000) cautioned that "any analysis of achievement must consider the nature of measurement because testing is not ideologically innocent and differential outcomes may well be the product of biases in the procedures and content of assessment measures" (p. 104).

The dispute over genetic inferiority and superiority started in the late 1960s. Jensen (1969) suggested that intellectual ability is determined 80% by heredity and 20% by environment. He based this notion on genetic factors. However, later scholars disputed and criticized his claim. But perhaps Jensen's controversial suggestions have become embedded in the minds of some people who are mean-spirited. Similarly, Murry and Herrnstein (1994) introduced the "Bell Curve," claiming that students of color are less intelligent than their White counterparts. These writers did not carefully consider all aspects of testing and cultural diversity.

Multicultural educators should pay close attention to these kinds of problems when reading about any analysis and interpretation of the achievement gap. They need to examine the validity and reliability of each instrument used to assess students academically and culturally before forming an opinion. Misapplications can be made, sometimes inadvertently, and the results can misguide curricular efforts and cause students from different racial and income groups to be mislabeled.

Construct bias exists in most tests. For instance, consider the test construct below:

1. A house is made of …
   A. Steel
   B. Cement
   C. Adobe
   D. Wood
   E. All the above

2. A man dressed in a suit is going to…
   A. Work
   B. Church

C. School
D. Funeral
E. All the above

If these sample questions were on a test, many minority students would choose A, B, C, or D as correct answers, but not E because of their cultural backgrounds. However, students from European cultures would choose E as the correct answer because of their experiences. Keep in mind that most tests are Euro-centric and are written on the basis of White, middle-class values. The ways educators and policy makers approach the challenges of cultural diversity depend on their framework for understanding that diversity. In other words, what is their paradigm of multiculturalism?

What Is a Multicultural Paradigm?

A multicultural paradigm is simply a model, a pattern, or a lens for explaining cultural diversity. It is important because the way in which someone looks at a particular phenomenon, such as cultural diversity, determines that person's behavior toward the phenomenon. Banks (2008) eloquently described the multicultural paradigm as follows:

> An interrelated set of facts, concepts, generalizations, and theories that attempt to explain human behaviors or a social phenomenon and that imply policy and action …which is also a set of explanations, has specific goals, assumptions, and values that can be described.…Explanations such as at-risk students, culturally deprived students, and culturally different students are paradigms.

Banks introduced two distinct paradigms to explain why low-income students and students of color perform poorly in school and have low academic achievement—the cultural deprivation model and the cultural difference model. The cultural deprivation paradigm suggests that children who are socialized in the culture of poverty lack something in their culture. The cultural difference paradigm rejects the idea that minority students have a cultural deficit, asserting instead that students of color have rich cultures that are simply different from that of the majority. Experts believe that educators who espouse the cultural deprivation model blame low-income students and students of color for their academic problems, and educators who apply the cultural difference paradigm believe that the larger society is responsible for the academic problems of these students.

Regardless, educators need to learn different perspectives for dealing with the needs of all students. It is difficult to apply a one-model-fits-all approach to teaching and learning because cultural diversity is complex in nature. Educators should consider different models and respond to the needs, cultural traits, and learning styles of all their students.

What Is the Cultural Deficit Paradigm?

In the cultural deficit model, students of color are assumed to be deprived and disadvantaged because their social behaviors, languages, beliefs, values, customs, and identities are different from those of middle-class students (Manning & Baruth, 2009). Lessow-Hurley (2000) observed that the cultural deficit model, introduced in the 1960s, was then known as the deficiency model. It suggests that minority students fail because of some inadequacy on their part. Lessow-Hurley explained that children of color were said to be language deprived because they did not have adequate language development at home. She explained, however, that this way of thinking is basically cultural tunnel vision. In this model, students who fail are often blamed for the failure. Educators should not blindly adopt this view because the cultural deficit model fails to consider all factors associated with the process of teaching and learning; it does not really address issues of cultural diversity. The concept of remediation for "cultural deficits" does not work either. Experts suggest that educators need to account for the social and political context of schooling (Boykin, 1984; Manning & Baruth, 2009).

What Is the Cultural Mismatch Paradigm?

The cultural mismatch model begins with the assumption that students of color do not fare well or succeed in school because their cultural characteristics are incongruent or incompatible with those of mainstream students and the school system (Lessow-Hurley, 2000). In other words, culturally different students fail to achieve academically due to their lack of cultural traits that match those of the dominant culture in school. According to Manning and Baruth (2009), educators who operate according to this model believe that the better the match, the greater the likelihood of academic success. Lessow-Hurley observed that this model is supported by research not because it is valid, but because the cultural traits and learning styles of students affect classroom dynamics. However, because of the complexity of different cultures, learning styles, and student characteristics, educators should be cautious about rushing to judgment without carefully considering all aspects of cultural diversity. What they see could be just the tip of the iceberg, and educators should realize that what lies under the water's surface could be of far greater importance.

What Is the Cultural Difference Paradigm?

In contrast to the cultural deficit paradigm, the cultural difference model recognizes and appreciates differences in race, ethnicity, class, culture, language, religion, and socioeconomic status as strengths, not weaknesses, and these strengths enrich school culture. This model discards the ideas of deficiency and mismatch and embraces cultural diversity. It sees value in helping all students to learn about differences. Manning and Baruth (2009) pointed out that cultural compatibility and awareness between teachers and students are crucially important regardless of cultural differences, personal expectations, or interests.

Summing Up

This chapter presented the major dimensions of contemporary cultural diversity and examined different concepts, paradigms, and models of cultural diversity. It also explored socio-cultural issues related to racism, sexism, stereotyping, discrimination, ethnicity, social class, and socioeconomic status. Prospective educators need to know that cultural diversity is a complex topic; understanding it requires deliberate and consistent effort. Most importantly, prospective educators should not forget to learn more about their own cultures and traditions so they can contribute to the richness of cultural diversity in their classrooms.

Chapter Three

Becoming Multicultural Educators

All of us have two educations:
One which we receive from others;
another and the most valuable, which we give ourselves.
—John Randolph

Overview

In recent years, a debate on bilingualism started in California when someone asked teaching professionals for input on whether all future teachers should be bilingual. A brief survey flew around the state via e-mails asking teachers about their feelings on the subject. The final result was stunning. Most respondents voted against the idea that all teachers in California should be bilingual or multilingual.

So far, no one is taking a survey asking people how future teachers should feel about becoming multicultural educators, even in states with great cultural diversity such as California, Florida, Texas, Arizona, Oregon, and New York. If such a survey were taken, it would show that the majority feel apprehensive and inadequate. Most teachers today have limited training and skills in multicultural education that would equip them to deal with the diverse needs and diverse abilities of culturally, linguistically, religiously, and economically diverse students.

Keep in mind that critics of multicultural education would not say that teachers should acquire knowledge in multicultural education or that teachers should prescribe multicultural curricula to help students of color because critics see cultural diversity as a weakness or threat to the nation's educational system rather than as a strength or enrichment. Their views should be respected to some extent; however, their views are not consistent with those of educational psychologists. The number of minority students is growing, and soon these students are going to constitute the majority of the student population in the American school system.

This chapter takes prospective educators back to basics to examine socio-cultural issues related to the educational psychology of multicultural education. The purpose is to help educators move from a mono-cultural perspective to a multicultural perspective in a pluralistic society and eventually become responsive and appreciative multicultural educators for today's diverse student population.

Why Academic Inequality Exists

To help prospective educators feel the pain of students of minority backgrounds is not to deny that academic inequality exists in today's schools. The problem of social and academic inequality is not new. In the mid-1800s Karl Marx wrote that division of labor, social conflict, and the existence of private property gave birth to inequality in society. He believed that as long as these three phenomena continued, inequalities of all kinds would remain in society (Marks & Engels, 1848). Certainly, inequality can be seen vividly in public schools and many other places.

Michels' (1915/1962) Iron Law of Oligarchy can be applied to the organization, government, and domination of today's American public schools. The school system is ruled and controlled by members of one particular group in society. The dominant racial group's hegemonic action earns it the privilege and power to control how children should be educated as well as how resources should be distributed throughout the system. The group's prestige separates the poor from the rich. Consider, for example, that those who control the schools blindly sort students into different academic tracks and prescribe academic curricula that fit their contemporary lifestyles. This sorting distributes graduates racially and economically into the various occupations of the employment system and eventually into various places in the economic system based on contemporary values and ideals. Because of academic inequality, working-class students learn to comply with the norms and values of the dominant culture while upper-middle-class students, who have unearned privilege, prestige, and power, learn leadership roles and innovations that enable them to perpetuate their hegemony in society.

To understand the foundations of the American education system, educators should learn about the court cases and landmark decisions that have addressed illegal separation and educational discrimination. Most importantly, they should study the civil right actions that sought to eliminate inequalities in public schools. The public educational system appears to be getting more complex as the number of students of color increases. Inequality is now part of the socio-academic framework of the educational system.

The School Culture

One of the most difficult challenges facing today's teachers is the necessity of dealing with the diverse needs and diverse abilities of language-minority students from different racial and income groups. This pressing concern raises many unanswered questions for new teachers who are about to enter the classroom. Are they equipped cross-culturally to deal with the realities of critical pedagogy in multicultural education?

According to Hussar and Gerald (1998), national data on student enrollment show that approximately 54 million K-12 students are enrolled in public and private schools in the U.S. Of that number, 38 million are in grades K-8 and 16 million are in Grades 9-12. Furthermore, the U.S. Department of Education reported that approximately 5.2 million students ages 6 to 21 enrolled in public and private school in the U.S. have some kind of disability. And approximately a half million students aged 3 to 5 enrolled in schools have already been diagnosed with some kind of disability. Manning and Baruth (2009) pointed out that approximately 6% of students are classified as having a learning disability and approximately 12% of all students have some kind of disability.

National data indicate that approximately 5.2 million students in U.S. schools are classified as limited English Proficient (LEP), and half of those, or approximately 1.5 million, are in California (California Department of Education, 2006; Lessow-Hurley, 2000; Macias & Kelly, 1996; Manning & Baruth, 2009). Besides the 1.5 million LEP, another 1 million students in California are classified as Fluent English Proficient (FEP) students.

As Banks (2008) reported, language-minority students of diverse backgrounds make up 43% of the school population in the U.S. If current trends continue, in the next 20 years, the number of students of color—Hispanics, Asians, Arabs, Native Americans, and African Americans—will outnumber White students—European Americans. Earlier, Banks (1991) pointed out that "students of color constitute a majority in 25 of the nation's largest school districts and in California, our most populous state with a population of thirty million people" (p. 1). Banks predicted that "students of color will make up nearly half (46 percent) of the nation's school-age youth by 2020, and about 27 percent of those students will be victims of poverty" (p. 1).

Ovando et al. (2006) noted that in 2000, approximately 54,700 children of immigrants were enrolled in K-12 schools. Of this number, 2,700 were foreign-born first-generation and 7,800 were U.S.-born second-generation.

Moreover, parents of 44,200 of these children were U.S.-born, whereas parents of 10,500 were foreign-born. The researchers warned that "it is crucial that educators, researchers, and policymakers listen attentively to the inner voices of language minority students, who may be prisoners of silence in English dominant classrooms" (p. 8).

As experts of multicultural education predicted, school culture is continuing to change as the number of language-minority students continues to rise. Wars in Iraq, Afghanistan, Pakistan, and elsewhere have brought more diverse cultures, traditions, languages, races, ethnicities, classes, and religions to the U.S., a nation that already had a rich mix of cultures and traditions before the recent influx. If teachers are not prepared to teach diverse students, who will be able to help newcomers when they arrive in the U.S.? The blood of cultural diversity in school is going to be thicker in the next 2 decades when a new wave of refugees arrives in America.

Brief History of Bilingual Education

The demographics of the American student population have changed dramatically over the 40 years since the passage of the federal Bilingual Education Act (BEA) of 1968. For educators to detect misconceptions and misperceptions about the needs of LEP students in the American school system, they need to understand the evolution of legislative and judicial support for bilingual education. This will allow them to learn about the struggle for equality in the public school system. Also, this information will help them become knowledgeable about significant developments in bilingual education. This section provides an overview of major laws, policies, and landmark decisions of the U.S. Supreme Court as well as other actions in other federal and state courts in regard to the political debate on bilingual education in the U.S. and in California.

Multicultural educators should have fundamental knowledge about federal laws, decisions, and policies that affect today's public education in order to advocate for educational equality for all students. Experts, scholars, and researchers of multicultural education often cite and discuss with educators the following landmark decisions at the federal level (Banks, 2008; Gollnick & Chinn, 2009; Lessow-Hurley, 2000; Manning & Baruth, 2009; Ovando et al., 2006; and Ryan & Cooper, 2001):

1. The 14th Amendment to the U.S. Constitution established the constitutional basis for the educational rights of language-minority students and guaranteed that no state may make or enforce any law

abridging the privileges or immunities of citizens; nor deprive any person of life, liberty, interest, or property interest without due process of law; nor deny equal protection of the laws.

2. The U.S. Supreme Court's 1954 ruling in *Brown v. Board of Education*, 347 U.S. 483, was a landmark decision that overruled the 1896 decision in *Plessey v. Ferguson* that had permitted "separate but equal" education for Negro (now African American) children. This decision declared the separation of Negro and White students to be unconstitutional and ordered desegregation of U.S. schools. It then established the principle of equal educational opportunity for all students. For instance, it said, "Where a state has undertaken to provide an opportunity for an education in its public schools, such opportunity is a right which must be made available to all on equal terms."

3. Title VI of the Civil Rights Act of 1964 prohibited discrimination in federally funded programs. This act has been one of most frequently cited in court cases throughout U.S. history ever since. The core of this act gave constitutional protection to all students in public schools and basically stated that a student has a right to meaningful and effective instruction.

4. The Bilingual Education Acts of 1968 and 1974, also known as Title VII, provided supplemental funding for school districts interested in establishing programs to meet the special educational needs of large numbers of children of limited English speaking ability. In 2001, Title VII was renamed as part of the No Child Left Behind Act.

5. The federal Department of Housing, Education, and Welfare (HEW) issued an interpretation of the Title VII regulations known as the May 25, 1970, Memorandum; it prohibited the denial of access to educational programs because of a student's limited English proficiency.

6. The Equal Educational Opportunity Act of 1974 provided specific definitions of what constituted denial of equal opportunity. For instance, section 1703 (f) described as a denial "the failure by an educational agency to take appropriate action to overcome language barriers that impede equal participation by students in an instructional program."

7. The landmark decision in *Lau v. Nichols* in 1974 was a reaffirmation of the constitutionality of the 1970 Memorandum. It addressed the denial of access and participation in an educational program due to inability to speak or understand English in a class action suit brought by Chinese speaking students in the City of San Francisco against the city's school district. The judges stated that because of two factors—(a) providing students who do not understand English with the same facilities, textbooks, teachers, and curriculum does not constitute equality of treatment because the students are effectively cut off from any meaningful education, and (b) basic skills are at the very core of what public schools teach—imposition of a requirement that before children can effectively participate in the educational program, they must already have acquired basis skills would make a mockery of public education.

8. In 1975 the *Lau* remedies prompted HEW to establish some basic guidelines for schools with LEP students; however, these guidelines were discontinued in the early 1980s.

9. In 1974, in the case of *Keyes v. School District No. 1*, the federal court issued a desegregation order that precluded a bilingual education maintenance program because desegregation involved reassignment of staff, teachers, and personnel needed for a bilingual classroom.

10. In 1975, in the case of *Morgan v. Kerrigan*, the federal court issued guidelines for preserving the integrity of established bilingual programs and the reassignment of LEP students as a cluster.

11. The Civil Rights Language Minority regulations of 1980 specifically mandated schools to service language-minority students in four basic components: identification, assessment, services, and exit. The regulations included the requirement that bilingual instruction be given by qualified teachers.

12. The landmark decision in the case *Castafieda v. Pickard* in 1981 set standards for the courts in examining programs for LEP students and required school districts to have (a) a pedagogically sound plan for LEP students; (b) sufficient qualified staff to implement the plan, which might mean hiring new staff and training current staff; and (c)

a system for evaluating the program. However, this case did not require bilingual education programs to meet these standards; it required only that appropriate action to overcome language barriers be taken through well implemented programs.

13. The landmark decision in *Idaho v. Migrant Council* in 1981 established the legal responsibility of state departments of education to monitor implementation of programs for LEP students.

14. In 1983, in *Denver v. School District No. 1*, the court allowed the standards established in the *Castafieda v. Pickard* decision to be used to evaluate the district's program for LEP students.

15. The landmark decision in *Illinois v. Gomez* in 1987 required the state to establish and enforce minimum standards for implementation of language remediation programs and established requirements for the redesignation of students from LEP to FEP status. The effects of this case and other federal decisions were the following basic guidelines for servicing LEP students:

    a. Schools need to develop programs based on a sound theoretical rationale or research.
    b. Schools need to provide professional training or development for teachers, staff, and other personnel.
    c. Schools need to provide sufficient materials or resources to help implement the programs.
    d. Schools need to develop or devise an evaluation system or assessment instrument for the programs that measures student learning as well as language proficiency.
    e. Schools need to refine or modify instructional strategies or programs in accordance with the data gathered from evaluations of student learning.

16. In 1987 the decision in *Teresa P. v. Berkeley Unified* allowed the standards established in *Castafieda v. Pickard* to be used for evaluation of the district's program for LEP students.

17. In 1994 Public Law 103-382, Improving America's School Act of 1994, was signed, reauthorizing for the fifth time the Elementary and Secondary Education Act of 1965 and including Title VII, the Bilin-

gual Education, Language Enhancement, and Language Acquisition Programs.

18. In 1998 Public Law 105-78 provided approximately $29 billion in discretionary funds for the U.S. Department of Education to use to fund educational services at all levels. Of that amount, approximately $200 million was allotted for instructional services to LEP students, and another $150 million was designated for servicing immigrant children. A portion of these funds was directed toward after-school programs, financial assistance for college students, school reform, technological innovation and programs, and school improvement initiatives.

In addition to federal legislative and judicial action, a number of state laws, policies, and mandates affect bilingual education. The following are important in the legal history of bilingual education in California:

1. In 1967 Senate Bill 53 overturned an 1872 law that required English only instruction; it allowed the use of other languages of instruction in California public schools.

2. In 1974 the Chacon-Moscone Bilingual-Bicultural Education Act established transitional bilingual education programs to meet the needs of LEP students and required that such programs follow federal guidelines for identification, program placement, and reclassification of students as FEP.

3. In 1981 the Bilingual Education Act was strengthened to require that school districts provide specific programs and fulfill other obligations to language-minority students.

4. In 1987 the governor of California rejected a reauthorization of the Bilingual Education Act. This rejection left school districts in limbo, but they continued to enforce the provisions of Chacon-Moscone without a clear mandate to do so. In other words, the state could not enforce previous state mandates, and school districts were left to fend for themselves in meeting the needs of language-minority students.

5. In 1996 the California Board of Education granted waivers for four school districts, exempting them from compliance with the provisions of the Bilingual Education Act. The waivers allowed the districts to establish sheltered English immersion programs and to dismantle their bilingual education programs.

6. In 1997, in *Quiroz et al. v. State Board of Education*, the plaintiffs claimed that LEP students' rights were violated by the Orange Unified School District's waivers for English-only instruction. In March 1998 the court ruled that the State Board of Education was not authorized to grant waivers to the expired Bilingual Education Act. At the same time, the court ruled that the Orange Unified School District did not have to provide bilingual education under California law because only federal legal requirements for educating language-minority children applied.

7. In May 1998 the governor of California vetoed Senate Bill 6 that added new ingredients to the provisions of Chacon-Moscone. If passed, this law would have granted flexibility to school districts to use either bilingual education or English immersion in accordance with local needs and preferences.

8. On June 3, 1998, the voters in California approved Proposition 227 that virtually banned bilingual education except under certain special conditions and established a 1-year sheltered immersion program for all LEP students. In July 1998, in *Valeria G. v. Wilson*, the court denied a request for an injunction against implementation of Proposition 227. The court ruled on the basis of precedents established in *Castafieda v. Pickard* that allowed sequential programs for teaching English language first followed by academic content, sequential programs such as the structured English immersion design of Proposition 227. The effects of this ruling clarified school districts' obligation to language-minority students to recoup within a reasonable period of time any academic deficit that occurred while students were learning English until the LEP students achieved academically at a level comparable to their English-speaking peers.

9. In April 1999 the State Board of Education eliminated the redesignation criteria formerly in place for classification of LEP to FEP and

allowed school districts to establish or set their own criteria for re-classification of LEP students to FEP status. At the same time, the state sponsored the English Language Development (ELD) test, also known as the California English Language Development Test (CELDT) with ELD standards.

10. In July 1999 the State Board of Education finally adopted the ELD standards that coordinated with the Language Arts/Reading Content Standards.

11. Standards in Senate Bill 2042 and Senate Bill 1059 required that teacher preparation programs include college methodology courses that address the needs of English language learners (ELs).

12. Under the California Commission on Teaching Credential's (CCTC) teacher performance expectations (TPEs), standards, and teacher performance assessment (TPAs) tasks, future teachers are required to use appropriate adaptations to target and address the needs of ELs and students with special needs.

13. In 2009 new bilingual standards required teacher preparation programs to develop specific college courses and pedagogical content to prepare future teachers to deal with the needs of language-minority students in California.

Educators must keep in mind that federal laws, court decisions, and state laws regarding the education of students of color are still somewhat controversial. No specific court order or legal remedy sets clear and concise academic standards for school districts to follow. Thus, the designs of most services to LEP students are based on interpretations of the court decisions, laws, education codes, and mandates. Most importantly, the responsibility to meet the challenges of educating students of color falls on teachers and administrators at the state and local levels.

Multicultural educators should bear in mind that different states have different programs for meeting the learning needs of LEP students. For example, in California, the prospect of legislative support has faded since the passage of Proposition 227. This means that the requirement to provide bilingual education for students of color is uncertain unless a new law is enacted. Even though federal laws support bilingual education programs, current programs are capriciously implemented throughout the nation. A few

Spanish bilingual programs or models can be found in schools today, and selection of bilingual curricula remains a local issue even if a state requires that higher education institutions adequately prepare new teachers to deal with the needs of English learners. In other words, minority parents and students have to ask school districts to provide a bilingual curriculum, and, perhaps, parents have to sign a waiver in order for the school to offer such a program in California.

Bilingual Program Models

Since the 1960s, bilingual education models have been available. Each program has its strengths and weaknesses. Multicultural educators should understand that the majority of the bilingual programs or models in U.S. schools were not designed to help students of color speak fluently in their primary and secondary languages. The goal of most programs is to help bilingual students and monolingual students become proficient in English. Despite the claims of bilingualism, these models are not designed to be taught in two languages. Some programs are considered subtractive and others are considered additive. However, keep in mind that different students require different instructional approaches and task strategies. The program models may not have instruction in all primary languages (L1) in place; therefore, a goal of bilingualism or even of biliteracy is unrealistic. The main program models are illustrated briefly in Table 3.1.

The subtractive and additive outcomes listed in Table 3.1 may not be entirely possible for students with first languages other than Spanish because not all primary languages (L1) are taught in school. For instance, schools do not generally offer programs in Punjabi, Vietnamese, Chinese, Hmong, Japanese, Hindi, Tagalong, and German. Therefore, students from these cultural backgrounds who are placed in one of these programs are expected to learn and become proficient in English, but not in their primary languages. Also, keep in mind that the ultimate goal of these programs is English proficiency, not proficiency in the primary language. The only one of these programs that can help students achieve academic proficiency is the transitional bilingual education model.

The Socialization Process Part 1: Cross-Cultural Adjustment

Life in the New World transits through trial and error, sadness and joy, uncertainty and excitement, expectations and disappointments, rejection and adjustment, discrimination and prejudice, frustration and motivation, exclusion and inclusion, and imbalance of life and mental disequilibrium (Park & Chi, 1999). The process of cross-cultural adjustment teeters between acceptance and rejection.

Table 3.1. Bilingual Education Program Models

Model	Goal	Possible Outcome	Target	Socialization Process
Transitional	Achieve English proficiency (L2)	Subtractive bilingualism—losing L1	Language-minority students of diverse backgrounds	Assimilationist approach
Maintenance	Achieve bilingualism and biliteracy (L2 and L1)	Additive bilingualism—L2 and L1	Language-minority students of diverse backgrounds and mainstream students	Pluralist approach
Enrichment, or two-way immersion	Achieve bilingualism and biliteracy (L2 and L1)	Additive bilingualism—L2 and L1	Language-minority students of diverse backgrounds and mainstream students	Pluralistic approach, but L1 may not be available
Enrichment immersion	Achieve bilingualism and biliteracy (L2 and L1)	Additive bilingualism—L2 and L1	Language-minority students of diverse backgrounds and mainstream students	Pluralistic approach, but L1 may not be available
Two-way immersion	Achieve bilingualism and biliteracy (L2 and L1)	Additive bilingualism—L2 and L1	Language-minority students of diverse backgrounds and mainstream students	Pluralistic approach, but L1 may not be available
English immersion, or saturation	Achieve English proficiency (L2)	Subtractive bilingualism—losing L1	Language-minority students of diverse backgrounds	Assimilationist approach

Note. Information from *The Foundations of Dual Language Instruction* (3rd ed.), by Lessow-Hurley, 2000, New York: Addison Wesley Longman.

Socialization is a two-part process that consists of cross-cultural adjustment and cross-cultural functioning. Completing this process in the first 5 years after arrival forms a critical foundation because the cognitive, affective, and academic development of people who come from diverse cultural backgrounds is dependent on the ability to adapt to and function in the new reality.

It is very important for today's multicultural educators to understand the social adjustment process of students from diverse backgrounds. Undergoing the socialization process significantly affects their academic performance as well as their social maturity. Today, the student population consists of a mixture of U.S.-born and foreign-born children whose parents are Americans, immigrants, refugees, and visitors. They often feel uncomfortable and strange when they have not learned to differentiate the appropriateness of various actions in all the cultures present in America. In other words, they make mistakes inadvertently, and the mistakes can cause embarrassment. Multicultural educators who understand the stages of the socialization process have an advantage in dealing with these students' educational needs and learning styles.

Newcomers to America go through 10 stages of cross-cultural adjustment. First is the *arrival* stage. Parents and children are exploring, discovering, and learning about their new environment, life, culture, traditions, and people. Most newcomers are pleased to be in America. They have come for different reasons and, regardless of their personal ambitions, political or social status, they all adjust differently.

Second is the *family reunification* stage, which is actually part of the arrival stage. However, this stage has a different feeling for those who have family members already in the U.S. Parents and children or other family members are happy to see one another again after years of separation; they want to enjoy one another and start celebrating. Of course, adults and children experience this stage differently. Some adults appear to have more difficulties adjusting to the new environment than children. Children adapt to a new way of life much more quickly. In some instances, children fit in without expressing or exhibiting any personal feelings.

Third is the *culture shock* stage. Parents and children almost immediately encounter both positive and negative events as they learn, change, misunderstand, like, dislike, complain, disbelieve, mistrust, and modify life situations to accommodate the new environment. Culture shock could result in feelings of personal guilt, embarrassment, shame, humiliation, devastation, and discomfort. Sometimes some shocking events are life-threatening. For example, Hmong refugees who experienced Halloween with its practice of trick or treating when they first arrived were terrified. They had not been told about the customs, and they believed there are ghosts in America. On the other hand, those who arrived in the month of December were very happy when they received many gifts.

Fourth is the *blaming* stage. People who come to America either through force or because of war experience this stage even if the first three stages of adjustment are relatively pleasant. For instance, Hmong refugees blamed the Secret War in Laos for their loss of lives, family members, homes, livestock, and family wealth. The feeling of blame that accompanies learning to cope with social and cultural pressures is a gut feeling. For instance, parents must figure out how to deal with the clash of values, seeing their children become Americanized, the inability to communicate in English, and unexpected health problems, especially stresses related to post-traumatic disorders.

Fifth is the *coping* stage. Newcomers must learn to deal with new life situations in order to adjust, accommodate, and acculturate. Issues that surfaced in Stages 1 through 4 are now reality, and parents must cope with everyday life. Children emulate their parents at home while imitating their peers in school. Communication between parents and children can be strained as younger children lose their native language and older children attempt to balance two cultures. Some kind of mixture of languages, values, and communication is unavoidable. For instance, some Latino children speak "Spanglish" and some Hmong children speak "Hmonglish." Many parents learn as much English as they can to improve communication at home.

Sixth is the *accommodation* stage. Newcomers learn to accommodate the differences in the two cultures and parents and children figure out how to adapt to differences between them caused by different levels of acceptance of the new culture. The accommodations must be made by both children and parents. For instance, Hmong parents may slowly change the food menu at home to accommodate their children, who are used to the food served at school and are less inclined to eat Hmong traditional dishes at home. Hmong parents learn to hug, kiss, and comfort their children physically and publicly. They find that celebration of birthdays, Mother's Day, Father's Day, and Christmas, for example, brings joy to all the family members. In the accommodation stage, newcomers appreciate, adjust, and embrace aspects of the new culture.

Seventh is the *mixture* stage. Parents and children let go of some cultural practices and retain others as they learn to accept American ideals and values. Parents want their children to preserve the family's values embodied in marriage customs, funeral services, religious rituals, cultural ceremonies, and social structures such as a clan system. Children want their parents to understand the new social phenomena, including curfews, expectations of others on them, social temptations, and adolescent courtship. Most parents realize that their children will fall behind if they are expected to fulfill some of their traditional roles, which may involve strict performance of household chores, heavy family responsibilities, and limited parent/child interaction at home. Both parents and children acculturate at home first in order to gain greater advantage outside the home. However, each family is different, and acculturation occurs at different paces.

Eighth is the *acceptance* stage. Parents and children enter a comfort zone. Open communication is likely to take place at home. Sharing is constant and instant. Some of the traditional barriers between parents and children are removed although certain limitations and restrictions remain. But for the most part, parents and children embrace new views and new family roles. The new value system brought home by the children is not viewed as odd or as an external pressure. For instance, Hmong Americans accomplish this stage by acknowledging that learning to adjust to the values of the mainstream society brings economic as well as educational opportunities. In other words, they see their children lagging behind if the parents remain stubborn in demanding adherence to old ways. In this stage, parents show more interest in their children's education, social development, and goals. In some cases, parents encourage their children to aim high to achieve their personal goals. Some of the characteristics of this stage are presented in Figure 3.1.

Ninth is the *rejection* stage. Parents and children compromise to reject or rebut certain attitudes, traits, social norms, and customs that they view as inappropriate. For instance, Hmong Americans reject the traditional view of determining the value of daughters and sons expressed in the old cliché "Nine moons will equal a sun" (which means nine daughters are equal in value to one son). This rejection fosters a positive attitude toward both female and male children, declaring they are worthy of equal economic opportunities. Similarly, Hmong children reject the traditional view that females should get married, rear children, and stay home. Instead, the children break away from their traditional gender roles to pursue higher education and become professionals who work outside the home. In some families, wives are the breadwinners or primary wage earners. However, regardless of status or educational level, most Hmong Americans adamantly reject the notion of a gay or lesbian lifestyle. Why? They believe this lifestyle is the worst curse a person could have. However, this belief may change in time. Some of the characteristics of the rejection stage are shown in Figure 3.2.

Positive Interdependence	Promotive Interaction	Positive Relationships
Having feeling toward others	Promoting self-pride, self-concept, self-image, self-esteem	Realistic expectations and objectives, attainable goals
⇩	⇩	⇩
Engaging in frequent and open communication	Empowering productivity, success, and achievement	Maintaining positive communication with others
⇩	⇩	⇩
Understanding different perspectives	Aware of bias, prejudice, racism, stereotypes	Embracing differences through accommodation
⇩	⇩	⇩
Interpersonal attraction	Pluralism	Cultural diversity

Figure 3.1. Characteristics of acceptance

No Interdependence	Oppositional Interaction	Negative Relationships
Little or no communication	Monopolistic views	Unrealistic expectations
⇩	⇩	⇩
Egocentric attitudes	Low self-concept and self-esteem	Lack of communication
⇩	⇩	⇩
Resistance to influence	Lack of cross-cultural experience	Blaming and scapegoating

Figure 3.2. Characteristics of rejection

Tenth is the *maintenance* stage. Even without full assimilation, parents and children can enrich, accommodate, acculturate, and integrate mainstream society's values to a large extent at the same time they preserve their own culture and traditions. Each cultural group maintains its own cultural heritage uniquely. In some cultures, people share a common belief system and congregate to worship in a well established setting. Maintaining cultural identity is an extremely important part of life. Cultural groups hold commemorative celebrations, honor special holidays, and organize family gatherings. Teaching the group's native language is one way of maintaining culture. For instance, Hmong Americans offer special classes to teach young children Hmong traditional rituals and customs. In church, Hmong parents and children learn how to read and write the Hmong language as part of their Bible study. The Hmong community holds New Year's celebrations each year to expose the young generation to Hmong traditional values. Each culture has its own way of maintaining itself. However, maintaining a culture requires persistent effort in order to keep up with social changes and the generation gap.

The Socialization Process Part 2: Cross-Cultural Functioning and the Process of Saturation

Once newcomers have completed the ten stages of cross-cultural adjustment, they learn to function cross-culturally as they become saturated in the dominant culture. The process of saturation is complex and plays a big role in the entire socialization process. In the school setting as well as in life, saturation is pretty much a series of swim-or-sink situations. Newcomers have to deal with a myriad of cultural dilemmas. They may encounter confusing expectations at school, in the workplace, at social events, in hospitals, in social service agencies, and in community centers. Multicultural educators should understand that during the process of saturation students may feel uncomfortable or rejected simply because they lack basic interpersonal communication skills and cognitive academic language proficiency needed to answer specific questions or perform specific tasks. Saturation could be traumatic for some; therefore, unrealistic expectations may be counterproductive and may cause students to completely reject the desire to function cross-culturally.

Despite newcomers' difficulties with cross-cultural adjustment and functioning, members of the dominant culture expect newcomers to saturate themselves in the American culture as quickly as possible, stressing the *unum* of the *e pluribus unum* motto. Today, however, the emphasis is on *pluribus* as leaders move to promote cultural diversity. As Gollnick and Chinn (2009) noted, placing unreachable expectations on minority students can create irreparable damage to those students. When they internalize the feelings that arise from failure to meet expectations, they believe they are not socially accepted by members of the dominant school culture and they become marginalized and alienated from school.

What Is the "Melting Pot"?

The concept of a melting pot is an eighteenth century ideology. Whether melting pot is an assimilationist metaphor or an Anglo-conformity fantasy, at one point in the history of this great nation, all people were expected to eventually dissolve themselves into the macro-culture, which was presumed to be the culture of the dominant group. This idea is sometimes referred to as the *unum model*. However, the melting pot ideology is no longer considered valid. Sociologists, scholars, and researchers now consider the melting pot concept to be not only misleading, but also discriminatory in practice because it never leveled the socio-cultural or racial playing fields in America (de Melendez & Beck, 2010; Lessow-Hurley, 2000; Manning & Baruth, 2009; Ovando et al., 2006). The melting pot concept has been replaced with the idea of cultural pluralism, which holds that individuals can maintain their distinct cultural identities without being dissolved into a larger identity.

What Is Xenophobia?

America is a land of immigrants and refugees. For hundreds of years, thousands of people of many different cultural groups from around the world came to America for a fresh start. The influx of immigrants posed societal threats and discomforts to the European settlers who arrived in America first. The rejection of new immigrants is referred to as *xenophobia*, a fear of strangers or foreigners. Whether the fear is for national security or other reasons, America was a very racist nation until the 1960s. Xenophobic feelings still exist in different communities across America. For instance, in 2008, a county in Florida expressed antagonism toward President Obama, saying its people could not support his presidency because he is Black. As mentioned previously, Birmingham, Alabama was referred to as Bombingham in the mid-1960s because of actions motivated by blatant racism. Even though much overt racism has disappeared, xenophobic feelings and actions may reemerge because people are not free of cultural bias, prejudice, racism, and bigotry. Despite the positive societal changes, these feelings could resurface, and they are contagious. Educators should plan to provide multicultural curricula to help reduce painful memories and ingrained psychological fears caused by xenophobia.

Who Are the Minorities?

Literally, minority groups include women, low-income families, the less privileged, the economically disadvantaged, the working class, underrepresented groups, certain racial groups, and the poor. However, in America, some groups fare better than others academically, politically, socially, and economically. Among minority groups, some have greater social and political status in the community. Ogbu (1978) divided racial minorities into three major categories; his work is old, but his definitions are still applicable today.

Ogbu (1978) classified as *autonomous* minorities those people who came to America with religious and political advantages. He used Jews and Mormons to illustrate his categorization, even if their numbers were relatively small. Ogbu explained that these two groups represent a small number of immigrants and each is a minority in the numerical sense; however, in reality, others do not perceive them to be second-class citizens because they possess power, privilege, prestige, and recognition. Therefore, members of these groups are at ease maintaining their cultural identity without isolating themselves from the political and social arenas. In other words, members of these groups do not have to undergo as much cultural identity change as those of other groups.

Ogbu (1978) categorized as *immigrant* minorities people who came to America for a variety of reasons without religious or political advantage. Some came voluntarily to seek educational and economic opportunities. However, many made perilous ventures across the ocean or border for survival. Despite challenges, voluntary immigrants strive to maintain their cultural identities and self-concepts and thus adjust slowly. Some who are educated and have professional status might enter the mainstream society without facing much difficulty.

Ogbu's (1978) third classification, *caste-like* minorities, who are also referred to as indigenous or traditional groups, came to America involuntarily through slavery, conquest, colonization, or for other political reasons. For instance, Southeast Asian groups that have political ties with the U.S. government resettled in America for survival because they had no choice but to leave their native countries; otherwise, they would have been persecuted, tortured, imprisoned, or executed. Other traditional groups, such as African

Americans, Mexican Americans, and Native Americans, underwent the subjugation of slavery, conquest, or colonization. In some cases, caste-like minorities continue to encounter serious structural assimilation challenges in America.

At present, approximately 20 million illegal aliens, or undocumented immigrants, live in the U.S. This number is steadily increasing, and that means that the number of minority families is continuing to grow.

What Is Pluralism?

The term *pluralism* refers to the many different cultures in America. Cultural pluralism is a movement to promote the manifestations and maintenance of all cultures without dissolution to form a macro-culture or dominant culture. As Ovando et al. (2006) and de Melendez and Beck (2010) explained, to keep all cultures parallel and equal to the dominant culture, cultural pluralism encourages cultural groups to maintain their cultures and languages while embracing and adopting differences. In other words, newcomers do not have to give up their cultural identities in order to be accepted into the dominant culture. Cultural pluralism emphasizes the multicultural motto *E Pluribus Unum*, meaning we are "one out of many" (Lessow-Hurley, 2000).

What Is a Salad Bowl?

The salad bowl concept emerged from the cultural pluralism movement. Similar to the image of a rainbow, it is used as an analogy to depict cultural diversity. In a salad bowl, individuals maintain their culture and language while embracing the cultures and languages of others, forming a new and complex society that reflects differences in race, ethnicity, culture, language, religion, socioeconomic status, and class. Each ingredient in the salad bowl contributes to the whole while maintaining its original form and remaining distinct from all other identities inside the bowl.

What does this mean for educators? It means that in American society today, people of color are maintaining their cultures and languages regardless of their social status, and that fact should be part of multicultural education. Multicultural educators are like the dressing that enhances every single ingredient in the salad bowl. Without multicultural educators who understand and teach how unity is achieved in diversity without destroying the diversity, colorblind educators mislead their students and distort the salad bowl into a melting pot.

What Is Integration?

Integration is the concept that newcomers should blend in as quickly as possible at the experiencing stage while still maintaining their cultural identity. Newcomers often have cross-cultural experiences that are superficial, brief, and uncomfortable. These may include social greetings, handshakes, hugging, and facial expressions. They may be asked questions, expected to express feelings, and asked to introduce themselves. These experiences help them develop the social, people, and interpersonal skills needed for survival in America; however, people of diverse backgrounds may not be ready to respond or act in the American way quickly. For instance, Hmong women did not generally shake hands with men or women before arriving in America. They greeted one another by using their husbands' first names, their husbands' professional titles, or their first children's names. Shaking hands is still culturally taboo between Hmong men and Hmong women in non-Western countries. The purpose of integration is to unite individuals into a whole, bringing people of diverse backgrounds into one culture.

What Is Accommodation?

Accommodation is an adaptation or reconciliation for dealing with drastic changes at the incipient stage of life in the new country. Parents and children are expected to voluntarily or involuntarily accept the customary practices of other cultures without having full knowledge of those practices. People are often uncomfortable adopting or adapting to the symbols or characteristics of a culture outside their own ethnic group. For instance, Hmong refugees who resettled in isolated cities quickly adopted the mainstream culture without considering its impact on their family values. Accommodation can take place by choice or force, voluntarily or involuntarily. In the sink-or-swim situations in which accommodation often occurs, students who fail to swim along with their peers face imminent danger. Those who sink have difficulty catching up with their peers, and many never do. Hmong families that adapted without reconciliation with family members suffered substantial loss of their cultural heritage years later.

What Is Acculturation?

Acculturation is a process whereby a cultural group adopts new cultural values in order to embrace differences between cultures. An example is celebrating special days that are not a part of the group's culture, such as

Independence Day, Thanksgiving, Halloween, Christmas, Cinco de Mayo, President's Day, or New Year's Day. Adoptions can be made in formal and informal settings. Children learn U.S. history and the traditions and languages of other cultures in school. Minority parents often need to take English classes in adult school for survival and employability. Their ability to speak a second language empowers them to engage in social processes. Children gain social skills and conversational skills through cooperative learning and on the playground. Watching television or listening to radio programs can help parents and children learn English. However, even with acquisition of language skills, acculturation may proceed slowly because it takes time for people to use their skills in the family circle.

Acculturation is facilitated by the establishment of linguistic, religious, and economic ties with the larger community. For instance, affiliation with a religious group in which members of a minority group share the same belief system with members of another group helps people acculturate more quickly. Formal schooling helps minority students acculturate as they share with others in their studies. Actually, most newcomers to America do become acculturated and assimilated at least in some ways because they understand that adopting aspects of the new culture helps them advance through the social ladder. Becoming U.S. citizens, for example, helps parents and children become acculturated because they wish to exercise civic responsibility, especially voting.

What Is Assimilation?

Assimilation is the process of complete adoption of another culture so as to be transformed from one culture to the dominant culture. Ovando et al. (2006) and Ryan and Cooper (2001) described assimilation as a process of absorption in which a cultural group completely takes on the traits, patterns, traditions, and values of another culture by abandoning its own ancestral culture. First- or second-generation children are usually completely assimilated.

However, the extent of assimilation varies among individuals who were foreign-born. Some assimilate economically and politically, but not religiously or culturally, because they have strong religious or cultural ties to their cultural community. For instance, Hmong professionals of the third generation typically have strong ties with their community organization and would not alienate themselves from their cultural traditions.

Keep in mind that involuntary immigrants look at assimilation differently from voluntary immigrants. Among involuntary immigrants, structural assimilation does not happen as quickly as it generally does among voluntary immigrants. Those who came to the country through slavery or conquest have less motivation to assimilate.

What Is Enculturation?

Enculturation is a socialization process in which a cultural group has successfully acquired the symbols, characteristics, traditions, values, and traits of the dominant culture and, at the same, has become completely competent in the new language, culture, and traditions. Second-generation children of virtually every cultural group are enculturated; they were born in the U.S. and raised in accordance with American ideals and values. Foreign-born children can become enculturated; however, their ways of behaving, acting, respecting, learning, and honoring family traditions could be much different from those of native-born children because they value the group above the individual.

Regarding the stages of cross-cultural adjustment and the process of saturation, much is still to be understood about learners' attitudes and stages of cognitive development in order to pinpoint how an individual processes, learns, and comprehends the information given in class. Multicultural educators should design multicultural curricula and/or educational experiences that reaffirm these stages of development to recognize their cross-cultural capabilities and cultural perspectives.

What Are Values?

Quite often, people tout American values, ideals, and culture; however, few can really explain what these are. Imagine what goes on in the mind of a child who was not born in the U.S., who came to America as an immigrant or refugee, and who hears such expressions. Educators should realize that values, like beliefs, are held in the heart as true or correct. In the classroom, teachers share their values with their students, and sometimes the teacher's values clash with the values in the child's home because different cultures have their own sets of values. People's values are reflected in their actions, feelings, and interactions with others.

In professional practice, values are conduct standards by which people judge their own acts and the acts of others. In other words, classroom values are standards of what is appropriate to be given, shared, required, and forbidden in the presence of students.

Moreover, values can be measures of what is honorable, shameful, beautiful, or ugly. Educators should understand that values are manifest in one's social and professional life by the judgments they make about other people. Values, like ideas, feelings, beliefs, rules, and stereotypes, are cultural and sometimes philosophical. Most people defend their values as true and correct regardless of the consequences of holding them.

Exploring Multicultural Philosophy

Here are some questions for potential teachers to ponder while exploring their philosophy regarding multicultural education:

- How would I deal with students who do not speak English?
- How would I deal with students who do not have middle-class values?
- How do I feel about working with students who may not understand my directions or teaching?
- How can I help them if they cannot tell me what they really need?
- How do I know their feelings about being in my class?
- How would I reach out to them if I do not speak their language?
- How can I treat all my students the same way if they have different needs and abilities?
- Am I a teacher of and for all students?

Perhaps it is hard to imagine the answers to these questions. If one were asked to describe one's philosophy of multicultural education for today's schools, the answer may be easy. But implementing that philosophy on a practical level requires more thought. For the most part, there are no simple, right or wrong answers to the questions above. Earlier in the book, the author laid out the broad foundations for multicultural education to help educators broaden their professional horizons. In fact, however, the philosophy is based on a gut-level understanding of the psychology of multicultural education.

Like other philosophies and theories of education, multicultural philosophy is a humanistic approach toward public education in a pluralistic society that recognizes, respects, includes, and embraces cultural diversity in the learning environment with diverse learners who have diverse needs and abilities. It encourages professional practices that foster cultural enrichment of all children and adolescents from different racial and income groups. Multicultural educators plan instructional approaches and educational experiences that address psychological issues related to social injustice, racism, sexism, discrimination, and economic inequality by reducing cultural bias and racial prejudice in order to appreciate, respect, and accept cultural diversity, foster positive attitudes toward diverse learning styles, and show cross-cultural tolerance throughout the total formal curriculum. Moreover, multiculturalism is based on the philosophical movement of *E Pluribus Unum*, which holds that the cultural diversity in a pluralistic society should be reflected in all the institutionalized structures of the educational system (de Melendez & Beck, 2010).

The Humanistic Approach of Multicultural Education

In educational psychology, attitude is very important; however, in multicultural education, personality is the single most important factor that influences student learning. As in other school programs, multicultural education takes a humanistic approach to teaching and learning. Understanding the psychosocial dimensions of humanistic education, educators need to cultivate the psychological and professional attitudes advocated by Carl Rogers (1967): (a) be genuine or real; (b) give positive, unconditional regard; and (c) display empathy.

The genuineness or realness of an educator encompasses his or her professionalism, feelings, and behaviors toward the students, subject matter, lesson plan design, and delivery mode. In some situations, teachers should be students, and students should be teachers; in other words, students and teachers sometimes play reversible roles in the learning circle. However, for the most part, the teacher should be regarded as a real professional. Teachers should know that their responsibility is to be role models and educators for their students, and they are available to all their students regardless of who they are.

Why should teachers give positive, unconditional regard to their students? Simply put, teachers should help their students feel like worthy individuals, treating them with respect regardless of their race, ethnicity, religion, social class, culture, language, traditions, gender, and socioeconomic status. As with medical patients, students of color could be rich, poor, or homeless; regardless, teachers are educational "doctors" who administer the very best care to each student. In other words, in a room of diverse needs and diverse abilities, the teacher's attitude could be real medicine that heals students' internal struggles and pain. As Nelson Mandela once said, "Wounds that can't be seen are more painful than those that can be seen and cured by the doctors." Positive, unconditional regard is the caring and curing that teachers can give their students without preconditions.

Most importantly, teachers should show empathy when teaching in a pluralistic society. Why? Because many children do not come to school prepared; they are hard pressed to read, write, and listen. Their struggles, pains, barriers, and disabilities brought from home seem insurmountable without teachers who are willing to guide them every step of the way. In some cases, children need to be disciplined academically and responsibly in order to accomplish learning goals. Setting high expectations for learning does not guarantee that all students of color will be able to achieve; teachers must understand how different students learn and process information. Empathy requires profound effort on the part of teachers, forcing them to put themselves in the students' shoes in order to feel and understand their pains and struggles.

To help prospective teachers put themselves in their students' shoes, one university professor required his credential-candidate students to watch a TV program in a language other than English for at least 30 minutes and write a two-page reflection on the content of the program. Nine of 10 students reported that the assignment was a real eye-opener, helping them realize how English learners feel when they sit in class all day long but do not understand what the teacher is talking about. Multicultural educators know that all children deserve the very best education, and that education is available in the hearts of teachers.

What Are Some Disadvantages and Advantages of Multicultural Education?

Earlier in the book, the author asked whether multicultural education is a talent or a handicap. In chapter two, the author discussed the myths, misconceptions, and misperceptions of multicultural education. He also addressed issues related to the foundations of multicultural education. Critics of multicultural education argue that cultural diversity is a handicap or a weakness for a number of reasons. However, experts, scholars, and researchers such as Banks (1991, 2008), Crawford (1981), Gollnick and Chinn (2009), Hakuta (1985), Manning and Baruth (2009), and Nieto have no difficulty rebutting their claims. Of course, multicultural education is a talent or a strength.

The psycho-social dimensions of multicultural education can be oversimplified and thereby its impact on all aspects of the education of culturally diverse students underestimated; however, for the most part, multicultural education has been viewed as a salient part of public education in America and elsewhere in the West. Most importantly, multicultural education does not require anything that schools do not have or cannot offer; in fact, multicultural education advocates for equal opportunity and educational equality for all students. Students of color are still subject to receiving lip service, cosmetic education, empty promises, and capriciously administered curricula. The academic achievement gap is widening while the number of students of color is increasing exponentially. Educationally disadvantaged students are being blamed for their failure to achieve.

As Ovando et al. (2006) warned, language-minority students will continue to be prisoners of silence in English instruction classrooms if nothing is done to change the status quo. Furthermore, language-minority students will also be nothing more than seat warmers in class, included in head counts but not in learning. In essence, the whole school system benefits from the multicultural education approach. Too often, however, schools downplay multicultural curricula and disregard the needs of students of color because of the use of measurement-driven curricula, which focus on testing and results, but not on the process of teaching and learning that involves equality.

Is Multicultural Experience Important?

Multicultural experience is not merely a critical element, but it is a universal requirement in many if not most professions. In banking, athletics, elected office, teaching, police service, and social services, the racial makeup of employees reflects the communities in which they serve. Similarly, when college students apply to a program in pursuit of a teaching credential, a multicultural questionnaire is used as part of the initial interview. The questionnaire solicits information not about what new teachers are going to do, but about how they feel about what they are going to do. Credential applicants are often asked to respond to items relative to their psycho-social profile as follows:

1. Reasons for wanting to become a teacher
2. Experiences with minority students
3. Dealing with English learners
4. Working with bilingual parents
5. Issues in a multicultural classroom
6. Teacher's roles
7. Attitudes toward cultural diversity
8. Special attributes and qualities
9. Gender issues in the classroom
10. Maturity level and preparedness

In addition, students are asked to provide evidence of cross-cultural experiences and satisfaction of foreign language requirements as prerequisites that play a role in their cognitive and professional preparation for becoming multicultural educators. Figure 3.3 illustrates the various spheres of life in which students may experience cultural diversity.

Figure 3.3. Circles in which cultural diversity is learned

In most cases, students respond to the questionnaire by sharing personal experiences, family heritages, school experiences, community involvement, national events, and global matters. For example, students may describe traveling to different nations; eating different foods; having friends from different groups; observing or participating in cultural celebrations, wedding ceremonies, religious events, and social and family gatherings. These experiences help people learn about and understand cultural diversity in America; however, they do not prove that the students are ready to deal with the needs of students of color, who face difficult challenges in the classroom.

College courses such as Methods in Multicultural Education and Foundation of Education in a Diverse Society expose college students to a variety of teaching techniques, strategies, applications, and methodologies that add to their teaching repertoire. Such courses give them skills for addressing issues of inclusion of all students in the total school curriculum for content-obligatory curricula rather than separating students into homogeneous groups for content-compatibility curricula. Consider, for example, that some schools use pull-out activities to group students on the basis of reading ability but not academic needs, and others group all LEP students in one classroom based on level of English proficiency but not academic needs. In most cases, these students are subject to impoverished and watered down curricular activities. In other words, issues of full inclusion remained unresolved in today's schools.

The Rainbow Classroom

Today, most classrooms contain students from a variety of racial and income groups. Schools reflect the national makeup, a mixture of races, ethnicities, languages, cultures, classes, genders, socioeconomic statuses, and religions. Whether teachers are colorblind or not, the variety of students in the typical classroom is like the colors of a rainbow. Each color is unique, and each group of students may require different teaching modalities to engage them in academic tasks. The different feelings of students and teachers have direct and indirect impacts on teaching and learning. Consider, for example, how teachers feel when they cannot reach their students who are non-English speakers. At the same time, how do students feel when they are not able to do their tasks because they do not understand their teacher?

How do teachers feel about teaching and dealing with all students in the rainbow classroom? Their feelings are professional commitments, and these feelings are reflected in their actions in the classroom. Experts, researchers, and scholars have laid out general approaches for helping educators articulate their planning instructions by considering different domains when dealing with students who may not speak English well enough to perform daily tasks in the classroom (Bloom, 1956; Harrow, 1972; Howe, 2002; Krathwohl, Bloom & Masia, 1964). Adding the academic and cross-cultural domains to the list makes it more inclusive. Table 3.2 presents an overview of five basic domains of student learning.

These domains do not explicitly indicate how students feel in class; however, how students feel about a teacher plays a significant role in cognitive, social, and academic development. Whether the feelings are negative or positive could be critical in determining the extent of the child's engagement in academic tasks and the learning process. Although understanding these domains is important, it is not the panacea for learning problems and challenges. Teachers need to consider all the aspects of student learning in order to address the needs of each student. One of those aspects is the fact that academic inequality in the classroom will remain until teachers change their attitudes and actions to fit the reality of a multicultural world.

Finally, to become a multicultural educator is to become a culturally competent professional. Cultural competence is the ability to function effectively in the realm of differences in race, ethnicity, class, language, religion, gender, socioeconomic status, culture, needs, and abilities.

Table 3.2. Factors and Instructional Approaches Associated with Five Domains of Learning

Domain	Associated Factors	Instructional Approaches
Cognitive	Comprehension, knowledge, skills, processing, and application	Knowing what and knowing how and expressing in written or verbal forms
Affective	Emotions, feelings, attitudes, personalities, behaviors, and values	Reflective responses to tasks, sharing with peers, interaction, communication, and expressing in verbal form
Psychomotor	Motor skills, coordination, comprehension, expression, and muscular control	Diagramming, mapping, manipulation, connection, idea web, and application
Social	Basic interpersonal communication skills, sharing, socialization, citizenship, and cooperation	Cooperative learning, teamwork, group activity, role and responsibility, and project
Academic	Cognitive academic language proficiency, literacy, constructivism, and context-reduced	Logical, arbitrary, social, physical, and constructive knowledge

Summing Up

This chapter reviewed the multicultural aspects of cultural diversity to provide prospective educators with some background knowledge helpful in becoming multicultural educators for all children of color. Keep in mind that becoming a multicultural educator requires a passion for learning and an understanding that America is a complex world and its inhabitants are unique and diverse in so many ways. Learning to become a multicultural educator is similar to acquiring a taste for different foods and drinks. Each item has a unique taste, and one may or may not like the taste of a particular item. Regardless of whether someone likes the taste of a product, the product was made to a certain quality standard. Therefore, one should not try to change the taste by altering the product's ingredients; one should not attempt to change the product into something it is not. Similarly, educators should not try to subtract primary languages from their students by educating them in another language. Losing one's language is truly the loss of one's identity.

To reduce cultural biases, stereotypes, prejudices, and judgments, educators should at the very least be open-minded enough to acknowledge any personal ignorance in the area of multiculturalism. Such acknowledgment would aid them in learning ways to embrace cultural diversity. To help their students overcome the psychological hurdles that so often come with minority status, educators must recognize their own ethnocentrism. With this in mind, educators can view diversity as a great strength rather than as a weakness.

PART TWO

THE STUDENT DIVERSITY DOMAIN

Chapter Four

European American Children and Their Families

> Ask not what your country can do for you —
> ask what you can do for your country.
> —President John F. Kennedy, 1961

Overview

When Christopher Columbus discovered the Bahamas in 1492, he came upon a new world. When John Cabot discovered and explored the northeast coast of Delaware in 1497, he opened the New World to European nations. Soon after, other explorers from many countries also reached the new land, and the New World eventually gave birth to a new country, the United States of America.

Like so many other groups since, the various Europeans brought their differences in race, culture, tradition, religion, dialect, custom, language, and way of life to the New World. From all different nations in Europe, they formed a new fabric and began America's rich cultural diversity that has been a part of the nation from the late 1400s to the present day. Multicultural educators should learn and appreciate this plethora of cultural differences. This chapter focuses on European Americans and their heritages, examining the diversity in their origins, cultures, socioeconomic status, families, children, religions, gender roles, languages, and ways of life.

The Origins of European Americans

Since the discoveries of Christopher Columbus, John Cabot, Juan Ponce de Leon, Giovanni da Verrazano, and Hernando De Soto in the late 1400s to the mid-1500s, immigrants have come to the New World from European nations both voluntarily and involuntarily. The European Americans originated in several different countries: England, France, Germany, Greece, Hungary, Ireland, Italy, Netherlands, Norway, Poland, Portugal, Russia, Spain, Sweden, Switzerland, and others. Immigrants have come from eastern and western Europe and different locations in the eastern portions of the Soviet Union.

During the colonial period, from the 1600s to the late 1700s, most European immigrants came from Great Britain, Ireland, and surrounding nations. Until the early 1800s, Germans, French, Norwegians, Swedes, Italians, and other groups immigrated to the United States for social and economic reasons.

Massive immigration from European nations took place during the 100-year period from 1830 to 1930, the Century of Immigration. In that time span, millions of people from different nations in Europe headed for the New World to start new lives. European nations faced difficulties because of a scarcity of land, the abolition of feudalism, economic pressures, and social upheavals. This large-scale immigration built the new nation's labor force and contributed to great industrial growth. For instance, a sizable number of German and Polish immigrants were skilled workers, tradesmen, merchants, farmers, weavers, carpenters, shoemakers, tailors, blacksmiths, locksmiths, miners, dressmakers, and prospectors.

In the late 1800s to the early 1900s, millions of immigrants came from Italy. Prior to the start of World War I, Italian immigrants made up a quarter of all immigrants, and after World War II, a sizable number of German immigrants arrived in the New World (Manning & Baruth, 2009).

A later wave of immigration from Europe consisted largely of Jews. From the late 1800s to the early 1900s, a great number of Jewish refugees fled the Soviet Union and immigrated to the United States. Approximately 40,000 settled in the west, and many went to Israel after it became a nation in 1948 (Abrams, 1993; Manning & Baruth, 2009). As a result of the Six Day War, the Leningrad Trial, and religious persecution in the Soviet Union, nearly 100,000 Soviet Jews immigrated to the United States.

To help educators understand the origins of European Americans, Table 4.1 presents some demographic information on the ancestry of the major groups. Keep in mind that it is impossible to account for all aspects of the history of European Americans; their cultural backgrounds as well as their immigration histories are complex. This discussion is intended to give a brief overview of their history. Educators should be encouraged to learn more about European Americans and specific groups in order to gain in-depth knowledge about the roots of European Americans.

Table 4.1. Numbers of European Americans by Country of Ancestry

Country	Number in millions
England	24.5
Germany	42.8
France	8.3
Latin American nations	16.0
Ireland	30.5
United States	20.6

Note. Data from U.S. Census Bureau, *Census 2000 Demographic Profile Highlights.* Numbers are rounded.

Who Are European Americans Today?

The massive transfer of people from the Old World to the New World involved primarily European Americans. No doubt the many differences among them created great cultural diversity in America. However, this group is the least examined in multicultural education. Neither teachers nor students are taught about the cultures of European Americans. To date, no one offers a workshop for teachers, students, or parents on European American Culture; such training is available on other cultures. This is a missing link that educators must ponder when working with students of color.

Today, European Americans constitute one of the most diverse and complex groups in America, but most people assume they are all part of the dominant culture. Their cultural heritages are more intricate today than they were hundreds of years ago. For many European Americans, family roots, cultural traditions, and lineages were forgotten or lost after generations in the New World. However, according to the 2000 U.S. census, there are approximately 211 million contemporary European Americans, or Whites, living in the U.S., as shown in Table 4.2.

European Americans do not make up a homogenous group. The eight leading groups of European Americans are listed in Table 4.3 together with the portion of the population each constituted in 1990. Keep in mind that these figures may have changed somewhat since then. Among the eight largest groups, six are the most commonly identified European heritages of current U.S. citizens. These are shown in Table 4.4.

Table 4.2. Populations of Selected Racial Groups in the U.S.

Group	Number in 2000, in Millions	Projected Number in 2010, in Millions
Whites	211.0	221.0
Blacks	34.0	37.0
Asians	10.0	13.0
Native Americans	2.3	2.4
Hispanics	35.2	44.0

Note. Data from U.S. Census Bureau, *Census 2000 Demographic Profile Highlights.* Numbers are rounded.

Table 4.3. Leading European American Groups in 1990

Group	Percentage of European American Population
English	27
German	27
Irish	22
French	7
Italian	6
Scottish	4
Polish	4
Dutch	3

Note. Data from *Ethnic Identity: The Transformation of White America*, by R. D. Alba, 1990, New Haven, CT: Yale University Press.

Table 4.4. European Heritages Most Commonly Identified by Americans

Heritage	Percentage of European American Population
German	17
Irish	12
English	10
Italian	6
Polish	3
French	3

Note. Data from U.S. Census Bureau, *Statistical Abstract, 2006.*

As with other racial groups, European Americans live scattered throughout the 50 states; however, some reside close to where their ancestors first settled. Among the largest populations of European Americans, approximately 35% live in the Western states, 31% in the Southern states, and 15% in the Northeastern states (Manning & Baruth, 2009). Wherever they live today, European Americans, classified by race as "White," still constitute the largest group in America, as illustrated in Table 4.2.

The gender distribution of European Americans is fairly even, with slightly more females than males in nearly every national group. Tables 4.5 and 4.6 show the population by gender for the total and for the 12 largest groups.

Table 4.5. Number of European Americans in 2000, by Gender

Gender	Number (in Millions)
Male	103.8
Female	107.7
Total	211.5

Note. Data from U.S. Census Bureau, *Census 2000 Demographic Profile Highlights*. Numbers are rounded.

Table 4.6. Number of European Americans in 2000 in 12 Most Populous Groups, by Gender

Group	Number, in millions	Males, in millions	Females, in millions
German	43	21	22
Irish	31	15	16
English	25	12	13
American, heritage not specified	21	10	11
Italians	16	8	8
Polish	9	4.4	4.5
French	8.5	4	4.5
Scottish	4.9	2.6	2.3
Dutch	4.5	2.2	2.3
Norwegian	4.5	2.2	2.3
Swedish	3.9	1.8	2.1
Russian	2.7	1.3	1.4

Note. Data from U.S. Census Bureau, *Census 2000 Demographic Profile Highlights*. Numbers are rounded.

European Americans are not immune to stereotyping, discrimination, racism, and sexism. However, Manning and Baruth (2009) explained that European Americans suffer these societal problems in a way that is different from minority groups. They noted that "insidious acts or feelings can result from reasons other than the color of peoples' skin or the language they speak" (p. 147). In other words, European Americans are not free of racial conflicts among themselves or with others. In fact, in U.S. history every European group except, perhaps, the English, experienced prejudice and discrimination. European Americans can suffer from social inequality just like any other group in America.

The Cultural Characteristics of European Americans

Although many people think of European Americans as having one culture, each national group has its own values, beliefs, religion, language, traditions, and customs. Most of these differing cultural characteristics are unknown to other racial groups because so little is taught about European American cultures and traditions. This scarcity of information led Manning and Baruth (2009) to qualify their characterization of European American culture. They generalized, "European Americans place importance on time, cleanliness, hard work, material comforts, material wealth, and an orientation toward working and the future" (p. 148). But then they added, "The most important cultural description of European Americans comes from considering individual cultures" (p. 148).

There are some cultural characteristics that appear to be fairly common across European American groups. These include an emphasis on the individual and individual rights, a belief in freedom, and open and assertive communication (Kitano & Perkins, 2000). Some of the basic characteristics of European American culture are given in Table 4.7.

The values of European Americans are listed in Table 4.8. However, because the number of European American groups is so large and the groups are so diverse, all European Americans may not subscribe to these values. The level of family assimilation also affects the degree to which any particular value is important to an individual. To avoid overgeneralizing, educators should note that there is room for differences in the application of each value.

To learn more about the cultural characteristics of European groups, educators might compare some values between groups to understand the differences as well as the similarities. As an example, some of the cultural characteristics of Americans of Greek ancestry and Italian ancestry are compared in Table 4.9.

Table 4.7. Characteristics of Selected Culture Components of European Americans

Culture Component	Characteristics
Values	Individuality, personal achievement, independence, control one's environment, self comes first
Beliefs	Inalienable rights, privacy, free enterprise, private property, self-actualization
Interaction	Roles of specialization, status, self-sufficiency, competition, personal success
Communication	Direct, informal, formal, assertive, expressive, opinionated

Note. Information from "Gifted European American Women," by M. K. Kitano and C. O. Perkins, 2000, *Journal of the Education of the Gifted, 23*(3), pp. 288–310.

Table 4.8. European American Values

Value	Examples
Primacy of individual	Personal success or achievement
Democratic orientation	Egalitarianism, equality, election, or majority rule
Nuclear family structure	Small family, few children, live alone or remain single
Emphasis on youth	Show more respect for youth than for elders
Independence	Self-actualization, materialism, inquisitiveness, wealth
Assertiveness	Venting anger, opinionated, asking, expressing
Nonconformity	Choose one's own identity, values, or lifestyle
Competition	Goal-oriented, best of the best, gold medalist, ability
Conflict	Advocate for self or others, privacy, rights, possessions
Freedom	Speech, religion, assembly, marriage, education, choice, career

Note. Information from Vicente & Associates, *Planning for Diversity*, 1990, UC, Davis: University of California.

This illustration is just one example of the differences in cultural characteristics and values of different European American groups. Again, educators should be warned that within the European American designation there are a variety of subcultures, religious groups, and political affiliations. European Americans occupy various rungs on the socioeconomic ladder, and they experience generation gaps as do all other groups.

Moreover, to help prospective educators gain specific understanding of European Americans, the traditional cultural characteristics of Portuguese Americans are described below:

Table 4.9. Characteristics of Italian and Greek Americans

Group	Characteristics	Efforts
Greek American	Family oriented, less coopera-tive, self-centered, competitive efforts, frugality, saving, strong work ethics, patriarchal control, defined roles, status	Know and solve family problems, persistent efforts to deal with problems, pride, individuality, kin-ship, networking, family honor, philotimo (love of honor)
Italian American	Allegiance to family, group oriented, family oriented, age cohort, young learn from eld-ers, cooperative, allegiance to church	Suspicious, filial obedience, emphasis on career and occupation, extended fam-ily, congenial and social

Note. Information from *Multicultural Education of Children and Adolescents* (5th ed.), by L. M. Manning and L. G. Baruth, 2009, New York: Pearson Education; *Ethnic Identity: The Transformation of White America*, by R. D. Alba, 1985, New Haven, CT: Yale University Press; *The Greek Americans*, by A. Scourby, 1984, Boston: Twayne.

1. Religious adherence: The majority of Portuguese Americans, nearly 94%, are Roman Catholic, and religious values play a big role in their cultural, social, and professional well-being.

2. Social formality: Most Portuguese Americans are traditional and conservative, have a strong sense of formality with one another, and show extreme politeness and gratitude toward one another.

3. Family values: In Portuguese culture, family is the principal founda-tion of social structure and stability. Extended family members are quite close and respected. The family unit serves as a social network with other family relatives in the community. The individual's loy-alty to the family is extremely important before establishing personal and professional relationships. As in other ethnic groups, nepotism is considered a good thing in Portuguese culture.

4. Appearance matters: Portuguese Americans consider physical ap-pearance to be very important, especially in the cities, because per-sonal appearance determines social standing and success; it reflects family and personal values. Portuguese Americans take great pride in

wearing good fabrics and clothes of the best standards or design they can afford.

5. Societal and social hierarchy: Portuguese Americans show great respect for the hierarchical system established in their family and community. Their societal and religious values also play a role in their social stratification and structure. Not only is social rank honored and respected, but Portuguese Americans also have great respect for authority. Sometimes decisions are made on the basis of authoritarianism. For instance, in business, Portuguese Americans rely on the power and authority that generally resides with a leader or leaders who make decisions with little concern for building consensus with subordinates.

6. Cultural etiquette and social customs: As in other ethnic groups, cultural etiquette and customs are important. All initial social and professional greetings are reserved but polite and gracious in nature. For instance, Portuguese Americans greet one another with handshakes accompanied by direct eye contact and a greeting appropriate for the particular time of day. However, once a personal relationship has been established and has developed cordially, social greetings become quite personal. For instance, men may greet each other with a hug and a handshake, and women may kiss each other twice on the cheek.

7. Professional titles: As mentioned earlier, the hierarchical system is extremely important in Portuguese culture. The proper form of social address is the honorific title "senhor" and "senhora" with the surname or family name. Anyone with a high academic degree is referred to by the honorific title "doctor." In social settings, an individual may delay using another's first name until invited or introduced by the other party. In most situations, one is expected to use the formal rather than the informal case until the other party, especially a Portuguese friend, suggests otherwise.

8. Gift giving etiquette: As in other cultures, Portuguese Americans honor and respect their way of life dearly. If a Portuguese family invites an individual to the home for dinner, it is a good idea to bring flowers, good quality chocolates, or brand-name candy to the hostess. Wine is a good idea if one knows which brand of wine the host

or hostess prefers. Moreover, be aware of cultural superstitions such as the number 13, red flowers, lilies, and chrysanthemums. Usually, gifts are graciously opened when received.

9. Dining etiquette: Time is extremely important; however, one should not arrive for dinner more than 15 minutes after the stipulated time; otherwise, punctuality displays respect for the person one is going to meet. One should dress conservatively. It is important to know that one may engage in discussion about business in social situations or events. However, if one should forget to bring flowers for the hostess, it is a great idea to send flowers the next day. At the dining table, manners are extremely important and formal. For instance, wait to be seated by the host or hostess and do not eat until the hostess says "bom appetito." Using utensils correctly is also important. The fork is held in the left hand, the knife in the right. No elbow rests on the table; hands must be visible, and keep the napkin to the left of the plate while dining. When finished eating, place the napkin to the right of the plate, leave some food on the plate, lay the knife and fork parallel on the plate with the fork's tines facing up and handles facing to the right. If not done with dining, cross the knife and fork on the plate with the fork over the knife.

10. Communication: Portuguese Americans do not like impersonal communications such as written notes or telephone calls; they prefer to have face-to-face meetings to resolve issues. Most communications are considered to be formal and should be conducted according to strict rules of protocol. Because of the hierarchical system, Portuguese Americans defer to those in senior or higher positions and maintain a sense of formality in written communication. Most importantly, Portuguese Americans do not appreciate direct criticism even if it is justified.

Prospective educators should keep in mind that these are only a few of the cultural characteristics of Portuguese Americans, and there are more to be learned. Having firsthand contact is more helpful than reading the information in a book. In addition, teachers need to get to know their students personally since students of any cultural group are diverse, depending on their socioeconomic status and immigrant situation. Some children and adolescents come from Americanized families and some come from more traditional families, and the differences bring challenges to the classroom.

European American Families

Discussing the family characteristics of European Americans is quite difficult because there are so many different kinds of family structures in this group. The family structure of one European American group may not adequately reflect that of other groups. Although this discussion runs the risk of over-generalizing and stereotyping, presenting some generally common character-istics is necessary to help educators learn about the families of European Americans.

Typically, families of European Americans are not much different from families of other racial groups in America. Family characteristics such as how the family is headed; what the roles of husband, wife, and children are; how children are reared; what the family lifestyle is like; what work ethics are followed; and how relatives, extended family, and the nuclear family function are essentially common. However, the parent/child relationship in the European American family seems far different from that of other racial groups. Manning and Baruth (2009) observed that European American par-ents tend to get more involved in their children's education than parents in other groups, and they put greater emphasis on early independence, achieve-ment, decision making, assigning household chores, and expecting youth to work outside the home. On the other hand, Kitano and Perkins (2000) noted that European American parents expect their children to establish their own cultural identities, to make their own decisions, to create their own families, and finally to leave the homes of their biological families.

To help educators learn more about the families of European Americans, the roles and responsibilities of family members of six different European cultural groups are presented in Table 4.10. These are given merely as an illustration of the variety that exists within the larger European American culture. They are by no means inclusive of all the many groups or of all as-pects of family functioning.

Educators should bear in mind that there is still much to learn about European Americans and their families. Understanding family roles and ex-pectations is crucial to dealing with children in the classroom. As in any other racial groups, family values play an integral part in children's educa-tion as well as their social behaviors.

Gender Roles of European Americans

As briefly depicted in Table 4.10, different European cultural groups have different sets of values, but all expect their children to conform to those val-ues. In the children of European Americans, as well as the children of other racial and income groups in America, there are some differences in roles and expectations between boys and girls. These differences, however, may not be overt; they may not be seen clearly with the naked eye. Assumption can lead to misinterpretations.

Table 4.10. Roles in Families of Selected European American Groups

Group	Father	Mother	Children
German	Head, leader, stern, strict, reserved, stubborn, sentimental, self-controlled	Dutiful, subservient, comply to father's role, family pride	Emulation of parents' roles
Greek	Provider, breadwinner, authoritarian, disciplinarian, family honor, revere mother	Fulfill husband's wishes, motherhood, social prestige, child rearing	Strict gender role, gender inequity (son over daughter)
Irish	Shadowy, absent figure, avoidance, limited role	Dominant, leader, run the family	Egalitarian, gender equity, polite, respect, obedience, behave, limited praises
Italian	Head, authority, leader, serious,	Submissive, family oriented, motherhood	Gender inequity (daughter over son), respect elders, extended family focus
Polish	Leader, head, decision maker for family	Leader, head, fulfill family wishes	Defined role for family members, strict, obedience, use physical discipline
Portuguese	Emotional combatant, head, leader, family strength	Purity, honor, obey, and fulfill husband's wishes	Self-controlled, respect, obedience, gender inequity (girls receive overt discipline whereas boys do not)

Note. Information from *Multicultural Education of Children and Adolescents* (5th ed.), by L. M. Manning and L. G. Baruth, 2009, New York: Pearson Education.

Boys and girls have different learning styles, motivations, opinions, views of the world around them, perceptions of objects, and thinking patterns. In the past, these differences and different expectations of and limitations on the genders led to unequal educational opportunities, achievement, and success. For example, science was once considered a subject primarily for males. But today, these gender restrictions are no longer present; females can study and become scientists as well. Today, children of both sexes are equally capable of achieving solid educational goals.

As mentioned earlier, European American parents put great emphasis on early independence, achievement, individuality, competition, freedom, hard work, and assertiveness. Because of the different gender roles in the family, male and female European American children may not exhibit these desired characteristics equally. Females may be dependent on others because they lack confidence in themselves and their abilities. Some females may feel guilty because they cannot be equal to males, more commonly in regard to physical tasks that require strength rather than in academics. Gender roles are not the same in every family, and in some families parents prefer one gender over the other. The subject of gender roles of European Americans is still a gray area that needs further research.

Religions of European Americans

European Americans have different religious affiliations, like members of so many other racial groups in America. Christianity seems to be the most widely practiced religion among European Americans. Table 4.11 shows the numbers of European Americans who adhere to various Christian denominations in the United States. The figures indicate that European Americans are among the most religious of all groups in America, and their family values and belief systems appear to be based on the principles of Christianity.

Table 4.11. European American Adherents to Selected Religious Denominations

Denomination	No. Adherents
Assemblies of God	1,900,000
Church of the Nazarene	475,000
Evangelical Lutheran Church	4,800,000
Int. Pentecostal Holiness Church	184,000
Mennonite Church in US	99,000
Presbyterian Church	2,200,000
Roman Catholic Church	41,800,000
United Methodist Church	7,200,000

Note. Data from Association of Statisticians of American Religious Bodies, 2002. Numbers are rounded.

Languages of European Americans

European Americans are linguistically diverse. Perhaps contrary to popular belief, this group, as a group, is both multilingual and multicultural. There are at least 23 different prominent culture/language groups among European Americans. Figure 4.1 lists these major groups as identified by U.S. Census Bureau (2000a) *Census 2000 Demographic Profile Highlights.* However, educators should bear in mind that there are other European American groups and subgroups whose members speak different languages and dialects.

Austrian	Australian	British	Danish
Dutch	English	European	French
German	Greek	Hungarian	Irish
Israeli	Italian	Norwegian	Polish
Portuguese	Russian	Scandinavian	Scottish
Swedish	Swiss	Yugoslavian	

Figure 4.1. Most prominent culture/language groups of European Americans

The variety of languages spoken in European American homes suggests that the children of European Americans are not immune to language difficulties in school and elsewhere. As with students from all other racial groups, European American children bring challenges to the classroom having to do with learning English as the academic language, and educators should be prepared to meet their linguistic needs. To help educators understand the language difficulties faced by European American students, Table 4.12 shows that a large number of Indo-Europeans in America have difficulty with the English language.

Table 4.12. Numbers of Indo-Europeans in U.S. at Various Levels of English Speaking Ability

Speaking Ability Level	Number of People
Very well	6,600,000
Well	2,100,000
Not well	1,100,000
Not at all	220,000

Note. Data from U.S. Census Bureau, *Census 2000 Demographic Profile Highlights.* Numbers are rounded.

European American students may have difficulty with the English language; however, keep in mind that students in the different European American groups may experience different language difficulties. A number of external and internal factors influence the learner's ability to learn and speak English. For instance, some families live in language enclaves where parents speak their native language at home. European children who are surrounded by their native language have more difficulty with the English language than those whose parents speak English at home. Table 4.13 illustrates the fact that large numbers of European Americans speak a language other than English in the home.

Table 4.13. Numbers of European Americans Who Speak Selected Languages at Home

Language	Number of People
French	1,100,000
Italian	1,000,000
Portuguese	565,000
German	1,400,000
Greek	365,000
Russian	706,000
Polish	667,000

Note. Data from U.S. Census Bureau, *Census 2000 Demographic Profile Highlights*. Numbers are rounded.

Keep in mind that proficiency in speaking a language is not a sufficient condition for academic achievement. To succeed in school, students must not only be competent in conversational English, but they must also learn the English academic language.

Socioeconomic Status of European Americans

European American students come from diverse family, cultural, linguistic, economic, educational, religious, and educational backgrounds. Some are wealthy, some are poor, and some are middle class, just as in any racial group in America. Socioeconomic status (SES) is often associated with prestige, pride, privilege, power, and influence in life as well as in school. Whether high or low SES has much to do with school performance and achievement, educators should keep in mind that all children deserve the best education possible regardless of their family income.

Generally, race is associated with class in America, and thus with SES. One indicator of SES is home ownership. Owning a home enables families to live in good areas with good schools, to find jobs, to go to college, and to perpetuate the life cycle. Table 4.14 shows the home ownership disparities among racial groups.

Table 4.14. Racial Disparities in Home Ownership

Racial Group	Percentage Owning a Home
White	75
Black	46
Asian	60
Hispanic	48

Note. Data from U.S. Census Bureau, *American Community Survey*, 2005.

Racial disparities continue to plague SES figures in America. Since 1980, the income gap among racial groups appear to have narrowed somewhat; however, incomes in White households are two thirds higher than in Black households and 40% higher than among Hispanics. Table 4.15 shows the racial disparities in median household income.

Table 4.15. Racial Disparities in Median Household Income

Racial Group	Median Income
White	$50,000
Black	$30,000
Asian	$60,000
Hispanic	$36,000

Note. Data from U.S. Census Bureau, *American Community Survey*, 2005. Numbers are rounded.

Another indication of SES disparity is the difference in poverty rates among racial groups in America. In 2005, the U.S. Census Bureau reported that the poverty rate for Whites was 8.3%; for Blacks, 24.9%; for Hispanics, 21.8%; and for Asians, 11.1%. Educators should bear in mind that income should not determine whether students of color have an opportunity to succeed in school or go to college. Regardless of the color of skin, every single child deserves a good education. This is true for European American children as much as for any others.

Promoting Academic Achievement for European Americans

Academically, U.S. Census 2000 reported that of the population 25 years and over, nearly 119,587,422 European Americans have earned high school diploma or higher, and about 37,291,563 have a bachelor's degree or higher. This means that of the 211.4 million European Americans living in the U.S., approximately 57% graduated from high school or similar schools, and 18% have graduated from college.

Almost all children of immigrants have greater difficulties with English in school than first- or second-generation native-born children. However, this does not mean that second- or third-generation European Americans do not have learning problems in school. European American students can encounter challenges at the same time they bring their individual and unique needs to schools.

However, their cultural background could play an important role in how they feel about school and the academic support they either do or do not receive. To promote the academic progress of European American students, prospective educators should be aware that there is little or no paraprofessional help available to these students. Most bilingual aides and paraprofessionals are skilled at helping children from other language groups. Very few schools have paraprofessionals who speak the languages or dialects of European Americans.

Furthermore, to promote pride in the cultural identities of European American students, prospective educators should carefully consider the following issues:

1. Does the school have bilingual staff or paraprofessionals who can speak the child's native language?
2. Are bilingual curricula available to assist European American students or do school personnel need to develop some?
3. Should the school let struggling European American students fend for themselves through the sink-or-swim process of saturation?
4. Should these students be placed in a classroom with expectations that are either too high or too low for them?
5. Should the school provide primary support when necessary to help these children learn English when they do not fully understand the language of instruction?

Prospective educators should bear in mind that multicultural curricula is effective in promoting positive self-esteem, self-image, self-concept, and cultural identities in children of diverse cultural backgrounds, including European Americans. To promote cultural diversity in the classroom, prospective educators should consider the following:

- Helping children learn and understand other students' cultures
- Recognizing differences in race, cultures, traditions, class, and gender
- Appreciating different viewpoints
- Providing relevant materials that enable all students to learn about cultural diversity
- Providing teaching and learning experiences that help dispel cultural myths, distortions, misperception, prejudice, and stereotypes appropriately and academically

It may seem a bit odd to learn that European American students could be considered to belong to a group of English learners that should be included in the cultural diversity curriculum. However, in fact, a surprisingly large number in this group of students are really English learners. And, coming from a wide variety of cultural backgrounds, they are as diverse as any other racial group of students in American schools.

Summing Up

This chapter presented the cultural characteristics of European children and families to provide prospective educators with some fundamental understanding of the diverse needs and abilities of children who have a European ancestry. European Americans came from different nations and brought diverse cultural practices to America; however, for years, the educational curricula dwelt more on the cultural characteristics of students who do not share the European ancestry and who speak languages at home other than English. As this chapter demonstrated, European American children and adolescents are not linguistically and academically immune to having difficulties with the English language. Children of Italian immigrants continue to face challenges in school, as do the children of Greek, French, Portuguese, Russian, German, Armenian, and Irish immigrants. European American children and adolescents should be recognized as integral to the nation's cultural diversity because they are culturally and linguistically diverse.

Despite the inadequacies of past educational practices, European American children and adolescents deserve educational programs that recognize their cultural characteristics with regard to motivation and learning; otherwise, like other children of other cultures, they become prisoners of silence in multicultural-dominant classrooms. Prospective educators need to consider European American children's language differences, learning styles, school success, cultural characteristics, self-esteem, and cultural identities to be part of the multicultural approach in order to design academic curricula that will benefit all students of all cultures.

Chapter Five

Hispanic American Children and Their Families

> Dream of what you can become and rejoice.
>
> —Cesar Chavez, President
> United Farm Workers of America

Overview

In 2006, in the midst of immigration reform in Washington, DC, Hispanic leaders in America called for a peaceful march in every city and state, a march they called "A Day without Immigrants." This monumental event captured the nation's attention and headlines because of the huge socioeconomic impact of Hispanics on American life.

Hispanic Americans constitute the second largest and one of the most diverse racial groups in America. Prospective educators need to understand the racial, ethnic, cultural, class, religious, family, language, and economic characteristics of Hispanic American children as well as their ways of life. The contributions of Hispanic Americans to the nation's educational system and cultural fabric should also be recognized and appreciated.

This chapter focuses on Hispanic Americans and their heritages. It explores the diversity in their origins, cultures, socioeconomic status, families, children, religions, gender roles, languages, and ways of life.

The Origins of Hispanic Americans

As with European Americans, it is impossible to describe in great detail the origins of all Hispanic American cultural groups and subgroups. Hispanic Americans originated in different places, such as Mexico, Central American nations, South American nations, and European nations. Taken together, Hispanic Americans comprise a diverse group with rich cultural heritages that include Chicanos, Latinos, Mexican Americans, Central Americans, South Americans, Spanish Americans, Latin Americans, Costa Ricans, Cubans, Puerto Ricans, Guatemalans, Salvadorans, Panamanians, Bolivians,

Hondurans, Colombians, Argentineans, Ecuadorians, Paraguayans, Uruguayans, Peruvians, and Venezuelans.

The various Hispanic American groups share many similar cultural values, characteristics, and belief systems. Depending on the country of origin, each group or subgroups has its own unique way of expressing itself and behaving. However, as a whole, Hispanic Americans share a fairly common cultural history, language origins, values, customs, traditions, religions, and way of life. But in America, Hispanics sometimes exhibit differences in ways that characterize them as members of heterogeneous cultural groups as well as individuals of distinct subgroups.

The Spaniards Juan Ponce de Leon, Hernando Cortez, Hernando De Soto, Vasco Nunez de Balboa, Cabeza de Vaca, Francisco Vasquez de Coronado, and Francisco Pizarro were among the first explorers to discover the New World in the 1400s and 1500s. At different times in history, Hispanic Americans were considered to be native inhabitants of this land because they were living in the Americas for many years before settlers came from the Old World. The western and southern states of the United States once belonged to Mexico or Spain.

To help educators understand the origins of Hispanic Americans, Table 5.1 lists the countries of origin of Hispanic Americans with the largest populations in the U.S. The table does not show every country of ancestry; however, all the groups not included together account for approximately 6 million people. Beyond simply celebrating Cinco de Mayo in May of each year, prospective educators should learn about the complex origins of their Hispanic American students by examining the cultural diversity among the different groups.

Prospective educators should keep in mind that only some origins of prominent and prosperous groups of Hispanic Americans are examined in this section. It is a great idea to learn more about individual students and their respective countries of origin to gain more insight into their cultural characteristics and nationalities.

Who Are Hispanic Americans Today?

After European Americans, Hispanic Americans constitute the largest ethnic or racial group that for several centuries has contributed the rich texture of cultural diversity to the fabric of America. By the year 2025, experts believe, one in four children in American public schools will be Hispanic (Manning & Baruth, 2009; Zehr, 2000).

Table 5.1. Hispanic Americans' Countries of Origin and Population Size in 2000

Country	Number
Mexico	20,600,000
Puerto Rico	3,400,000
Central America	1,600,000
South America	1,300,000
Cuba	1,200,000
Dominican Republic	765,000
Salvador	655,000
Colombia	471,000
Guatemala	372,000
Peru	234,000
Honduras	217,000
Argentina	101,000
Spain	100,000

Note. Data from U.S. Census Bureau, *Census 2000 Demographic Profile Highlights.* Numbers are rounded.

As mentioned earlier, the Hispanic American student population is projected to outnumber the student population of African Americans and European Americans because of high birth rates and cultural preservation in Hispanic American communities. If the trends continue, the Hispanic student population will soon be the majority, and the descendents of European Americans and African Americans will be minorities (see Table 5.2).

Table 5.2. Major Racial Groups in the U.S.

Group	Number in 2000, in millions	Projection in 2010, in millions
Whites	211.0	221.0
Blacks	34.0	37.0
Asians	10.0	13.0
Native Americans	2.3	2.4
Hispanics	35.2	44.0

Note. Data from U.S. Census Bureau, *Census 2000 Demographic Profile Highlights.* Numbers are rounded.

According to the 2000 U.S. census, there are approximately 35 million Hispanic Americans living in the U.S. The number of Hispanic Americans is expected to rise from 35 million to 44 million in 2010. If this trend continues

—and there is no reason to suspect that it will not—the number of Hispanics will increase substantially in the next few decades. Table 5.3 illustrates the gender distribution of the current and projected Hispanic American population.

Table 5.3. Gender Distribution of Hispanic American Population

Gender	Number in 2000, in millions	Projection in 2010, in millions
Male	18.1	23.0
Female	17.1	21.0
Total	35.2	44.0

Note. Data from U.S. Census Bureau, *Census 2000 Demographic Profile Highlights.* Numbers are rounded.

Prospective educators should bear in mind that tremendous variations as well as similarities exist among all Hispanic groups in America. For instance, cultural and linguistic differences exist between Mexican Americans and Panamanian Americans and between Chicanos and Latin Americans.

The Cultural Characteristics of Hispanic Americans

As with people from any racial group, Hispanic American students possess their own unique identities as well as cultural traits that could be identical to, different from, or somewhat similar to those of other students. Prospective educators should be open-minded to examine the stereotypes associated with Hispanic Americans. Some mistakenly perceive Hispanic students as less well behaved, less intelligent, less docile, less peaceful, and less cooperative than students of other racial groups. As Manning and Baruth (2009) point out, these negative perceptions produce inaccurate stereotypes that often result in self-fulfilling prophecies.

Prospective educators have a critical role to play in the development of self-image in Hispanic students as well as in students from other racial groups. Self-image is enhanced by genuinely deserved praise, sincere acceptance, understanding, and appreciation of differences. On the other hand, self-image is damaged by criticism, stereotyping, prejudice, bias, and unwarranted disapproval. Self-image is important because it helps students develop their cultural identity. For instance, for Hispanic students, the cultural value of *machismo* plays an important role in behaviors and attitudes, as shown in Table 5.4.

Table 5.4. Significance of Machismo to Cultural Identity

Positive/Negative	Significance
Positive	Clear-cut distinction between sexes
	Give privilege and rights to males, but not females
	Manhood, toughness
	Honor; dignity; protector of self-image, name, and possessions
	Social status, respect
	Family oriented, altruism
	Self-esteem
Negative	Consider others as untrustworthy
	Threat, fear, hostility, suspicion
	Disrespect

Note. Information from *Multicultural Education of Children and Adolescents* (5th ed.), by L. M. Manning and L. G. Baruth, 2009, New York: Pearson Education.

Self-image, like machismo, is not innate; it is learned. Self-image is shaped or molded by an individual's social and life experiences. All cultural characteristics are inculcated through continual reinforcement throughout the development process. Table 5.5 lists the cultural values that are important to most Hispanic Americans. Prospective educators should learn about the intricacies of Hispanic American cultural values and at the same time take into consideration other issues not mentioned here when dealing with the educational needs of their Hispanic American students.

Hispanic American values appear to affirm the practice of resiliency theory when dealing with cultural and language barriers in school. Manning and Baruth (2009) noted that resiliency theory identifies socio-cultural factors associated with families, schools, and communities of successful children and adolescents of diverse backgrounds. These coping skills are often absent in the lives of troubled children and adolescents. Resiliency theory is based on four basic attributes: social competence (people skills, human relations, interpersonal skills, and resources), problem-solving skills (having technical skills to find assistance, being proficient, thinking positively, and learning how to cope), autonomy (self-concept, pride, self-reliance, self-confidence, self-image, and self-esteem), and goal-orientation (setting up objectives, knowing tasks, self-discipline, and self-motivation).

Table 5.5. Common Hispanic American Values

Value	Examples
Responsibility	Taking care of family, siblings, gender roles
Family	Bonding, interaction, pride, kinship
Extended family	Grandparents, parents, in-laws, other relatives
Community	Living close to family members and promoting cultural heritage
Sincerity	Being honest, respectful, trustworthy
Sacrifice	Family oriented, group oriented, honor
Spirituality	Belonging to a religious group or affiliation
Generosity	Giving, caring, sharing, helping
Respect	Revere elders, grandparents, parents, authority
Cooperation	Team work, group work, community efforts
Harmony	Happy, congenial, strong bonds
Endurance	Hard working, altruistic, benevolent, responsible

Note. Information from Vincente and Associates: *Planning for Diversity*, 1990. UC, Davis: University of California.

Family factors include familial support system, parental guidance, and parental involvement. School factors are good teachers, learning adaptability, academic success, and supportive relationship with school personnel. Community factors include educational programs, good neighborhoods, location of residence, and social influences. Most importantly, personal factors include motivation, expectation, self-esteem, responsibility, social skills, and adaptability. These sociocultural factors play a role in cognitive maturity and social development.

One sociocultural factor that is important to most Hispanic students and parents is the ability to speak Spanish at home and in school. Sometimes Hispanic students use code switch while conversing in or learning English. However, some monolingual teachers encourage Hispanic students to speak less Spanish and more English in order to learn English more quickly. In the past, Hispanic students were punished for speaking English in class. In the assimilationist view, discouraging students from speaking a language other than English appears to be sound practice; however, in the pluralistic view, forcing someone to stop speaking Spanish is unacceptable. Even today, some teachers still disallow students to use Spanish as BICS or CALP in class.

To gain in-depth knowledge about the cultural backgrounds of diverse students, prospective educators should consider doing one or more of the following:

- Visiting local social organizations or community cultural events to gain firsthand experience.

- Interviewing or conversing with educators who have good knowledge about Hispanic culture.
- Being open to learning more and reading objective literature about the Hispanic culture to gain broader perspectives on historical background.
- Learning more about extended families, immediate families, family traditions, customs, and values.
- Taking the time to learn about individual students and their differences.
- Being aware of cross-cultural insensitivities, misinterpretations, and misapplications.
- Stopping using professional generalizations about Hispanic students.
- Considering entanglement of values and cultural orientations.

Prospective educators also need to take the clash of cultures into consideration when working with Hispanic children and adolescents. For instance, some teachers may encourage specific students to excel academically above their peers; however, this kind of encouragement could cause the students to stand out as being Americanized or different among their peers in opposition to their cultural expectations and values. However, in some cases, this kind of encouragement may be appropriate because individual students may need it in order to break away from the barriers that keep them from advancing.

Hispanic American Families

Although Hispanic Americans are culturally, linguistically, economically, and religiously diverse and come from different backgrounds, the traditional family features of the various groups are quite similar in many aspects. The importance of extended family seems to be a pervasive cultural characteristic; the extended family plays a major role in members' social and professional lives. Family comes before group or individuals, and group usually comes before the individual. Table 5.6 illustrates that Hispanic families are similar in size to families of other cultural groups.

Manning and Baruth (2009) noted that traditional Hispanic American families train their children early in life about the importance of five family values: (a) family responsibility, (b) clear-cut gender roles, (c) respect and reverence for elders and others in authority, (d) adherence to a patriarchal family structure, and (d) cooperation.

One cultural practice related to family structure that prospective educators should understand is the selection of godparents. Hispanic American parents arrange for godparents for their children and grandchildren. Godparents serve as additional authorities who care for the children's spiritual well-being and often take an active role in other aspects of their lives. This practice strengthens the family bond.

Table 5.6. Average Household and Family Sizes, by Racial Group

Group	Average Household Size	Average Family Size
Native Americans	3	4
Arab Americans	3	4
Hispanics	4	4
Whites	2	3
Asians	3	4
Blacks	3	3

Note. Data from U.S. Census, *Census 2000 Demographic Profile Highlights.*

Gender Roles of Hispanic Americans

Most Hispanic American families have clearly defined roles for fathers and mothers as well as for male and female children in the home. As stated earlier, Hispanic families place strong emphasis on the family structure and on communication, interaction, and cooperation within the family. For instance, Hispanic women generally assume a supporting role and occupy subordinate positions in the family circle, whereas Hispanic men are accorded honor, prestige, and authority in accordance with the fact that they are or will become heads of families in the patriarchal structure. Despite strong family values, Hispanic American families are not immune to divorce, separation, and raucous relationships. Still these disruptions of family are not as common as in European American and African American groups. As Table 5.7 shows, Hispanic Americans have the second lowest divorce rate, with the lowest divorce rate occurring in Asian American families.

In Hispanic families, male and female children have well defined family roles. Male children seem to have more and earlier social independence than female children. In some cases, male children are not subject to strict family curfew rules as are female children. As mentioned earlier, these differences in gender roles shape and mold the cognitive development of the self-image, self-concept, and academic self-image. It is crucial for prospective educators to design instructional activities, multicultural curricula, and teaching experiences that address gender inequity in order to promote positive cultural identity.

Table 5.7. Divorce Rates Among Selected Racial Groups

Group	Divorce Rate in 2000
European Americans	9.8%
African Americans	11.3%
Hispanic Americans	7.6%
Asian Americans	3.0%

Note. Data from *What's the Real Status of Divorce in America?* by M. Wojdacz, 2009, retrieved June 15, 2009, from http://www.legalzoom,com/legal-articles

Religions of Hispanic Americans

Hispanic Americans come from diverse religious backgrounds, and they do not all belong to just one religious denomination. At times, differences in religious affiliations flare up among Hispanic groups. A large number of Hispanic Americans were brought to the New World by their faith in Catholicism, but many Latinos decline the religious attachment to Catholicism, choosing instead evangelical or Protestant denominations. Prospective educators should be cautious about assuming they know the faith of their Hispanic American students. As Manning and Baruth (2009) pointed out, stereotyping religious affiliations for Latino Americans could be inaccurate, misleading, and damaging. Nonetheless, to help prospective educators learn more about the religious diversity of Hispanic Americans, Table 5.8 lists the most common religious affiliations of Hispanic Americans.

Table 5.8. Religious Affiliations Among Hispanic Americans

Denomination	Number of Adherents
Assembly of God	474,000
Nazarene	16,000
Evangelical Lutheran	39,000
Int. Pentecostal Holiness	23,000
Mennonite	4,000
Presbyterian	29,000
Roman Catholic	18,000,000
United Methodist	60,000

Note. Data from the Association of Statisticians of American Religious Bodies, 2002. Numbers are rounded.

As Table 5.8 illustrates, religious affiliation plays a central role in the family, social, political, and professional life of many Hispanic Americans, as it does with European Americans. Religion has been a part of Hispanic American culture from the very beginnings of that culture. Spanish missionaries arrived in the southwestern regions of the New World in the mid 1500s. Many of the Spanish missions that were founded along the California coast in the late 1700s and the early 1800s remain today.

In their religious practices and devotions, there are distinctions in the gender roles of men, women, and children. These distinctions are similar to the role differences in the family. Men assume roles of church leadership, serving, for example, as pastors or priests, and women serve as devout participants in subordinate positions (Manning & Baruth, 2009).

Languages of Hispanic Americans

As with members of other racial groups in America, Hispanic Americans speak many languages and dialects because they came from different places. Foreign-born and native-born Hispanic Americans often have linguistic differences in meanings, sounds, phonemes, intonations, cheremes, and emphasis depending on their immigration status, nation of origin, and current place of residence. For instance, in Spain the word *Castellano* denotes a regional dialect or culture that originated in the province of Castile, but in Latin American, the word refers to all Spanish in general (Lessow-Hurley, 2000).

Keep in mind that dialects are linguistic variations of a language used by certain groups of people who may have the same national origins. The Spanish word for *peach*, for example, is *durazno* in Mexico, but *melocoton* in Puerto Rico. In greeting people when answering the phone, Argentineans say *Allo*, Latin Americans say *Diga*, and Mexican Americans say *Bueno* (Lessow-Hurley, 2000).

Prospective educators should not assume that all Spanish words or vocabularies connote the same meanings in the minds of Mexican Americans, Latino Americans, Central Americans, and South Americans. For instance, in Panama the Spanish word *raspar* means to scratch or scrape, but in other parts of the world it means to have something to do with diarrhea (Haapanen, personal communication, 2009). Furthermore, consider that the Spanish word for *boy* is *niño*. But a number of other words are used for *boy* in different countries: in El Salvador, *cipote*; in Guatemala, *patojo*; in Peru, *chibola;* in Honduras, *hischoco*; in Mexico, *chabalo*; and in Argentina, *pibe*.

Undoubtedly, Hispanic American students face linguistic challenges in school. The English language is a complex form of communication, especially for learners from other cultures. Students' difficulties in learning English may have tremendous impact on their self-esteem and self-concept as well as the cognitive development of their cultural identity. For instance, Hispanic students who live in language enclaves may have academic problems when they hear Spanish spoken at home on a regular basis and feel pressured to learn and speak English in school. The struggle could degrade their feelings and attitudes toward their schoolwork.

Even if the majority of LEP students in the U.S. had Hispanic cultural backgrounds, that fact cannot be used to evaluate groups of students academically or linguistically. Prospective educators need to know that not all Hispanic students have difficulties in learning English or are limited in English proficiency. Caution needs to be taken when using visual assessment as assessment of perceived ability to determine language proficiency in students of color. Careless assessments can lead prospective educators to make inaccurate assumptions and thus to overlook students' academic needs.

Socioeconomic Status of Hispanic Americans

As is true in all ethnic groups, some Hispanic Americans live in poverty in America. The U.S. Census Bureau reported in 2006 that approximately 21% of Hispanic families lived in poverty, slightly lower than the 22% figure for the previous year. The two prominent contributors to family poverty of Hispanic Americans are (a) a high unemployment rate and (b) a high number of female-headed households (Manning & Baruth, 2009). However, as Table 5.9 illustrates, the poverty rate for Hispanic Americans in 2005 was lower than for African Americans but higher than for Whites and Asians.

Table 5.9. Poverty Rates Among Selected Racial Groups

Group	Rate
Whites	8.3%
Blacks	25.0%
Asians	11.0%
Hispanics	21.0%

Note. Data from U.S. Census Bureau, *American Community Survey,* 2005.

Even if Hispanic children are more likely to live in poverty and less likely to have health insurance coverage than European Americans, the narrowing disparities in home ownership and family income show positive signs of socioeconomic growth among Hispanic American families. As Table 5.10 indicates, Hispanic home ownership in 2005 was higher than for Blacks, but lower than for Whites and Asians. Moreover, in 2006, household income was higher for Hispanic families than for Black families (see Table 5.11).

Table 5.10. Percentages of Families Owning
Homes, by Racial Group

Group	Percentage
Whites	75
Blacks	46
Asians	60
Hispanics	48

Note. Data from U.S. Census Bureau,
American Community Survey, 2005.

Table 5.11. Percentages of Households at Selected Income Levels, by Racial Group

Group	$35,000 to $49,000	$50,000 to $74,000	$75,000 to $99,000	$100,000 and over
Whites	14.6	18.8	11.8	20.2
Blacks	14.8	15.2	7.7	9.1
Hispanics	17.5	17.3	8.9	10.5
Asians	NA	NA	NA	NA

Note. Data from *Income, Poverty, and Health Insurance Coverage in the United States* (U.S. Census Bureau Current Population Report P60-233), by C. DeNavas-Walt, B. D. Proctor, and J. Smith, 2007, Washington, DC: U.S. Government Printing Office.

Another way to help prospective educators understand the SES of Hispanic Americans is to compare the median family income of this group with that of other racial groups. Table 5.12 illustrates that the median income of Hispanics is higher than that of Blacks but lower than those of Whites and Asians.

Whether these SES factors are indicators or predictors of wealth and class in America, the racial disparities in income, education, home ownership, and family poverty level will continue to be substantial if current trends prevail. Regardless of any of these factors, prospective educators should bear in mind that income should have no bearing on whether students of color have an opportunity to succeed in school and go to college. Irrespective of the color of a child's skin, every single child deserves a good education, Hispanic children as well as all others.

Table 5.12. Median Household Income, by Racial Group

Group	Median Income
White	$50,000
Black	$30,000
Asian	$60,000
Hispanic	$36,000

Note. Data from U.S. Census Bureau, *American Community Survey,* 2005. Numbers are rounded.

Promoting Academic Achievement for Hispanic Americans

Almost all children of immigrant and minority families have some kind of language difficulties in school as compared with students coming from affluent families and majority backgrounds. Hispanic American students often encounter significant challenges, and their cultural backgrounds may play an important role in how they feel about school. The dropout rate for foreign-born Hispanics is 44%, a figure twice as high as the 22% for native-born Hispanics (Manning & Baruth, 2009). If nothing is done to stop this trend, foreign-born Hispanic students could be heading toward academic calamity.

As reported by U.S. Census Bureau 2000, of the population of 25 years and over, 9,577,031 Hispanics have a high school diploma or higher, and 1,908,039 have graduated from college. Moreover, this means that of the 35 million Hispanics living in the U.S., approximately 27% have graduated from high school or similar schools and only 5% have a bachelor's degree or higher.

To promote the academic progress of Hispanic American students, prospective educators should be aware of the factors that contribute to school dropout. Manning and Baruth (2009) suggested that Hispanic students who attend schools that have the following characteristics are susceptible to a higher rate of dropout, or lower rate of school completion: (a) overcrowded classrooms, (b) poor and inferior instruction, (c) insufficient bilingual staff to help students, (d) breeding grounds for antisocial activities or gang affiliations, and (e) location in poor inner city or other rundown area.

Self-fulfilling prophecies may form another layer of problems for Hispanic students if prospective educators make inaccurate assumptions about their students. Hispanic students are frequently subjected to debilitating stereotyping, social prejudice, cultural bias, blanket discrimination, and capricious implementation of curricula. These negativities lower their self-esteem, self-concept, and cognitive academic development. Dejected attitudes or despondent feelings could lead children to believe that formal education cannot improve their daily lives, and they lose the internal desire to succeed.

To promote positive cultural identity formation, prospective educators should carefully consider doing the following:

1. Have bilingual staff or paraprofessionals who can speak the child's native language.
2. Offer bilingual curricula instead of letting students fend for themselves.
3. Place students in classroom with teachers who can provide primary language support.
4. Provide primary support when necessary to help children learn English when the language of instruction is a language they do not fully understand.
5. Encourage the child to use the primary language for learning other subject matter while learning English.
6. Help children learn and understand other students' cultures.
7. Recognize differences in race, cultures, traditions, class, and gender.
8. Appreciate different viewpoints.
9. Provide relevant materials so all students can learn about cultural diversity.
10. Provide teaching and learning experiences that dispel cultural myths, distortions, misperceptions, prejudices, and stereotypes appropriately and academically.

When dealing with students of color, prospective educators should bear in mind that multicultural curricula can be integrated in ways that promote positive self-esteem, self-image, self-concept, and cultural identities in children. Nonetheless, to promote cultural diversity in the classroom, prospective educators should be honest, genuine, respectful, and kind.

Summing Up

This chapter gave an overview of Hispanic American children and their families to provide prospective educators with some background understanding of the diverse needs and abilities of children who share a Hispanic ancestry. As discussed in this chapter, educators should promote positive feelings in learners regarding their self-concept, self-image, self-esteem, and cultural identity because these cultural characteristics influence school achievement, cognitive development, and the socialization process. Recognizing language differences, language problems, difficulties with English, and learning styles will help prospective educators plan and implement educational programs and academic curricula that reflect cultural diversity. To help Hispanic students develop strong cultural identity, educators should create a multicultural environment that empowers individual students to respect the Spanish language and culture and, at the same time, counters labeling on the basis of myth, stereotypes, racism, prejudices, generalizations, discrimination, and biases.

Chapter Six

Native American Children and Their Families

If a white man wants to live in peace with the Indian, he can live in peace....Treat all men alike....Give them all the same law....Give them all an even chance to live and grow....All men were made by the same Great Spirit Chief....They are all brothers....The earth is the mother of all people, and all people should have equal rights upon it....Let me be a free man, free to travel, free to stop, free to work, free to trade where I choose my own teachers, free to follow the religion of my fathers, free to think and talk for myself, and I will obey every law, or submit to the penalty.

—Chief Joseph, Heinmot Tooyalaket, Nez Perce Leader

Overview

In 1621, at Plymouth, Massachusetts, the Pilgrims held their first Thanksgiving dinner to give thanks to God for everything that they had accomplished in the New World. Their special guests were some Native Americans who had helped them plant and harvest their crops. At that event, the Pilgrims did not have turkeys for dinner; in fact, they had mashed potatoes.

Many people have long forgotten that Native Americans were in this land before settlers arrived from different parts of the Old World. Soon after the settlers came, the lives of Native Americans were changed forever. Their way of life was destroyed, they were forced off their land, and thousands were either killed or relocated. However, some groups survived terrible ordeals and they preserved their cultural heritages. Today's Native Americans form as diverse a group as any other racial group in America. This chapter describes Native Americans and their differences in race, ethnicity, culture, class, religion, family, language, economics, and ways of life. Their long history and invaluable contributions to the American fabric has enriched this nation.

The Origins of Native Americans

Despite different and sketchy accounts of scholars who cannot determine who actually lived in the New World before the Europeans arrived, archaeological evidence reveals some information about the ancestors of today's Native Americans. The terms Native American, American Indian, and Native American Indian have been used interchangeably throughout the last 3 centuries to refer to these people. These names speak for themselves; without a doubt, Native Americans inhabited this land before anyone else.

The names of many U.S. states are taken from Native American words, as shown in Table 6.1. These names that designate states in every part of the country—from north to south and east to west and including Alaska—indicate that Native Americans lived throughout the land long before European Americans arrived. Native Americans did not claim ownership of the land the way European Americans did, but they obviously occupied much, if not all, of the country.

Historically, Native Americans underwent cultural changes at different times in history as a result of political domination by European Americans. Portman and Herring (2001) identified five major phases of change.

1. From the late 1600s to the early 1800s Native Americans were removed from their lands by the federal government.
2. From the mid-1800s to the early 1900s, Native Americans were restricted to living on reservations.
3. From the 1930s to the early 1950s, the federal government established schools on the reservation to put an end to the political and cultural repression of Native Americans.
4. From the mid-1950s to the late 1960s, Native Americans underwent rapid socio-cultural changes in a bittersweet process of socio-political integration as they tried to terminate their political dependence on the federal government.
5. From the early 1970s to the present time, Native Americans have engaged in the process of self-determination to retain their tribal sovereignty. They reorganized their social system to preserve their cultural heritages as well as their family traditions, values, and spirituality.

Lessow-Hurley (2000) observed that although Native American tribes were located in different regions across America during Phase 1, the southeastern tribes appeared to be successful in dealing with cross-cultural contacts with European Americans. They were called "civilized tribes" because the European Americans perceived them as capable of self-governance, and they were granted some political autonomy. As a result, some tribes developed writing systems for their languages. The Cherokee Sequoya created a writing system for the Cherokee language in the early 1800s that was implemented successfully in schools for many years. Eventually, however, political expediency overrode all else, and the Indian school systems were eradicated in the late 1800s (Lessow-Hurley, 2000; Weinberg, 1977).

Table 6.1. Native American Origins of the Names of Selected U.S. States

State	Origin/Meaning
Alabama	Indian for tribal town, a tribe of Alabamas, or Alabamans of Creek Confederacy
Alaska	Aleutian or Eskimo for "peninsula, great lands," or "land that is not an island"
Arizona	Pima for "little spring place" or Aztec Arizuma for "silver bearing "
Connecticut	Mohican or Algonquin for "long river place"
Illinois	Algonquin for "men or warriors"
Indiana	Means "land of the Indians"
Iowa	Indian for "here I rest" or "beautiful land"
Kansas	Sioux for "south wind people"
Kentucky	Indian for "dark, bloody ground, meadowland," or "land of tomorrow"
Massachusetts	Indian for "large hill place"
Michigan	Chippewa for "great water"
Minnesota	Dakota Sioux for "cloudy water" or "sky tinted water"
Mississippi	Chippewa for "great river" or "gathering in all of the waters"
Nebraska	Omaha or Otoe for "broad water" or "flat river"
North Dakota	Dakota is Sioux for "friend" or "ally"
Ohio	Iroquois for "fine or good river"
Oklahoma	Choctaw for "red man"
Texas	Caddo for "friends" or "allies"
Utah	Navajo for "upper" or "higher up"
Wisconsin	Indian for "grassy place"
Wyoming	Algonquin for "large prairie place, at the big plain," or "on the great plain"

Note. Data from Origins of the Names of U.S. States, *World Almanac and Book of Facts 1998*, New York: Simon and Schuster, 1997.

Who Are Native Americans Today?

Today, Native Americans may be found living on reservations, on rancherias, off the reservation, and in the non-Indian communities. The current Native American population is linguistically, culturally, religiously, and economically diverse. It is varied in tribal size, clan systems, residency on or off the reservation, educational attainment, and socioeconomic status. Many Native Americans are moving off reservation lands to non-Indian settings; however, they often face greater societal problems than those who remain on reservation lands. Moving off the reservation frequently strains family relationships and causes children to develop drastic social behaviors that are contrary to their traditional norms. Moreover, many Native Americans live below the poverty line (U.S. Census Bureau, 2000).

In 2006, the U.S. Census Bureau estimated that approximately 1% of the U.S. population was of Native American or Alaska Native descent. In the 2000 census, 2.5 million Native Americans were reported to be living in the U.S.; however, this number was unevenly distributed across the 50 states. According to 2006 demographic data, the 10 states with the highest proportions of Native Americans are Alaska, where Native Americans make up 13.1% of the population, New Mexico (9.7%), South Dakota (8.6%), Oklahoma (6.8%), Montana (6.3%), North Dakota (5.2%), Arizona (4.5%), Wyoming (2.2%), Oregon (1.8%), and Washington (1.5%).

Manning and Baruth (2009) observed that the 2.5 million Native Americans are distributed among approximately 500 different tribes of varying sizes. In 2000, the most prominent and largest tribes were the Cherokee, Choctaw, Apache, Blackfeet, Iroquois, Pueblo, Navajo, Chippewa, and Sioux. Tribal sizes range from 10,000 to 21,000 people; however, many small tribes of fewer than 10,000 people exist. The U.S. Census Bureau estimated that in 2003 one third of all Native Americans lived in California, Arizona, and Oklahoma. About one half lived west of the Mississippi River, and more than half reside in Alaska, Arizona, California, New Mexico, Oklahoma, and Washington (Manning & Baruth).

The tribes of Native Americans, the indigenous people of North America, are classified into four cultural regions: Alaska Native, western, central, and eastern regions. The Alaska Native region includes the Arctic or Eskimo-Aleut and Subarctic or Northern Athabaskan groups. The western United States region consists of the California tribes (Yok-Utian, Pacific Coast Athabaskan, Coast Miwok, Yurok, and Palaihnihan), the Plateau tribes (Interior Salish and Plateau Penutian), the Great Basin tribes (Uto-Aztecan), the Pacific Northwest Coast or Pacific Coast Athabaskan and Coast Salish, and the Southwestern tribes (Uto-Aztecan, Yuman, and Southern Athabaskan). The central region is comprised of the Plains Indians (Siouan, Plains Algonquian) and Southern Athabaskan. The eastern region includes the Northeastern Woodlands tribes (Iroquoian, Central Algonquian, Eastern Algonquian) and the Southeastern tribes (Siouan, Catawban, and Iroquoian).

The Cultural Characteristics of Native Americans

Traditionally, most Native Americans appear to center their personal well-being, demeanor, attitudes, behaviors, honor, peace, and respect on their relationship with nature, God, and guiding spirits. Children are taught early in life that in all actions nature and man are connected, and their behaviors, attitudes, and social welfare must be in harmony with nature. Native Americans follow 10 codes of ethics in their personal relationship with people and nature. One of the codes contains 15 different admonitions that highlight the concept of "respect" that Native Americans have for themselves and toward others. For Native Americans, to respect means to feel or show honor or esteem for someone or something, to consider the well-being of or to treat someone or something with deference or courtesy. Showing respect is a basic law of life, as the following 15 instructions, taken from "The Sacred Tree" in The Four Worlds Development Project (1982), demonstrate:

1. Treat every person, from the tiniest child to the oldest elder, with respect at all times.
2. Special respect should be given to elders, parents, teachers, and community leaders.
3. No person should be made to feel "put down" by you; avoid hurting other hearts as you would avoid a deadly poison.
4. Touch nothing that belongs to someone else, especially sacred objects, without permission or an understanding between you.
5. Respect the privacy of every person; never intrude on a person's quiet moment or personal space.
6. Never walk between people who are conversing.
7. Never interrupt people who are conversing.
8. Speak in a soft voice, especially when you are in the presence of elders, strangers, or others to whom special respect is due.
9. Do not speak unless invited to do so at gatherings where elders are present except to ask what is expected of you should you be in doubt.
10. Never speak about others in a negative way, whether they are present or not.
11. Treat the earth and all of her aspects as your mother and do nothing to pollute our Mother; rise up with wisdom to defend her.
12. Show deep respect for the mineral world, the plant world, and the animal world.
13. Show deep respect for the beliefs and religion of others.

14. Listen with courtesy to what others say, even if you feel that what they are saying is worthless; listen with your heart.
15. Respect the wisdom of the people in council.

Without a doubt, adherence to these values will put Native American children at a disadvantage in settings with European Americans. These values do not give rise to the typical social behaviors expected among European Americans. Native American children experience culture shock, cultural confusion, and cultural mismatch in the larger U.S. society.

Mutual sharing is another cultural characteristic of Native Americans. Cooperation gives a sense of a social self-image and self-concept that is associated with personal ability, worth, and social status, whereas competition is seen as selfish and prideful. This emphasis on cooperation rather than competition can appear as passiveness and lead to a misperception of Native American children as having low self-esteem when actually they are simply being considerate of and respectful toward others.

As Manning and Baruth (2009) pointed out, Native American cultural characteristics of patience, passiveness, soft voice, respect, and sharing can mistakenly lead others to portray Native American children as strange, uncaring, or lacking middle-class values. In fact, respect, which is the basis of these cultural traits, is integral to Native Americans' lives. One of the codes of Native American ethics says, "The hurt of one is the hurt of all; the honor of one is the honor of all." Genuine respect for others is part of their unique cultural identity; it causes them to take responsible action to work with others toward achieving a common goal for the greater good of all in harmony with nature.

Native American Families

Some Native American families are patriarchal and some are matriarchal. Children learn oral traditions and cultural values from their parents, grandparents, elders, and spiritual healers. Native Americans have immediate and extended family structures, and their tribes, clan systems, and cultural values play integral roles in the development of their cultural identity and social self-image.

Native Americans place a high value on group or family welfare. Children are taught obedience and respect, and they are taught about the privileges, rights, and social position of elders and parents. As Manning and Baruth (2009) explained, even if some measure of self-sufficiency is taught early in life, adolescents look up to the older members of the family or group for social acceptance and approval. To preserve their cultural heritage, older members are responsible to acquaint the young with family traditions, customs, rituals, legends, history, and myths.

The average household size and average family size of Native Americans are not much different from those of other racial groups, as illustrated in Table 6.2. The household size for Native Americans is the same as for Arab Americans, Asians, and Blacks, but smaller than that of Hispanics and larger than that of whites.

Table 6.2. Average Household and Family Sizes, by Racial Group

Group	Average Household Size	Average Family Size
Native Americans	3	4
Arab Americans	3	4
Hispanics	4	4
Whites	2	3
Asians	3	4
Blacks	3	3

Note. Data from U.S. Census Bureau, *Census 2000 Demographic Profile Highlights.*

Gender Roles of Native Americans

As with other racial groups, Native Americans teach their sons and daughters how they expect children of both sexes to behave, think, and act. The children learn gender roles in accordance with their tribes' cultural beliefs and values. Prospective educators need to understand gender differences in roles of Native Americans to avoid making the inaccurate assumption that the two sexes are socially alike in the academic setting.

Regardless of whether they live off the reservation or on the reservation, many Native Americans maintain traditional gender roles. However, cultural variations regarding gender roles exist among the different tribes, clan systems, and subgroups. Some tribes practice polygamy. Some follow a matriarchal system, whereas others prefer a patriarchal system. In some groups, a blend of the two is followed. Cherokee tradition, for example, is that women own the family property, and men hunt, trade, and make war against their enemies. At home, the women are expected to gather plants, care for the children, look after the elders, fashion clothing designs, make instruments, and cure meat.

Native American women generally have subordinate positions in the family. Nevertheless, they serve crucial roles that are essential to the survival of their tribes. Women make tools and weapons, take care of the home, help their men hunt, gather herbs to help cure the ill, and safeguard the family unit. Even though fighting and hunting are male activities, Sioux girls are allowed to learn how to ride, hunt, and fight.

The socio-cultural changes that have been thrust upon Native Americans have altered their gender roles. For instance, forced assimilation shattered the customary male-female relationship; today's Native American men are concerned about losing their traditional and tribal image as their wives enter the labor force. This concern has led males to put great pressure on women, which sometimes results in deadly consequences. Portman and Herring (2001) observed that the suicide rate among Native American women increased as they entered the labor force.

Keep in mind that information about Native American cultures and traditions is relatively new in the education community. Much has been learned about gender roles and differences among those who live on the reservation, but little is known about those who live off the reservation. Prospective educators should be cautious to avoid overgeneralization when dealing with male and female Native American students.

Religions of Native Americans

Today, a large number of Native Americans claim adherence to some form of Christianity, and they belong to different religious denominations. Traditional spiritual rites and ceremonial rituals are still practiced by various tribal groups to preserve tribal identity or personal primary religious identity.

As diverse as the cultures, beliefs, traditions, customs, rituals, values, and religions of Native Americans, so far no formal religion or religious tradition has emerged as hegemonic among the tribes in the United States. Each tribe has its own rites and rituals and modes of healing, worship, and praying. However, most tribal religious practices are tied to an almighty God and perceive all beings in the world to be interconnected and live according to the same processes.

Native Americans view nature as the essence of God; God controls all nature and gives people access to it. They see the natural world and its beauty as spiritual and physical and spiritual entities as of equal value regardless of their living or non-living status. Axelson (1999) and Manning and Baruth (2009) noted that Native Americans perceive God as the great power above everything, the one who created people, nature, and the universe and instructs people how to live on the land he made. They see God as positive, altruistic, benevolent, and powerful. His power is healing and provides benefits for daily life. Each tribe has a distinct word for *God*, or the inner spiritual power (see Table 6.3).

Table 6.3. Word for God Among Selected Native American Tribes

Tribe	Word
Iroquois	Orenda
Algonquian	Manitou
Powhatan	Alone
Sioux	Wakan, or wakonda, or wakan tanka

Note. From *Multicultural Education of Children and Adolescents* (5th ed.), by L. M. Manning and L. G. Baruth, 2009, New York: Pearson Education.

During the colonization of the United States, many tribes were introduced to Christianity. Catholic missionaries brought the Christian faith to Native Americans as early as the late 1400s. Contemporary Native American children and families are adherents of various modern religious denominations, as shown in Table 6.4. Catholicism appears to be the dominant religious affiliation among Native Americans.

Table 6.4. Religious Affiliations of Native Americans

Denomination	Number of Adherents
Assemblies of God	35,000
Nazarene	1,600
Evangelical Lutheran Church	7,200
Int. Pentecostal Holiness	400
Mennonite	470
Presbyterian	6,800
Roman Catholic	640,000
United Methodist	28,000

Note. Data from Association of Statisticians of American Religious Bodies, 2002. Numbers are rounded.

Although Native Americans are religiously diverse, religious faith appears to be an integral part of the lives of most Native Americans. It is ingrained in their codes of ethics. One of the codes reads as follows:

To serve others, to be of some use to family, community, nation, and the world is one of the main purposes for which human beings have been created....Do not fill yourself with your own affairs and forget your most important talks....True happiness comes only to those who dedicate their lives to the service of others.

Languages of Native Americans

Of the 2.5 million Native Americans, about 630,000 still speak a language other than English at home according to the 2000 census data. This statistic suggests that in many tribes people are still using their native languages for daily communication with their offspring. According to Manning and Baruth (2009), Native Americans speak 2,200 different languages; however, it is unknown how many languages are in oral form only and how many are in both oral and written forms.

So far, the only known Native American language that has a writing system is the Cherokee language. In 1827, the Cherokee nation published its first bilingual newspaper, called the *Cherokee Phoenix*. After its creation, the Cherokee established schools and academies to teach both Cherokee and English. As a result, by 1852, the southwestern Cherokees in Oklahoma had a high literacy rate in English as compared with tribes that did not have a writing system. Of the 11,000 students enrolled in the Cherokee schools and academies, 90% were literate in the Cherokee language as well (Lessow-Hurley, 2000).

Because so many languages are spoken in the home, Native American children today are prone to difficulties with English. Prospective educators need to be aware that their communication styles, both verbal and nonverbal, affect learning for these students. For instance, Manning and Baruth (2009) pointed out that Native American children appear to speak more softly and at a slower rate than others, and they use head nods and demonstrate respect between speaker and listener.

Native American children are quite likely to experience a clash of culture at home if their communication with their parents and elders is limited due to the fact that the children choose to use English over their primary language. For their monolingual parents, the inability to converse with their children could lower their self-esteem and self-image and interfere with their cultural development as well as their cognitive development. Cultural identity is very important to Native Americans.

Manning and Baruth (2009) reported that very few Native American children are able to speak excellent English, and the majority speak the language either fairly or poorly. However, despite the linguistic complexities, prospective educators should not assume that the only means to success for them is mastery of the English language. As mentioned earlier, proficiency in a language is not a sufficient condition for academic achievement. In other words, all children must learn the academic language needed to perform academic tasks.

Socioeconomic Status of Native Americans

Despite all the gambling casinos built on Indian reservation property, Native Americans are still among the poorest groups in America. As Manning and Baruth (2009) wrote, Native Americans are among the poorest, least employed, least healthy, and worst-housed groups, with the lowest income and lowest educational attainment. To compare Native Americans with other racial and income groups in America in SES, Table 6.5 lists the 1999 per capita income of the main racial groups.

Table 6.5. Per Capita Income in 1999, by Racial Group

Group	Per Capita Income
Native Americans	$12,893
Arab Americans	$24,061
Hispanic Americans	$12,111
Whites	$23,918
Blacks	$14,437
Asians	$21,823

Note. Data from U.S. Census Bureau, *Census 2000 Demographic Profile Highlights.*

As a group, Native Americans were not as poor as Hispanic Americans in 1999 in terms of income; however, SES includes other socio-cultural factors. Different cultures have different values concerning wealth, health, housing, and employment. What is considered healthy in one culture may not be seen the same way in another culture. For instance, living in a remote area, such as on a reservation, could be thought of as unhealthy and undesirable by some European Americans; however, for many Native Americans, it is a way of life that has been passed from one generation to the next and therefore of high value. Moreover, traditional foods that might be considered strange or even unfit to eat in one culture might be prized by another cultural group.

To help prospective educators understand the SES of Native Americans, Table 6.6 provides a comparison of median family incomes among the major racial groups.

As the table illustrates, Native American families are not far behind Black families and Hispanic families in median family income. The income disparities among these three groups do not appear significant. However, family income is not the only indicator of economic success. Prospective educators should bear in mind that success means different things to different people.

Table 6.6. Median Family Income in 1999, by Racial Group

Group	Income
Native Americans	$33,144
Arab Americans	$55,673
Hispanic Americans	$34,397
Whites	$53,456
Blacks	$33,255
Asians	$59,323

Note. Data from U.S. Census Bureau, *Census 2000 Demographic Profile Highlights.*

Promoting Academic Achievement for Native Americans

In 2000, the U.S. Census Bureau reported that of the population 25 years and over, 958,078 have high school diplomas or higher, and 155,069 have earned a bachelor's degree or higher. This information indicates that of the 2.5 million Native Americans living in the U.S., about 39% graduated from high school or similar schools and only 6% have earned college degrees.

Many educators have limited knowledge, understanding, and encounters with Native Americans because they are among the least studied, least identified, most underreported, and most misunderstood cultural and racial groups in America. Political stereotypes exhibited in the cries "The only good Indian is a dead Indian" and "Kill the Indian but save the person" are derogatory and inappropriate. However, misperceptions about Native Americans persist. Prospective educators need to avoid educational decisions and curricula based on unsound judgments that would trigger stereotypical generalizations.

Native American children are not immune to academic problems and cross-cultural challenges. They need to acquire time management skills, study skills, coping skills, interpersonal skills, and language proficiency. They struggle with cultural barriers and personal needs. As with any other students, they bring their diverse needs and abilities to school. Their personal feelings are not much different from those of other students of color. Living in an environment of cultural differences could make them feel unfit, incompatible, isolated, lonely, rejected, dejected, anxious, worried, and bored. As Manning and Baruth (2009) explained, these internalized feelings could contribute to social alienation, poor self-image, low self-esteem, withdrawal, and relationship problems. These predicaments could mislead others to believe that they are uncaring, indifferent, unsociable, and irresponsive. In fact, they are probably unmotivated for a variety of reasons.

To promote the cultural identity and academic progress of Native American children and adolescents, prospective educators need to take all cultural factors and academic issues into careful consideration. For instance, no program is available to help these children if they do not understand the English instruction given in class. Most paraprofessionals are hired to aid other students with different language needs, such as Hispanics and Asians. Nel (1994) suggested using the following strategies to accommodate the cultural characteristics of Native American students:

1. Emphasize sharing, generosity, and cooperation.
2. Praise privately.
3. Avoid public praise.
4. Teach coping skills.
5. Show how to cooperate and how to compete.
6. Be flexible about time.
7. Offer opportunity.
8. Deal with feelings of alienation.
9. Show how to overcome isolation.
10. Improve self-image and self-esteem.

As Manning and Baruth (2009) asserted, loss of confidence, decline in motivation, hopelessness, confusion, frustration, anxiety, and peer pressure exacerbate the already existing problems faced by minority students. In some cases, prospective educators mistakenly label Native American students as lazy, shy, reserved, inactive, inattentive, unmotivated, and dawdling. With these students as well as with all others, educators should apply the following understandings when dealing with student behaviors:

1. Understand harboring feelings.
2. Understand sensitivity of language barriers.
3. Understand clash of cultures.
4. Understand culture identity development.
5. Understand anxiety and confusion.
6. Understand personal comfort zone.
7. Understand cultural orientation.
8. Understand unassertiveness.

9. Understand respect.
10. Understand involuntary efforts

Applying these understandings will go a long way toward promoting students' self-esteem and cultural identities; however, results may vary according to individual students. In addition to understanding the differences among students, prospective educators should also be aware of actions that are counterproductive while dealing with Native American students. Some of these actions to avoid are as follows:

1. Avoid self-talk, self-assessment, and self-report activities, unless used in the group.
2. Avoid competitive activities unless they are taught as activities.
3. Avoid direct eye contact unless absolutely necessary.
4. Avoid extensive verbal reporting, verbal interaction, and oral presentations unless required.
5. Avoid homogeneous grouping unless needed for a meaningful purpose.

Understanding these cultural characteristics should be beneficial to prospective educators. Native American children are facing a downward trend in academic achievement after the fourth grade (Manning & Baruth, 2009). In addition, as Montgomery (2001) found out, Native American students who are gifted and talented have not been identified by schools as such for a variety of reasons. School reform is direly needed to address the diverse needs and abilities of Native American students. In truth, it is long overdue.

Summing Up

This chapter discussed the cultural characteristics of Native American children and families to provide prospective educators with some understanding of children who share Native American ancestry. As with other cultural groups, promoting positive self-image, self-concept, self-esteem, and self-worth for Native American children and adolescents is one of the most important ways to empower academic achievement and reduce behavior-related school problems. Prospective educators should adapt their teaching styles and academic curricula to address the learning styles, cultural characteristics, and individual differences of all children to improve the academic progress and the overall school success of Native American children and adolescents. Teachers should incorporate the historical accomplishments and contributions of Native Americans into the school curricula and, at the same time, provide academic curricula and instructional practices that promote multicultural views and reflect learners' cultural identities.

Chapter Seven

African American Children and Their Families

I long for the day when we will be judged not by the color of our skins,
but by the content of our character.
—Dr. Martin Luther King, Jr., 1963

Overview

In 2008, 40 years after the death of Martin Luther King, Jr., and 145 years after the abolition of slavery, Barack Obama was elected to the highest office in the land, the first African American to accede to the presidency. In so doing, he made history and changed the mosaic of national leadership. As Obama said at the 2004 Democratic National Convention, "This is not about red or blue states; it is about the United States of America." This chapter examines African Americans and describes their differences in ethnicity, culture, class, religion, family, language, economics, and ways of life. African Americans have contributed much to the country's cultural diversity and serve as symbols of the greatness of this nation.

The Origins of African Americans

People from the nations of Africa were brought to the New World by European Americans. The first African Americans, or black laborers, were captured and transported against their will to a land that was totally foreign to them. Ogbu (1978) classified African Americans as one of the caste-like minority groups in America because they came to the West involuntarily.

In the early 1600s, the Blacks brought from Africa were indentured servants under European masters, but within a few decades, by the mid-1600s, they were slaves in a system that was legalized in the New World. African Americans did not come to America seeking economic or religious opportunities as did other immigrants. Many were forced to work on plantations and lived under horrible, cruel, and inhumane conditions. African Americans deserve understanding and appreciation because they suffered in ways that no other racial group in America did. Even after slavery, they endured brutal sociopolitical injustice, racial inequities, mistreatment, and discrimination that are difficult to imagine.

American history shows that the inhumane treatment led to slave revolutions. In the first revolution, in 1712, 6 African Americans in New York committed suicide and 21 were executed. In a second revolution, in 1741, also in New York, 13 African Americans were hanged, 13 were burned to death, and 71 were deported to their native land.

Just over 100 years later, in 1863, President Abraham Lincoln issued the Emancipation Proclamation, which freed all slaves in the Union. Two years later, the 13th Amendment to the U.S. Constitution abolished slavery. However, these measures did not end the prejudice against African Americans. It continued through the civil rights movement of the 1950s and 1960s, which was a quest for equal rights. In 1963, Dr. Martin Luther King, Jr., organized the largest event in the civil rights movement, a "March on Washington" to demand equality for all citizens. About 250,000 people participated in the march, and Dr. King delivered his famous "I Have a Dream" speech. The march was a turning point in American politics and domestic policy.

The election of President Obama in 2008 was a victory in the African American struggle against racial inequities, from slavery through oppression, marginalization, repression, and racial discrimination. At his election, many prominent African American leaders and elected officials expressed tearful elation that a dream had finally been realized. Many had not expected to see a Black president in their lifetime. But it happened.

Who Are African Americans Today?

Today's African Americans are socially, economically, religiously, linguistically, and politically diverse. They comprise the third largest racial group in America, behind European Americans, the largest, and Hispanic Americans, the second largest. After more than 400 years in the New World, African Americans have become enculturated as well as successfully assimilated into the mainstream of society. Today, about 36 million African Americans live in the U.S. (U.S. Census Bureau, 2000a). Of that number, 19 million are female and 17 million are male.

The term *African American* should not exclude people who came somewhat recently and voluntarily from African nations and regions such as Ethiopia, Nigeria, Sudan, Darfur, Congo, Kenya, Algeria, Ghana, Tanzania, Uganda, Somalia, Liberia, Senegal, South Africa, and Zambia. However, the term usually refers to the Black Americans who are descendants of slavery and are now monolingual in English. Recent immigrants and refugees could be considered as subgroups that originated in different nations in Africa; most of these are bilingual or multilingual. In other words, prospective educators should understand that the contemporary term *African American* could encompass more than just Black Americans.

As with other racial groups, African Americans today are successful in some areas and struggle in others. Manning and Baruth (2009) observed that despite gains since the civil rights movement of the 1960s, fundamental socio-political, socioeconomic, and health disparities remain between Whites and Blacks. They listed some of those disparities as follows:

1. Blacks get sick more easily.
2. Blacks stay sick longer.
3. Blacks die sooner than Whites.
4. African American babies have a shorter life expectancy.
5. African American babies are born weighing less.
6. Blacks are less likely to survive the 1st year after birth.
7. Blacks face a higher risk of having medical conditions.
8. Blacks are twice as likely to die of a stroke.
9. Blacks are more likely to die of heart disease.
10. Blacks have a higher incidence of cancer.
11. Blacks are twice as likely to be without health insurance.
12. Blacks have more stresses.
13. Blacks have a less healthy diet.
14. Blacks often mistrust doctors and healthcare providers.
15. Blacks earn less money than Whites.
16. Blacks possess less wealth.

Although these claims are true, some differences are not statistically significant. Sometimes the differences are overgeneralized in an attempt to demonstrate that African Americans are at risk in many social areas. All the claims cannot be applied to every African American subgroup. Generally, however, these disparities exist and indicate that African Americans continue to suffer social and racial inequities. To help prospective educators understand some of the disparities between today's African American and other racial groups, Table 7.1 compares disability in populations 5 years and older of different racial groups.

According to the data shown in Table 7.1, African Americans have the second highest percentage of children with disabilities, with Native Americans having the highest. Nonetheless, it is prejudicial to compare African

American children with White children on the basis of a 5% disparity and a huge difference in the size of the total populations. Interestingly, Whites have a higher percentage of children with disabilities than Arab Americans, Asian Americans, and Hispanic Americans. When compared with populations of similar size, African Americans have a far greater portion of children with disabilities—21.1% as compared with 14.7% for Hispanic Americans, for example. African Americans are improving in many areas; however, some socio-cultural issues are difficult to overcome.

Table 7.1. Numbers of People 5 Years and Above with Disabilities, by Racial Group

Group	In 2000	Projected in 2007	Percentage
Whites	36,000,000	221,000,000	16.3
Blacks	7,600,000	36,000,000	21.1
Native Americans	531,000	2,500,000	21.2
Arab Americans	169,000	1,200,000	14.1
Hispanic Americans	6,500,000	44,000,000	14.7
Asian Americans	1,600,000	12,000,000	13.3

Note. Data from U.S. Census Bureau, *Census 2000 Demographic Profile Highlights.* Numbers are rounded.

The Cultural Characteristics of African Americans

The cultural characteristics of African Americans are unique and diverse. For instance, social stratification among African Americans is evident, with some African Americans falling into the underclass; some in the lower, middle, or upper-middle classes; and others in the higher socioeconomic brackets.

As Manning and Baruth (2009) pointed out, African American children usually find themselves in the middle of two distinct cultural norms: the culture of the home and neighborhood where they grow up, and the cultures of the schools and social organizations where they learn to socialize with different people of other cultures. In other words, like other students of color, African American children often experience conflict between their families' values and the values of other people. Educators need to affirm and reaffirm in African American children, as well as in all other children of diverse backgrounds, that being different does not imply being wrong. At the same time, students need to learn the normal and acceptable behaviors that are expected of all children.

To help prospective educators understand African American cultural characteristics, Table 7.2 illustrates the primary values that are recognized as appropriate among African Americans. However, educators need to remember that misapplication of these values could result in inaccurate generalizations.

Table 7.2. Values of African Americans

Values	Examples
Mutual aid	Sharing, helping, loving, caring
Adaptability	Accommodating, flexible, changeable, movable
Family	Mother, father, and children; relationships
Extended family	Having large family, living together, village or group
Natural goodness	Beauty, originality, purity, genuineness
Inclusivity	Group efforts, group oriented, for all
Unconditional love	Commitment to one another
Religion	Bonds that bind all together, faith, sacrifice, rituals
Respect for elders	Showing gratitude toward grandparents, parents, and leaders
Restraint	Self-control, self-restraint, patience
Reciprocity	Exchanging, sharing, caring, giving
Interdependence	Group oriented, security, bonding, networking
Cooperation	Sharing, group, team work, interdependence

Note. Information from Vincente & Associates: *Planning for Diversity*, 1990, University of California, Davis.

As Table 7.2 shows, African Americans are traditionally family, group, and community oriented. Contemporary African American children are taught early in life to show respect for the elderly, parents (especially mothers), community leaders, relatives, extended family members, and siblings. Manning and Baruth (2009) observed that African American children and adolescents tend to be highly talkative, expressive, assertive, emotional, verbal, and opinionated in dealing with peers and adults. In some situations, they avoid eye contact and may interrupt the speaker even if interjecting sometimes appears to be rude or inappropriate in other cultures. Body language, nonverbal cues, and hand gestures also play a role in how children and adolescents communicate and socialize. Keep in mind that some of these social traits may seem odd to people of other cultures, but they are not wrong.

One troubling cultural characteristic among today's African Americans is the lack of positive male role models either in the home or in the community. This remains a pressing social issue in the African American community.

African American Families

Most African American families are closely bonded. In the past, African Americans had large nuclear families as well as large extended families. Today, African American family and household sizes are not much different from those of other races, as shown in Table 7.3. The average African American family size is the same as that of Whites; however, it is slightly smaller than those of Native Americans, Arab Americans, Hispanic Americans, and Asian Americans. The average household size for African Americans, which may include members of the extended family, is the same as for Native Americans, Arab Americans, and Asian Americans. It is slightly higher than that of Whites and slightly lower than that of Hispanic Americans.

Table 7.3. Average Family and Household Sizes, by Racial Group

Groups	Number in Household	Number in Family
Native Americans	3	4
Arab Americans	3	4
Hispanics	4	4
Whites	2	3
Asians	3	4
Blacks	3	3

Note. Data from U.S. Census Bureau, *Census 2000 Demographic Profile Highlights.*

Having a stable family unit is the most important societal value for children because the family unit is the nest in which they grow up and are fed daily. In a June 2009 speech addressing the importance of Father's Day, President Obama lamented the fact that about half of African American children do not have positive male role models in the home.

To help prospective educators understand this pressing issue, Table 7.4 lists the divorce rates of different racial groups. Based on data for 2000, African Americans have the highest divorce rate, followed by Whites, Hispanics, and Asians.

Table 7.4. Divorce Rates, by Racial Group

Group	Percent Divorced in 2000
European Americans	9.8
African Americans	11.3
Hispanic Americans	7.6
Asian Americans	3.0

Note. Data from National Center for Health Statistics, *Marriage and Divorce Statistics*, 2002, Washington, DC: U.S. Census Bureau.

Culturally, family members and close relatives play an important role in the African America family unit; they help care for children. Despite the number of people living in poverty and the lack of positive male role models in the home, the cultural tradition of multi-generational families that function cooperatively is likely to continue and be a strength in the African American community.

Gender Roles of African Americans

Information on gender roles of African American males and females is limited. Based on the cultural characteristics and family values, it appears that many African American females are the heads of their households; they take care of their children and sometimes extended families without the presence of adult males. The absence of males in many homes does not indicate that all African American males are not family oriented or are irresponsible. More importantly, it does not indicate that African Americans prefer families without adult males. Furthermore, it does not preclude other racial groups from having the same situation. No culture, family structure, or people function perfectly according to their values. All have to learn to survive and adapt to changes each and every day.

According to Manning and Baruth (2009), African American females could benefit from school settings with behavior management systems with positive consequences and positive learning environments. Cooperative strategies should work well with African American children; however, the tasks need to be prescribed according to the students' abilities and needs. For instance, strategies that promote development of positive self-image, self-concept, and self-esteem would elevate individuals' feelings and motivate students to cooperate as well as to compete. At the same time, these strategies would reduce or eliminate false perceptions of self. Moreover, African American females need to understand socially acceptable behaviors in order to develop self-confidence, self-image, and self-reliance. Educators should model appropriate behaviors for both sexes through actual educational learning experiences.

Furthermore, academic problems facing African American males need to be addressed on an ongoing basis and in a timely manner; otherwise, the problems could lead to detention, suspension, expulsion, retention at grade level, placement in alternative education programs, and dropout. As mentioned earlier, being different is not the same as being wrong. However, if students fail to differentiate what is merely different and what is unacceptable, the difference does matter. For instance, modulating one's voice or practicing proper grooming may need to move from expectations to requirements because these behaviors reflect the school's norms.

Prospective educators should keep in mind that African American children are more likely to be placed in special education programs than children of other cultures for a variety of reasons. Sometimes, however, the placement is not the correct academic prescription. Two out of every three students in special education are African American. This statistic is alarming and troublesome and deserves careful assessment.

Prospective educators who sincerely wish to motivate African American students should recognize that both the physical environment, which is the school setting, and professional behavior, which includes the actions and attitudes of the teacher, play major roles in the development of positive self-image and the achievement of academic success.

Religions of African Americans

Undoubtedly, religion is the tie that has bound African Americans together for centuries. Religious faith and principles have taken them through cultural oppression and repression and enabled them to overcome many obstacles. Today, their religions are as diverse as their cultures and traditions. A large number of African Americans are affiliated with Christianity; some of the denominations are shown in Table 7.5. As indicated, the largest religious affiliation of African Americans is Roman Catholicism. This table does not show the number of African Americans who follow Islam, Buddhism, Hinduism, or other types of religions.

As mentioned previously, the cultural values and traditions of African Americans are rich and strong. For African Americans, religious affiliation plays an important role in the personal life, social status, development of self-image, and psychological well-being.

Table 7.5. Religious Affiliation of African Americans

Denomination	Number of Adherents
Assemblies of God	183,000
Church of Nazarene	22,000
Evangelical Lutheran Church	53,000
Int. Pentecostal Holiness Church	934
Presbyterian Church U.S.A	73,000
Roman Catholic Church	2,500,000
United Methodist Church	427,000
Mennonite Church	6,300

Note. Data from Association of Statisticians of American Religious Bodies, 2002. Numbers are rounded.

Languages of African Americans

African Americans may or may not speak a language other than English, but for most, English is the primary language. However, some of the subgroups of African Americans speak other languages. The language of African American children is sometimes referred to as Black English, Ebonics, various vernaculars of African American English, or simply English. Some African Americans speak English with distinct grammatical structures or dialects, depending on the person's social status, geographic location, level of acculturation, educational level, and profession. The way African Americans speak the English language reflects their culture, personality, attitudes, family values, and community norms, all of which play roles in the development of their cultural identity, social behaviors, academic achievement, psychological well-being, and cognitive maturity. Under no circumstance should educators denigrate the language with which a child was raised.

Manning and Baruth (2009) cautioned that African American children sometimes encounter a dilemma when the language they speak is acceptable at home but is seen as different and unacceptable in other environments. Even though English is a flexible language and can be expressed in a variety of ways, the home language that African American children bring to school can be misunderstood by others. This conflict might result in lower self-esteem, self-image, and social self-concept in African American children.

Whether African American children speak Standard English or non-Standard English, the language they speak is the language of the home, of their community, and of their people. Educators can show appreciation for and recognition of different dialects when African American children enter school speaking a dialect different from the speech of the majority. Keep in mind that regardless of what students speak, educators cannot assume that students who cannot speak English correctly or do not use Standard English cannot achieve or succeed academically. Moreover, children's inability to speak English well does not warrant a decision not to teach them Standard English.

Most importantly, prospective educators should keep in mind that no child was born with a language; all children have to learn their mother tongue. Educators should take into consideration that the first language children learn to speak is the language of the home, not the language of the school. Children of all colors are able to learn the accepted and predominant form of communication if the opportunity is given to them without negative attitudes that can affect their cognitive process and psychological development.

Socioeconomic Status of African Americans

The American people continue to believe that SES plays a major role in academic success for all children. America has a caste system that stratifies people into SES classes by placing them in different positions on the wealth and riches scale. This caste system is based on several factors: power, privilege, prestige, justice, income, wealth, occupation, education, leadership, and intelligence.

As the result of decades of cultural oppression and repression, many African Americans are still trying to overcome social inequities, prejudice, discrimination, and injustice. Unfairness has deprived them of equal opportunities to improve their SES and advance economically, educationally, socially, and politically. According to the caste system in America, a large number of African Americans are disproportionately classified as on the lower rungs of the socioeconomic ladder.

To help prospective educators understand the SES of African Americans, Table 7.6 compares median family incomes of racial groups from data gathered in 1999. As indicated in the table, African American families trail families of all other racial groups except Native American.

Table 7.6. Median Family Income, by Racial Group

Group	Income in 1999
Native Americans	$33,144
Arab Americans	$55,673
Hispanic Americans	$34,397
Whites	$53,456
Blacks	$33,255
Asians	$59,323

Note. Data from U.S. Census Bureau, *Census 2000 Demographic Profile Highlights.*

This means that more African Americans are living at or below poverty level than members of nearly every other group. Table 7.7 compares the number of individuals in various racial groups who lived below the poverty level in 2000. Of the six major racial groups, African Americans have the second highest proportion of families in poverty, with Native Americans having the highest.

Table 7.7. People Living Below Poverty Level in 2000, by Racial Group

Group	Number of People	Percentage
Whites	18,800,000	8.7
Blacks	8,100,000	23.4
Native Americans	607,000	24.2
Arab Americans	163,000	13.5
Hispanic Americans	7,700,000	21.8
Asian Americans	1,200,000	11.7

Note. Data from U.S. Census Bureau, *Census 2000 Demographic Profile Highlights.* Numbers are rounded.

An important component of SES is employment. The rate of unemployment for African Americans, both men and women, is higher than for White men and women. The unemployment rate for African American men is 9.5%, as compared to 4.0% for White men; for African American women the unemployment rate is 8.5%, as compared to 4.1% for White women (Manning & Baruth, 2009).

Another way to look at SES is to examine the number of individuals who participate in the food stamp program. Table 7.8 gives these figures for 2005. According to the U.S. Department of Agriculture, about 24.8 million people participated in the federal food stamp program in Fiscal Year 2005. Of that number, 10 million were male and 14 million were female. Among all racial groups, Whites had the highest level of participation, followed by African Americans. Keep in mind that this number alone does not reflect whether more Whites or Blacks are living in poverty.

Table 7.8. Food Stamp Participants in 2005, by Racial Group

Group	Number of Participants	Percentage
Whites	10,727,000	43.1
African Americans	8,299,000	33.4
Hispanics	4,786,000	19.2
Asians	594,000	2.4
Native Americans	367,000	1.5
Unknown race	68,000	0.4

Note. Data from U.S. Department of Agriculture, 2006, *Characteristics of Food Stamp Households: Fiscal Year 2005* (Report FSP-06-CHAR). Numbers are rounded.

However, generally speaking, poverty seems to affect more African Americans than members of any other racial group regardless of what economic factors are examined. Despite this fact, prospective educators must bear in mind that there are many African Americans who are wealthy, just as in other groups. It is also important that income alone not be the sole determining factor as to whether someone should have an opportunity to earn a good education or go to college.

Promoting Academic Achievement for African Americans

The problems currently faced by African American children can be viewed in a number of ways. Of course, African American children are not immune to the ups and downs all students experience in education. Typically, children are good in some areas and struggle in others. Very few children are good in all areas. As with children of all other cultural groups, African American students have diverse needs and abilities.

The U.S. Census Bureau reported in 2000 that of the population 25 years and over, 14,350,401 African Americans had received a high school diploma or higher, and 2,831,269 had earned a bachelor's degree or higher. These numbers reveal that of the 34 million African Americans, nearly 41% graduated from high school or similar schools and only 8% percent earned a bachelor's degree or higher.

Manning and Baruth (2009) cautioned prospective educators to bear in mind that even if the fundamental approach to promoting the academic achievement of African American children is objectivity, teaching styles need to correspond with learners' learning styles. Sometimes, this correspondence is cultural and academic. Incongruity between teaching and learning styles can affect African American children's sense of self-worth, self-image, self-concept, and, most importantly, their academic self-image. In essence, it is not what they need to learn that is most important, but it is how they are taught to learn what they need to know, and equally important, how they feel about learning things from teachers who may not be open to meeting their needs.

Hundreds of studies provide ample evidence as to why African American children trail White students in all tested areas as well as in most academic subject areas. Discussion of these findings here might undermine teachers' expectations regarding teaching African American children. Whether the causes are disparities in writing proficiency, lower standardized test scores, the widening achievement gap, the lack of quality teachers, physical conditions of schools, unequal opportunities, or stresses, little will change the status quo unless teachers are willing to fulfill so-far broken promises to these students, eliminate prejudice, deal with covert discrimination, stop blaming the victims, and understand learners' feelings. When teachers do not consider the development of their students' cultural identities important, they do not provide a good education.

Culturally, African American children respond better to teaching styles that are people-oriented, relational, sensitive, and field dependent as opposed to the analytical, abstract style that is common in schools today. To promote the formation and maintenance of cultural identity as well as the academic progress of African American students, teachers should employ culturally relevant teaching strategies and culturally relevant pedagogy to keep learners interested in the learning process.

Manning and Baruth (2009) and Howard (2001) suggested that the following instructional strategies may work well with African American children:

1. Validate cultural identity.
2. Promote self-worth.
3. Suspend use of the cultural deficit model.
4. Show appreciation for cultural differences.
5. Recognize different learning styles.
6. Instill trust and self-image.

7. Use cooperative learning methodologies.
8. Use group activities.
9. Create a positive learning environment for all.
10. Use culturally relevant pedagogy.

Prospective teachers should bear in mind that some African American children perform poorly in school because they are hindered by internal and external factors associated with their daily lives. For the most part, they may not have control over these factors. Consider, for instance, family poverty, poor health, family dysfunction, family difficulties, divorce, separation, community violence, abuse, and inadequate supervision; any and all of these can lead to low academic achievement. Even with the best instructional strategies and the most qualified teachers, African American children may not perform well in school unless they receive formal intensive interaction with educators who establish good rapport, give unconditional support, and provide social affection.

Most importantly, prospective educators should bear in mind that continuing to compare the academic successes of Blacks and Whites does more harm than good because pointing out the gap in achievement sows seeds of doubt in African American children concerning their ability to compete in school. Even if the information is used only as a guide, the tendency to permit these children to settle for a second-class education is strong. Rather, prospective educators need to give all their students equal opportunity as well as provide them with the highest quality of instruction.

Summing Up

This chapter reviewed the sociocultural characteristics of African American children and their families to provide prospective educators with some understanding of children who share African American ancestry. African American children and adolescents continue to feel the crisis of credibility due to many broken promises and inequalities in public education. Time and time again, African American students struggle to overcome the low expectations teachers and public schools place upon them because covert and overt discrimination is commonly practiced against them. In some cities, African American children still encounter serious problems in the socialization process because their immediate cultural values are considered unimportant when compared to those of other cultures. Prospective educators should examine their perceptions of others and their own cultural values that inhibit them from gaining better cross-cultural understanding of themselves and others in a pluralistic society. Most importantly, African American children and adolescents need to improve their self-perception in order to increase their self-concept, self-image, self-esteem, and self-worth in the learning environment, where race may still be a factor.

Chapter Eight

Arab American Children and Their Families

> He who grows on something will grow old with it.
> —Arabian proverb

Overview

Without a doubt, Arab Americans are among the most unrecognized, misunderstood, and invisible racial groups in America. Their cultural heritages and family values are often ignored and overlooked by public schools. As Wingfield and Karaman (1995) noted, in some situations, Arab American children and adolescents seem to be lost sheep in the American educational system. Unless someone "shows them the ropes," they will fall through the cracks because of overt ignorance and covert hegemony that denigrate their diverse needs and abilities. This chapter explores Arab American cultural groups, describing their differences in race, ethnicity, culture, class, religion, family, language, economics, and ways of life. Arab Americans are among the fastest growing racial and income groups in America. U.S. educators need to know who they are and appreciate their contributions to the national fabric that enriches our country's cultural diversity.

The Origins of Arab Americans

As with other racial groups in America, Arab Americans have differences in religion, language, economics, class, ethnicity, nationality, culture, and family values. Arab Americans came to the United States from one of 22 Arab countries located in the Middle East and Northern Africa. The Arab countries of the Middle East are Lebanon, Syria, Jordan, Iraq, Yemen, the United Arab Emirates, Kuwait, Saudi Arabia, Bahrain, Oman, and Qatar (Manning & Baruth, 2009). In the Northern regions of Africa, the Arab countries are Morocco, Tunisia, Mauritania, Somalia, Sudan, Algeria, Niger, Nigeria, Senegal, Guinea Bissau, and Gambia. The origins of Arab Americans are complex. Not everyone who immigrated to the U.S. from an Arab country is considered an Arab, and not all Arab Americans look the same; they could be Black, White, or a mixture of one or more races. Moreover, there are many Arab American subgroups, including Berbers, Druze, Kurds, and Kildanis.

Despite their differences, most Arab Americans speak Arabic as their primary language and share common historical roots with other people of the Arab world. Most Arabs are Muslim, or adherents of the religion of Islam. Nevertheless, prospective educators should understand that Islam is a world-wide religious faith that is also followed by many who are not Arabs. In fact, the world's largest Muslim community is located in Indonesia, which is not an Arab country, and minority Muslim communities are located in other Asian and European nations. Arabs make up 12%–18% of the world's population.

Arab Americans came to the United States in two waves. The first wave of immigration occurred in the late 1800s to the early 1900s. The early immigration originated in Syria, which included modern-day Libya, Palestine, Jordan, and Iran. The people in this wave of immigrants were economically poor and undereducated; they were farmers or from the working class. Some worked as slaves on plantations and others were traders, peddlers, industrial workers, and farmers. These early immigrants assimilated into the mainstream culture, losing their cultural heritage. Many distanced themselves from their Arab roots and adopted Western views, religions, and ways.

During and between the two world wars, immigration from the Arab world slowed due to restrictive immigration laws. After the Second World War, however, a new wave of immigration from Arab countries began and continues to the present day. The immigrants of the second wave are mostly from Egypt, Iran, Lebanon, and Palestine. They were more educated; many were professionals with college degrees. These Arab Americans practiced the Muslin faith. As they maintained ties to their native lands, they were able to retain their heritages and cultural identities.

Who Are Arab Americans Today?

According to the 2000 U.S. census, there were approximately 1.2 million Arab Americans living in the U.S. However, this figure may not be accurate because of the likelihood of undercounting. Some Arab American organizations estimate the actual number at between 2.5 and 3 million, and others estimated it to be as high as 5 million.

Arab Americans live throughout the 50 states. More than half reside in the following large U.S. metropolitan areas: New York; Los Angeles; San Francisco; Detroit; Washington, DC; Houston; Chicago; and Jacksonville. Of the 1.2 million reported in the census, approximately 649,000 are male and 640,000 are female. Most Arab Americans appear to be young; 834,000 are 18 years and older, and only 85,000 are 65 years and older.

Even if Arab Americans are identified on the basis of Arabic-speaking ancestry, not all individuals with this ancestry consider themselves to be Arabs. Many from this region of the world have a mixture of racial and economic backgrounds. To help prospective educators learn more about them, Table 8.1 shows the numbers of Arab Americans living in the U.S. from various racial groups.

Table 8.1. Racial Origins of Arab Americans

Racial Group	Number of People
Arabic	206,000
Egyptian	143,000
Iraqi	38,000
Jordanian	40,000
Lebanese	440,000
Moroccan	39,000
Palestinian	72,000
Syrian	143,000
Armenian	386,000
Assyrian (Chaldean/Syrian)	82,000

Note. Data from U.S. Census Bureau, *Census 2000 Demographic Profile Highlights.* Numbers are rounded.

Manning and Baruth (2009) observed that 54% of the U.S. Muslim population is male and 46% is female. It is worth noting that among Arab Americans as a whole, males outnumber females. This is not the case with other racial groups in America. Among Hispanic, Asian, and European Americans, the number of females is greater than the number of males.

The Cultural Characteristics of Arab Americans

Many Americans do not have a clear understanding of Arab culture. Animations, movie characters, action figures, and media cartoons often characterize Arabs as violent, alien, exotic, cruel, magical, greedy, and villainous. These are not accurate representations of the cultural characteristics of Arab Americans. In reality, these characterizations are distortions of the Arab world.

The Arab American community consists of different ethnic groups with different nationalities of origin and different languages, cultures, traditions, classes, socioeconomic status, and religions. It is a heterogeneous group with a wide range of heritages. The cultural characteristics of the various Arab American groups could be easily misunderstood and misinterpreted as a result of inadequate information. Consider, for example, that wearing a *galabiya* or *hijab* could be viewed as odd by some racial groups; however, these are traditional or religious outfits that are customary to Arab Americans.

Prospective educators should understand that Arab American children may follow a restricted food menu and specific diets as required by their religions. During the month of Ramadan, they might participate in ritual fasting to follow the dictates of their faith.

The most prominent characteristic of Arab American culture is "saving face." Arab Americans are non-confrontational. They solve conflicts in ways that avoid embarrassment, discomfort, humiliation, and insult. Asking Arab American children to look someone in the eyes while talking is in direct opposition to the concept of saving face. If this cultural characteristic seems odd, educators must realize that it is appropriate in Arab cultures because it demonstrates respect, patience, and politeness

Arab American children are traditionally raised with a group orientation and a high value placed on collectivism. However, as is the case with Hispanics, Asians, and Native Americans, Arab American children need to learn to be somewhat more individualistic in order to compete in the Western world. In school, Arab American children and adolescents face definite challenges because the current U.S. educational system is operated on the basis of individual orientation. In other words, the system heavily emphasizes individualism.

To help prospective educators understand the cultural characteristics of Arab American children and adolescents, Table 8.2 lists some of the general characteristics of Eastern cultural values, illustrating how collectivism supersedes individualism. However, keep in mind that these values are also held by Asian cultures with slight differences in accordance with practices of each particular cultural and racial group.

Keep in mind that each cultural trait listed in Table 8.2 may not be characteristic of a specific Arab American population. The different ethnic groups may have different sets of cultural values, and the same values can take different forms in accordance with a group's needs and everyday practices. Educators should take other issues into consideration when dealing with Arab American children and adolescents because the backgrounds of the many groups are quite diverse. Learning about these values should mini-

mize the harboring of negative perceptions of and attitudes toward Arab
Americans.

Table 8.2. Eastern Cultural Values

Cultural Value	Examples of Cultural Characteristics
Primacy of relationship	Family ties, lineage, group orientation, collectivism
Authoritarian orientation	Hierarchy, patriarchy, order of birth, respect elders
Extended family structure	Grandparents, parents, children, body, unit, community
Emphasis on maturity	Age cohort, respect elders, social status
Interdependence	Group orientation, community, collectivism, networking
Compliance	Follow orders, emulation, imitation, submission
Conformity	Saving face, attitude suspension, sacrifice, group oriented
Cooperation	Group oriented, family honor, sharing,
Harmony	Peace for all, sacrifice, faith, privacy, religious values
Security	Sacrifice, protector, saving face, space, peace

Note. Information from Vincente & Associates, *Planning for Diversity*, 1990. UC, Davis:
University of California.

Arab American Families

As the cultural characteristics shown in Table 8.2 indicate, Arab American
families play key roles in instilling familial pride, developing dignity, and
maintaining religion in both individuals and groups. Today's Arab American
families appear to be a little larger than those of Whites and Blacks, as shown
in Table 8.3. However, Hispanics, Asians, and Native Americans have the
same family size as Arab Americans. Similarly, the average household size is
not much different for Arab Americans than for other racial groups, except it
is slightly larger than that of Whites and slightly smaller than that of Hispanics. Generally, Arab families in the U.S. are smaller than traditional families
in the Arab countries. Despite such adaptations to Western life, Arab American families remain a unifying force, tying members together as indivisible
units. Many Arab Americans hold the religious value of *umma,* an Islamic
concept that all Muslims are brothers and sisters. Because of this value, Islamic Arab Americans embrace other Muslims as one body, a cultural collectivism that promotes the welfare of the whole group as a collectivistic
community.

In the Arab world, a large family is desirable because the larger the family, the greater is that family's economic contribution to the larger commu-

nity. In America, however, large families present a variety of economic concerns. Of the 1.2 million Arab Americans in the U.S., approximately 32,000 families were living below poverty level in 2000, as shown in Table 8.4.

Table 8.3. Average Household and Family Size, by Racial Group

Group	Average Household Size	Average Family Size
Native Americans	3	4
Arab Americans	3	4
Hispanics	4	4
Whites	2	3
Asians	3	4
Blacks	3	3

Note. Data from U.S. Census Bureau, *Census 2000 Demographic Profile Highlights.*

Table 8.4. Families Living Below Poverty Level, by Racial Group

Group	Number of Families	Total Population
Whites	3,500,000	211,000,000
Blacks	1,700,000	34,000,000
Hispanics	1,500,000	35,000,000
Asians	226,000	10,000,000
Native Americans	122,000	2,400,000
Arab Americans	32,000	1,200,000

Note. Data from U.S. Census Bureau, *Census 2000 Demographic Profile Highlights.* Numbers are rounded.

Keep in mind that the different Arab American groups are connected by a common culture but have different faiths. No current statistics are available regarding divorce among Arab Americans; however, divorce is uncommon but permitted as a last resort in the Arab world. Some faiths permit divorce, whereas the laws of others forbid it. Culturally as well as religiously, some Arab American men can obtain a divorce simply by saying "I divorce you" three times in front of witnesses. A woman, however, needs to go through court proceedings to obtain a legal divorce.

The family structure of Arab Americans has changed over time as they have undergone the process of socialization. In the past, a patriarchal system dictated that most major decisions were made solely by the father; however, in America, these decisions are often reached jointly by both the father and the mother. As in other cultures, children sometimes aid parents in making decisions for the family when necessary. This cultural shift is common in most cultural groups. Culture shock is a common occurrence among Arab Americans as is a clash of cultures. Intergenerational conflicts are quite common. Educators need to heed issues of acculturation, language differences, and clash of value systems when working with both parents and children.

Gender Roles of Arab Americans

Depending on the cultural origins of a particular family, boys and girls may be treated differently in different Arab cultures. However, like most children, regardless of cultural background, Arab American parents and children often experience generational conflicts as they cope with social changes.

Traditionally, women are respected in the Arab world. The distinct characteristics of females are appreciated. However, gender and age are significant in the family circle. Each member has a defined family role with distinct responsibilities. For instance, the father is usually the head of the household, and he provides for the family's needs, and the mother has the primary responsibility in raising the children, taking care of the house, and managing the family's everyday functioning. Sons and daughters are taught to follow their family traditions and gender roles.

On the one hand, sons are expected to be the protector of their sisters and brothers and assume the masculine role of helping their fathers with all familial duties inside and outside the family circle as much as possible. On the other hand, daughters are taught to be supportive and good helpers, assisting their mothers with household chores and responsibilities.

Arab American children are taught to behave conservatively in public. Unlike many other Americans, they display affection only privately and secretly. Adults hardly ever show affection in public, and such a thing as public romance is nearly nonexistent among Arab Americans because they strongly believe displays of affection should be private. Moreover, they also believe disputes between family members should be kept private as well. Traditionally, Arab Americans prefer to convey information in ways that guarantee privacy between disputing parties; they engage in mediation or intervention rarely and only if absolutely necessary. Prospective educators should keep in mind that privacy is an extremely important value among Arab Americans.

Therefore, great sensitivity should be exercised when communicating with children and parents.

The social greeting is a matter that deserves special attention. Unlike Americans, Arab American females traditionally do not greet one another with a physical hug or kiss; however, they may shake hands. In most cases, a verbal greeting is culturally appropriate and sufficient. However, depending on the family, some are accustomed to Western greetings.

Similarly, verbal and public compliments of a person's physical beauty might be considered an insult; however, praise and encouragement can be acknowledged privately. A gift should not be opened in front of the giver. Keep in mind that these actions may seem like small details to some people, but they could be significant to Arab Americans and may affect Arab American students' social behaviors in the classroom. Violating these conservative values could jeopardize a student's social self-image, self-concept, and self-identity.

Religions of Arab Americans

Educators need to be careful in making assumptions about the cultural and religious identity of Arab Americans. Keep in mind that not all Arab Americans are Muslim and not all Muslims are Arab American. As Manning and Baruth (2009) observed, uninformed people often assume that all Arab traditions are Islamic and that Islam unifies all Arabs; in fact, this is a wrong perception. The faiths of Arab Americans are many. Nearly 70% of Arabs in the U.S. are affiliated with Christianity and only 30% practice Islam. Islam itself is a diverse religion. Of the foreign-born Muslims in the U.S., 53% are Sunni, 21% Shiite, and 26% other (Miller, 2007).

In addition to the diversity in religious beliefs, Arab Americans differ in how serious they are about the beliefs they hold. Miller (2007) reported that only 22% of foreign-born Muslims are highly committed to their faith, 49% are moderately committed, and 29% had low commitment. The religious picture of Arabs in the United States does not reflect the situation in the Arab world. In some countries, such as Iran and Indonesia, Islam is the faith of nearly 90% of the people. Manning and Baruth (2009) warned, "Labeling all Arabs as Muslims is a sweeping false generalization" (p. 112). In fact, the two main religions of contemporary Arab Americans are Christianity and Islam.

Because Islam has many adherents among Arab Americans, prospective educators should learn the aspects of the faith that affect the cultural identities of their students. According to a report by the Fort Gordon Equal Opportunity Office (2009), in the nations that are united by the Islamic faith, people believe in the following religious commonalities:

> In One, Unique, Incomparable God ... in the Angels created by Him ... in the Prophets through whom His revelations were brought ... in the Day of Judgment and individual accountability for actions ...in God's complete authority over human destiny and in life after death ... God's final message to man was revealed to the Prophet Muhammad through Gabriel.

Moreover, five distinct pillars form the framework of Muslim life:

1. Faith—No god is worthy of worship except God, and Muhammad is His messenger.
2. Prayer—Obligatory prayers are performed five times a day and constitute a directed link between the worshipper and God.
3. The Zakat—All things belong to God, and wealth is held by human beings in trust.
4. The Fast—In the month of Ramadan all Muslims fast from first light to sundown.
5. Pilgrimage, or hajj—Those who are physically and financially able make an annual obligatory pilgrimage to the city of Makkah.

One way to accommodate the diverse needs and abilities of Muslim Arab American children and adolescents as well as their social constraints is to learn more about their Islamic views. Some vocabulary that might be helpful here is given in Table 8.5. Some Islamic terms have been misunderstood. For example, many Westerners think of the word "Jihad" as connoting holy war, but the word actually means "strive for a better way of life."

There are other sociopolitical issues facing the Arab American community as a whole; however, prospective educators should keep in mind that harboring misperceptions that equate terrorists with Arabs is not only wrong, but is prejudicial and harmful. Political terms such as radical extremist, fundamentalist, and terrorist may be accurately applied to a number of people who are not necessarily from the Arab world. The most pressing issue right now for many Arab Americans is their feeling that they are being discriminated against because they are Arab even though they have nothing to do with global terrorism. This backlash is totally unfair and is damaging to Arab American children and adolescents.

Table 8.5. Selected Islamic Terms and Definitions

Term	Meaning
Allah	Creator of the universe, God
Arab	Native of Arab world who speaks Arabic and believes in Arabic culture
Ayah or Ayat	A miracle or a sign
Azan	Daily prayers
Birth	People are born free of sin
Aqiqah	Festivity, a dinner reception after a child is born
Walimah	Festivity, a dinner reception after a marriage is consummated
Islam, Silm or Salam	A religion of peace, greeting, salutation, obedience, loyalty, allegiance, and submission
Jihad or Jahada	Strive for a better way of life
Muslim or Moslem	One who submits to God, or a believer in Islam, a follower
Quran	A holy book for Muslims, a book of the Word of God
Ramadan	The ninth month, the month of fasting, self-discipline, and purification
Imam or sheik	Leader of prayer at a Mosque, leader
Umm	Refers to mother
Abu	Refers to father

Note. Information from *Arab American Experience and Middle Eastern Culture*, by Gordon Equal Opportunity Office, 2009, retrieved June 14, 2009, from http://www.gordon.army.mil/eoo/arab.htm

Languages of Arab Americans

Most Arab Americans are multicultural and multilingual. There are 57 Islamic nations with approximately 1.3 billion people, of which 22 are Arab nations with nearly 300 million people. Arabic is the sixth most commonly spoken language in the world; it is spoken by nearly 200 million native speakers and 235 million people worldwide. Most Arabs speak Arabic as a universal language; however, a number of other languages are spoken throughout the Arab world. The four major language groups of the Middle East are Arabic, Hebrew, Persian, and Turkish, or Herber. Variations of these languages, colloquial languages, are also spoken. In the Arab world, linguistics is as intricate as religion.

In the complex multicultural and multilingual Arab world, there are seven distinct dialects or language groups. The first dialect is Aramaic, a well known language spoken by many. The second is the Levantine dialect, spoken by Jordanians, Syrians, Palestinians, and Lebanese. The third linguistic group is the Egyptian, or Northern African dialect. The fourth is the Khalijji, or Gulf dialect, a regional dialect spoken by tribal and village people. The fifth dialect is Coptic, a native Egyptian language spoken mainly in Egypt. The sixth dialect is Quranic Arabic, a spoken and written form of Arabic with a writing style and lexicon different from other written languages in the Arab world. Finally, Modern Standard Arabic, somewhat similar to Quranic Arabic, is a pan-Arabic writing system using formal letters; it is the most recognized and widely used dialect in verbal and written forms in the Arab world, used for textbooks, newspapers, press, and national media.

One country normally thought of as Arab does not have any of these languages as its primary language. In Iran, the language most commonly spoken is Farsi. Arabs do not consider Iran to be part of the Arab world, even though a large number of Iranians are Muslims and follow the Islamic faith, because it is a newer country with its own unique cultural and national heritage (Allied Media Corp., 2007). This may be surprising to Westerners.

Socioeconomic Status of Arab Americans

Arab Americans immigrated to the United States for a variety of reasons. Like those in many other racial groups, they came to the land of opportunity seeking economic and educational betterment. Contemporary Arab Americans work in all professions; however, 60% of Arab professionals serve as executives in big corporations (Allied Media Corp., 2007). As mentioned previously, the first Arab immigrants were poor and uneducated. Many worked on plantations and others were primarily peddlers, traders, merchants, industrial workers, and farmers. The second wave of Arab immigrants entered the work force with better economic opportunities because many were professionals with college degrees.

According to the 2000 U.S. census, Arab American families had a median income of $55,000 per year in 1999, placing them second highest in family income, behind Asian American families (see Table 8.6). Both these groups had median family incomes higher than that for Whites.

Not surprisingly, Arab Americans had a low proportion of individuals living below poverty level, as illustrated in Table 8.7; only Whites and Asian Americans had lower proportions. Keep in mind, however, that among Arab

Americans, as in all other racial groups, annual household incomes vary widely. Some individuals are able to achieve financially, whereas others struggle to climb the economic ladder. Some Arab Americans are recent immigrants who are starting all over in the U.S., and others are first-, second-, or later-generation Arab Americans who have adjusted or assimilated to the Western culture.

Table 8.6. Median Family Income in 1999, by
Racial Group

Group	Income
Native Americans	$33,144
Arab Americans	$55,673
Hispanic Americans	$34,397
Whites	$53,456
Blacks	$33,255
Asians	$59,323

Note. Data from U.S. Census Bureau, *Census 2000 Demographic Profile Highlights.*

Table 8.7. People Living Below Poverty Level, by Racial Group

Group	Number of People	Percentage
Whites	18,800,000	8.7
Blacks	8,100,000	23.4
Native Americans	607,000	24.2
Arab Americans	163,000	13.5
Hispanic Americans	7,700,000	21.8
Asians	1,200,000	11.7

Note. Data from U.S. Census Bureau, *Census 2000 Demographic Profile Highlights.*
Numbers are rounded.

The SES of Arab Americans is illustrated by their annual household incomes, which are reported for 2006 in Table 8.8. It is apparent from these figures that Arab Americans trail their White counterparts in annual household income; however, they are far better off than Hispanics and Blacks. Nonetheless, keep in mind that a greater proportion of Arab American families earn $29,000 or less per year than in all other racial groups. This statistic suggests that a large number of Arab American families live only slightly above the federal poverty level.

Regardless, prospective educators should bear in mind that income should not be a factor in whether Arab American children and adolescents receive the same opportunities in school as others. Neither should income be a factor that determines whether these or any other students have an opportunity to go to college. Just like children of every other racial group, Arab American children deserve fair and equal access to public education.

Table 8.8. Percent of Populations with Selected Annual Household Incomes, by Racial Group

Group	$100,000 and over	$75,000-$99,000	$50,000-$74,000	$30,000-$49,000	$29,000 or less
White	20	12	19	15	11
Arab	16	10	15	24	35
Hispanic	10	9	17	17	14
Black	9	8	15	14	13

Note. Data from *Income, Poverty, and Health Insurance Coverage in the United States* (U.S. Census Bureau Current Population Report P60-233), by C. DeNavas-Walt, B. D. Proctor, and J. Smith, 2007, Washington, DC: U.S. Government Printing Office.

Promoting Academic Achievement for Arab Americans

In 2000, the U.S. Census Bureau reported that of the population 25 years and over, 611,279 Arab Americans have earned a high school diploma or higher, and 297,842 have graduated from college with a bachelor's degree or higher. This means that of the 1,189,000 Arab Americans living in the U.S., 51% have at least a high school diploma, and 25% have an undergraduate or higher college education.

As sensitive as some of the cultural characteristics of Arab Americans are, as complex as their religious beliefs, and as modest as their family values, prospective educators should at least be prepared to share educational experiences that would elevate Arab American children's self-concept, self-image, and self-esteem toward the development of positive cultural identity in the learning community. Remember, public schools are geared toward individualism, a mindset that is part of a Euro-centric culture, but Arab American children grow up in a culture that values collectivism, or group orientation. However, simply growing up with a group orientation should not keep Arab American children from being trained or disciplined to be competitive as well as cooperative in both environments.

While dealing with Arab American children and adolescents, educators need to consider the strictness and rigidity of their faiths as well as their cultural characteristics. For instance, their loyal compliance with cultural and religious values may strain their social and personal interactions, and the resulting conflict may affect their internal feelings and self-concept. In other words, Arab American students could face a dilemma when it comes to adjusting to or choosing to accept or reject a new set of values learned in school. Consider, for example, students' difficulty looking a teacher in the eyes when the teacher is talking to them.

The unique cultures of Arab American children and adolescents are still unknown to many educators because this group has been unintentionally ignored as a distinct cultural group until recently. Undoubtedly, the diverse needs and abilities of Arab American children have been neglected and overlooked in many ways. Arab American children are still the most misunderstood and invisible students in public schools as a result of cultural ignorance and negative media information about the Arab-Israeli conflict. As they must do in teaching the offspring of Native Americans, Blacks, Hispanics, and Asians, prospective educators need to overcome these sociopolitical barriers that keep them from being able to reach out in an informed way to educate Arab American students and embrace their differences in ethnicity, culture, language, religion, class, and economic status.

Keep in mind that although much research has done on other racial groups, such as Hispanics, Asians, Blacks, Whites, and Native Americans, little has been done to inform educators about the unique needs of Arab American children and adolescents. This means that public schools and prospective educators lack meaningful and practical information about this particular group of students, including their learning styles, communication styles, cultural identity, cognitive development, psycho-social feelings and experiences about schooling, and contributions to the total school culture. No child should be allowed to fall through the cracks because teachers do not have adequate information to help that child. Experts warn that English language learners may be silent and voiceless in the educational system because not many people are willing to show them the ropes so they can pull themselves out of the ditch of ignorance.

Where there is a will, there is a way to help children learn. Arab American children can achieve in school as well as any others as long as schools provide social justice, culturally appropriate instructional strategies, cultural enrichment activities, social empowerment, prejudice reduction, integrated content, and a culturally appropriate curricular design. To address the academic needs and challenges facing Arab American children and adolescents, educators could consider taking the following steps:

1. Develop school curricula that reflect community and school values.
2. Remove the professional barriers and personal biases that hinder social acceptance and equal respect for all.
3. Create a positive learning environment that embraces cultural differences.
4. Overcome the one-model-fits-all approach and use adaptations to enhance learning.
5. Apply multiple approaches to accommodate diverse learning styles.
6. Supply relevant materials that enhance cross-cultural learning.
7. Prescribe cooperative learning and student-centered instruction.
8. Address inappropriate remarks that are considered culturally and religiously insensitive.
9. Promote self-image, self-concept, and self-esteem.
10. Recruit or hire bilingual staff who speaks Arabic to promote good home-school relationships.

Keep in mind that although these suggestions are helpful for any racial group, they are not a panacea that will solve all academic problems. Educators will have to provide individualized instruction whenever necessary in order to ensure that what is taught is learned.

Summing Up

This chapter gave an overview of the sociocultural characteristics of Arab American children and their families to provide prospective educators with some understanding of children who share Arab American ancestry. No doubt, many Arab American children and adolescents are the lost sheep in the educational system because they have been ignored, overlooked, and neglected. Their invisibility is due to the cross-cultural ignorance of people who fail to recognize the differences and cultural distinctives Arab American students bring to the classroom. Arab Americans are culturally and linguistically diverse; they do not constitute a unified, single ethnic group. Prospective educators need to recognize the sociocultural characteristics and needs of Arab American children and adolescents in order to provide academic curricula and instructional practices that reflect their culture, art, literature, and sociopolitical accomplishments. Doing so will promote the development of positive self-esteem, self-image, self-concept, and cultural identity in these students.

Chapter Nine

Asian American Children and Their Families

Tell me, I will forget; show me, I will remember;
involve me, I will understand.

—Chinese proverb

Overview

Like Hispanic, Arab, and Native Americans, Asian Americans constitute a mixed group. Asian Americans have different national origins, cultures, traditions, religions, heritages, classes, languages, customs, and socioeconomic status. There are approximately 30 major subgroups among Asian Americans, each a distinct and unique ethnicity with distinct dialects, religions, customs, and traditions. These 30 groups can be categorized into four major groups based on geographic place of origin: (a) East Asian—Chinese, Japanese, Korean, Taiwanese, and people of Hong Kong; (b) Pacific Islander—Filipinos, Samoans, Tongans, Chamorro, Malaysians, Indonesians, and Hawaiians; (c) Southeast Asian—Vietnamese, Thai, Cambodians, Laotians, and Hmong; and (d) South Asian—Indians, Pakistanis, Burmese (people of Myanmar), Nepalese, and people of Bangladesh.

This chapter focuses on the East Asians—Chinese, Japanese, Koreans, and Pacific Islanders (mainly Filipinos). It examines the socio-cultural differences among these groups in race, ethnicity, culture, class, religion, family, language, economics, and ways of life. Among all Asian groups in the U.S., East Asians and Pacific Islanders are the most prominent in the U.S. Chapter Ten will describe Southeast Asians and South Asians. Dividing Asian Americans into these two broad categories will permit deeper examination of all groups. Otherwise, study of Chinese, Japanese, Koreans, and Filipinos would mask the various socio-cultural issues of people from Southeast Asia and South Asia.

East Asians and Pacific Islanders have achieved notable successes in the United States and have contributed to the national fabric of America, just as other groups have.

The Origins of Asian Americans

Politically, *Asian American* is a broad term used to describe people whose ancestry is in countries in Asia such as China, Japan, Korea, Philippines, Hong Kong, Taiwan, India, Pakistan, Vietnam, Thailand, Laos, and Cambodia. However, this term is often understood in a more limited sense. It usually refers to Chinese, Japanese, Koreans, Filipinos, and other Pacific Islanders because these were the first groups of Asians in America. Using this term carries with it the mistaken assumption that these people are homogenous, whereas, in fact, they are quite diverse.

Prospective educators should understand that the various Asian groups immigrated to America for different socio-cultural reasons. As Manning and Baruth (2009) explained, some were middle-class people in stable countries, some were poor people from war-torn nations who came to America with nothing, and a small number came with skills and affluence to start a new life. To understand the similarities in these groups and recognize and appreciate the differences, the four main groups will be described separately. The characteristics of one should not be used to generalize the traits of other Asian American groups or subgroups.

Chinese Americans

The first group of Chinese immigrated to America in the late 1700s, and a large number arrived in the mid-1800s (Cheng, 1999). Most took jobs as farmers, miners, railroad workers, or performing other physical labor. Chinese Americans settled along the West Coast of California, where they first arrived and could find employment. Chinese Americans suffered much social, economic, and political discrimination. The Chinese Exclusion Act of 1882 and the Oriental Exclusion Act of 1924 were very harsh.

After World War II, a second wave of Chinese arrived from Hong Kong and Taiwan seeking educational opportunities, reunification with family members, or economic ventures in America.

A third wave of Chinese immigration took place in the second half of the 1900s, the largest Chinese immigration in U.S. history. In the 45 years between 1920 and 1965, 417,000 immigrants came to the U.S. from China (Sung, 1967), but in just 11 years between 1966 and 1977, approximately 255,000 Chinese immigrants resettled in the U.S. from Hong Kong and Tai wan (California Department of Education, 1989). Moreover, in the 1980s, a large number of Chinese professionals and businesspeople moved to the U.S. from Hong Kong in fear of what would happen when Hong Kong was returned to Communist China in July 1997. Thereafter, Chinese immigrants continued to arrive in the U.S. as exchange students or scholars.

Korean Americans

Compared with the Chinese, Koreans were latecomers to the U.S. The first wave of Korean immigrants arrived in the early 1900s as contracted workers on sugar plantations in Hawaii. However, Koreans had contact with Americans as early as 1871 when the U.S. briefly occupied a Korean island. Between 1903 and 1905, 65 ships carried approximately 7,200 Koreans to America (Choy, 1979). Like the Chinese, the first Korean immigrants were bachelor men.

The second wave of Korean immigrants arrived between 1906 and 1920. The number was small; most were students and political exiles (Lyu, 1977). As with Chinese immigration, Korean immigration slowed in the 1920s as a result of passage of the Oriental Exclusion Act in 1924. This legislation severely limited immigration from Asia for decades, until the 1950s.

In 1952, Koreans resumed immigration to the U.S. A quota system limited the number of immigrants to 100 persons per year. In 1965, the passage of immigration reform laws opened the door for more Korean immigrants. Starting in 1973, approximately 20,000 Korean immigrants were admitted to the U.S. annually (Lee, 1975).

Koreans immigrated to the West for reasons similar to those of Chinese Americans. As Kim (1978) noted, most wanted economic opportunities; an example is the men who came alone as contracted laborers to work in the sugar plantations of Hawaii. Some sought better educational opportunities for their children and themselves. Still others wanted to improve their standard of living and build a brighter future for their families. Most of the single men who came intended to work long enough to earn enough money to return to their native land and begin a better life there. However, many did not return, but decided instead to stay in the U.S. Like the Chinese, Korean Americans sponsored their family members to join them in America. In fact, this chain of immigration and subsequent sponsorship of relatives brought many Korean immigrants to the U.S.

Japanese Americans

Japanese American immigration to the U.S. took place in two periods—from 1885 to 1907 and from 1908 to 1924 (Ichioka, 1988). People of the first generation of Japanese Americans are referred to as *Issei*, and those of the second generation, as *Nisei*. Young Japanese laborers looked to America as the land of promise, and they hoped it would give them economic opportunities they did not have in Japan. Their intention was to stay only long enough to earn a good sum of money and then return home. But like the Koreans and Chinese, their life situations changed and many stayed.

As the Japanese settled on agricultural land in the U.S., they established new lives, making the transition from laborers to farmers. Most resided along the Pacific Coast, where they could find employment. Like the Chinese and Koreans, Japanese Americans suffered discrimination. In 1907, under the Gentlemen's Agreement, Japan agreed to a limitation on the number of unskilled workers emigrating from Japan in exchange for better treatment for the Japanese already in the U.S. But again, like the Chinese and Koreans, the Japanese were victims of the anti-oriental sentiment of the Oriental Exclusion Act of 1924, which completely barred all Asian immigration to the U.S.

At the inception of World War II, the Nisei, or second generation, suffered another political setback in one of the darkest moments in U.S. history. After the Japanese attack on Pearl Harbor in 1941, President Franklin Roosevelt issued Executive Order 9066, which was stamped with legal approval by the U.S. Supreme Court and supported by public anti-oriental sentiment, forcing evacuation of approximately 110,000 Japanese Americans to internment camps. Forty-some years later, the U.S. government finally offered monetary reparations and a public apology; however, as Yamano (1994) reported, the pain and suffering of that ordeal forever altered the lives of thousands of Japanese Americans psychologically, culturally, linguistically, and politically.

Filipino Americans

From the Pacific Islands located in Southeast Asia, Filipinos appear to be the largest and most prominent group in the U.S. However, limiting discussion of Pacific Islanders to one group is not intended to devalue the origins of other groups or exclude them from recognition.

Filipinos first arrived in what would become the United States in the mid-1500s. During the Spanish occupation of the Philippines, some Filipinos worked as crewmen aboard Spanish ships. Because they were brutally mistreated, many jumped off the ships when they arrived in Mexico. They made homes in present-day Louisiana and made livings as fishermen (Litton, 1999; Macaranas, 1983).

Filipinos became familiar with the West through the colonial relationship that took place throughout the first half of the 1900s; in 1898 Philippines had become a U.S. territory. Even after Philippines gained independence from the U.S. in 1946, American influence continued to affect life on the islands in many ways. Litton (1999) divided the history of Filipino immigration to America into three different waves, each with unique reasons for Filipinos coming to the U.S.

The first massive wave of Filipino immigration occurred during U.S. occupation of the Philippines from the very late 1800s to the mid-1900s (Macaranas, 1983). During the 1900s, Filipino immigrants were primarily college students, called *pensionados*. These students came to the U.S. to pursue higher education through federally funded programs. Many pensionados returned to their native land to assume leadership roles.

The second wave of Filipino immigration, during the 1900s, filled the high demand for inexpensive labor in the U.S. labor market. Low-paying jobs were available because other Asian groups had been excluded from entry into the country. Filipinos, however, were not subject to the anti-oriental restrictions because they were classified as American "nationals" on the basis of the status of Philippines as a U.S. territory. They were not, however, free from discrimination and strong anti-Filipino sentiment throughout the 1900s.

The third wave of immigration from the Philippines took place following the passage of the Immigration Reform Act of 1965. This legislation established an immigration quota system; approximately 20,000 Asians were allowed to enter the U.S. per year (Litton, 1999). Taking advantage of this new opportunity, Filipino immigrants of the first and second wave sponsored family members to join them in the U.S. The Filipino population more than tripled after 1965. At that time, Filipinos referred to America as the land of milk and honey.

The above is merely a general overview of the origins of Asian Americans from East Asia and the Southeast Pacific Islands. Prospective educators should remember that this discussion does not cover all subgroups of East

168   *Educational Psychology of Methods in Multicultural Education*

Asians. The histories of immigration to the U.S. of the various groups could be different or similar to the ones described. Discourse should be encouraged in school so all students can learn from one another.

Who Are Asian Americans Today?

Today, East Asian Americans include Chinese, Japanese, Korean, Taiwanese, and people of Hong Kong and the Pacific Islands. Pacific Islanders are mainly Filipinos, Samoans, Tongans, Chamorro, Malaysians, Indonesians, and Hawaiians. According to the U.S. Census Bureau (2000), the total Asian American population is 10.2 million, with 4.9 million males and 5.3 million females. The bureau predicts that in 2010 the total population will reach 12.5 million. The growth rate of the Asian American population is steady. Table 9.1 lists the populations of the major groups of East Asians, and Table 9.2 shows the populations of the most prominent groups of Pacific Islanders.

Table 9.1. East Asian Population, by National Group

Group	Population	Percentage
Chinese, including Hong Kong	2,300,000	22.0
Japanese	767,000	7.5
Korean	1,100,000	10.7
Taiwanese	118,000	1.1
Total	4,285,000	41.3

Note. Data from U.S. Census Bureau, *Census 2000 Demographic Profile Highlights.* Numbers are rounded.

As Table 9.1 shows, the largest East Asian group is the Chinese American group, followed by Korean American as the second largest, Japanese American as the third largest, and Taiwanese American as the smallest. Combined, East Asian Americans account for 41.3% of the total Asian American population in the U.S.

Table 9.2 illustrates that among the Southeast Asian Pacific Islanders, Filipino Americans outnumber members of all other groups as the largest group, followed by Native Hawaiians as the second largest, Samoans as the third largest, and Guamanians as the fourth largest. Malaysians constitute the smallest group. Together, all Pacific Islanders represent 20.28% of the total Asian American population in the U.S.

Thus the East Asian groups and the Pacific Islanders make up approximately 62% of the Asian American population in the U.S. As Tables 9.1 and 9.2 illustrate, neither is a homogenous group. Asian Americans are sometimes called a "model minority," but use of this term overgeneralizes the academic and business success of Asian Americans in general. In fact, the term is actually used to acknowledge the hard work and academic success of second-generation Taiwanese Americans exclusively.

Although East Asian Americans and Pacific Islanders live scattered throughout the 50 states, a large number are located in the large metropolitan areas of the West, especially in California. They constitute one of the fastest growing minority groups in America, and they continue to enrich the national fabric of this great nation. In the past, they suffered severe mistreatment and, for some, those memories remain.

Table 9.2. Pacific Islander Population in U.S., by National Group

Group	Population	Percentage
Filipinos	1,800,000	17.00
Malaysians	10,000	.09
Native Hawaiians	140,000	1.30
Samoans	91,000	.80
Tongans	27,000	.20
Guamanians or Chamorro	58,000	.50
Fijians	9,700	.09
Indonesians	39,000	.30
Total	2,174,700	20.28

Note. Data from U.S. Census Bureau, *Census 2000 Demographic Profile Highlights.* Numbers are rounded.

The Cultural Characteristics of Asian Americans

From the Western point of view, the East Asian and Pacific Islander groups appear to be very different—from Westerners and among themselves—in race, ethnicity, language, culture, religion, economic status, and family traditions. Asian Americans come from diverse backgrounds, but they share many similarities in cultural characteristics and beliefs. In fact, commonalities span most Asian cultures. Most have similar family values, such as respect for elders, importance of extended family, and filial piety. Social structures, such as the patriarchal family and clan systems, are similar. Most Asian Americans are alike in personal conduct and social behaviors.

Many Asians are affiliated with Confucianism or Buddhism. Even among Asians who practice religions other than Confucianism or Buddhism, Asian cultural characteristics were influenced greatly by the philosophies of these two systems of thought prior to the introduction of Christianity. Regardless of their religious affiliation, most Asian parents tend to have similar aspirations and expectations for their children.

In the U.S., most East Asian groups work diligently to keep their cultural characteristics and identity alive. They establish weekend schools where their offspring learn their cultural heritages, especially their native languages—Chinese, Korean, and Japanese.

To illustrate the cultural characteristics of contemporary Asian Americans, Table 9.3 presents some differences between Asian culture and American culture. In some areas, Asian and non-Asian American cultural characteristics may overlap. This illustration should help prospective educators gain insight into the complexities of the socio-cultural issues Asian American children might bring to school. However, keep in mind that these examples of cultural values may not necessarily be held in all Asian American cultures and families. Educators should provide all children the opportunity to gain a broader and deeper understanding of different cultural values through formal school discourse.

Asian American Families

Family is the center of Asian American life. The family projects an image of personal and professional success outside the family circle. In Asian culture, family honor is important, and honor comes from the image of the family. One indication of the strength of the family is the 2007 report of the U.S. Census Bureau that 87% of Asian American families were two-parent households and only 13% were single-parent households. Of the single-parent households, 10% were headed by mothers and 3% were headed by fathers. These figures indicate the heavy emphasis Asian Americans place on family.

Filipino American cultural values and families are somewhat different from those of Chinese and Japanese Americans because different outside forces influenced their cultural development. Filipino society and culture were influenced by the Malay, the Spanish, and Americans (Ponce, 1980). These conflicting influences have created much diversity within Filipino culture and families. Nevertheless, Filipinos are able to preserve their cultural characteristics and family values through the maintenance of a kinship system, a system of consanguineal, or blood, bonds.

As Table 9.3 illustrates, the traditional family values of Asian Americans include fulfillment of duties and responsibilities, interdependence, sacrifice, kinship, extended family life, two-parent households, offspring, and posterity. As has happened to people in other racial groups, Asian Americans have had to cope with different life situations in America, and the coping has resulted in adjustments of traditional values. An example is family size. Parents in the first generation of Asian American immigrants generally have larger families than those in subsequent generations. According to the 2000 U.S. census, the average household size for Asian Americans is 3 and the average family size is 4 (see Table 9.4). In comparison with other racial groups, Asian Americans family and of household sizes are similar to all except Hispanics, who have larger families and households.

The proportion of Asian American families living below poverty level is lower than those of all other racial groups except Whites (see Table 9.5). Perhaps this is related to the fact that nearly 8 out of 10 Asian American children live in homes with two parents.

Another way to look at family structure and values is to examine the divorce rate. As Table 9.6 illustrates, the divorce rate for Asian Americans in 2000 was 3%, which is the lowest of all racial groups. On the one hand, this number may be a true indication of the situation in Asian American families. On the other hand, it may be lower than the actual rate of marital separation because Asian divorces do not generally appear in court but are handled within the community according to traditional customs.

In other words, marriage dissolutions may have been mediated outside the courts. Nevertheless, most Asian Americans hold strong family values and place a heavy emphasis on marriage. In fact, marriage and family are probably the highest priorities at the core of Asian American culture.

Gender Roles of Asian Americans

As with Hispanic and Arab Americans, Asian Americans learn gender roles and family responsibilities early in life. Usually, parents guide their children through the process of understanding gender roles and responsibilities. In a patriarchal society, daughters learn household chores as early as possible so they can help their mothers around the house, and sons emulate their father's roles as much and as early as possible. Even if these gender roles are unequal and seem not to fit in America, these expectations are still high in Asian American families regardless of the level of acculturation of the children.

Table 9.3. Comparison of Asian and American Cultural Perspectives

Cultural Area	Asian Culture	American Culture
Community value, worldview, or global image	Family centered, family comes first, group welfare	Individual centered, individual comes first, self-actualization
Human relationship or social civility	Hierarchical or patriarchal relationship, age-centered, authority, consanguineal relationships	Egalitarianism, personal quality, ability centered, power, privilege, status
Cultural and family values	Duties, responsibilities, interdependence, sacrifice, posterity, kinship, extended family, two-parent household	Individualism, independence, self-centered, nuclear family, single-parent household, personal choice of lifestyle
Personal attitudes	Respect, deference, obedience, patience, conformity, open, flexible, considerate, yielding, humble, caring, sensitive	Self-assertive, opinionated, expressive, question authority, disagreement, rules, policies, time oriented
Self-identity	Group oriented, status in group, honor in group, reserved, inner strength, introverted feelings	Personal ability, individual success, self-achievement, materialistic, inquisitive, extroverted feelings
Socialization process	Filial piety, obedience, emulation, observation, hesitation, reluctance, smiling, facial expression, body language	Active involvement, engagement, trial and error, taking initiative, volunteer, heroism, vocal
Thinking styles	Global, impressionistic, considerate, cooperation, sharing, self-reservation, spiral approach, reflexes approach, memorization	Analytical approach, specification, concrete details, direct, impulsive approach, logical consequences
Personal attitude toward education	Achievement to honor, respect, proud, bring honor to group	Individual success, personal growth, social maturity, self-actualization, self-fulfillment
Personal behaviors and attitudes	Self-control, self-restraint, avoiding confrontation, silence is golden, patience, suspension, refine attitude, humble, modesty, internalizing, save face	Venting feelings, overt expression, assertive, freedom of speech, personal rights, confrontation, forgive, apology
Parents/children relationship	According to gender role, covert aspiration, unveiling support, lacking process, aiming at outcome, expect positive final result, lifetime commitment to help parents, parental control	Ongoing support, sufficient encouragement, positive reinforcement, early independence, limited commitment, personal freedom, curfew

Table 9.4. Average Household and Family Size, by Racial Group

Group	Average Household Size	Average Family Size
Native Americans	3	4
Arab Americans	3	4
Hispanics	4	4
Whites	2	3
Asians	3	4
Blacks	3	3

Note. Data from U.S. Census Bureau, *Census 2000 Demographic Profile Highlights.*

Table 9.5. Number of Families Below Poverty Level, by Racial Group

Group	Number of Families	Total population in 2000
Whites	3,500,000	211,000,000
Blacks	1,700,000	34,000,000
Hispanics	1,500,000	35,000,000
Asians	226,000	10,000,000
Native Americans	122,000	2,400,000
Arab Americans	32,000	1,200,000

Note. Data from U.S. Census Bureau, *Census 2000 Demographic Profile Highlights.* Numbers are rounded.

Table 9.6. Percentage of Couples Divorced, by Racial Group

Group	Percentage
European Americans	9.8
African Americans	11.3
Hispanic Americans	7.6
Asian Americans	3.0

Note. Data from National Center for Health Statistics, *Marriage and Divorce Statistics*, 2002, Washington, DC: U.S. Census Bureau.

Regardless of religious affiliation, most Asian Americans base their gender roles on the system of kinship and filial piety that guides them every step of the way in life. In the kinship system, males are patriarchal figures. In the family hierarchy, the father is the head of the household and is responsible for the welfare of his family economically and physically, and the mother is in charge of taking care of the children and household chores, maintaining the family as a unit, and managing the family.

The filial piety system is designed to develop good behaviors and responsible attitudes in children. Children of both sexes are expected to be obedient to parents, not question parents' wishes and expectations, act politely, show respect for elders, not talk back, not challenge authority, maintain family harmony, learn to express themselves, control their emotions and avoid outbursts, present themselves appropriately in front of others, show desirable demeanor even under difficult circumstances, and avoid confrontation. Moreover, children are told to control any expressions of anger, hostility, aggression, and self-pity to keep from being exposed to humiliation and insult, to avoid losing face. In other words, they are taught the value of self-effacement.

To help prospective educators gain insight into the intricate kinship and filial piety system of Asian American children and families, some differences in gender roles in dealing with family matters are given in Table 9.7. The roles listed are typical roles and may not necessarily represent the situation in all Asian American families. The gender roles of some subgroups or subcultures of Asian Americans may be totally different from those given here. However, even if these roles are not the ones followed in a given Asian American family, the family has clearly defined gender roles. Discussions should be introduced in school to allow students of various cultural groups to share with others academically and formally the ways their families function.

Consider, for example, Manning and Baruth's (2009) claim that Asian American females do not receive the same respect that males receive and females are valued less than males. Perhaps this is the case in some Asian American cultures, but many Asian families in America have discarded the rigid idea of male dominance in order to accommodate the new life situations in the U.S.

It should also be noted that Asian American women are notably successful in many areas, and their professional achievements have altered the gender roles and responsibilities in the family circle as well as in the communities in which they live. For instance, several Asian American women have been elected as city council members, state senators, local supervisors, and school board trustees. Many Asian American women are lawyers, doctors, professors, dentists, chiropractors, teachers, nurses, and business owners. Without a doubt, changes in gender roles have caused disruption in family life and conflict with traditional views. However, mothers who work outside the home have provided financial relief and stability to their families.

Table 9.7. Asian American Gender Roles in Dealing with Family Matters

Family Matter	Male	Female	Compromised
Religious activities	xx		
Household chores	x	xy	y
Decision making	xx	x	y
Leadership	xx	x	
Discipline	x	x	y
Finances	x	x	y
College education	x	x	y
Major purchase	x	x	y
Childrearing	x	x	y
Marriage of children	x	x	y
Family conflicts	xx		y
Cooking	x	xy	y
Family contact person	xx		
Attend parent/teacher conference	x	xy	y
Doctor's appointment for children	x	xy	y
Pay household bills	x	xy	y
House repairs	xx		
Family recognition and image	xx	x	

Note. xx = mostly male, x = both or equally male and female, y = could be compromised, xy = mostly female.

Religions of Asian Americans

As with other racial groups in America, contemporary Asian Americans are religiously diverse. As Table 9.8 shows, East Asian Americans and Pacific Islanders have different religious affiliations. The largest affiliation is Catholicism, followed by the Assemblies of God.

Many Asian Americans follow the teaching of Confucianism, whereas others primarily practice animism, fatalism, Taoism, Hinduism, Buddhism, Islam, Shintoism, Christianity, ancestor worship, and other indigenous beliefs. Religious diversity is great in some Asian groups because of strong outside influences. For instance, Filipinos were influenced heavily by the Malay, the Spanish, and Americans religiously as well as economically. Table 9.9 lists some of the religions Asian Americans brought with them to the U.S.

Table 9.8. Religious Affiliations of Asian Americans

Denomination	Number of Adherents
Assemblies of God	99,700
Church of the Nazarene	6,600
Evangelical Lutheran Church in America	22,000
Int. Pentecostal Holiness Church	5,300
Mennonite Church	1,000
Presbyterian Church U.S.A	65,800
Roman Catholic Church	290,000
The United Methodist Church	90,200

Note. Data from Association of Statisticians of American Religious Bodies, 2002. Numbers are rounded.

Religiously and culturally, the religions of the countries of origin shaped the cultural identity and family values of each group. However, most Asian Americans center their faith and belief systems around kinship and filial piety. Their moral principles and values include a deep reverence toward ancestors and high priority on personal obligation, duty, responsibility, loyalty, kindness, honor, and harmony. To some people, Asian Americans' religious values appear to be rigid, harsh, strict, and odd; however, these values form their standards of morality. As a monk once said, "The wall is low, but the power of Buddha is high."

Table 9.9. Religions of East Asian Countries

Country	Major Religions	Other Beliefs
China	Atheism, Buddhism, Taoism, Islam, and Christianity	Indigenous beliefs
Japan	Buddhism and Shintoism	Christianity
Korea	Christianity (49%) and Buddhism (47%)	Others (4%)
Philippines	Christianity (92%) and Malay (4%)	Others (4%)

Note. Data from U.S. Census Bureau, International Data Base, 1997.

Languages of Asian Americans

Asian Americans are linguistically diverse. The many Asian American languages or dialects can be classified into groups on the basis of their linguistic origins: Altaic languages that are polysyllabic; Austronesia; Malayo-Polynesian languages that are polysyllabic; Sino-Tibetan languages with tonal, monosyllabic, and non-inflection characteristics; pre-Sinitic languages; and Austro-Asiatic languages (Anderson & Jones, 1974; Arlotto, 1972; Huffman & Proum, 1978; Llamso, 1978; Miller, 1967).

As Table 9.10 shows, each major Asian American group speaks a language entirely different from the others even if the languages or dialects originally came from the same family. The primary language experiences of Asian Americans may not directly transfer to their learning of English because the linguistic differences between English and Asian languages are so great. This means that most Asian Americans learn English as a brand new language, unlike students of Hispanic and European backgrounds.

Table 9.10. Origins and Families of Languages of East Asia

Country	Number of Languages	Origins	Language Families
China	7 major ones	Sino-Tibetan languages	Mandarin, Cantonese, Wu, Xiang, Kan, Hakka, Minnar, and Yue
Korea	1	Altaic languages	Manchu, Mongolia, Turkish, and Japanese
Japan	1	Altaic languages, similar to Korean	Manchu, Mongolia, Turkish, and Korean
Philippines	8 major ones	Austronesia or Malayo-Polynesian languages	Tagalog, Cebuano, Ilocano, Hiligaynon, Bicol, Waray, Pampango, and Pangasinan

Note. Information from *Asian-American Education: Perspectives and Challenges*, by C. C. Park & Y. M. M. Chi, 1999, Westport: Bergin & Garvey.

Manning and Baruth (2009) reported that of the 4 million Asian American children 5 years and older, approximately 56% speak English poorly or not very well, and 35% are linguistically isolated, meaning they are unable to speak English at all because they grow up in non-English speaking homes. This is not a surprise. In 2000, the U.S. Census Bureau documented that at least 7.5 million Asian Americans 5 years and older spoke a language other than English at home; that figure represents nearly three-fourths of all Asian Americans.

As complex as their languages are, Asian Americans living in ethnic enclaves find learning English extremely difficult because, unlike their languages, English is a temporal language with different verb tenses. Asian American children living in these environments have difficulty learning English because they hear their parents, their relatives, and bystanders speak their native language most of the time. Without a doubt, linguistics is the most difficult challenge of Asian American children and adolescents. Difficulties with English hinder their academic achievement and educational attainment in some ways. However, keep in mind that proficiency in spoken English alone is not a sufficient condition for academic achievement. All students need to learn the English needed for academic tasks.

As is true for students of most minority cultures, public schools leave Asian American English learners to fend for themselves, and teachers expect them to overcome language barriers even though the school system is operated under Euro-American hegemony with measurement-driven curricula. More significantly, the American educational system is not prepared to work with these linguistically diverse students.

In summary, Asian American students with their diverse linguistic backgrounds appear to have tremendous difficulties breaking a word into inflectional or intonated syllables. For instance, Asian American students from monosyllabic, tonal, and non-inflectional linguistic backgrounds struggle to put stress on the appropriate syllables in English while learning to speak.

Socioeconomic Status of Asian Americans

In 1999, the U.S. Census Bureau reported that the per capita income of Asian Americans was $21,823. This was lower than for Whites and Arab Americans but higher than for Blacks, Hispanics, and Native Americans, as shown in Table 9.11. As a whole, Asian Americans appear to do well financially; however, some struggle. Manning and Baruth (2009) reported that in 2004, 438,000 Asian Americans families had annual family incomes between $75,000 and $99,000; 145,000 families earned less than $10,000; and 152,000 families earned $100,000 and over.

In 2000, the proportion of Asian Americans living below poverty level was 11.7%, a figure higher than that of Whites but lower than those of Arab Americans, Blacks, Hispanics, and Native Americans (see Table 9.12). This indicates that Asian Americans are striving hard for economic survival and success, and, more importantly, they make up the second most employed racial group in America. However, as Table 9.11 shows, they do not earn the highest incomes.

Table 9.11. Per Capita Income in 1999, by Racial Group

Group	Income
Native Americans	$12,893
Arab Americans	$24,061
Hispanic Americans	$12,111
Whites	$23,918
Blacks	$14,437
Asians	$21,823

Note. Data from U.S. Census Bureau, *Census 2000 Demographic Profile Highlights.*

Table 9.12. Number of People Living Below Poverty Level, by Racial Group

Group	Number of people	Percentage
Whites	18,800,000	8.7
Blacks	8,100,000	23.4
Native Americans	607,000	24.2
Arab Americans	163,000	13.5
Hispanic Americans	7,700,000	21.8
Asians	1,200,000	11.7

Note. Data from U.S. Census Bureau, *Census 2000 Demographic Profile Highlights.* Numbers are rounded.

As mentioned previously, even if 145,000 Asian American families earned less than $10,000 in 2004, they appear to be adequately self-sufficient based on several socioeconomic factors. As Table 9.13 shows, the total number of Asian Americans who were eligible for and received food stamps was 594,000, or 2.4%, a proportion higher than for Native Americans but considerably lower than for all other groups. This could mean that Asian Americans who are not as fortunate as others depend on some sort of public assistance, or the figure could represent recent immigrants and refugees from Asian countries.

It should be noted that despite all the political setbacks, pain, and suffering of the past, many Asian Americans have achieved impressive SES and have overcome severe prejudice and discrimination. However, as with other racial groups in America, there are many who still need to take advantage of the educational opportunities available to them in order to conquer the barriers that keep them from achieving their highest potential.

Table 9.13. Number of Food Stamp Participants, by Racial Group

Group	Number of Participants	Percentage
Whites	10,727,000	43.1
Blacks	8,299,000	33.4
Hispanics	4,786,000	19.2
Asians	594,000	2.4
Native Americans	367,000	1.5
Unknown race	68,000	0.4

Note. Data from U.S. Department of Agriculture, *Characteristics of Food Stamp Households: Fiscal Year 2005* (Report FSP-06-CHAR), 2006. Numbers are rounded.

Promoting Academic Achievement for Asian Americans

In 2000, approximately 5.3 million Asian Americans reported having high school diplomas or higher education, and nearly 2.9 million Asian Americans had received a bachelor's degree or higher degree (U.S. Census Bureau, 2000a). In 2007, the U.S. Census Bureau reported that the number of Asian American college graduates was up from the number in the previous census. Approximately 54% of Asian American males and 46% of Asian American females earned college degrees in 2005, up from 47% for males and 40% for females in 2000.

Most foreign-born Asian American students and adolescents do not possess middle-class American values when they enter public schools, but U.S.-born Asian American children usually do. Many fare well in school, and others do not because of social, psychological, educational, cross-cultural, economic, neurological, and linguistic factors associated with their life situations. For instance, some have medical conditions; some have learning problems that are not modifiable; some come to school unprepared and lack motivation; some lack proficiency in English; some are poor and have inadequate resources; some are new arrivals from other countries; some are disabled; some are gifted and talented; some have behavioral problems; some are too shy, too humble, too modest, and too nice; and some are rebellious, antisocial, and antiauthority. These are characteristics that can be found in any group of students. However, Asian American children as a whole have attained success in public schools (Manning & Baruth, 2009).

Typically, the challenges with learning English that Asian American children and adolescents encounter are not terribly different from those experienced by students of other ethnic groups in the public schools. Asian American students place a heavy emphasis on filial piety and the social and cultural values derived from the philosophical principles of Confucianism. These values are the bases of their self-concept, self-image, self-esteem, and self-worth, but, for the most part, they are contrary to the American values needed for success in school. For example, schoolteachers are more likely to respond to students who are assertive and opinionated and less likely to find time to deal with students who are quiet, shy, respectful, humble, and modest.

Prospective educators should bear in mind that Asian Americans could be ambivalent; they might smile or slump, they might be very quiet. They may need to be prompted to overcome such barriers. Otherwise, they might develop patterns of hesitation and reservation. Asian American students should at least learn to adjust to the difference between Asian culture and American culture by leaving their self-effacing behaviors at home and becoming more assertive in school. For instance, deferring to answer questions in order to avoid drawing attention to oneself or avoid the possibility of losing face will not help them advance academically in the American school system. Moreover, they should understand that listening respectfully does not preclude one from speaking considerately and carefully. In fact, most children do not learn by listening, but by doing. Schooling is a formalized process of trial and error; Asian American students are not trained at home for this process.

Most importantly, educators should work to preserve Asian American students' cultural identities in order to respect and protect their personal dignity. However, cultural identity should not be exploited as an excuse to limit students' access to learning opportunities, nor should differences in cultural backgrounds keep students from receiving academic services.

To promote the academic achievement of Asian American children and adolescents, educators should consider the following actions:

1. Focus on the students' needs rather than their cultural identities.
2. Create a learning environment that fosters cultural diversity.
3. Use eclectic teaching techniques to engage students.
4. Use differentiating instruction to benefit all.
5. Prescribe cooperative learning.
6. Allow student-centered instruction.
7. Stop using surface level assessment.

8. Eliminate homogenous grouping.
9. Use hands-on and minds-on activities.
10. Use ELD, SDAIE, TESOL, or sheltered English instruction to improve BICS and CALP.
11. Hire bilingual staff or bilingual instructional aides.
12. Use obligatory content standards, not compatibility content.

These are suggestions that also work well with other ethnic students if applied appropriately. Prospective educators should bear in mind that children of these cultures are as deserving as any children in the educational system. Of course, most students are trained by their parents to behave; school is the time for educators to formally discipline them to be educated.

Summing Up

This chapter presented the sociocultural characteristics of Asian American children and families to provide prospective educators with some understanding of children who share Asian American ancestry. The label "model minority" has stereotypical connotations; however, children of Asian immigrants and first-generation Asian immigrants deserve to be praised for their sacrifices, struggles, and sociopolitical determinations in the U.S. Prospective educators need to understand that positive self-image, self-concept, self-esteem, self-worth, and cultural identities are critical to the psychological, cognitive, and social development of most Asian American children and adolescents. Family values have great influences and play a significant role in their daily lives. Prospective educators should recognize that Asian American students have distinct cultures, languages, and sociocultural factors that make individual students unique, and grouping all of them together as one large cultural group is inaccurate.

Chapter Ten

Southeast Asian Children and Their Families

The beauty and struggle of one's present life is pre-determined
and pre-destined by his goodness or evil in his previous life.
—The Karma in Buddhism

Overview

The experiences of refugees from French Indo-China should not be forgotten because stories about the "boat people" from Vietnam, the "soldiers of the Sky" or "guerrilla soldiers" from Laos, and the "bloodbath" or "killing field" survivors from Cambodia still chill the hearts and souls of Southeast Asian families. But many Americans still do not know why the Southeast Asians are here in the U.S.

This chapter describes Southeast Asian Americans (SEAA)— Vietnamese, Cambodian (Khmer), Laotians, Hmong, Thai—as well as South Asian Americans (SAA), specifically people from India. It presents the socio-cultural differences in race, ethnicity, culture, class, religion, family, language, economics, and ways of life.

Who Are Southeast Asian Americans?

The political designation "Southeast Asian (SEA)" became well known to the West during the Vietnam War in the French Indo-China countries of Vietnam, Laos, and Cambodia (Vangay, 2004). At the end of the Vietnam War and the Secret War in Laos in 1975, the United States conducted massive emergency evacuations in these war-torn nations to save the lives of former officials and freedom fighters who cooperated in American foreign policy missions. Many were airlifted to safe havens in Thailand and elsewhere, and others were abandoned to fend for themselves. Hundreds of thousands became war refugees. Similar to those on the Native American Trail of Tears, refugees sought their own ways to leave their homelands for Thailand, the Philippines, Hong Kong, Australia, Canada, and the United States. After a time in temporary shelters in Asian nations, most refugees wound up in the West—the United States, Canada, France, and Australia.

One cautionary note: Although Thailand has always been part of Southeast Asia, the Vietnam War did not involve Thailand, and its inhabitants immigrated to the West for reasons other than those of the refugees from Vietnam, Laos, and Cambodia. Moreover, Thailand was the nation where most refugees from Indo-China found temporary havens.

The term *Asian Indian* was created by the U.S. Census Bureau in 2000 to identify people from the country of India. Asian Indians include people who speak Hindi, Punjabi, and Urdu. Prospective educators should keep in mind that among all SEAA groups, Vietnamese, Cambodian, Hmong, and Laotians account for the largest numbers of SEAA students in public schools. Among the South Asian groups, Indians, also called Asian Indians,are the most noticeable group in public schools. However, there are other SEA subgroups in the U.S. with distinct cultures and traditions, such as Iu Mien, Lahu, Khamu, Lao Theung, Pakistanis, Burmese (from Myanmar), Nepalese, Bengals, Sri Lankans, Malaysians, Indonesians, and Bangladeshi.

The Origins of Southeast Asian Americans

Unlike other Asian Americans who are immigrants, Southeast Asian Americans are refugees who underwent the process of diaspora. They are in the U.S. because of the loss of their countries, not because they searched for religious freedom, economic opportunities, or the American dream. The refugee immigrations from Vietnam, Cambodia, and Laos took place from 1975 to the mid-1990s. For Hmong refugees, the latest wave to come to the U.S. arrived in 2003.

Vietnamese

When the Vietnam War ended in 1975, the first large group of SEA refugees to leave their homeland was Vietnamese. The Vietnam evacuation was a last-minute rush to escape communist rule. Thousands of Vietnamese left unexpectedly, quickly, quietly, hurriedly, in shock and anxiety. The evacuation was total chaos, but there were no other choices. There was not time to prepare. Some left with their family members, but many left by themselves. The majority abandoned everything they had in life. They took suitcases, handbags, precious items, and some clothes. In their shocked states of mind, many wondered about their final destination. But when they learned they were traveling to another country, they were even more fearful, worried about what would happen to their loved ones left behind. The lucky ones were airlifted or traveled by boats to safety in neighboring countries and finally came to the United States (Training Center, 1982).

Shortly after the swift evacuation, thousands of Vietnamese and Chinese Vietnamese who refused to live under the communist reign risked their lives to escape by sea; they were called "boat people." Many men, women, and teenagers embarked on a treacherous journey by sea, drifting in the dark to find freedom. Pirates took advantage of them. Many were beaten and tortured physically and mentally. Women were raped repeatedly. Some were drowned, some died of starvation, and some were shot to death. Sadly, many watched members of their crew die slowly. To survive, some resorted to cannibalism because there was no other source of food available in the middle of the sea. Those who survived the deadly escape reached Malaysia and Thailand. There, they were imprisoned for entering a country illegally. However, their hope was greater than their fear. They were allowed to live in temporary refugee camps prior to resettling in Western nations.

Cambodians (Khmer)

The Cambodian people faced a similar plight following the fall of Vietnam in 1975. Within a few months, Cambodia fell under Pol Pot. Under his communist rule, the Khmer Rouge regime, millions of people were subject to hard labor, imprisonment, torture, and genocide. The bloodbath took place in killing fields through the entire nation. Approximately 25% of the nation's civilians were annihilated. Some lucky ones were able to escape the bloody killings; they made their way to Thailand and sought political asylum. Like the Vietnamese, they were beaten, tortured, and imprisoned for trespassing; however, most were allowed to remain in the temporary refugee camps in anticipation of coming to the Western nations (Training Center, 1982).

Um (1999) noted that the Khmer Rouge's infliction of brutal "systematic class persecution, endemic starvation, and hard physical labor resulted in the death of hundreds of millions of people, of which one-seventh of the population with a disproportionate percentage of the educated, professionals, and urbanites being killed" (p. 264). Most Cambodian refugees came to the U.S. from the early 1980s to the late 1990s.

The word *Khmer*, pronounced "Khmai," refers to the primary language or mother tongue of the Cambodian people. The word *Cambodian* is usually used of the people who speak Khmer. Khmer is the spoken language and writing system of the Cambodian people.

Laotians

Following the fall of Vietnam and Cambodia in 1975, Laos became the third domino to fall under communist rule in Southeast Asia. All Laotians faced the same plight as Cambodians and Vietnamese. The term *Laotian* encompases a mixed group of highlanders and lowlanders, including Hmong, Laotians, Iu Mien, Lahu, Lao Lue, Khamu, and Lau Theung. Life was in great turmoil for all these groups (Training Center, 1982). The largest Lao refugee group was the Hmong, and the second largest the Laotians.

As part of the Vietnam War, Laos was engaged in a Secret War against communist North Vietnam sponsored by the United States Central Intelligent Agency (CIA) from 1960 to 1973. The purpose of the Secret War was to prevent the extension of the Ho Chi Minh Trail to South Vietnam. When the U.S. reached an agreement with North Vietnam to withdraw its military from Laos in 1973, the Royal Army of Laos and Hmong guerrilla forces were left to fend for themselves during another 2 years of heavy warfare. Following the fall of Vietnam, Laos, like Cambodia, also fell under communist rule.

On May 14, 1975, the "final rescue effort" took place at the air base of Long Cheng, the CIA military base in Region 2 in Laos. Like the scene in Vietnam, it was a sudden and chaotic evacuation. In fact, it was a last-minute rush to airlift U.S. officials to safety. Thousands of Laotian Hmong left their villages to board the planes; however, the number of flights was limited and thousands of Laotian Hmong refugees were left behind. Moreover, hundreds of families were torn apart because of the rescue. Some left with their families, but many left by themselves. Hundreds of thousands living in the cities had already crossed the Mekong River by boat to Thailand. The lucky ones arrived in Thailand, and the unlucky ones retreated to their villages and hid in the jungle to evade capture and imprisonment. After 1975, hundreds of thousands of Hmong refugees trekked through the jungle and found their way to Thailand.

Hmong refugees started arriving in Western countries in late 1975, and they continued coming through 2003. Several thousand Hmong refugees living in northern Thailand are still awaiting international rescue more than 30 years after the end of the war. These displaced refugees hope to resettle in the Western nations and start new lives.

The heartache of Laotian refugees has not ended even nearly 35 years after the fall of Laos because the ethnic cleansing and killings are still going on in the countryside against those who were associated with the insurgent resistance and those who had or have ties with the United States.

Asian Indians and Thai

Unlike the SEA groups, Asian Indian and Thai immigrants entered the U.S. to seek opportunities in education, employment, and religion, and to pursue the American dream. Many came to the U.S. long before the arrival of SE-AAs. However, over the last 35 years, the numbers of both groups have increased substantially, especially the number of Asian Indians. The Punjabi population in public schools is large, perhaps the largest among all SEAA and SAA groups. Among SAA groups, there are four major cultural groups, such as the Indo-Aryans—high class; Dravidians—middle class of the southern region of the peninsula; Negrito—low class or tribal groups; and Mongolian of Himalayan region—low class or mountaintop people. This relatively new group of students speaks three different dialects: Punjabi, Hindi, and Urdu. The number of Thai students is relatively small compared with the numbers of Laotian, Hmong, Vietnamese, Cambodian, and Punjabi. However, in certain cities, such as Los Angeles and New York, the Thai student population is quite sizeable.

It is important to examine these two groups briefly as part of the SAA population because of their significant numbers in public school. However, more information is needed than will be supplied here to fully understand their diverse academic needs and abilities.

Who Are Southeast Asian and South Asian Americans Today?

There are six SEAA groups and six SAA groups with significant numbers of students in American schools, as shown in Tables 10.1 and 10.2. According to the U.S. Census Bureau (2000), approximately 3.5 million SEAA and 1.8 million SAA were living in the U.S. in 2000. These figures do not include all subgroups of the major groups. A rough estimation of all SEAA and SAA minority groups adds another million to these numbers. As of 2000, the total U.S. Asian population was 10.2 million; this means that SEAA and SAA constitute almost half of the total Asian American population.

Among all SEA refugee groups that immigrated to the U.S. since 1975, Vietnamese constitute the largest group, followed by Cambodians, Hmong, Laotians, and Thai. One cautionary note should be made here regarding the total numbers of Hmong and Laotians in the census numbers. The number of Laotians is higher than experts believe is accurate, and the number of Hmong is lower. This discrepancy may be caused by the fact that some Hmong iden tify themselves as Laotian Hmong instead of Hmong and the census category *Laotian* includes otherwise unidentified ethnicities such as Iu Mien, Lue, Lahu, Khamu, and Lao Theung. The *Hmong Tribune Newspaper* (2008) estimated the number of Hmong in the U.S. to be at least 300,000. If this number is correct, Hmong constitute the second largest SEA group, with Vietnamese the largest. In fact, this is consistent with national data on the total number of Hmong LEP students in public schools in California. Hispanic students constitute the largest group, followed by Vietnamese students and then Hmong students.

Table 10.1. Southeast Asian American Population, by Racial Group

Group	Total Population	Percent of Total Asian American Population
Vietnamese	1,122,000	11.00
Thai	112,000	1.10
Laotians	168,000	1.64
Hmong	169,000	1.65
Cambodia	171,000	1.67
Iu Mien	10,000	.09
Total	1,752,000	17.15

Note. Data from U.S. Census Bureau, *Census 2000 Demographic Profile Highlights.* Numbers are rounded.

Table 10.2. South Asian American Population, by Racial Group

Group	Total Population	Percent of Total Asian American Population
Asian Indians	1,600,000	15.68
Bangladeshi	41,000	.40
Indonesian	39,000	.38
Malaysian	10,000	.09
Pakistani	153,000	1.50
Sri Lankan	20,000	.19
Total	1,863,000	18.24

Note. Data from U.S. Census Bureau, *Census 2000 Demographic Profile Highlights.* Numbers are rounded.

As Table 10.2 shows, Asian Indians constitute the largest SA group, followed by Pakistani a distant second and Bangladeshi. Moreover, the Asian Indian population in the U.S. is larger than that of Vietnamese. This means that among all SEAAs and SAAs, Asian Indians constitute the most populous group. Moreover, a noticeable growth has occurred in the Asian Indian student population in the public schools. Indeed, more teachers coming from this particular cultural group are needed; otherwise, students who speak Hindi, Punjabi, or Urdu are left to fend for themselves. The failure of schools to prepare to meet the needs of culturally and linguistically diverse students is very common.

The Cultural Characteristics of Southeast Asian and South Asian Americans

The SEAA and SAA groups are demographically and politically diverse; even non-Asian individuals can distinguish some of their differences in race, ethnicity, language, culture, religion, economic status, and family traditions. Like members of other racial groups, SEAAs and SAAs come from diverse backgrounds, but they share many similar cultural characteristics and beliefs. In fact, they share some of the same cultural characteristics as other Asian Americans, such as respect for elders, patriarchal family system, hierarchical social system, extended family, filial piety, patience, obedience, and kinship and clan systems. They also have similar social behaviors. Many of their cultural characteristics were influenced greatly by Confucianism and Buddhism. Buddhism started in India; Asian Indian culture was heavily influenced by Buddhist beliefs and practices regarding nirvana and the rules of Karma.

To help prospective educators gain insight into the cultural characteristics of SEAAs and SAAs, Table 10.3 illustrates some of the basic social values of the six major cultural groups with respect to societal stratification. The highest position in the hierarchy, or social ladder, in Asian cultures does not appear in the table; it is reserved for deity or God.

Socially, Asians consider it odd and unacceptable for women of Asian cultures to shake hands. However, Asian Americans consider the practice permissible in the U.S. between Asian women and people of other races. Within a race, however, women shaking hands is still taboo, but sometimes it is accepted, depending on the individual's assimilation level. Verbal acknowledgment is the most common form of greeting. The position of teach ers in the social strata varies slightly among all groups, but most consider teachers to occupy a higher societal position than parents because of their prestigious position in society. In most groups except Vietnamese, the king has the highest position in the caste system or social order. Vietnam has never had a royal family or dynasty, whereas all the other countries were once ruled by royal families.

Table 10.3. Values of Selected SEAA and SAA Cultures Related to Caste System

Value	Viet-namese	Cambo-dian	Lao	Thai	Hmong	Asian Indian
Hierarchy of social stratifica-tion	Scholar, farmer, fisherman, laborer, business-man	King, monk, adminis-trator, technician, business-man, farmer, and la-borer	King, monk, adminis-trator, technician, business-man, farmer, and la-borer	King, monk, adminis-trator, technician, business-man, farmer, laborer	King, shaman, military leader, civic leader, clan leader, farmer, laborer	King, scholar, civic leader, business-man, clan leader, farmer, laborer
Places of teachers and par-ents	Teachers more re-spected than par-ents	Parents more re-spected than teachers	Parents more re-spected than teachers	Parents more re-spected than teachers	Teachers more re-spected, than par-ents	Teachers more re-spected than par-ents

Note. Information from Fresno County Department of Social Services, *Indochinese Cultural Awareness Training for Social Work Services*, 1993.

Table 10.4 presents additional cultural values of SEAAs and SAAs that are essential for prospective educators to consider when working and dealing with students who are coming from these cultural backgrounds.

Keep in mind that some of these traditional values have changed over time. Time orientation has changed drastically since arrival in America because people have had to learn to keep appointments and follow schedules. Writing with the left hand and other uses of the left hand are still taboo in some cultures, considered unacceptable or evil in some cases; however, this has changed in other cultures to accommodate biological difference in children. Raising feet high and even showing the feet are culturally inappropriate in most Asian cultures because the foot is the lowest and dirtiest part of the body. In some cultures, people wash their feet before entering a house and people hide their feet while worshiping or paying respect to others.

Table 10.4. Cultural Characteristics of Selected SEAA and SAA Groups

Cultural Matter	Vietnamese	Cambodian	Lao	Thai	Hmong	Asian Indian
Showing respect	All—Bow head					
Passing object to another	All—Use both hands					
Saluting person of particular status	Join both hands at chest	4 levels: equal status, join hands at chest; older status, join hands at chin; higher status, join hands at nose; authority or royalty, join hands over head			Shake hands or bow head. To show higher respect, left hand touches right wrist when shaking hands	Shake hands, bow head, or hug, kiss on the cheeks (varied)
Eye contact	All—No direct eye contact when talking to someone					
Touching head of students	Considered rude					
Calling someone	All—Use all fingers, facing down					
Putting feet on desk while talking	All—Rude or impolite					
Writing with left hand	Not allowed	Not allowed	Not allowed	Not allowed	No limitation	Not allowed, religious interpretation
Time orientation	All—Time is flexible, no hurry, punctuality not necessary unless extremely important situation					

Note. Information from Fresno County Department of Social Services, *Indochinese Cultural Awareness Training for Social Work Services*, 1993.

Using a single finger to summon someone is considered rude and impolite because in Asian cultures this gesture is used to call an animal, not a person. Using the whole hand, with fingers facing down, is the accepted way to call someone. This thought might be new to many, including Asian American children.

Patting and touching are social compliments, but sometimes touching someone's head is not allowed because the top of the head, the highest point of the body, is considered sacred. Parents are allowed to touch their children's heads to praise or comfort them.

Finally, although making eye contact is extremely important in American culture, in Asian cultures looking in the eyes is seen as direct facial intimidation and insult. Educators should remember these cultural characteristics when working with Asian American families. Keep in mind that these are only some of the cultural values of SEAAs and SAAs.

Southeast Asian and South Asian American Families

SEAA and SAA families are not much different from any other families; however, some are quite a bit bigger than those of Whites, Blacks, Arabs, Native Americans, and other Asians because most SEAA and SAA families contain several children. The average size of the Hmong American family is six, the largest of all SEAA and SAA groups (see Table 10.5). This size is smaller than that of the parents or the first generation to arrive in America (Personal communication, Vang, 2009). An Americanized Hmong family generally consists of four children and two parents. A traditional Hmong family typically has at least 8 to 10 people. Many non-Hmong consider this large family size unmanageable, but for Hmong, it is desirable. For other SEAA and SAA groups, the household sizes of the first families to come to the U.S. as refugees were relatively similar (Personal communication, Mouanoutoua, 2009; Mouen, 2009; and Sayaseng; 2009).

As mentioned in Chapter Nine, family is the center of the lives of Asian Americans, and they spend tremendous energy keeping families from breaking apart. As noted in previous chapters, Asian Americans have the lowest divorce rate of all cultural groups. Eight out of 10 Asian American children live in a two-parent household. To help prospective educators recognize typical family names and associate them with the corresponding cultural group, Table 10.6 lists the predominant family names of the major SEAA and SAA cultural groups.

Keep in mind that some given names, or first names, are common among more than one Asian group. For instance, Tong, Thong, Keo, Phan, Ly, Lee, and Le are common in many Asian cultures. Sometimes, in some cultural groups, first names and family names are the same. For example,

Vang could be either a first or last name, as could Ly, Le, or Lee. One cautionary note is in order: As a result of interracial marriage, last names, or given names, sometimes do not identify the individual's nationality, family, or ethnicity.

Table 10.5. Average Household and Family Sizes, by Racial Group

Group	Average Household Size	Average Family Size
Asian (overall)	3	4
Cambodian	5	5
Hmong	6	6
Laotian	4	5
Thai	3	3
Vietnamese	4	4
Mien	5	5
Asian Indian	4	5
Chinese	3	3
Filipino	3	4
Japanese	3	3
Korean	3	3

Note. Data from U.S. Census Bureau, *Census 2000 Demographic Profile Highlights.*

Table 10.6. Typical Family and Given Names in Selected Racial Groups

Group	Typical Family Names	Typical Given Names
Vietnamese	Nguyen, Tran, Doan, Ho, and Vu	Linh, Hoa, Tri, Truc, and Loc
Cambodian	Sambo, Touch, Vuthy, Chak, Sok	Serey, Chea, Samlei, Narong, Dara
Lao	Sayaseng, Bouphasiri, Khamphoukeo, Sisavong, Koulavongsa	Keo, Bounmy, Thong, Bounsouam, Phouchan
Hmong	Vang, Lee, Her, Lor, Thao, and Vue	Chia, Pao, Yee, Blia, May
Thai	Konsivilai, Ratanassen, Aphechat, Pommavongsai, Nasirichantanara	Thongphan, Keo, Phin, Daralai, Loun
Asian Indian	Singh, Ramesh, Dhaliwal, Sodhu, Soni	Ajaib, Jairam, Hardeep, Charan, Baldeep
Iu Mien	Saechao, Saetern, Saelee, Saephan, Saefong	Kao, Nai, Chee, Farm, Feuy

Note. Information from Fresno County Department of Social Services, *Indochinese Cultural Awareness Training for Social Work Services*, 1993.

One of the ways to learn more about SEAA and SAA families is to take a look at the number of families living below poverty level in 2000, as shown in Table 10.7. Among all SEAA and SAA groups, Cambodian and Hmong families are the poorest and are the most likely to live below poverty level. On the other hand, Thai families are the least likely to be poor, followed by Asian Indian families as the second least likely to live below poverty level. Perhaps the reason Hmong and Cambodian families are the poorest among these groups is that they have larger households and bigger families than other Asian groups. Another reason may be that their employment rates are probably lower than for other groups.

Table 10.7. Numbers of Families Below Poverty Level in 2000, by Racial Group

Group	Number of Families	Total Population
Vietnamese	34,900	1,122,000
Cambodian	9,500	171,000
Laotian	5,700	168,000
Thai	2,100	112,000
Hmong	8,900	169,000
Asian Indian	27,900	1,600,000

Note. Data from U.S. Census Bureau, *Census 2000 Demographic Profile Highlights.* Numbers are rounded.

Gender Roles of Southeast Asian and South Asian Americans

SEAA and SAA children have well-defined roles in the family circle, as do parents. Family expectations for both male and female children are high in accordance with the value of filial piety and the kinship system. Boys and girls are not free to do what they want. Girls are generally under strict supervision and must observe a curfew. In some communities, segregation of sexes is still the common social rule. For example, in Hmong culture, at family social gatherings, males usually dine together separate from females. The culture has changed a bit, but segregated dining is still a preferable practice when in a group.

In some cultures, brothers and sisters do not touch or kiss each other socially in public; such behavior would be a public embarrassment or an insult to the family. As in other Asian American cultures, sons are apparently valued more than daughters because sons remain in the family, whereas daughters will someday marry outside the family clan.

To help prospective educators gain insight into the gender roles in SEAA and SAA cultures, Table 10.8 contrasts the views of the parent/children relationship in Asian cultures with the views in the American culture. Keep in mind that these cultural values and behaviors represent only some of the many possible variations that may exist within all Asian cultures. Learning more about a specific culture to gain in-depth knowledge about gender roles is highly encouraged.

Table 10.8. Views of Parent/Children Relationship in SEAA and American Cultures

Family Matter	Southeast Asian American Culture	American Culture
View of children	Children are extensions of parents	Children are individuals
Decision making	Family makes decision for the child	The child is given many choices
Self/sibling responsibility	Older children are responsible for their siblings' actions and deeds	Each child is responsible for his or her own actions and deeds
Family dependency	Children should remain dependent on the family for most needs	Early independence is encouraged and practiced
Group harmony	Children should submit to structure	Children should think what is right for themselves
Dealing with feelings	Young children do not have well-formed feelings or individual needs	Young children have well-defined feelings and personalities
Self-control of anger	Children should express anger, frustration, or contempt toward parents or authority	It is better to vent anger and frustration than let it sit inside
Methods of discipline	Punishment includes shaming and withdrawal of love if appropriate	Punishment should involve logical consequences
Filial piety system	Questioning adults or asking why is not accepted	Curiosity and individualization are encouraged
Parental roles	Parents provide authority, supervision, and decisions	Parents provide guidance, support, and explanations

Note. Information from *Psychoeducational Model,* by Special Education Resource Network, 1985.

The cultural attitudes, social behaviors, and family values listed in Table 10.8 shape the gender roles in Asian cultures. The gender roles as well as the cultural values and behaviors of SEAAs and SAAs are very similar to those of Asian American families discussed in Chapter Nine.

In Punjabi cultural traditions and customs, family relationships are significant in explaining the roles and responsibilities of kinship. For instance, different sets of terms are used to formally address the paternal and maternal kinfolk, such as *taya* for the father's elder brother, *chacha* for the father's youngest brother, *bhua* for the father's sister, *mama* for the mother's brother, and *massi* for the mother's sister. Moreover, the relationship between brothers is friendly and cordial, whereas the relationship between brothers and sisters is considered to be the warmest and cleanest of all human relations. Sisters always look up to their brothers for protection and assistance.

Religions of Southeast Asian and South Asian Americans

In SEAA and SAA cultures, the eldest son has a duty to perform the rituals of ancestor worship at home and to take charge of larger family religious rituals and ceremonial events As mentioned in Chapter Nine, religious activities are generally the responsibility of men in Asian cultures. Nonetheless, many Asian women are incredible healers and honorable experts in medicine. To help prospective educators understand the importance of religious practices in Asian cultures, Table 10.9 shows the major religions in the countries of origin of SEAAs and SAAs. As with other racial groups, most Asian Americans are very religious when it comes to family values, respect, social behaviors, and cultural preservation.

Although SEAA and SAA groups are religiously diverse, the majority followed Buddhism, Hinduism, or Islam prior to coming to the U.S. Vietnam has a mixture of several religious groups; however, no indication of the percentage of religious adherents for each belief system was available. It should be noted that Morocco is the only country with only one dominant religion, which is Sunni Islam. Most countries have at least three major religions.

Today's SEAAs and SAAs are still strongly committed to the religious practices and affiliations their parents brought with them to the U.S. As Table 10.10 illustrates, the major religions of these groups are Buddhism, Hinduism, Islam, and Christianity. One cautionary note: Generally speaking, many Asians practice two or more religious faiths at the same time. For example, Hmong believe in a mixture of Buddhism, Hinduism, animism, ancestor worship, and Christianity.

Table 10.9. Major Religions of Southeast Asian and South Asian Countries

Country	Religions
India	Hinduism (80%), Islam (14%), Christianity (2%), Sikh (2%)
Cambodia	Buddhism (95%), others (5%)
Vietnam	Buddhism, Taoism, Catholicism, indigenous beliefs
Thailand	Buddhism (95%), Islam (4%), Christianity (1%)
Laos	Buddhism (60%), animism (25%), others (15%)
Myanmar (Burma)	Buddhism (89%), Christianity (4%), Islam (4%)
Bangladesh	Islam (83%), Hinduism (16%), others (1%)
Nepal	Hinduism (90%), Buddhism (5%), Islam (3%)
Morocco	Sunni Islam (99%), others (1%)
Sri Lankan	Buddhism (69%), Hinduism (15%), Christianity (8%), Islam (8%)

Note. Data from U.S. Census Bureau, *International Data Base: The World Factbook 1998*, 1997, Washington, DC.

Table 10.10. Religions of SEAAs and SAs, by Racial Group

Group	Major Religions	Most Commonly Practiced Religions
Vietnamese	Christianity, Buddhism, Taoism, Confucianism, ancestor worship, animism	Buddhism and ancestor worship
Cambodian	Buddhism and Christianity	Buddhism
Thai	Buddhism, Christianity, Islam	Buddhism
Laotian	Buddhism and Christianity	Buddhism
Iu Mien	Buddhism, animism, Christianity	Buddhism and animism
Hmong	Buddhism, Hinduism, animism, ancestor worship, Christianity	Buddhism, animism, and ancestor worship
India	Hinduism, Islam, Christianity, Sikhism	Hinduism

Note. Information from *Asian Pacific Islander Cultural Awareness Training*, Fresno County Department of Social Services, 1998.

Generally, Buddhism, ancestor worship, and Hinduism are the dominant religious forces in most Asian families. Regardless of which faith they identify with closely, most families worship tirelessly, diligently, faithfully, and humbly toward the end of achieving an internal feeling of bliss in a transcendent state. Most believe that the cycle of life, death, and rebirth for an individual will cease only when that individual has finally been able to get rid of earthly desires and attain a state of spiritual liberation. Similar to the religious beliefs of some Native Americans, animism is practical, with religious values that some families consider each and every day; animism holds that all people are supposed to live in harmony with nature and not dominate nature.

The core of religious devotion among SEAAs and SAAs is spiritualism. For men, spiritualism is the highest point in life and the dominant force in society. Men are to honor God with sacrifices in order to fulfill the rules of Karma, in which one's present life is pre-determined and pre-destined by the good or bad deeds done in his previous life.

Languages of Southeast Asian and South Asian Americans

Unlike the cultural and religious values, the languages of SEAA and SAA groups are distinctly different; however, some languages share the same origins and have linguistic similarities, as shown in Table 10.11. Most of the languages of these two groups originated from one of two major language families: Sino-Tibetan languages or Austro-Asiatic languages. The large number of languages spoken by these groups indicates the linguistic complexities among them. In addition to English, most of the groups with the exception of Cambodians speak two or more languages. Although the groups are multilingual, Thais and Laotians appear to be more linguistically diverse because each has four major language families.

Nonetheless, keep in mind that every distinct language and dialect spoken by SEAA and SAA subgroups is not displayed in Table 10.11. For instance, although most contemporary Hmong in the U.S. speak either White Hmong or Blue Hmong, several other Hmong dialects are also spoken, such as Red Hmong, Stripe Hmong, Black Hmong, and Green Hmong. Similarly, in India, the universal native language is Hindi; however, most contemporary Asian Indian students in public schools in America speak Punjabi or Urdu and other regional dialects. Of course, the multitude of diverse languages poses difficult challenges for teachers and schools since the system is not ready to deal well with linguistic and cultural diversity.

Among SEAA and SAA groups, language similarities and differences exist. Vietnamese and Hindi have almost no commonalities with other SEA or SA languages, as shown in Table 10.12. Some languages are similar to others in the way they sound when spoken; however, only Thai and Lao are similar in their written forms as well as verbal utterances. Thus a Lao speaker can understand a Thai speaker readily. Moreover, both Thai and Lao speakers can easily understand Cambodian colloquial language because some of the words sound exactly the same as Lao and Thai words with the same meanings. Some Cambodian words not only sound the same as Thai and Lao words, but actually have the same derivative roots.

Table 10.11. Languages of SEAA and SAA Groups

Group	Number of Major Languages	Language Origin	Languages
Cambodian	1	Austro-Asiatic	Khmer
Vietnamese	2	Sino-Tibetan	Vietnamese, Chinese
Thai	4	Austro-Asiatic	Thai, Lao, Chinese, Malay
Lao	3	Austro-Asiatic	Lao, Khamu, Lao Theung
Asian Indian	3	Gurmukhi script, Perso-Arabic Script, Sino-Tibetan, or Austro-Austro-Asiatic	Hindi, Punjabi, Urdu, Assamese, Bengali, Gujarathi, Kannada, Kashmiri, Malayalam, Marathi, Oriya, Sanskrit, Sindhi, Tamil, and Telugu
Mien	2	Sino-Tibetan	Mien, Chinese
Hmong	2	Sino-Tibetan	White Hmong, Blue Hmong

Note. Information from *Asian Pacific Islander Cultural Awareness Training*, Fresno County Department of Social Services, 1998, and U.S. Census Bureau, *International Data Base: The World Factbook 1998*, 1997.

Socioeconomic Status of Southeast Asian and South Asian Americans

Unlike most racial groups in America, nearly all SEAAs are refugees from war-torn countries—Vietnam, Laos, and Cambodia. People from Thailand and the South Asian countries—India, Bengal, Nepal, Malaysia, Indonesia, Morocco, and others—are not refugees. Most refugees arrived in the U.S. with little or nothing with which to start new lives. Therefore, most were desperately poor, and many are still poor because of multiple barriers, including language and cultural differences, lack of educational background, inability to learn and speak English, lack of employment skills, and the experience of culture shock. Economically, a large number of SEAA families lag behind the general population, as the 1999 per capita income figures in Table 10.13 demonstrate. The overall per capita income for Asian Americans in 1999 was $21,823, considerably higher than the incomes of any of the five major SEA groups—Vietnamese, Cambodian, Laotian, Thai, and Hmong. Only the Asian Indians, members of a nonrefugee SA group, come close to the overall Asian American per capita figure; in fact, this group surpasses the aggregate figure.

Table 10.12. Similarities Among SEA and SA Languages

Language	Languages with Sound Similarity	Languages with Written Similarity
Vietnamese	None	None
Cambodian	Lao, Thai	None
Lao	Thai, Cambodian	Thai
Thai	Lao, Cambodian	Lao
Hmong	Mien	None
Iu Mien	Hmong	None
Hindi	None	None

Note. Information from *Asian Pacific Islander Cultural Awareness Training*, Fresno County Department of Social Services, 1998.

Among the four refugee groups listed, Vietnamese appear to be the most economically successful, followed by Laotian and Cambodian. Hmong is the poorest group of all.

Table 10.13. Per Capita Income in 1999, by Racial Group

Group	Income
Asian (overall)	$21,823.
Vietnamese	$15,655.
Cambodian	$10,366.
Laotian	$11,830.
Thai	$19,066.
Hmong	$6,600.
Asian Indian	$27,514.

Note. Data from U.S. Census Bureau, *Census 2000 Demographic Profile Highlights*.

Another way to learn more about refugee families is to take a closer look at the number of SEAA and SAA individuals living below poverty level in 2000. The overall proportion of Asian American individuals living below poverty level in 2000 was 11.7%. As indicated in Table 10.14, by this measure, Hmong are still the poorest, as 37.6% live below poverty level; they are followed by Cambodians (29.8%). This ranking may be related to the fact that Hmong have larger family and household sizes than other groups. Cambodian and Hmong families seem to share similar economic struggles in their new homeland. They have high rates of unemployment, lack educational background, have higher numbers of teenage parents, and have many non-English speaking individuals living in the home.

The groups with the smallest proportions living below poverty are Asian Indians (9.3%), Thai (13.8%), and Vietnamese (15.6%). In contrast to Hmong and Cambodians, these groups appear to have a higher rate of employment, more educational background, and smaller family and household sizes.

Table 10.14. Number of People Below Poverty Level in 2000, by Racial Group

Group	Number of People	Total population	Percentage
Asian (overall)	1,200,000	10,200,000	11.7
Vietnamese	175,900	1,122,000	15.6
Cambodian	51,000	171,000	29.8
Laotian	30,600	168,000	18.2
Thai	15,500	112,000	13.8
Hmong	63,600	169,000	37.6
Asian Indian	157,500	1,678,000	9.3

Note. Data from U.S. Census Bureau, *Census 2000 Demographic Profile Highlights.* Numbers are rounded.

Furthermore, based on these statistics, most SEAA families are economically disadvantaged and still struggle to become self-sufficient. Undoubtedly, a myriad of economic factors contribute to their socio-cultural difficulties; however, it is clear that many have not been as fortunate as others and certainly need better educational opportunities in order to gain greater access to economic opportunities. In other words, some SEAA families have achieved socioeconomic success and other have not because of differences in educational levels.

Promoting Academic Achievement for Southeast Asian and South Asian Americans

The U.S. Census Bureau 2000 reported that of the population 25 years and over, nearly 1.5 million SEAA and SAA have received high school diplomas and some higher education, and approximately 882,900 have earned their bachelor's and higher college degrees. For non-Asian Americans, these numbers are small, but for SEAA and SAA groups, they are encouraging and promising.

Like other Asian Americans, SEAAs and SAAs face difficulties in public schools. Their foreign born children and adolescents do not possess middle-class American values when they enter public schools, but their U.S.-born children do. In some cases, foreign-born children appear to fare better than U.S-born children. Some perform well in school, and others do not because of social, psychological, educational, cross-cultural, economic, neurological, and linguistic factors in their daily lives.

Generally speaking, some children of these groups present quite difficult challenges for teachers because of the complex nature of their families' experiences in war-torn countries. These students are linguistically, religiously, economically, and socially diverse. Parents expect them to succeed, but their personal situations often hinder that success. For instance, Hmong parents usually expect their children to achieve good grades and attend college; however, many children have difficulties learning English and are placed in ESL classes where they can easily earn "As" and "Bs." They appear to be doing well, but as they proceed to higher grades, many struggle academically.

To help prospective educators learn more about the academic achievements and successes of SEAAs and SAAs, Table 10.15 illustrates the total numbers of high school and college graduates of each group as reported in 2000 by the U.S Census Bureau. Of all the groups, Thai have the highest proportion of people who received their high school diplomas, followed by Asian Indians and Vietnamese. On the other hand, Asian Indians have the highest proportion of people who earned bachelor or higher degrees, followed by Thai and Vietnamese.

Regardless of differences in education, Hmong have made impressive progress at both high school and college levels of education. The reason for the progress is that public education is relatively new to Hmong both in Laos and in the West. Hmong gained access to public education in Laos in the late 1930s, and Hmong adults and children did not enter U.S. public schools until 1975. In other words, of all the groups, Hmong have had severely limited educational or academic experiences. Only 10% of Hmong parents could read and write when they first came to the U.S. in 1975, whereas other groups had hundreds of years of academic experience in education. Some, such as Vietnamese, Asian Indians, and Thai, were even Westernized.

Table 10.15. Number of People Earning Diploma or Degree in 2000, by Racial Group

Group	High School Diploma or Higher		Bachelor's Degree or Higher		Total Population
	Number	%	Number	%	
Asian Indian	906,400	54	668,000	39	1,678,000
Vietnamese	429,000	38	143,800	13	1,122,000
Thai	62,000	55	30,000	27	112,000
Laotian	43,000	225	6,700	4	168,000
Hmong	21,900	13	4,000	3	169,000
Cambodian	40,200	23	7,900	5	171,000

Note. Data from U.S. Census Bureau, *Census 2000 Demographic Profile Highlights.* Numbers are rounded.

Educators should realize that SEAA and SAA students may be ambivalent, timid, and quiet. However, teachers need to guide them in overcoming these reserved attitudes, which are culturally biased. Otherwise, students' verbal and nonverbal behaviors could be viewed as odd based on middle-class American values. Keep in mind that SEAA and SAA children and adolescents internalize personal feelings rather than vent them. However, if and when they do express their pent-up feelings, they may be viewed by teachers as out-of-control or rebellious students. Rather, they are probably frustrated because no one seems to care about how they feel about their self-concept, self-image, self-esteem, and self-worth.

To promote the academic achievement of SEAA and SAA children and adolescents, educators should consider following actions:

1. Do not wait for students to initiate dialogue.
2. Be open to talk about their feelings.
3. Decode the "I don't care attitude."
4. Respect gender issues.
5. Make sure assignments are clear and understood.
6. Encourage students to ask for help.
7. Focus on the students' needs, not their cultural identities.
8. Use positive reinforcement to break the code of silence.
9. Interpret body language and nonverbal reactions.
10. Create a learning environment that fosters cultural diversity.

11. Use eclectic teaching techniques to engage students.
12. Use differentiating instruction to benefit all.
13. Prescribe cooperative learning.
14. Allow student-centered instruction.
15. Stop using surface level assessment.
16. Eliminate homogenous grouping.
17. Use hands-on and minds-on activities.
18. Use ELD, SDAIE, TESOL, or sheltered English instruction to improve BICS and CALP.
19. Hire bilingual staff or bilingual instructional aides.
20. Use obligatory content standards instead of compatibility content.

Remember, these are suggestions that are also effective with other ethnic students. However, these suggestions do not cover everything that will help English learners learn. Teachers need to address issues involving students appropriately and according to their individual needs. Also, bear in mind that if there is a will, then there is way to deal with linguistically, culturally, and religiously diverse students. In most cases, SEAA and SAA children and adolescents are trained at home to behave courteously, to respect their teachers, to exercise control-self, and to aim high. With this foundation, educators simply need to discipline them academically.

Summing Up

This chapter highlighted the sociocultural characteristics of Southeast Asian American (SEAA) and South Asian American (SAA) children and families to provide prospective educators with some understanding of children who share Southeast Asian and South Asian ancestry. Most SEAA and SAA children and adolescents are relatively new to the American educational system, with the exception of some descendents of SAAs who immigrated to the U.S. before 1975. The immigration status of SEAAs is different from that of SAAs. Most SEAAs are children of war refugees who immigrated to the U.S. after the loss of their native countries in 1975. Most SAAs are children of immigrants who came to the U.S. in search of economic, educational, and other opportunities. Prospective educators should recognize the unique and diverse self-image, self-concept, self-esteem, self-worth, and cultural identities of these groups in order to provide academic curricula and instructional practices that accommodate individual students' needs in order to promote their psychological, cognitive, and social development.

PART THREE

THE AT-RISK STUDENTS' DOMAIN

Chapter Eleven

At-Risk Students in Public Schools

The roots of education are bitter, but the fruit is sweet.

—Aristotle

Overview

Why are so many language-minority students far from academic success and still at-risk in public schools in the 21st century? Costello (1996) and Vang (2001) noted that public schools identify students who are considered at-risk due to socio-cultural issues related to socioeconomic status, poverty, race, ethnicity, language, behavioral problems, low achievement, and other factors. The dilemma is that when these children do not achieve in school, policy makers, educators, and parents disagree about who and what is to blame for their academic underachievement. The number of at-risk students is rising in public schools, and current school curricula needs to be restructured to respond to the pressing academic needs created by student diversity. This chapter explores the socio-cultural issues of students who face a multitude of complex academic problems in public schools to gain more insight into how they become at-risk students. Knowing the characteristics of at-risk students can help teachers identify and address the factors that impact their academic success or lack of success.

The Greatest Influence on Student Learning

Teachers play an important role in all children's education. Prospective educators should believe firmly that every child deserves a good education, and every teacher should be committed to meeting every child's academic needs and providing all with the highest quality learning opportunities in the classroom. Quality teachers who deliver meaningful instruction have great influence on student learning and success. Nearly 54% percent of Americans believe that the greatest influence on student learning is the quality of the teacher, 30% believe the greatest influence is academic standards, and 14%

believe it is achievement tests in core academic subjects (Haselkorn & Harris, as cited in Ryan & Cooper, 2001).

Because teachers have such great influence, they must be willing to change themselves when necessary in order to see changes in the classroom. Understanding research findings involving at-risk students is the first step in applying pedagogical skills in ways that address the needs of at-risk students and assist them so they excel academically. For instance, asking a reflective question, such as why at-risk students are not learning at greater speeds, will inspire teachers to adapt teaching mechanisms to reach all their students. Perhaps asking such questions will motivate teachers to use a flexible teaching style to accommodate diverse learning styles. Of course, there is more than one way to teach students, and not all students learn the same way.

Despite the difficulties children have in school, teachers still hold the key to success. Society holds teachers accountable for being part of either the solution or the problem.

Knowing the Characteristics of Diverse Learners

It is true that not all learners of diverse backgrounds should be straight-A students because people differ in their learning styles, abilities, interests, and comprehension. However, prospective educators should bear in mind that all children should have the opportunity to learn whatever they can, to personally achieve their learning objectives, and to reach their personal learning goals in school. Contemporary students have different learning characteristics that determine their attitudes toward learning, and most importantly, these characteristics contribute to their desire to do well in school. As Heacox (1991) noted, teachers usually know their students belong to one of the two groups characterized in Figure 11.1.

Keep in mind that whether students belong to the achievement group or are trapped in the underachievement cycle, they can all experience the positive rewards of school success, building feelings of personal and academic confidence and competence and succeeding in the academic achievement game (Heacox, 1991). If teachers fail to help them overcome academic failure, the students become at-risk, and they form strong negative feelings about themselves and about school. In some cases, underachievement further leads to continued failure in school and beyond.

Furthermore, many educators are not equipped with the skills and knowledge needed to deal with students with learning disabilities. To help prospective educators understand the basic needs of these students, Mercer and

Pullen (2005) described the behaviors associated with students with language-learning disabilities; these are shown in Table 11.1.

Characteristics of Achievement Group	Characteristics of Underachieving Group
Arrive on time	Late to class
Coming to class prepared	Underprepared
Follow directions	Going off task
Active	Passive
Attentive	Not participating
Enthusiastic	Frustrated
Willing to try	Unsure
Concerned and conscientious	Complacent
Motivated	Irresponsible
Well-organized	Poor risk taker
A self-starter	Procrastinating
Task-oriented	Daydreaming
Goes the extra mile	Defensive
Confident	Distracted
Competitive	Bored
Adaptive and flexible	Have irritated behaviors

Figure. 11.1. Characteristics of diverse learners
Note. Information from *Up from Under-Achievement: How Teachers, Students, and Parents Can Work Together to Promote Student Success,* by D. Heacox, 1991, Minneapolis, MN: Free Spirit Publishing.

Keep in mind that students with learning disabilities often have characteristics other than those listed in Table 11.1. They may be emotionally disturbed or have motor problems, perceptual deficits, attention deficits, memory disorders, conduct disorders, social perceptual disorders, and more (McNamara, 2007). Without understanding these characteristics of diverse learners, prospective educators could make mistakes, labeling students as at-risk for many reasons other than their disabilities.

More Language-Minority Students in Schools

America is a multilingual and multicultural nation rich in cultural diversity. Today, language-minority students comprise one of the fastest-growing segments of the total student population in America, a culturally and linguistically diverse group. In Fiscal Year 2003-2004, nearly 5.2 million limited English proficient students were enrolled in public schools (Batalova, 2006).

Table 11.1. Behavior Characteristics of Students with Language-Learning Disabilities

Behavior	Characteristic	Possible Cause
Peer relations	Poor	Being a loner or playing alone
Adjustment to change	Poor	Easily upset or confused
Perseveration	Persistent	Spending too much time on a task
Emotional control	Poor	Easily angered or emotional
Dealing with frustration	Poor	Stamping foot or sulking
Asking for assistance	Poor	Sitting quietly or delaying assistance
Communication in general	Poor	Reserved, quiet, or self-centered
Physical comfort	Excessive	Need hugs, touches, or comfort from others
Hyperactivity	Excessive movement	Problems settling down
Learning style	Variable performance	Doing well on one task and poorly on the other
Task completion	Poor	Starting a task but cannot finish it on time
Maturity level	Immature	Behaving below age level
Learning new concepts	Poor or reduced vocabulary	Understanding issues and prefers the use of object labels
Responding to question	Delay or need wait time	Requiring extra time to process thought
Situational behaviors	Inappropriate and funny	Laughing or talking to self
Dealing with dysnomia	Unable to recall words	Difficult time recalling needed words
General attitude	Impulsive	Responding without thinking through
Following directions	Poor, unable to follow	Need to be told to behave

Note. Information from *Students with Learning Disabilities* (6th ed.), by C. D. Mercer & C. P. Pullen, 2005, Upper Saddle River, NJ: Merrill/Prentice Hall.

According to a report by the National Education Association, nearly 425 dialects are spoken by public school students each and every school day (Flannery, 2006). In California, approximately 80% of limited English proficient students (LEP) speak Spanish and the other 20% speak Vietnamese, Hmong, Cantonese, Tagalog, and other languages, as shown in Table 11.2. More than 100 languages are spoken daily by the children in California's public schools. In Los Angeles County alone, approximately 114 different languages are spoken by public school students.

Table 11.2. Top Five Non-English Primary Languages of California Public School Students

Language	Number of Students	Percentage of Enrollment
Spanish	1,341,000	21.3
Vietnamese	34,200	.5
Hmong	21,900	.3
Filipino (Tagalog)	21,400	.3
All other groups	129,600	2.1

Note. Information from: http:// www.schoolmatters.com: California Department of Education, 2005-2006.

Moreover, of the 6 million students enrolled in California public schools, approximately 1.5 million are LEP students. At least 38% of the students in public schools in the U.S. belong to an ethnic minority, and a large portion of this group comes from a language-disadvantaged family. Zehr (2000) projected that in 25 years, one in every four elementary students will be Hispanic because Hispanics constitute the nation's largest racial minority. Moreover, 58% of the nation's LEP student population were born in America, and of that number, 74% are from a Hispanic background (Manning & Baruth, 2004). For example, in California's Stanislaus County, 50 different languages are spoken at home by students; in Fresno County the number is 66, and in Santa Barbara County it is 54. These numbers illustrate the rich cultural diversity in the state's and the nation's public schools.

A large number of language-minority students in public schools are classified by the school as at-risk for facing language and cultural barriers. Place of birth of students and of their parents is a significant factor in the potential at-risk status of students. However, merely being born in the U.S. does not necessarily lessen the risk. Batalova (2006) noted that nearly 64% of LEP students are U.S.-born and 40% are foreign-born.

Immigration status also affects academic performance. The foreign-born children of foreign-born parents account for nearly 36% of the total LEP student population, the U.S.-born children of foreign-born parents account for 42%, and U.S.-born children of U.S.-born parents account for 22% (Batalova, 2006).

Classification of students as at-risk or LEP may not be an accurate portrayal of every student so designated. The classifications may be based on a sorting paradigm or surface level assessment that is not appropriate or precise. Once sorted, some students receive instruction based on high expectations and others are relegated to lower quality education and lower quality futures (North Central Regional Educational Laboratory [NCREL], 1999).

Tracking of Students Not for Academic Purposes

Traditionally, LEP students are tracked into substandard courses of study in meaningless programs holding little or no expectations for learning (NCREL, 1999). By federal mandate, public schools are required to classify language-minority students as LEP or fluent English proficient (FEP) following an initial assessment process. California uses the California English Language Development Test (CELDT) to measure English proficiency in second-language learners. LEP students are classified according to five English-Language Development (ELD) levels: Level I (pre-production), Level II (early production), Level III (speech emergence), Level IV (intermediate fluency), and Level V (advanced). However, since 2006, ELD standards in California use the following five basic categories to classify English proficiency: Beginning, Early Intermediate, Intermediate, Early Advanced, and Advanced. Table 11.3 gives descriptions of each of these levels.

Public schools sometimes offer LEP students primary language instruction, bilingual tutoring services, English language development or specifically designed academic instruction in English, or bilingual instructional assistance. Most public schools are more likely to classify language-minority students as LEP than FEP and place them in three main categories: (a) students identified by school districts as limited English proficient, (b) students who were foreign-born and entered public schools for the first time in the U.S. but learned English quickly, and (c) adolescents who were foreign-born and came to America between the ages of 11 and 18. Sedlacek and Kim (1995) stated that the labeling of bilingual students is often done for social control; they called the practice "the quest for the golden label" because public schools sometimes misuse the label to "solve" academic problems.

As a result of the school's inability to deal with these students' diverse needs and abilities, a large number of bilingual students fall into the at-risk category, and furthermore, their cultural and linguistic backgrounds put them at a disadvantage in the American educational system and place them in a position in which school, second-language learning, academic achievement, and cross-cultural adjustment can be difficult. Miranda, Halsell, and Debarone (1991) reported demographic statistics that indicated that at risk students are usually poor and of ethnic minority status. Similarly, Horn, Chen, and Adelman (1998) found that risk factors for academic difficulties often correlated highly with a student's gender, race, and socioeconomic status. These authors listed six personal risk factors: low socio-economic measurement, single parent family, family history of dropout, mobility, average grades of "C" or lower, and repeating an earlier grade.

Table 11.3. CELDT Proficiency Levels

Level	Basic Descriptions with Unmodified Instruction
Beginning	Presenting little or no receptive or productive English skills, understand a few concrete details, respond to some communication and learning demands, have many errors, oral and written production is limited, and have difficulties communicating in English.
Early intermediate	Developing receptive and productive skills, being able to identify or understand concrete details, making fewer errors, oral and written production is limited to phrases, and having frequent errors in communicating in English.
Intermediate	Beginning to tailor with English skills, meeting communication and learning demands, understanding more concrete details or major abstracts, responding to questions, making fewer errors, oral and written production expands to sentences and paragraphs, and having some complicated communication in English.
Early advanced	Understanding complex details, being able to use English in content area learning, identifying and summarizing in details, having elaborating discourse, being able to write full paragraphs and composition, and making fewer errors and having rare complicated communication.
Advanced	Being able to communicate effectively with peers, attaining proficiency at level of native speaking students, being able to summarize in details, oral and written production reflects discourse appropriate, having competence in learning all content areas, and making fewer errors without reducing communication in English.

Note. Information from http://www.cde.ca.gov/ta/tg/el/documents.

What Types of Students Are At-Risk?

Academically, the term *at-risk* is still controversial and is not new to some experienced classroom teachers; however, the meaning and implications of the term may be relatively new to some teachers who may not know how to deal with students so identified. The National Institute for the Education of At-Risk Students (1998) reported that many students were at risk of educational failure because of limited English proficiency, poverty, economic disadvantage, or specific race or geographic location. The institute cited many definitions of the term *at-risk,* some based on economic and cultural characteristics. Some of the definitions were based on an ecological view of educational risk, systemic failure, or the inequity of access to educational opportunity and academic achievement.

Researchers have found that at-risk students come from every part of the community and have varied needs (Barr & Parrett, 1995; Lange and Lehr, 1999). Lee-Pierce, Plowman, and Touchston (1998) observed that not all children have a childhood filled with a variety of experiences and not all begin school with a library of knowledge or pre-reading or science skills. These authors suggested that children raised in poverty are especially at-risk.

Wright (1997) and Tugent (1986) described an at-risk student as an individual who was chemically dependent, a dropout, suicidal, either sexually active or pregnant in the teenage years, or alcoholic. Brown (1986) defined an at-risk student as someone in one of the following categories: chronically truant, underachiever, troublemaker, economically disadvantaged, poor student, minority young person, runaway, delinquent, unemployed teen, or lacking motivation to do well in school or work (p. 13).

Brown (1986) proposed two definitions for *at-risk.* The first considered an individual's background, social, and emotional characteristics. The second was based on problematic behaviors, including low grades, skipping classes, disruptive actions, underachievement, and lack of academic progress. Brown suggested that behavioral traits were crucial in identifying at-risk students. Moreover, Brown confirmed that the term *at-risk* was normally applied to students rather than children in general, since educational institutions commonly use the term *at-risk* to predict students' academic success or failure.

Dougherty (1989) defined as at-risk those students who, for a variety of reasons, did not perform well in school and were likely to drop out. Slavin, Karweit, and Madden (1989) widened the definition to take in those students who were in danger of dropping out or leaving school without adequate skills. The term *at-risk* has also been applied to students with a high probability of school failure or learning problems.

Siu (1996) observed that *at-risk* was not synonymous with dropping out; some high school students graduate but have inadequate academic competencies. Siu noted that many Asian American students do not drop out, but quietly fail in school. Siu also expressed concern regarding the number of Asian American students who leave school with less than adequate proficiency in English. Siu cautioned that researchers, school districts, and state agencies define *at-risk* differently, each having its own operational definition of the term. This creates difficulty when comparing academic statistics and research data on at-risk students.

Typically, inside the classroom, educators identify at-risk students according to one of five different approaches:

1. In the achievement approach, an at-risk student is one with two or more failing semester course grades.
2. In the age approach, an at-risk student is one who is 2 or more years older than grade-level peers.
3. In the attendance approach, a student is at-risk who misses more than 20% of required classes.
4. In the discipline approach, an at-risk student has one or more school suspensions.
5. In the transiency approach, a student who moves three or more times in one school year is at-risk.

Furthermore, some classroom teachers feel that language-minority students are more likely to be at-risk because they lack the academic language needed for performing academic tasks in school.

Language-Minority Students Lack Language Skills

The current school system is not designed or prepared to serve, deal with, and educate students of color who have a multitude of cultural and language barriers. Clearly, the system is made for students who have American middle-class values and come from similar cultural backgrounds. Therefore, most language minority students are at a disadvantage in school.

At the outset of their formal education, when language-minority students first enter the public school system, they usually lack the academic background, English skills, and appropriate learning styles needed for school success. Public schools face a multitude of challenges with these students because appropriate placement and instructional methods are not always in place to meet their academic needs. Language deficiency is generally the biggest handicap, and the lack of language skills leads to low scholastic achievement, low test scores, and credit deficiencies. Furthermore, language-minority students face difficult social challenges in the classroom because they speak one language at home and must function in a new language at school.

English speaking ability alone is not a sufficient language condition for academic success. Researchers have linked academic underachievement to the lack of academic language (Cummins, 1981; Kuehn, 1996; Stotsky, 1979; Wright, 1997). The nature of academic language is still a subject of debate among linguists, researchers, and scholars, but most experts, educators, and scholars agree that academic language is a distinct type of communication used in textbooks and classrooms (Wright). Students who are unfamiliar with it or fail to develop it, these educators say, could be academically at-risk. In most cases, second-language learners have difficulty with academic language. As Kuehn and Wright observed, acquisition of academic language is vital regardless of a student's native language or cultural background.

Importance of Academic Language

Cummins (1981) distinguished between cognitive academic language proficiency (CALP)—language used for critical thinking and reasoning—and basic interpersonal communication skills (BICS)—language used for conversational purposes. He explained that academic language is context-reduced in nature and conversational language is context-embedded in nature. In context-reduced circumstances, students do not have situational or paralinguistic cues, but they think and reason based solely on comprehension of a situation. In context-embedded scenarios, students are able to enhance situational and paralinguistic cues through a variety of means: body language, speech intonation, sequence of events, meaning, understanding of phrases, and interpretation.

Similarly, Stotsky (1979) suggested that academic language refers to the language of mature, expository prose or the formal English in college textbooks. Stotsky characterized language as academic strictly on the basis of its linguistic features: abstract vocabulary, noun forms, verb forms, Latin/or Greek vocabulary roots, and other grammatical elements.

Academic language has unique language functions and structures that are difficult for language learners to master. Although the research on academic language is still very limited, scholars agree on the language functions of academic language: seeking information, analyzing, comparing, classifying, predicting, justifying, hypothesizing, persuading, solving problems, synthesizing, evaluating, generalizing, and abstracting (O'Malley, 1992; Wright, 1997). Students must be able to perform these functions and thus need academic language in order to achieve academically.

In 1993, the U.S. Department of Labor reported that elementary LEP students take at least 3 to 5 years to acquire English skills for social settings equal to those of their peers (American Council on Education, 1994). These same students require a minimum of 4 to 7 years to attain grade norms in academic English. The Department concluded that the lack of academic language is a major reason for academic failure among language-minority students and a major factor contributing to high dropout rates among these students.

Similarly, Thomas and Collier (1997) reported that the academic learning process will typically take U.S.-born bilingual school students who are achieving on grade level in their native language 4 to 7 years to make it to the 50th Normal Curve Equivalent (NCE) in English. For foreign-born, advantaged immigrant students with 2 to 5 years of schooling in their home country who were on grade level in their native language usually take at least 5 to 7 years to reach the 50th NCE in English when schooled in the U.S. Most importantly, these scholars suggested that the majority of students do not even make it to the 50th NCE without the support of native language academic and cognitive development at home.

Furthermore, a study on the academic language of college-bound at-risk secondary students exploring self-assessment, proficiency levels, and effects of language development instruction found the following characteristics among the at-risk students (Wright, 1997):

- The problems faced by at-risk secondary students were complex and often related to academic achievement in ways that were not under anyone's control.
- Lack of academic language proficiency was related to low academic achievement in high school.
- Students were generally under-prepared in the area of academic language.
- The development of academic vocabulary was necessary for good reading comprehension and writing.
- Academic language skills were generally not strongly related to grades in high school.
- Grades included elements of effort and persistence and were not reliable measures of language proficiency or academic achievement for LEP students.

Placement of ELLs Is Still a Problem

According to the NCREL (1999), the majority of at-risk students attend public schools, where they receive daily instructions from several different teachers who may or may not have proper teaching credentials. This kind of instruction arouses negative feelings in students, and many students taught in this manner tend to alienate themselves from their teachers and peers. The negative feelings and alienation exacerbate disciplinary and behavioral problems.

Findings such as these suggest that LEP students should be placed in primary-language instruction classrooms with primary-language teachers or bilingual teachers who have cross-cultural, language, and academic development (CLAD) or bilingual cross-cultural, language, and academic development (BCLAD) teaching credentials. However, a review of school practices prior to and after the passage of Proposition 227 in California, the "English-Only Instruction Initiative," revealed that many LEP students were placed in classrooms with teachers who did not have proper credentials or did not speak a second language. In California, approximately 30% of LEP students were in a bilingual program without a bilingual teacher. Approximately 70% of these students received no formal primary language instruction in academics, and approximately 25% of LEP students received no special services at all.

The NCREL (1999) described how a student is placed and tracked as at-risk in the school system:

> Students are placed at risk when they experience a significant mismatch between their circumstances and needs and the capacity or willingness of the school to accept, accommodate, and respond to them in a manner that supports and enables their maximum social, emotional, and intellectual growth and development. As the degree of mismatch increases, so does the likelihood that they will fail to either complete their elementary and secondary education, or more importantly, to benefit from it in a manner that ensures they have the knowledge, skills, and dispositions necessary to be successful in the next stage of their lives . . . that is, to successfully pursue post-secondary education, training, or meaningful employment and to participate in, and contribute to, the social, economic, and political life of their community and society as a whole. (p. 2)

Shockingly, researchers have found that LEP students, who require greater resources than English proficient students, are sometimes placed in classrooms with less qualified teachers, where expectations are lower, curriculum is watered down, and fewer classroom materials are available (Cooper, 2000; Hubbard & Mehan, 1999; Oakes, 1992). In contrast, White students are placed in high-track classrooms in disproportionately high numbers and receive more qualified teachers, greater classroom resources, and an enriched curriculum designed to prepare them to attend college (Hubbard & Mehan; Oakes, Gamoran, & Page, 1992). In some cases, placement becomes a tracking system.

Keep in mind that homogeneous grouping and heterogeneous clustering are not the most effective methods for teaching LEP students. School officials often characterize low achieving students as those whose cognitive structures have gaps in fundamental knowledge. School personnel should keep in mind, however, that language-minority students from different cultural backgrounds and sub-ethnic groups cannot be categorized by the same criteria as native-speaker students. They have different repertoires, learning styles, socioeconomic status, academic backgrounds, and cultural/language barriers.

Tracking Creates Unequal Access to Schooling

Segregation is legal and is commonly practiced in public schools today. The public education system remains separate and unequal despite extensive desegregation efforts over the past 50 years (Cooper, 1999; Darling-Hammond, 1995; Steele, 1992). Even though schools have achieved success with racial integration, many remain stratified by race and social class (Oakes, 1990; Schofield, 1991). The segregation of students in racially mixed schools is the result of tracking or grouping students by perceived abilities or surface level assessment (Oakes, 1990; Orfield, 1993; Wells & Grain, 1994). For instance, Table 11.4 lists the redesignation criteria used by public schools to track LEP students in the ELD programs.

Table 11.4. Criteria Used for Redesignation of LEP Students

Criteria	Examples of Required Activities
"C" average grade	Maintain a "C" average grade in all subject matter or classes.
Teacher evaluation and recommendation	Classroom teachers assess student progress periodically and write a recommendation for reassessment by the district.
Reassessment	The district reassesses the student's proficiency in English after receiving teacher's recommendation.
36th percentile scores on CST	Score at least in the 36th percentile or higher on the CST in all tested areas; otherwise, ineligible for redesignation despite meeting all other criteria.
Parental approval	Parents need to approve the redesignation from LEP to FEP after all other criteria are met.

Note. Information from *Histories and Academic Profiles of Successful and Unsuccessful Hmong Secondary Students*, by C. T. Vang, 2001, unpublished doctoral dissertation, University of California, Davis and California State University, Fresno.

These criteria are being used as secret weapons to keep LEP students in ELD programs for years. In most cases, the only criterion most LEP students fail to meet is the requirement of 36th percentile test scores on CST in all tested areas. Such tracking produces gross inequities.

Moreover, African American, Hispanic, and other language-minority students, placed in lower tracked classes in disproportionately high numbers, systematically receive fewer resources than their peers. Even though the merits of tracking continue to be debated, school segregation remains widespread, and an alarming number of students are at risk of school failure. Both parents and educators are extremely concerned about special education segregation in public schools because 70% of special education students are African American.

Sanders (2004) expressed her concerns about the practice of academic segregation:

> There is a disproportionate number of black children in special education, especially the black males, because it's easier to push them into special education and label them learning disabled than it is to work with them....Part of the problem is that those making the designation may not understand the black culture. Often, these decisions are culturally biased. (p. 9)

Researchers have suggested that tracking creates class and race-linked differences in learning and is a major contributor to the persistent achievement gap between disadvantaged and affluent students and the gap between students of color and Caucasians (Cooper, 1999; Oakes, 1992). According to a 2004 report from the California Teacher Association, the widening achievement gap in California's public schools raises many questions about educational equality. The report indicates that in 1990, the gap between the scores of Black and White students on the National Assessment of Educational Programs mathematics test at the eighth-grade level was 33 points, and by 2000, the gap had grown to 39 points. Similarly, Latino students were 28 points behind White students in 1990 and 33 points behind a decade later. In 2003, of the fourth- and eighth-grade students tested, African American and Latino students were found to perform, on average, 3 years behind their White counterparts in math and language arts.

McLaren (1998) noted that tracking fosters "the illusion of meritocratic competition while in reality it functions as a ranking system that legitimates differences based on race, gender, and social power and locks students into positions of limited opportunities" (p. 9).

Ogbu (1978) characterized this practice and the school organization that implements it as a type of caste system. Similarly, Dayton, Ruby, Stein, and Weisberg (1992) and Shorr and Horn (1997) described the educational system as a caste system that permeates every facet of student learning, academic performance, and school failure. They cited as evidence the following:

- The system tracks students by ability, thereby reinforcing and exacerbating social and class stereotyping.
- Size and impersonality of classes increase in high school.
- Low expectations are held for students who are not accepted culturally.
- Uninspiring curricula are offered that lack academic rigor and fail to develop skills students need after high school.
- Narrow vocational training is offered for jobs with little future.
- LEP students are not offered a successful transition into mainstream education.

Reyes and Jason (1993) observed that educational support for language learners is generally pulled out too soon, leaving these students with superficial skills because the public schools use different instructional methods for bilingual students. Although the goal for LEP students is to become proficient in English, some instructional methods are appropriate for reaching this goal and others are not. For instance, a Transitional Bilingual Education (TBE) program appears to be geared toward the academic standards and content area standards required for specific grade levels; however, other programs are taught based on content-compatibility language, not content-obligatory language (Lessow-Hurley, 2000).

Academic Gap Is Based on Socio-Academic Framework

Moreover, the academic gap between White students and students of color has pretty much remained the same over the last 2 decades. As long as the public school system continues to use norm-referenced tests to measure student learning, the gap will widen and eventually become meaningless. The California Teacher Association reported that the academic gap in public schools is widening as a result of family poverty, and schools with the lowest test scores are filled primarily with minority students living in poverty (Sanders, 2004).

However, the problem is compounded by the fact that public schools with minority students tend to have a greater percentage of teachers on emergency permits and high teacher turnover (Sanders). Family poverty is not the sole reason for the academic gap; schools with predominantly diverse minority students tend to have few minority teachers to whom they can relate and view as role models. The lack of minority teachers means that many of the teachers working in urban schools may not have sufficient training in poverty and race issues relative to academic responsibilities to work effectively with students of diverse backgrounds.

Need New Approaches to Working with Diverse Students

To improve instruction to at-risk students, teachers should consider using a variety of instructional and assessment approaches that accommodate a wide range of students' learning capacities, learning styles, and multiple intelligences. The fundamental approach to developing a culturally sensitive pedagogy is to empower ethnically diverse students through academic success, cultural affiliation, and personal efficacy (Manning & Baruth, 2004). It is very important for teachers to realize that some instructional practices may inhibit academic achievement in language-minority students. Any instruction needs to be prescribed with careful consideration of the learners; otherwise, learning can be cognitively undemanding and not academically relevant. In addition, if teachers are to provide effective, culturally responsive pedagogy, they ought to understand how ethnically diverse students learn and acquire a new language.

For instance, the English as a Second Language (ESL) methodology was developed primarily to teach English to university students rather than at secondary and elementary levels. However, the ESL methodology became prevalent in the public school system when a large influx of Indo-Chinese refugees and European immigrants arrived in the United States during the early 1960s to the late 1970s. The ESL guidelines at that time included a sheltered English methodology and content instruction in the student's primary language. The content instruction was used to teach new concepts in subject matter in a comprehensive manner and help students earn academic credits required for graduation. However, the tradition of bilingual curriculum and instruction was organized around subjects, or disciplines, and the subjects were presented as separate entities using facts and skills that were disconnected, fragmented, and disjointed (Del Vecchio et al., 1994). As McQueen (1999) explained:

> Poor students are not getting the same challenging schoolwork as other children, despite a federal law designed to bridge the learning gap between the haves and have-nots. Under the $8 billion federal program, the U.S. Department of Education gives states money to raise the historically low achievement levels of poor and other disadvantaged children. For years, many schools dumbed down the curriculum for poor children, believing such children couldn't be expected to do the same schoolwork as peers who didn't face the troubles they did. (p. A5)

In the late 1990s, ESL and content instruction methodologies were replaced by the ELD approach, which helps language learners improve language skills in reading, writing, and comprehension. ELD instruction helps students develop vocabulary skills that enhance their understanding of academic concepts. ELD is used to improve comprehension and speaking vocabulary (BICS), whereas content instruction and bilingual methods are used to develop academic language proficiency (CALP).

In 1994, California passed Senate Bill 1969 that authorized public school teachers to provide specially designed content instruction. This was done in response to the growing number of English learners. The law required teachers to have special training in order to be certified to teach ELD. More importantly, the law required that public schools provide specifically designed academic instruction in English (SDAIE) to English learners. The ELD and SDAIE methods are sheltered instructions and have been used in a variety of ways in dual-language instruction and other bilingual program models, including primary language instruction, whole language teaching, phonics instruction, and second language instruction, as shown in Tables 11.5 and 11.6. ELD and SDAIE lesson plans cannot be implemented without scaffolding techniques because hands-on and minds-on activities require bridging, contextualization, modeling, metacognitive development, and schema building, as illustrated in Table 11.7 (p. 227).

Starting in 2009, as required by the teacher performance assessment (TPA) in California, most teacher preparation programs require prospective educators to know how to use academic adaptations to teach and assess English learners and students with special needs in the classroom. For instance, teachers must learn what instructional strategies and student activities they will use to monitor progress and assess student learning. The academic adaptation process must include the following:

1. Identify two or more specific learning needs to focus on.
2. Identify challenging issues for the student.
3. Analyze student learning needs to overcome instructional challenges.
4. Design specific adaptation to meet learning needs.
5. How to use adaptation to monitor progress toward learning goal.
6. Monitor progress toward the development of English proficiency.
7. Use specific assessment to monitor progress toward the learning goal.
8. Give teaching rationale for choosing specific monitoring progress.
9. Steps to facilitate the process of English language development.
10. What would the teacher consider doing different next time?

Table 11.5. Example of Specially Designed Academic Instruction in English Lesson Plan

Procedural Process	Key Concepts	Examples of Activity
Title: Subject area: Grade level: Date: Time:	Create or choose a title for the lesson Science 4th grade December 12, 2009 15-30 minutes	Where do animals find food to eat? Life science.
Grade-level content area standard	4th grade life science, standard 2a. Food chain or food web	Introduce students to food chain or food web.
ELD levels: __Beginning __ Early intermediate __ Intermediate __Early advanced __Advanced	Choose ELD level to focus on, even though not all students are at the same level.	For 4th grade science, the lesson should be appropriate for intermediate level; however, take the lesson from concept to concrete approach.
ELD standards linkage	4th grade, ELD 1.2 or 4.1.	Vocabulary building and writing sentences.
Learning objective	List one specific objective or outcome.	Students will learn about basic food chain or food web and create a food chain using plants, animals, and people.
Key concepts	Herbivores, carnivores, omnivores, decomposers, producers, and consumers	Ask students to give examples for each group or write a sentence about each group.
Materials or resources	Video, handouts, worksheet, transparencies, books, crayons, markers, and posters.	Prepare hands-on activity for students to do in class with these materials.
Prior knowledge	Engagement, prompt, props, and intriguing questions.	Tap background knowledge into lesson and learning objective.
Procedures or steps	List specific steps for instruction: Preview, review, share, and then move into lesson plan.	What is food chain? What is food web? What is the difference between the two?

Table continues on next page

Table 11.5, continued

Procedural Process	Key Concepts	Examples of Activity
Scaffolding activities: 1. **Modeling** 2. **Bridging** 3. **Contextualization** 4. **Schema building** 5. **Representation of text** 6. **Metacognitive development** 7. **Summative assessment** 8. **Alternative assessment**	Follow scaffolding techniques and procedural process.	Give and provide students with examples according to each step and follow through.
Independent practice	Use book or computer for in class assignment and use worksheet for homework assignment.	Select a specific area for further practice: Creating a more complex food chain.
Reflection or reteaching	What is fun? What do students like best? Any changes?	Revise lesson plan and include new ideas for next time.

The process for dealing with students with special needs is similar; however, academic adaptation requires in-depth knowledge about specific learning disabilities of individual students included in the student profile.

LEP Students Need Quality Instruction

In 2006, the American Institute of Research (AIR) made the astonishing discovery that quality instruction is not based on the language of instruction but on the quality of instruction that language-minority students receive in the classroom. Keep in mind that regardless of academic plans and approaches, the number of ethnic and language-minority students in public schools continues to grow at a steady rate. Primary language instruction has failed to develop in students the academic vocabulary, understanding of concepts, cultural knowledge, and learning of abstract ideas of the English curriculum and textbooks; therefore, the transition to English has been a difficult hurdle for LEP students (Wright, 1997). Learning a second language is severely hampered when the transfer of literacy skills and knowledge from the first to the second language does not occur. This means that LEP students have problems reading and writing in English because the primary language instruction they received is not conducive to such learning.

Table 11.6. Example of English Language Development (ELD) Instruction Lesson Plan

Procedural Process	Key Concepts	Examples of Activity
Title: Grade level: ELD levels: __Beginning __Early intermediate __Intermediate __Early advanced __Advanced Date: Time:	Volcano Eruption 4th grade Choose an ELD level December 10, 2009 15-30 minutes	What causes volcanoes to erupt? Lesson is appropriate for grade level and learning ability level of ELD students. Instruction is in English without primary support (L1). Use thematic unit or 2-3 days lesson plan.
ELD standards	4th grade, ELD 1.2 or 4.1	Choose one appropriate language arts standard.
Content area standards	Link to other content area standards	Science or language arts.
Learning objective	List one specific objective or outcome.	Students will learn about volcano eruption.
Key concepts or vocabulary:	Magma, larva, eruption, explosion, temperature, fire, burning, gas, and fire.	List all vocabulary on the board and recite words and definitions with students.
Materials or resources	Video, handouts, worksheet, transparencies, books, crayons, markers, and posters.	Prepare hands-on and minds-on activities for students to do in class.
Prior knowledge	Engagement, prompt, props, and intriguing questions.	Ask students to share about volcano eruption before tapping into lesson.
Reflection or reteaching	What is fun? What do students like best? Any changes?	Revise lesson plan and include new ideas for next time.

Table 11.7. Scaffolding Techniques

Procedural process	Key Concepts	Examples of Activities
Modeling	Showing, demonstration, illustration, process, overhead projector, and examples.	Use step-by-step process to introduce key concepts to students.
Bridging	Prior knowledge, experience, tapping into, engagement, and prompt.	Ask thought-provoking questions to engage students before tapping them into the lesson.
Contextualization	Manipulatives, pictures, gestures, regalia, posters, visual aids.	Show students pictures, drawings, or books. Make visual connection.
Schema building	Clustering, grouping, mapping, interconnection, graphic organizers, compare, contrast, and classify.	Group students into groups, pairs, and centers for specific instruction or hands-on activities.
Representation of text	Retelling, recitation, repetition, asking, and sharing.	Review key concepts with students to make sure they understand learning expectation.
Metacognitive development	Process of thinking, solution, conclusion, and solving problems.	Use writing to increase thought process to describe what they have just learned or observed; no right or wrong answers.
Summative assessment	Evaluation, closure, testing, worksheet, independent practices, and reviews.	Recap learning objective with students, check for understanding, or complete worksheet independently.
Alternative assessment	Teacher-made test, group work, project, authentication, and performance.	Journal entries, writing sentences, defining words, or spelling test.

Language-minority students need to have English skills if they are to compete academically in the regular course of studies. Fluency in the primary language may not be necessary in later grades. Furthermore, researchers have found that the listening proficiency of English learners is about 80% of the proficiency of native-language speakers, and their writing and reading proficiencies in English are below 50% of those of native-language speakers (August & Hakuta, 1997). Table 11.8 gives some examples of sheltered strategies teachers can use to better deal with language-minority students in the mainstream classroom.

Table 11.8. Sheltered Strategies

Strategic Approaches	Examples of Activities
Seating arrangement	Seating language-minority students or at-risk students close to the teacher to keep them engaged at all times.
Peer support system	Using buddy system, cross-age peers, same-age peers, and cooperative learning to motivate students.
Controlling the rate of speech	Using expanded language or descriptive terms, slowing down, and applying multiple modes of communication.
BICS	Recognizing BICS in students to promote interaction and communication with peers.
CALP	Recognizing the development of CALP to monitor student progress and to assess student learning accordingly.
Kinetic involvement or hands-on activities	Using the five senses—sight, touch, taste, smell, and hearing—with visual aids, regalia, manipulatives, pictures, KWL charts, and graphic organizers.
Prior knowledge or background tapping	Connecting learning tasks to real-life experiences.
PQ5R's	Using preview, question, reading, reflection, recitation, review, and response to engage students at all levels.

Weslander and Stephany (1983) evaluated an ESL program and concluded that instruction in the English language was most effective during the first year of exposure to the language; they recommended that the amount of instruction decrease thereafter. Teaching academic English is crucial for helping second-language learners improve English skills. However, there is no uniformity in bilingual instruction in California's public schools.

Public schools have been criticized for the whole language approach to language learning ever since California students taught with the whole language approach had the lowest standardized test scores in the nation (Stein, 1995; Wright, 1997). Ferris (1996) and Stein observed that changes were being suggested to return language teaching to instruction in basic skills such as phonics because of the concern that the whole language approach does not use textbooks in the early grades. Students taught with this method are therefore not exposed to expository text until they face the difficult transition of needing to use textbooks for content learning in later grades. With whole language instruction, students failed to learn critical items in early grades, such as vocabulary, complex sentence structures, and academic language. Even though vocabulary knowledge is the single strongest predictor of reading comprehension scores and academic success, it was, with whole language instruction, "a long-neglected area of language instruction in both elementary and secondary contexts" (Wright, 1997, p. 26).

Detrack Language-Minority Students

For years, the school system has tracked language-minority students, offering them severely limited opportunities to learn what is needed to go beyond elementary and secondary schools (Oakes, 1990; Vang, 2001). It is time to call for a detracking system because language-minority students deserve better opportunities to acquire the skills and learn the information needed for academic tasks. Furthermore, the process called re-designation (reclassification from LEP to FEP) has been a real barrier for language-minority students; it is the most difficult hurdle an LEP student has to overcome in K-12 schools. Most LEP students cannot meet the requirements to be re-designated from LEP to FEP or to get out of the system schools use to place them in a low-level track year after year.

Each school has a master plan for providing educational services to LEP students. The Fresno Unified School District's (1995) master plan illustrates how difficult it is for many LEP students to advance through the levels of language proficiency. The plan lists five sources of data the district uses as the bases for making decisions about re-designation to a new language proficiency level: (a) data from an objective assessment of the student's English oral language proficiency, (b) a teacher's evaluation of the student's English language proficiency and academic grades of "C" or better on the student's report card, (c) a writing sample appropriate for grade level, (d) a record of the student's academic achievement on a standardized achievement test (at or above the 36th percentile in all tested areas), and (e) a record of approval from parents or guardians for re-designation. In some cases, bilingual students are trapped in a particular designation for as long as 4 to 6 years because public schools are inconsistent in monitoring and evaluating student progress (Loide, 1994).

In one study, Vang (2001) found that most bilingual students are lumped together at ELD V and are not re-designated because they do not meet all criteria for re-designation. As a result, language-minority students are academically at risk, lacking the language skills needed for academic success. Some LEP students remain in their initial ELD placements as long as they stay in school. In fact, not all schools have ELD programs and curricular activities. Moreover, many LEP students are never reclassified as FEP even after several years of education in U.S. public schools. Consequently, those LEP students who are not re-designated sometimes are required by school policy to repeat ELD classes in order to remain in bilingual education programs. School leaders and administrators should be urged to reexamine the re-designation process; otherwise, the tracking system will continue to bar bilingual students from entering mainstream classes and will set them up for failure.

Stop Using Watered Down Curricula for ELLs

It is evident that some language-minority students are at a greater risk for academic failure than others because they receive an impoverished curriculum and are subject to standardized testing for which the curriculum does not prepare them. The degree of risk also depends on where they live and what schools they attend. In recent years, research and political agendas drove public school policies; however, at the present time, standardized testing drives public school policy and the Academic Performance Index (API) is used to allocate funds.

Most public schools now operate under measurement-driven curricula. In other words, schools are tailoring their instruction to meet state requirements for monetary incentives rather than focusing on the needs of students in the classroom. In addition, state educational budgets are shrinking and educational services are being cut to meet fiscal demands. More testing and less funding for educational programs have divided school services and created new forms of school segregation, separating poor and affluent schools. This budgetary instability leaves many language learners at risk in the educational system because teachers are unable to deliver what is necessary to help them excel academically. This means that the academic gap is getting wider while public schools struggle to implement the No Child Left Behind Act of 2001. With dire budget situations, if schools do not find ways to eliminate educational disparities, more students, especially at-risk students, will drop out of school.

Stop Polishing the Golden Academic Label

To reduce the number of at-risk students and underachievers, public schools need to stop polishing the academic labels (LEP, EL, FEP, Title I, and academic at-risk students) that serve no academic purpose but are useful only for determining fiscal entitlements. Millions of dollars are spent each year to target these students' academic needs, but so far, little evidence exists to show that these students are better off with the tracking system. In some cases, they are real victims of the system. Statistically, bilingual students do not fare well in school because they are not taught what they need to learn. The academic gap needs to be narrowed and public schools must be equipped with tools that enable teachers to teach all students. Public schools need to stop placing bilingual students in classes that permit them to fulfill minimum graduation requirements only.

The labels placed on these students should be temporary; however, most schools brand language-minority students with this label for life, and this is not fair in practice. In fact, most parents do not know the symbolic meanings of this label. Some parents would remove their children from the ELD programs if they learned more about the label. The label is not beneficial to their children's education whatsoever. Keeping these students in the system to procure federal and state funds is not academically appropriate; the schools are failing to offer or provide them with meaningful academic curricula.

Moreover, the label is based on biased assessments and test results that have nothing to do with language proficiency. Most instruments used to assess these students were not designed to measure primary or secondary language proficiency. For instance, CAT6 scores and California Standardized Test scores have nothing to do with language proficiency. Schools need to review the validity and reliability of each test before implementing it or using it for a purpose for which it is not suitable; otherwise, these students are victimized by the system. Sadly, most parents have been defrauded to believe in bogus norm-referenced test results. Continuing to polish the label will cause more harm than good to language-minority students.

Minority students are still underrepresented in higher educational institutions. The academic achievement gap that separates African American students from their European and Asian counterparts is as much as four grade levels (Manning & Baruth, 2004). As a result of the passage of Proposition 209 in 2003, 25% of African American students, 22% of Latinos, and 23% of

American Indians completed course requirements for admission to the University of California and California State University systems. Every child deserves a chance to go beyond secondary school, and to have that chance a student needs to have excellent learning experiences. In fact, minority students make up the majority in remedial education courses to relearn English, reading, writing, and math skills. Bilingual students need academic language education that will provide them pathways to academic success. And most importantly, public schools need excellent teachers who can deliver excellent learning experiences to all students.

Need More Quality Teachers in the Classroom

As with every state, California definitely needs smaller class sizes, up-to-date textbooks, and more quality teachers in the classroom. School districts need to recruit high quality teachers who know *how* to teach rather than know *what* to teach. Perhaps public schools need to grow their own teachers in order to meet the specific needs of specific cultural groups of students (Vang, 1999). Good teachers are genuine heroes, mentors, role models, and lifesavers. They are life-long learners, and they can spark a fire of learning in their students. More importantly, good teachers develop teaching strategies that combine integration, creation, and transference of knowledge in ways that actively engage students in the learning process.

Regardless of what education policy mandates, the schoolteacher is the key to the success of the language-minority student. Without good teachers, the extra academic challenges facing second-language learners will drive them into a silent limbo in the educational system. Whatever language a student speaks, whatever culture a student is from, and no matter what class a student is in, that student, like every other child, deserves an opportunity to learn from a competent teacher. As Manning and Baruth (2009) put it,

> Racism, discrimination, and stereotyping continue to exist and to take a heavy toll on people of different cultural backgrounds. . . . Rather than accepting the status quo as the most equitable we can achieve, school curricula should deliberately instill in children and adolescents a sense of respect and acceptance for all people, regardless of their cultural and individual differences. (p. 214)

However, it is impossible for a teacher to save everyone . . . unless the teacher builds a bridge across the river or installs a barricade to prevent students from going into the water. So teachers need to provide the extra help students need and remove the hindrances that hold them back. Teachers are really the masters, and they must give their students the tools, life skills, academic knowledge, and guidance needed for success. Otherwise, students, especially language learners, will continue to drift in the system and will ultimately fail. In the end, the only time students cannot grow academically is when a teacher has not inspired them. Teaching is a challenging endeavor and a life-long learning experience. Let's teach *all* our students to aim high, dream big, and live to make a difference. And then let's give them what they need to reach those dreams.

To achieve all these, the current system needs to have more quality teachers who understand cultural diversity, diverse needs and abilities, and the characteristics of at-risk students. Tables 11.9 and 11.10 show the characteristics of various types of high and low achievers to help teachers reduce the likelihood of increasing the number of at-risk students.

Table 11.9. Characteristics of Various Types of High Achievers

Type	Characteristics
Goal-oriented	Know how to set up short-term and long-term academic goals and work toward them.
Positive thinkers	Expect to be successful because of prior experiences or have intrinsic and extrinsic motivation.
Confident	Have strong, positive, and believable feelings about personal abilities to achieve.
Resilient	Are not afraid to make mistakes and do not let failure get them down.
Self-discipline	Can resist distractions and diversions and stay focused to concentrate on learning tasks.
Have pride	Develop a sense of inner satisfaction, proud of accomplishments, believe in self, and more independent or less dependent.
Proficient	Develop skills to cope well, have necessary skills to be successful, and have what is required to do well.
Risk taker	Work on the edge, push the limit to learn new things, and have courage and confidence in self to achieve.

Note. Information from *Up from Under-Achievement: How Teachers, Students, and Parents Can Work Together to Promote Student Success*, by D. Heacox, 1991, Minneapolis, MN: Free Spirit.

As Heacox (1991) asked, who is responsible for students' academic success or failure? Perhaps most would think the teachers are; some would say the parents are; and others believe the students are. However, in most cases, it is the system that fails to provide teachers, parents, and students with adequate resources or proper tools to help students learn. Keep in mind that these characteristics should be used carefully and wisely because most students do need to experience both failure and success in order to enhance their learning. In other words, both lows and highs should have equal opportunity to become successful in school if teachers understand their special needs and know how to assist them to overcome their learning obstacles.

Table 11.10. Characteristics of Various Types of Low Achievers

Type	Characteristics
The rebel	See no relevance of classroom assignment and activities: Why do we have to do this anyway? This is a total waste of time.
The conformist	Decide doing well in school is just not worth it: I don't notice that I am smart.
The stressed learner or perfectionist	Have self-esteem that rises and falls depending on academic performance: It's not good enough.
The struggling student	Lack the basics of how to learn, how to manage, and how to organize schoolwork: I just don't get it.
The victim	Do not want to accept learning responsibility for the lack of success: It's not my fault.
The distracted learner	Have personal problems that affect school performance, such as influences, stress, life situations, and poor organizational skills: I just can't handle it all.
The bored student	Need more challenging tasks, have difficulties with tasks, or have advanced abilities: There is nothing new and exciting to learn in class.
The complacent learner	Content with the status quo, believe things to be normal, and go with the flow: I'm doing just fine.
The single-sided learner	Pick and choose subject matter to learn based on personal interests: It doesn't interest me.

Note. Information from *Up from Under-Achievement: How Teachers, Students, and Parents Can Work Together to Promote Student Success*, by D. Heacox, 1991, Minneapolis, MN: Free Spirit.

Suggestions for Reframing Current Practice

According to Goodman and Olivares (2004), teachers and administrators have vital roles to play in helping at-risk students deal with their problems and overcome their academic deficits. The authors gave several explicit ideas for working effectively with at-risk students in a multicultural setting:

1. Nothing will happen without the leadership of the teacher and support from the administration at high levels to find quality instruction for all students.

2. Find remediation strategies that address academic deficits, but include strategies that enhance critical thinking, coping skills, and problem solving skills.
3. Take action to address institutionalized and covert racism that disconnects students from their schools.
4. The content of multicultural education should include how the information is taught and shared rather than what is taught.
5. Make sure there is a direct connection between school curriculum and the emotional, psychological, and academic needs of students.
6. Money is not the answer for solving issues affecting the education of the disaffected.
7. Failure is not the fault of the victim, but it is rather the result of traditional, hegemonic pedagogy and leadership's inability to find sensible alternatives or methods of resolving problems.
8. Change the way of addressing the problems and pay attention to the disaffected.
9. Teachers and administrators need to overcome institutionalized racism based on biased school policies that favor one race over the other, such as zero tolerance policies.
10. Teachers and administrators need to tackle inequity and social injustice fairly and consistently.

Similarly, teachers and administrators can take actions to ameliorate the problems facing at-risk students. Some of those actions are as follows:

1. Build a collective vision or collaborative effort for working with parents and other people involved with at-risk students. Consider, for example, success for all programs, school development programs, accelerated school projects, reading recovery programs, and tutorial activities (NCREL, 2009).
2. Engage in professional development to learn more about at-risk students from experts.
3. Create a learning environment or school climate that promotes success for every student.
4. Develop academic programs that can be implemented within a school system.
5. Emphasize the belief that all students can succeed, and set high standards for all to learn.
6. Foster attitudes that promote learning and good behaviors.

7. Teach resiliency by focusing on student's strengths, not their weaknesses or deficits.
8. Eliminate the tracking system and other devices that place students in different groups for meaningless academic activities.
9. Offer and provide students with equal opportunities to compete for academic success.
10. Devise teacher-made assessments that truly measure student learning and progress.
11. Prescribe meaningful academic activities relevant to students' real life experiences.
12. Promote constructivism or constructivist teaching to engage students in solving real life problems.

Keep in mind that these suggestions may not work for all schools with at-risk students because each school may have different sets of goals for its students. Each prescription for an action plan can be adjusted to fit the needs of the students. As Goodman and Olivares (2004) suggested, teachers and administrators can strengthen their action plans with specific and measurable goals such as the following:

1. Promote, foster, and encourage resiliency or adaptability to achieve or to succeed.
2. Provide leadership and management to improve teaching and learning.
3. Deliver instruction that is rigorous, connected, and meaningful to real life experiences.
4. Utilize eclectic approaches or a variety of instructional approaches to engage students.
5. Use appropriate and accurate assessment to assess student learning.
6. Have a strong belief that students can succeed.
7. Assign challenging and difficult tasks to motivate students to develop high levels of thinking skills.
8. Honor positive attitudes that foster learning.
9. Maintain a positive learning environment or school climate in which all can succeed.
10. Collaborate with parents and community.

These suggestions, action plans, and goals are offered as practical and informative guides to encourage teachers and administrators to work diligently with at-risk students as well as all other students. Keep in mind that there is no academic panacea that will resolve all issues, solve all problems, and make up all deficits. Teachers are life-long learners; they learn as they teach. By the same token, students are not perfect human beings; they are learning through the process of trial and error.

Summing Up

This chapter provided a comprehensive overview of socio-cultural factors associated with the education of at-risk students. Keep in mind that the academic term *at-risk* is still controversial and has broad meanings in the educational field. However, a great number of at-risk students are language-minority students who speak a language other than English at home or whose primary language is not English. Without consistent effort, preferably a total school effort, to help this group of students, the number will increase substantially in the next decade. The current school system is under-prepared to work with these children; however, there is hope that teachers and school administrators can make a big difference in the students' lives by leading the way to change and improvement. Otherwise, the status quo remains and more students become at-risk.

PART FOUR

THE SCHOOL CURRICULAR DOMAIN

Chapter Twelve

Challenges in Curricular Approaches

Education and work are the levers to uplift a people....
Work alone will not do it unless inspired by the right ideals
and guided by intelligence....
Education must not simply teach work, it must teach life.
—W.E.B. Du Bois

Overview

Why do students of diverse backgrounds still face insurmountable academic issues and still struggle to understand the hidden messages within the American educational system? The argument is framed from the status quo, the so-called American way, of the hidden curriculum used in public schools. What should prospective educators know about the hidden curriculum relative to the ideal of academic equality for all children? Language-minority students are labeled and treated differently because of unfair professional practices that are part of the system. Education reform is a slow process, and it has not yet brought about the academic quality needed for success. Many children who deserve equal opportunity are subject to second-class educations offered by the current educational system on the base of deficient ideologies.

Without restructuring the system, reframing the practices, and addressing the hidden curriculum, the status quo will stand and language-minority students will continue to drift in the system. Eventually, most will fall through the cracks as a result of hegemonic practices and the covert utility of the hidden curriculum that inhibits equal opportunities. This chapter examines curricular challenges centered on the hidden curriculum.

The Ways Teachers Teach Still Matter

First and foremost, prospective educators need to understand the educational psychology of methods in multicultural education in order to demystify the misconceptions about cultural diversity. They need to examine their own personal beliefs about diversity and multicultural education in order to overcome academic barriers so they can teach all their students. Prospective educators should reflect upon what and how to teach all students equitably and justly. Consider, for example, what would make multicultural education or curricular approaches meaningful in assisting all students to become more tolerant, equitable, inclusive, collective, and respectful in the classroom where 1 in 10 children is a non-native English speaker and comes from a background that is incompatible with American ways.

Prospective educators should bear in mind the ongoing academic dilemma involving clashes between multiethnic and mono-ethnic ways of thinking in today's public schools. For instance, the hidden curriculum is more likely to be centered on individualism, whereas an understanding of student diversity is collectivistic. Furthermore, prospective educators should not deny that the U.S. is a multicultural and multilingual nation. Educators must see the U.S. as a salad bowl rather than a melting pot, a place where all people have significant and distinct roles in a united but varied whole rather than a place where everyone fades into a single identity. Otherwise, educators will choose curricular approaches that are covertly based on the hidden curriculum of the Western canon that reflects European egocentrism and ethnocentrism. The ways teachers view their country and their classrooms and the ways they teach still matter because it is not about *what* they teach; it is more of *how* they teach.

The Teacher's Beliefs About Students Still Matter

Without a doubt, the ways teachers believe or think about their students can make a pronounced difference in overall student performance and achievement. For instance, Winfield (1986) discovered that some teachers expected more from White students than from their counterparts, especially African American students, and other teachers expected more from middle-class students than from students of the working class. Interestingly, some teachers consider students of color incompetent or incapable of performing high-quality academic tasks.

Moreover, Birrel (1993) found that sometimes unrecognized or outright racism causes teachers to develop stereotypes, biases, prejudices, and negative feelings toward students of color and hold these unproven beliefs against their students. Birrel documented that teachers who have problems dealing with African American students' ethnic attitudes and lingo feel more comfortable with African American students who act White. These kinds of negative attitudes and beliefs reaffirm the practice of covert racism in public institutions, and most importantly, teachers with negative attitudes set lower expectations for academic achievement and success for African American students.

What Is the Hidden Curriculum?

Politics and education are inseparable, as are power and knowledge. Posner (1995) defined the hidden curriculum as the instructional norms and values not openly acknowledged by teachers or school officials. The hidden curriculum is also known as the informal or implicit curriculum. People generally assume no such thing as a hidden idea or behind-the-scenes agenda exists in schools, but there is something called *school culture*, which is a hegemonic value system present in all schools. As Manning and Baruth (2009) observed, the hidden curriculum impacts teaching in a number of ways: (a) most school policies recognize only middle-class values and expectations, (b) school media are oriented toward the mainstream culture, (c) instructional practices target the learning styles of the predominant culture, (d) extracurricular activities are dominated by one race, and (e) these hegemonic actions send negative messages to students of color.

Hidden curricula can play a significant role in educational leadership and management, undermining equality in public schools and producing policies and practices that are inadequate to meet the needs of all students. McLaren (1998) called this kind of action cultural imperialism, a situation in which the dominant cultural group exercises power by bringing other groups under its domination. The victims of cultural imperialism view themselves from the perspective of others.

McLaren (1998) thus saw the hidden curriculum as oppression. He warned poor and minority students to recognize the various manifestations of oppression because oppression disempowers them academically and politically. He classified as oppression the unconscious assumptions and reactions of well-meaning people in ordinary interactions, media, and cultural stereotypes. Moreover, he described the structural features of bureaucratic hierarchy and market mechanisms that affect the normal ongoing process of everyday life of powerless people as oppressive.

The Insidious Side Effects of Underachievement

Prospective educators should learn that the hidden curriculum can show itself in the illusion of progress. An example is the straight "A" ESL superstar story, a scenario in which a student receives excellent grades in substandard courses, creating the illusion that the student has achieved a high level of learning. Bilingual parents generally pay close attention to the grades their children receive and tend not to worry about the academic curricula and programs, often bilingual education or ELD programs, used in the classroom. They assume that if their children are bringing home good grades they are progressing well. In many cases, bilingual parents do not find out that their children cannot read, write, speak, or understand English sufficiently until later, in junior high school and high school.

At this point, parents complain to their children that they are lazy, disrespectful, shameful, and dishonoring for having failing grades, poor attendance, and language deficiencies. They cannot understand any other reasons their children used to be straight "A" students and their academic records changed over night when they entered junior high or high school. This misplaced blame creates conflict between parents and children that is very sensitive within many cultures, and neither parents nor children are able to understand or explain what has happened.

What has happened is that the children were given impoverished and improvised instruction with content-compatible language, not content-obligatory language. Students and parents need to know that although segregation has not been permitted in public education since 1954, segregation exists in the form of unequal instruction. In this legal form of segregation, minority children are separated from their peers and given substandard curricula and lower expectations.

Prospective educators should note the insidious side effects this creates in the minds of students of color. As McLaren (1998) explained, marginalized groups, such as poor, language-minority, and powerless individuals, are often marked on the basis of race and positioned by the dominant culture in relationships of dependency where they are excluded from equal rights and equal opportunities.

The Illusion of Bilingual Education

Prospective educators should know that over the last 30 or more years, strong emphasis has been placed on bilingual education for language-minority students, but in reality, bilingual education is a double-edged sword. Bilingual education is a legal public education program designated to help language-minority students in school. It does not always help students achieve academic success because many bilingual children are stuck in bilingual classes forever. English language learners (ELLs) are expected to learn their own languages and cultures to compete with the people who speak and write English. In fact, they have to learn English proficiently to transition from LEP to FEP or from bilingual classes to regular courses of study. Public schools usually assess, classify, and place ELL students in LEP or FEP categories.

The 1974 landmark *Lau v. Nicholas* decision established that public schools must provide non-native students the extra assistance they might need to excel in school. But the Court did not specify what public schools should do to help English language learners excel academically in school. The legal interpretation is so vague and ambiguous that no one knows what to do exactly to meet the needs and demands of disadvantaged students. Public schools were criticized for failing to teach ELL students. LEP curricula are in place today because of legal mandates, but the implementation of programs is somewhat capricious in nature. The curricula are inadequate and inconsistent. Schools are frustrated with federal and state mandates and bilingual education requirements, and language-minority students are often taught with low content instruction and materials that cannot help students meet standards and acquire content knowledge. Many language-minority students are not at grade level based on the tracking scales used by school districts, and many do not score well on the API.

Regardless of what bilingual programs these students are in, here is what prospective educators need to know: The goal of bilingual education is to transit language-minority students from poor English skills to becoming English proficient in order for them to compete academically in school; the goal is not to help them become proficient in their native languages. At the very least, the public schools need to stop following the hidden curriculum that leads to little or no academic learning for many.

The Illusion of Detrimental Curricular Efforts

Despite any criticism, cynicism, or idealism regarding multicultural education, no one really knows for sure whether the hidden curriculum will promote or destroy the educational opportunity that disadvantaged students really deserve. Above all, prospective educators should keep in mind that the answer is not easy because there is no academic panacea.

Furthermore, parents sometimes do not realize that good grades in bilingual classrooms may not be as academically sound as the same grades in regular classrooms. One cannot assume that the curricula in bilingual classrooms are of the same quality as the curricula in regular classes, and quality and excellence of teachers and curricula make the difference between passing and learning. All students, LEP and others, must have quality academic curricula, not curricula that merely teach survival skills related to BICS. What they really need is CALP. Bilingual parents do not understand the difference between reading comprehension and the ability to read, and good grades in ESL classes alone do not prepare their children for college educations. In practice, as Goldstein (1985) noted, schools do not prepare language-minority students academically to be college bound; they allow them simply to accumulate units for high school graduation.

Curricula can have either mixed or fixed applications. Posner (1995) described how content structures (spiral, discrete, flat, hierarchical, and linear) and media structures (parallel, convergent, divergent, and mixed) differentiate quality and effective methods of teaching and learning. Sometimes the curricula for ELL students are watered down by public schools. Educators need to give serious thought to the curricula they use when they teach bilingual students survival and social skills, drilling them on less academic topics that are not related to the operational curricula. The grades they earn with these types of curricula do not reflect genuine academic learning.

Furthermore, immigrant and refugee parents are unfamiliar with the American educational system because many did not have the chance to go to public schools in the U.S. Parents do not know how to ask or advocate for equity of education for their children who are drowning in school. Their children are suffering because of inconsistent implementation of programs that lack resources and qualified staffing. Schools encourage parents to get involved; however, once parents get involved, school personnel often label them disrespectfully. For instance, teachers call vocal parents who are concerned about their children's performance "helicopter parents." Many bilingual parents fear being misunderstood, and they therefore do not vocalize their concerns. So far, the curricula are so inadequate as to be considered, in some cases, academically inappropriate.

The Empty Promise of Trust

Prospective educators should pay close attention to the lack of public trust in teaching today that has resulted from the disingenuous representations of academia. Public schools have made so many empty promises regarding the needs of language-minority students. Bilingual students coming from diverse backgrounds are sometimes guaranteed academic services in accordance with federal, state, and local mandates. But in most cases, these are just empty promises; many students are being left alone to fend for themselves. In class, these students are often quiet and polite; however, their quiet and polite behaviors that may stem from the little understood cultural value of filial piety make it easy for culturally insensitive teachers to overlook and neglect their academic needs.

Despite the neglect, most parents regard their children's teachers highly. In the native countries of many of the parents, teachers are thought of like leaders and clergymen. Parents carry that tradition to the U.S., respecting schoolteachers and administrators as authority figures, firmly believing that teachers have great expertise in educating their children to become productive citizens. They do not know the difference between substitute teachers and regular classroom teachers, cannot tell what teachers have proper credentials, and do not understand academic standards. Perhaps, the word *teacher* means everything to them; they trust what they hear from a teacher.

Ironically, this attitude explains some of the problems bilingual children experience when they languish in the school system for many years. For example, ELL students face double jeopardy in public schools: teachers are not helping them learn and parents are not able to advocate for them. Neither parents nor schools know how to rescue them before they are undone by the hidden curriculum. The only time someone realizes the importance of education is when illiteracy occurs.

Prospective educators should bear in mind that all children in the U.S. are living in a culturally pluralistic society. Language-minority students are confused and grow up illiterate because they are not taught to take responsibility for themselves but to believe what schoolteachers have transferred to them in the classroom. Consider, for example, the null curriculum that public schools use that does not teach minority students about the American way of life. Most public schools teach "foreign" cultures and values, and students do not learn the culture of the society in which they live. Schoolteachers often have different socioeconomic backgrounds, but schools have not designed classroom curricula based on cultural perspectives even though some aspects of cultural values have been incorporated or integrated into social studies curricula. Unlike in other nations, no American public school teacher is allowed to teach specific cultural or religious values to students. Schoolteachers can express their views only implicitly, not explicitly.

The Secrecy of Socio-Academic Schooling

Prospective educators have learned that in our current society, poor children get a poor education and rich children get a richer education, even in public schools. McLaren (1998) brilliantly described this phenomenon as the result of powerlessness. The structures of social division and social status affect the lives of people who have little or no work autonomy, exercise little creativity or judgment in their work, have no technical expertise or authority, and express themselves awkwardly in public or bureaucratic settings.

Whether the hidden curriculum is a fair societal educational prescription for the diverse student population, parents are not aware of the problems until they see learning disabilities, illiteracy, frustrations, anxieties, and cultural alienation in their children's education. In general, the hidden curriculum mainly affects economically disadvantaged students. The hidden curriculum is especially evident in low socioeconomic areas in inner-city schools and rural school districts. Schools with high numbers of minority students seem to hire lower quality teachers to teach the LEP students. The instructional content and approaches may be whole language, phonics, or a participatory strategy. Teachers with low content knowledge are generally not able to deliver quality education to ELL students. As a result of inadequate preparation, many language-minority students are not able to compete for an education beyond 12th grade. Long before Grade 12, the dropout rates for minority students are three times higher than for other students in the public schools.

Moreover, poor education contributes to a poor society. For instance, the majority of minority dropout students are teenage girls. The majority of juvenile offenders are minority males who do poorly in school. Among the minority students who graduate from high school, how many are able to continue their education in college? How many are able to remain in college and complete their programs?

The socio-academic framework plays a large role in the future of language-minority students. Statistics indicate that economically poor minority students are at greater risk of dropping out of college due to many reasons related to poor academics, families, personal needs, under-preparation, and economic disadvantage.

The Betrayal of the Golden Academic Label

Prospective educators may not realize the hidden implications of the academic label public schools put on language-minority students when their parents enroll them in school. This golden label entitles schools to fiscal benefits; however, the recipients of this label receive few services those benefits are supposed to provide. As Goodman and Olivares (2004) pointed out, money is not the solution to academic inequity and social injustice. Prospective educators may rightly wonder why the academic label is more important in school than the education of language-minority students.

Actually, most identified LEP students carry the golden label needed for fiscal entitlements; however, public schools often divert the funds to purposes other than educating the identified students. For instance, in some schools, language minority students receive only sporadic ELD services. They are placed on a 2-year monitor list after being reclassified from LEP to FEP and are responsible for their own academic progress without help; if they fail to progress, they are classified as at-risk for having cultural and language barriers.

Many language-minority students are prisoners of silence in English dominant classrooms (Ovando et al., 2006). Many LEP students are placed in classes where they either learn to swim or sink academically. Consequently, the hidden curriculum is a covert mentality that relegates needy students to a minimum education, enabling them to accumulate minimum credits toward graduation. Many educators and policy makers overlook or ignore this practice.

Once LEP students are branded, blinders are put on their education. It is evident that the current attempt to continue promoting legal segregation, inequity of instruction, and colorblind instruction is part of the overt denial that these problems exist and that they are significant. Institutionalized and covert racism, discrimination, and prejudice continue to work to effectively sever connections between minority students and their schools (Goodman & Olivares, 2004). LEP students carry learning deficiencies throughout the life span of their education because of the label affixed to their academic records. The system has misused the golden label, serving itself instead of its students.

Test Scores Set Double Standards for Language Learners

New educators are hastily taught, as soon as they are hired for the job, to prepare to assess student learning; however, they rarely understand the reasons for spending so much time assessing students when they have so little time to teach them. Each year, schoolteachers spend at least 6 to 8 weeks assessing students' learning in order to meet state mandates and comply with requirements for various programs. Only a small number of prospective educators and parents know that public schools use the test scores to reclassify their ELD children; however, none of them knows that nearly 95% of these students will never be redesignated. They will not get out of the bilingual education program as long as they are enrolled in K-12 schools (Vang, 2001). In fact, they all are lumped together in ELD level V.

The hidden curriculum prejudges them as not as competent as their peers from the dominant culture. Sadly, schools tend to think of language-minority students as less civilized individuals who deserve only limited opportunity. Moreover, some public schools have attacked affirmative action and other education policies instituted to promote equity and social justice. In addition, ELL students have been discriminated against unconsciously because of their dialect, culture, and second language status; these characteristics often overshadow their learning in the classroom. Most importantly, language-minority students are being abandoned by the system because of their low test scores. School personnel feel frustrated that state mandates require them to educate these students, whose test scores lower the averages for their schools.

LEP students suffer not only from prejudging and cultural barriers, but also from the academic tests in their classes and the standardized tests, also called norm-referenced tests, used by public schools to predestine them in the system. As mentioned in Chapter Eleven, the reclassification criteria and redesignation process make it hard for LEP students to become FEP students based on their standardized test scores. This double standard is kept secret from parents and students. There is no doubt that the hidden curriculum carries many double standards that restrict LEP students from learning, advancing, and reaching their educational goals. Consider, for example, that the more LEP students who are reclassified or redesignated as FEP, the more funding the system loses. This fiscal dilemma causes the system to keep most LEP students in that classification for years.

Furthermore, year after year, the APIs of ELL students are in the bottom quartile in all tested areas. If the same criteria were applied to native speaking students, the result would be the same. Prospective educators should at least understand that norm-referenced testing is used not only to track language-minority students and place them in a lower position on the academic ladder, but it is also used to trap them in an academic limbo that prevents them from advancing.

The System that Traps Language-Minority Students

As much as is possible, educators should be strong advocates for all students because language-minority students are being tracked and trapped at the same time. McLaren (1998) referred to this as exploitation and likened it to the way in the labor arena in which working-class groups are transferred to benefit the wealthy by reproducing and causing divisions and unequal relationships.

As mentioned previously, public schools now are applying the SAT9 (CAT6) scores to redesignate students from LEP to FEP status. For an LEP student to be redesignated from LEP to FEP status, the student has to score in the 36th percentile on the SAT9 in all tested areas: language arts, reading, and math. This requirement is clearly an academic hurdle that many bilingual students cannot overcome. Even if students meet all requirements except the SAT9 score, they will remain at LEP classification regardless of their academic achievements. In fact, standardized test scores do not necessarily measure English communicative competence of LEP students; however, as a result, public schools link test scores to English proficiency anyway; that is an academic flaw that needs to change.

Redesignation means that students are mainstreamed out of the bilingual program and do not have to take ELD or ESL classes. However, their language skills are often not sufficient to permit them to do well in classes that require a high level of English skills, such as English, advanced math, or science. Therefore, redesignated students are discouraged from taking all but basic level courses.

Most parents do not know that bilingual students are required to take more classes than native speaking students to graduate. The current system requires that bilingual students take ELD classes in addition to their normal class load because the system is bounded by program rules and regulations. In other words, ELLs must take additional courses while enrolled in the regular course of studies unless they are redesignated completely from LEP to FEP status. This requirement creates a tracking system that traps students for no academic purpose; however, because of the funds that come with the LEP label, the students have to pay a price.

As mentioned previously, politics and education are inseparable; both are about domination and controlling the things that generate money. The fact of the matter is that schools need to procure state and federal monies in order to operate. However, as the old saying goes, the love of money is the root of all evil. Prospective educators should understand that primary language fluency is not an academic condition that determines academic ability, and being fluent in a language does not determine academic success in children. So far, no assessment instrument has been designed that predicts academic success in all aspects of students of color.

The System Only Pretends to Be Colorblind

Prospective educators study civil rights laws, court decisions, and the evolution of public policy in regard to public education. Civil rights issues are still present in public schools today. As mentioned previously, legalized segregation, racism, prejudice, bias, and inequality are alive and well. American society is still divided racially in some ways. For instance, the national mass media informed the world that race would determine the winner of the 2008 presidential election regardless of the results of any national poll. In fact, some asserted that the Bradley effect would be seen—Whites who publicly supported an African American presidential candidate would not cast their votes for him behind the curtain.

Skin color has played significant roles in the American way of life, politics, education, and societal values. Prospective educators should realize that going through the public school system is a difficult challenge for many language-minority students, especially ELLs, who may have cultural and language barriers. These children have to deal with two cultures and languages at the same time. Some have no help, and some have a number of services available. For LEP students with language barriers, navigating the school system is very frustrating. They find that perceived ability and surface assessments are the prime factors schools use to determine what academic support LEP students will receive. The system houses language-minority students in homogeneous groupings or cluster groupings on the basis of race for the purpose of providing them socialization with little or no regard for their academic learning.

Prospective educators should be concerned that the hidden curriculum consigns entire groups of students to prejudgment and discrimination solely on the basis of their manners of speech, learning, thinking, and talking. Schoolteachers often tend to believe that students who speak in a language other than English sound less intelligent than those who speak primarily English; therefore, they view LEP students as less likely to achieve in school. Sometimes teachers' judgments are based on test scores, but as Simmons (1991) observed, IQ tests and other Standard English language tests often are culturally and economically biased and do not give accurate pictures of student ability. Of course, teachers' beliefs about their students make a big difference in the way they teach, interact, assist, and share with those students.

Attempts to Denigrate Primary Language

At one time, speaking a language in school other than English was considered a violation of school policy. Some students were barred from speaking Spanish, Chinese, Korean, Russian, German, Greek, Yiddish, or other primary languages in school. Prospective educators should realize that this mindset still exists and is sometimes incorporated into professional practices that are discriminatory and incongruent with today's more democratic views. Those who follow the hidden curriculum tend to believe that the only way to teach students who speak languages other than Standard American English is to try to completely change the students' style of speech and learning by imposing one language and one culture. Thus, children who come from homes in which others speak broken, non-standard English, have heavy accents, or speak a different language altogether are subject to this form of language denigration.

Prospective educators should keep in mind that multicultural education does not prevent teachers from teaching all students Standard English. However, denigrating the language of the child's culture is like taking away the child's self-concept, self-image, self-worth, self-esteem, and cultural identity. Academically and socially, public schools should allocate time to allow students to make a voluntary transition instead of using hegemonic actions to force the transition. School administrators and teachers may not realize that changing a student's speech and learning style changes the cultural identity of that student. The negative impact on students' lives is maximized by policy implementations made on the basis of the hidden curriculum. Simmons (1991) mentioned that a moral dilemma is involved in making such a drastic change in people's lives. Almost all students use speech and learning patterns taught to them from birth.

Furthermore, prospective educators should understand that language differences are going to persist and perhaps grow as long as people live in a society as diverse as that of the U.S. Students identify the style of speech and usage of grammar in their native languages with who they are. The frustration in the hidden curriculum is that schools attempt to change the language of students by force because they perceive it as incorrect, as an insult to the language they are attempting to teach. In a practical sense, students should not be judged by their cultures and made to carry out a curriculum that seems sensible to the teacher, but they should be judged by the correctness of their academic attempts to master the dominant language. They should be taught the new language in a friendly way without compromising the quality and equity of education in other subjects. Whatever language students speak, the teacher should focus on the teaching of academic language, the language students are expected to learn in formalized processes.

Mistreating Students Is No Accident

Prospective educators should always keep in mind that professional attitudes and personalities play the biggest role in the teaching profession and are more important than anything else teachers bring to class. Curricular approaches, such as planning, lesson design, and assessment, are just parts of the show. The personality of a person is like a movie screen on which all children will be watching a performance. It could be black and white or it could be in color. Of course, teachers must teach whatever the school allows them to teach, but how they teach the curricula can make the show lively, intriguing, enjoyable, fun, engaging, enthusiastic, or very boring.

As experts have pointed out, the way schoolteachers treat children who are low achievers, have language barriers, struggle with learning difficulties, or require extra assistance has significant impacts on student learning. Sometimes teachers approach such students in ways that are academically biased. Ryan and Cooper (2001) and Good and Brophy (2000) listed some of the ways schoolteachers treat low achievers; these are shown in Table 12.1.

Researchers are not certain why teachers treat their low and high achievers differently in these ways, but experts have concluded after observations of many classrooms that teachers do in fact behave differently toward low and high achieving students. No doubt the differences are related to the implicit curriculum that teachers use in the classroom. Should parents know about these differences in treatment of students? Why not? And if they know, how would parents react to the information? They could be devastated.

Construct Bias in Assessments

Prospective educators should be aware that most assessment instruments are old and some are obsolete. Most importantly, most evaluative tools are not designed to measure academic development in children based on specific teaching methodologies or curricular approaches. Some instruments were developed by experts in educational psychology and related fields on the ba-

Table 12.1. Some Ways Teachers Treat Low Achievers

Treatment	Possible Causes
Give little time for lows to ask a question	Assuming lows don't understand the question, don't know the answer, or don't want to waste time.
Allow no clue, no hint, or no opportunity for lows	Expect lows to understand the question and know the correct answer right away.
Reward inappropriate behaviors or incorrect answers	Expecting lows to have middle-class values or focusing on the behaviors more than the needs.
Criticize lows for failure	Blaming the lows for not knowing or not understanding.
Praise them for success less frequently	Failing to promote lows, lacking cross-cultural education, or holding prejudicial biases.
Give less response and less public feedback	Holding stereotype, bias, prejudice, or rejection.
Pay less attention or interact less with lows	Avoiding lows for many reasons, focusing on other students, or ignoring lows' needs.
Call on lows less	Expecting the right answers, presuming incompetent, or holding cultural grudges.
Seat them farther away	Focusing on loud, noisy, rowdy, or assertive students and avoiding quiet and polite students.
Demand less from them	Assuming lows don't have skills, having problems speaking English, or won't know the answers.
Give lows more private than public interactions	Putting pressure on lows to learn, expecting lows to adapt, or making sure assignments are done.
Closely monitor lows in class	Focusing on lows' weaknesses, expecting lows to learn at the same rate, or having no time for lows.
Give lows more structured activities	Expecting lows to learn specific skills, giving lows different activities, or using strict rules.
Give lows no benefit of the doubt in borderline cases	Grading down instead of grading up, making errors is too serious, expecting to be like other learners.
Give lows less friendly interactions, fewer smiles, and less support	Presenting negative attitudes toward lows, shutting them off, or giving no attention at all.
Give lows shorter and less informative feedback	Failing to encourage lows, giving good, not good, or okay remarks, or sending "see me" notes.

Table continues on next page

Table 12.1, continued

Treatment	Possible Causes
Make less eye contact with lows and respond less attentively	Avoiding lows, considering lows to be "ghost like" students, or expecting nothing from them.
Use less effective lessons and less time-consuming instructional methods for lows	Giving content compatibility, not content obligatory, or watered down instruction.
Give less acceptance and lower use of their ideas and input	Assuming lows to be followers, not leaders, or expecting lows to be listeners, not actors.
Use impoverished and improvised curricula with lows	Using "whatever," giving lows easy assignments, expecting lows to do just enough, using lip services for lows, providing lows with cosmetic education, or offering lows nonacademic instruction.

sis of animal studies or other laboratory research. Moreover, most tests are not academically, linguistically, culturally, and cognitively sensitive to the different backgrounds and learning styles of a culturally diverse student population. One assessment, the IQ test, remains highly controversial, and in some cultures, the results of IQ tests are considered uneducated or nonacademic.

Furthermore, students who speak languages other than English are often viewed as having lower IQs. Hoover and Taylor (1987) observed that schools implement curricula and reach conclusions without any basis of fact in regard to students' culture and language. Kossak (1980) pointed out that teachers tend to assign lower grades to students who speak languages other than Standard American English. She also reported that teachers tend to respond more positively to higher achieving students, attractive students, female students, conforming students, and front-row students than students in minority groups who speak their native languages and sit in the back row.

Students with non-native English cultural backgrounds are often prejudged by public schools when IQ tests are administered before the test predetermines the results. Trick questions are often asked in language tests. Double negatives—such as "none of the following are true except..." or "all are false except..."—confuse LEP students and other language learners. Some have not been exposed to such questions in bilingual class or have not learned the grammatical meanings of the words. The wording and contexts of the questions are confusing to bilingual students who speak good or fluent English but lack test taking experience. Generally, standardized tests use super Standard English and vocabularies that are not taught in ESL or ELD classrooms. Some LEP students may not be able to ascertain the meanings because they have not heard the words before. Hoover and Taylor (1987) stated that about 34% of standardized language tests have language biases. This means that tests are based on one cultural value system, which is different from that of many minority students.

For instance, the *Negro Educational Review* (1992) reported that six out of seven language tests showed discrimination against Blacks, two out of seven discriminated against Latinos, and two out of seven discriminated against Southerners. Many students are being tested with materials that are obsolete. Bilingual students, especially refugee children, are being assessed on standardized language tests that are culturally mismatched to their backgrounds. The norm-reference test has no cultural or language values connected with the testing and measuring of students. Hispanic and refugee children are being tested for language proficiency because they speak languages other than English at home.

As indicated in the *Negro Educational Review* (1992) article, students might be understandably unable to answer questions that assume knowledge of a culture that is totally foreign to them. For instance, a standardized test question might ask students to identify the actions of a man in a suit. Students could give a reasonable answer from their cultural experience that is judged wrong because it is inaccurate from a Western cultural perspective. A middle-class White student may answer, "This man is going to work." Another student, whose male role model does not wear a suit on a daily basis, may answer, "The main is going to church." When a test shows a high rise building, some students might identify it as an office building, whereas others might say it is a home, referring to tall apartments in many cities. Their answers are based on their cultural experiences.

Exempting LEP Students from Taking Tests

Prospective educators should know that excluding students from taking tests could be illegal. Federal and state laws may exempt certain students and grades from taking the tests, but not on the basis of speaking a second or third language other than English at home. The excuses that public schools use to exempt language-minority students from examinations are not sound and need to be examined carefully. For instance, some public schools encourage language-minority students to evade testing because of the fear that their low test scores will bring the school's average scores down and because the school does not want these students to experience test anxieties. In fact, language-minority students are being excluded illegally and purposely for the sake of the schools' reputations.

Moreover, LEP students are not prepared adequately to take tests. They are taught one way and tested in another way. Schools seem to not want to deal with bilingual students' academic challenges but to give them a poor education that insufficiently prepares them for high-stakes testing. Occasionally, LEP students are excluded or exempt from taking standardized language tests because they are not proficient in English or because they speak two or more languages. Some schools are more concerned about the test results than about the students' learning and experiences. During testing weeks, some schools allow language-minority students to watch animated movies while others take tests. The hidden curriculum determines what is best for the schools and what is easy for the LEP students to do on test day. Who has the responsibility for academically preparing LEP students for the tests? Who knows? Maybe nobody is responsible but parents. Of course, the system should be held reliable and responsible for failing to meet their diverse needs and abilities.

Furthermore, the standardized tests—SAT, SAT9, ITAS, CAP, BSMIII, San Diego Model, WISC II/III, BENDER, CLASS, and others—are culturally and economically biased against the curricula taught in bilingual classes. Whether students receive straight "As" or "Bs" in their bilingual classes, this academic achievement is meaningless when they perform poorly on the standardized tests. School personnel often tell parents that the results of standardized tests do not predict or indicate potential success or lack of success in students, and that parents do not have to worry about the outcomes because they mean nothing to them or the students. In fact, however, these school personnel are being dishonest and hiding the value of test results from parents. Schools use the results, the empirical data, for statistical and funding purposes. Schools are afraid that low scores on standardized tests will harm their reputation for academic excellence. For this reason, schools engage in the frivolous practice of exempting and excluding many LEP students from taking the tests. It is about time to call this kind of hegemonic practice off for good.

The One-Model-Fits-All Leaves LEP Students Behind

As mentioned previously, education is very political. Prospective educators will feel the political pressure on their shoulders if their teaching does not align or coincide with the policy that governs daily life in the classroom. They may become frustrated as they struggle to overcome philosophical differences in policy, teaching, and assessing student learning. For instance, the No Child Left Behind Act of 2001 (NCLB) gives an educational model that benefits only those at the top of the academic scale. It requires testing and assessment of all students without considering their special needs and accommodations. This legislation does not give schools tools with which to do their job. Moreover, it fails to fund efforts to find the proper resources for teaching and testing students. School funding is going from bad to worse. As some experts put it, schools are merely "taming the beast," leaving many students untaught and untouched. Public schools are being controlled not only by test-driven curricula and research, but also by political machines and politicians who know very little about educating children. The goal of NCLB is to make sure that all students achieve passing scores by 2014.

Why are language-minority students being left behind in testing? Hoover and Taylor (1987) noted that standardized tests are developed by groups of educators and community members. About 80% of test developers are White, 4% are Black, 1% is Asian, 4% are Hispanic, and 3% are from various individuals of other ethnic groups. Nearly 100% have at least a high school education, about 77% have college degrees, and 90% have graduate degrees or educational experience beyond the bachelor degree level. Standardized test developers may have no cultural understanding of the students they measure. The test makers have absolutely nothing to do with the audience. This has caused some insensitivity in standardized testing.

As mentioned previously, the earliest tests designed for educational purposes were developed in the 1920s. These tests were developed with the support of educators and business corporations based on military alpha tests. The alpha tests measured values, morality, and job skills, not academic knowledge or skills. The tests were largely used for disciplinary purposes and social skills drills rather than for assessing teaching and learning. The tests had very little basis of fact in the domains of language development. In general, some interpretations can be drawn from these tests that they are not relevant to educational purposes. The content of the tests is racially, socially, and economically biased.

Undoubtedly, the Western canon plays a big role in designing tests for students; however, students of different cultures have different experiences. The tests need to consider the different cultural and academic backgrounds of students in order to accurately measure student learning. Students in rural areas may think train tracks are for transportation of machinery and equipment, whereas students in the inner cities probably think that train tracks are for transportation of people. This is an example of the type of differences test developers need to examine closely when they design testing instruments for students.

Kossak (1980) suggested that language difficulties stem from a lack of background knowledge and experiences from which to draw conclusions and make judgments. The hidden curriculum in the public school system ignores the fact that some children come to school with knowledge and experiences that differ from those of the majority. Some school administrators and teachers have missed this for years. They just do not care about the significance of cultural differences or different learning styles, and so they ignore the academic needs and challenges of the bilingual audience. In the end, the system gets what it wants by leaving many language-minority students stranded behind.

Cultural Baggage Inhibits Student Learning

Prospective educators should be aware of their own personal cultural baggage that may expose their personal biases in class. Keep in mind that no one is bias free or prejudice free; however, there are good biases and prejudices as well as bad ones. Teachers are not perfect human beings, but they are expected to act responsibly and professionally. They must be respectful of all cultures regardless of what they believe and value themselves. Personal cultural values cannot be allowed to overshadow one's professional values, such as student achievement, knowledge of learning styles, effective use of different communication styles, proper interpretation of testing outcomes, and socializing attitudes.

For instance, researchers and experts tend to agree that students whose first language is not English do not have severe academic problems comprehending materials written in Standard English when the curricula in the classroom and the standardized tests are related to their cultural backgrounds. The *Negro Educational Review* (1992) cited studies showing that groups dominant in vernacular Black English scored significantly higher when tested on materials related to Black cultural backgrounds. This shows that language-minority students perform and test as well as their peers when all else is equal.

Moreover, the perceptions of students regarding the tests influence their test taking behaviors and the outcomes of the tests. Some schoolteachers have preconceptions of their students' achievement levels before allowing them to perform academic tasks. As mentioned in the *Negro Educational Review*, in 1991, a study conducted by the Department of Teacher Education in California asked 52 second-grade teachers to listen to tapes of children who spoke both Standard American English and minority dialects. Nearly all of the teachers in the study were White. They judged most of the students with minority dialects to be slow learners with low IQs and low reading scores. Their conclusions were based solely on listening to audiotapes.

Later, according to the *Negro Educational Review*, a similar study was done with minority teachers. These teachers rated the minority-dialect students significantly higher than the White teachers rated them. The logical conclusion that can be drawn from these two studies is that White teachers tend to be biased against minority students. Students are being labeled solely on the basis of their cultures or languages. Whether the schoolteachers or test developers deal with these students fairly, the students themselves are destined to live out a self-fulfilled prophecy, becoming functionally illiterate adults if they are deprived of the opportunity to receive quality instruction.

Prospective educators should consider this: Societal bias is not easily removed, but test bias can be scraped away if students and parents understand the hidden curriculum in schools. The feeling that the language and culture of the dominant group is superior is difficult to change. But people can accept and incorporate diverse cultures and languages to broaden societal values and make judgments fairer and more reasonable. As Kossak (1980) observed, the Equal Education Act of 1974 stated that "no state shall deny educational opportunity by the failure of an educational agency to take appropriate action to overcome language barriers that impede equal participation by its instructional program" (p. 617).

Kossak (1980) argued that educators need to realize the value of a family's language and guide students to know how to use both their family language and their second languages in order to appease the language biases of society. The practical way of doing this would be to combine oral skills with language experiences and phonics skills with a strong emphasis on vocabularies and word meanings.

Most tests focus on assessing retention of information through recitation, memorization, and regurgitation. Rather, tests should assess construction of new knowledge and skills through comprehension, application, cognitive development, and implication. Bilingual students are subject to tests that do not measure any of these academic skills associated with their cultural backgrounds.

The Symbolic Struggle to Close the Academic Achievement Gap

Time after time, prospective educators read about the looming academic achievement gap between affluent students and economically disadvantaged students. Poor children get better grades than rich children, and children of rich families living in good neighborhoods score higher on tests than children of poor families living in high crime neighborhoods. The findings of these studies are convincing and troubling. Educators should ask what the system has done academically to help those students who cannot read the test questions before testing them. The research does not usually reveal the professional profiles of the teachers who teach these two different groups of students nor the curricula used to prepare the students for academic tests. Often the research findings are all about power, control, and politics. Therefore, prospective educators should not be distracted by the symbolic interpretations of normal curve results and should keep an open mind while working and dealing with all kinds of students.

To help minority students become successful in both languages and cultures, the schools have to give them the right tools from the start, tools that stimulate them academically rather than segregating them in groups where they see nothing new. The hidden curriculum—the unspoken instructional norms and values—should be the operational curriculum that meets student needs and fosters learning. Decisions should not be made behind closed doors. The denigrating of certain cultures and languages damages students' pride in learning both cultures and destroys their desire to do well in academic testing. When teachers help students take pride in and use the values and skills of both cultures and languages, they give them the confidence they need to build academic skills and the motivation to become successful and productive individuals in both communities.

To break through the many barriers they face, students need to experience both domains. The hidden curriculum denies them the ability to learn how to make educated choices, or informed decisions. Some schools use incentives and blurred explanations to get by students and parents. For instance, they tell parents that test results may not truly represent their children's academic ability or overall academic performance. In fact, the results are considered "done deal" when public schools disaggregate student achievement data by family income, race, ethnicity, disability, gender, and limited English proficiency.

Whether the hidden curriculum distorts beliefs about students, the cultural and language biases in academic testing must be eliminated; tests should be based on the teaching in the classroom and the life experiences of the students. The immoral practice in the educational system of discriminating against students on the basis of differences in culture and language should be eradicated for the sake of educating LEP and bilingual students.

For years, language-minority students have suffered academically from the hidden curriculum in schools. The power behind the hidden curriculum is a blanket policy that favors one group of students over the others. Prospective educators need to understand that bilingual children deserve the very best opportunity possible, the same as any other children. Children are sent to schools to learn, not to be spoiled by the system and trapped in the skewed practices that exist for the purpose of financial entitlement. Language should not be a barrier to children receiving a good education. Studies confirm that the quality of education is determined by the quality of instruction, not the language of instruction (American Institute for Research, 2006).

The Espoused Policy Versus the Policy in Use

Politics aside, prospective educators will soon learn that in many schools the espoused policy is contrary to the policy actually in use. When dealing with the academic needs of language-minority students, schools seem to add problem upon problem rather than solve problems. In some schools, the daily objective is not student learning, but social organization for the purpose of receiving entitlements. In those schools, bilingual children are housed in specially arranged classrooms, where little or no academic teaching takes place. The students in these classrooms are often taught by pre-credential paraprofessionals. Understanding that this grouping is frequently the result of policy driven by the hidden curriculum, Posner (1995) observed, "The hidden curriculum is not generally acknowledged by school officials but may have a deeper and more durable impact on students than either the official or the operational curriculum" (pp. 11–12). Citing Giroux and Purpel (1983), Posner further explained:

> The messages of the hidden curriculum concern issues of gender, class and race, and authority, and school knowledge about sex roles, "appropriate" behaviors for young people, the distinction between work and play, which children can succeed at various kinds of knowledge are considered legitimate. (p. 12)

As described previously, the label LEP ties a string to students that connects them to money for the school. In 1987 a majority of the voters of California passed Proposition 227, ending bilingual education in the state. Twelve years later, the state Board of Education voted to remove the criteria used in the measure to reclassify students from LEP to FEP. The state left to local schools the responsibility of coming up with well-conceptualized action plans to deal with the growing concerns of educating LEP students. In fact, nearly all public schools in California failed to develop any new plan; instead, they continued using the old criteria to track LEP students and trap them in LEP designations. Some school districts are afraid of losing thousands of dollars in funding if they abandon the current process. Some schools use the fact that they have bilingual students to establish a need for which to request categorical funding and compensatory programs.

Undoubtedly, fiscal instability affects school curricula in many ways. However, school administrators sometimes use the operational and official curricula not for educational purposes, but merely to satisfy commercial and legal requirements. Having stacks of curriculum binders on shelves does not mean that schools are implementing them. Sometimes the master plan calls for a particular curriculum only to be in compliance with federal and state mandates; no one is expected to actually use the materials. As Posner (1995) noted:

> Objectives may also act more indirectly by diverting attention from the hegemonic forces of the school as an institution. When we refocus our attention on the objectives of the official curriculum, we can lose sight of the fact that the school's hidden curriculum may have a more profound and durable impact on students than the official curriculum. . . . This hidden curriculum becomes even more hegemonic in its effect when different groups of children, segregated by "ability" or geography into socially, economically, or racially homogeneous schools or tracks, receive different hidden curricula preparing them for different positions in the social order. (pp. 12–13)

Educators may have a gut feeling that LEP students are being taught and trained for the purpose of filling the lower social order in society. These students are not encouraged or prepared to pursue higher education or aspire to high paying professions. Why? The great disappointment is to realize that the goal of their teachers is only to try to help these voiceless students survive, to satisfy their immediate needs, to enable them to meet the minimum requirements to graduate. No one is even thinking about their futures. Many public schools do not believe LEP students can or should go to college.

When considering curricula, prospective educators must consider the futures of all of their students. The shoddy education schools give to minority students is completely useless for them and for the larger community. If current curricular practices are not changed, many language-minority children will be left unserved in the system.

The Lack of Multicultural Curricula in School

Despite the arguments for and against multicultural education, prospective educators should know in their big hearts that something should be done about the way public schools educate children of diverse backgrounds. These children do not ask schools to craft new policies or come up with anything they do not have already or cannot offer to them. All they need is for schools to redress the wrongs of the hidden curriculum in order to provide all students with equal opportunity and equal access to quality education through multicultural lenses.

Otherwise, the hidden curriculum blocks or stalls attempts to meet the needs of the many bilingual and LEP students who are currently enrolled in the public school system. Parents have to be on the alert to evaluate their children's academic needs thoroughly and carefully, making sure that their children receive a good education. Even among students who speak English as a primary language, there are many cultures, many traditions, and many value systems. Schools do not teach values and children do not learn values in schools even though there is a day called the "National Day of Prayer." Therefore, very little inspiration is available in school for children to draw on to help them adjust and meet their social and emotional needs. Students experience little or no transformation unless they are able to plough through the instances of culture shock on their own. Consider, for example, that although the six pillars of character education are not embedded in the academic curricula or in the school's operational and official curricula, public schools expect students of color to adhere to these values without formally teaching them.

In U.S. history classes, children are taught that one of the reasons immigrants came to America was to find religious freedom; however, religion is nearly absent in the formalized school setting. Students are asked to pledge their allegiance to the flag of the United States as a patriotic action. The phrase "one nation under God" in that pledge says that Americans believe in God; however, different Americans may believe in different Gods, depending on their religious affiliations and practices. In fact, religious activities are extremely controversial in grades K-12, as shown in Table 12.2, but post-high school education often includes the study of religions. The point is that multicultural education, which respects and includes all cultures, prepares the younger generation to encounter other forms of faith and develop tolerance toward other people's cultures and traditions.

It appears that the hidden curriculum is the school's silent policy similar to the "don't ask, don't tell" policy regarding homosexuality. The implication and result of the hidden curriculum is that schools may continue in their hegemonic values and mentality.

Table. 12.2. Federal Guidelines on Religious Expression in Public Schools

Expression	Guideline
Student prayer and religious discussion	Students may pray in nondisruptive manner when not engaged in school activities or instruction and subject to the rules that normally pertain in the applicable setting.
Graduation prayer	Under current U.S. Supreme Court decision, school officials may not mandate or organize prayer at graduation nor organize religious baccalaureate ceremonies.
Official neutrality	Teachers and school administrators are prohibited by the U.S. Constitution from soliciting or encouraging religious activity and from discouraging activity because of its religious content.
Teaching about religion	Public schools may not provide religious instruction, but they may teach about religion, the history of religion, comparative religion, the Bible or other scripture as literature, and the role of religion in the history of the United States and other countries.
Religious holidays	Although public schools may teach about religious holidays and may celebrate the secular aspects of holidays, public schools may not observe holidays as religious events or promote such observance by students.
Student assignments	Students may express their beliefs about religion in the form of homework, artwork, and other written and oral assignments; such home and classroom work should be judged by ordinary academic standards.
Religious literature	Students have the rights to distribute religious literature to their schoolmates on the same terms as they are permitted to distribute other literature that is unrelated to school curriculum or activities.
Religions exemptions	Public schools enjoy substantial discretion to excuse individual students from lessons that are objectionable to the student or the student's parents on religious or other conscientious grounds.
Release time	Public schools have the discretion to dismiss students to off-premises religious instruction, provided that schools do not encourage or discourage participation, and public schools may not allow religious instruction by outsiders on school premises during the school day.
Teaching values	Though public schools must be neutral with respect to religions, they may play an active role with respect to teaching civic values and virtues.
Student garb	Students may display religious messages on items of clothing to the same extent that they are permitted to display other comparable messages.
The equal access act	Student religious groups have the same right of access to school facilities as is enjoyed by other comparable students groups.

Note. Information from U.S. Secretary of Education, Richard W. Riley, "Secretary's Statement on Religious Expression," released by the U.S. Department of Education in 1998, Washington, DC, retrieved from www.ed.gov/inits/religionandschools.

Reform to Promote Social Justice for All

The American educational system is one of the very best in the world. The compulsory educational system of this country was created on the basis of the democratic principles of the founding fathers who believed that equal opportunity in schooling would enrich the lives of the people and of the nation. Whether a child is born poor or rich, everyone should have equal opportunity to access quality education regardless of national origin, race, color, creed, gender, religion, and most importantly, immigration status.

Prospective educators should bear in mind that for the last three centuries, the people of this country fought for universal access to public education. But from now to the next century, the people of this country will contend politically for universal quality of schooling from which all children will benefit. The struggle now is not for equal access, but for equal quality.

To produce equal quality in today's culturally diverse public schools, schools must reform the hidden curriculum. They must develop a cultural enrichment curriculum within the instructional schemes to assist minority students in the saturation process to learn both their native and their new cultures and languages simultaneously. Total school reform may be impossible, but curricular reform is attainable. To ensure social justice for all, educators need to let go of the hidden curriculum; otherwise, the system itself will continue to undermine public trust in education.

Bilingual curricula should no longer be used as a political and legal mechanism to segregate LEP and bilingual students, denying them equality of education and opportunity. Legal segregation is what has caused the dichotomy of education in public schools. Instead, saturation would help schools eliminate segregation based on cultural and language differences, reducing prejudice and improving opportunities for all students. Keep in mind that America is a multicultural and multilingual nation that has historically welcomed change, reform, restructuring, and rethinking.

Multicultural Curricula for All Students

Instead of using one-size-fits-all instruction, prospective teachers could use integrated content area instruction as a multiple approach to reaching all students in all content areas, as shown in Table 12.3. Keep in mind that the strategies outlined in Table 12.3 should work well in all academic subjects and are appropriate for all students regardless of linguistic backgrounds.

Prospective educators should keep in mind that it will be extremely hard to meet all the needs and demands of each and every single student in the

Table 12.3. Integrated Content Area Instruction Strategies

Strategy	Activities	Examples
Preview/review	Introduce learning objective, key concepts, vocabulary, prior knowledge, and specific skills development.	What did we learn about the life cycle of a butterfly yesterday? Can anyone tell me something about it?
Simplify the input	Use clear enunciation, short sentences or questions; use simple vocabulary; apply body language; avoid idioms and complex language.	Explain each of the four stages of the life cycle: egg, cocoon, caterpillar, and butterfly.
Contextualization	Label everything, such as people, objects, pictures, key words, and diagrams.	Show a colored poster with the four stages of the life cycle of a butterfly.
Focus questions	Use anticipatory set for engaging prior knowledge and prompting curiosity.	How many kinds of butterflies are there? What are their colors?
Note taking strategies	Help jot down notes or key words or write key words on the board.	Make a list of key words: metamorphosis, chrysalis, cocoon, and pupa.
Outline guides	Prepare worksheet with specific tasks or activities for students to complete.	Use cutouts of the four stages for hands-on activity.
Tape or video record lesson	If legally permitted, tape or video record student activity and interaction and make copies for review at home.	Make videotape of students during hands-on activity to show how they put together the four stages.
Vocabulary book or journal entries	List key words on the board for students to copy.	Use key words to write simple sentences about the butterfly.
Cooperative groups	Divide students into groups of 2 to 5.	Give simple directions for group activities and allow each student to be part of the project.
Waiting time	Allow a few seconds for students to process the question before calling on someone to answer.	What is the first stage of the life cycle?

Table continues on next page

Table 12.3, continued

Strategy	Activities	Examples
Check for understanding	Monitor students throughout the entire lesson and adjust accordingly.	Move among students to make sure that all are doing hands-on activity.
Scripting or essay	Allow students to express in their own words their thoughts about the activity.	Ask students to write down what they learned today about butterflies.
PQ5R's	Use preview, question, reading, reflection, recitation, review, and response to recap key points with students.	What are the four stages of the life cycle of a butterfly? One is…, two is…, three is…, and four… is …. Also, recap key words, such as pupa, cocoon, and metamorphosis.

system; it is impossible to include all cultures and languages in the curriculum. Moreover, multicultural education is of value not just for LEP students or language-minority students; in fact, it is of great value for all students. The goal of modern multicultural education, which is to promote multicultural learning, can be reached through the following measures:

1. Develop integrated content instruction and curriculum. For instance, students should be guided to make learning connections through the units or themes the teacher has developed to teach all students. At the same time, integrate language instruction and content instruction so as to keep all students on the same page, objective, or goal.

2. Create social empowerment that promotes learning. For instance, engage students in meaningful and relevant communications during teaching to stimulate learning opportunities that allow students to use language as a medium of interaction to improve learning skills and social confidence. One useful strategy is to use cooperative learning or small groups to help students interact with one another while exchanging ideas.

3. Prescribe more hands-on and minds-on activities. For instance, instead of using rote memorization to encode and decode facts and information, the teacher designs a hands-on activity that engages students in firsthand experience and allows students to digest what they have just learned through the activity before asking them to share how they understand what has happened in oral or written form or both.

4. Set up clear, concise, and specific expectations for learning. For instance, for students with the family value of filial piety or with strict parental rules, teachers enforce their good and responsible behaviors in class by having clear classroom rules, routine procedures, assignment guidelines, and learning outcomes that keep students motivated. Consistency saves teachers time they can use to help students who need extra assistance. Classroom expectations should be reviewed on a regular basis as a disciplinary tool to hold students academically accountable.

5. Deal with issues of cultural diversity. Teachers who take the time to learn about their students' cultural identities have a greater chance of helping their students improve their self-concept, self-image, self-worth, and self-esteem because they build cultural connections with their students.

6. Combat prejudice in the learning environment. The teacher plays a vital role in reducing prejudice by modeling behaviors and attitudes and refusing to tolerate prejudicial or discriminatory remarks in the learning environment, demonstrating that all students are socially and culturally equal. Teachers can reduce or eradicate cultural misconceptions by introducing resources as well as instructional practices that help students learn from one another about their cultures and traditions.

7. Create equal opportunities for learning. For instance, teachers strategize teaching schemes that enable them to assist students who are having difficulties understanding assignments. This may mean devoting extra time in or out of class to certain students. Also, reflective teaching allows teachers to assess themselves based on student learning outcomes.

8. Provide equity of instruction. Some students may need individualized instruction regardless of how many times the teacher has covered or repeated a lesson. Individualized instruction is one of the most effective teaching modalities for helping language-minority students learn.

9. Use differentiated instruction modalities. For instance, to accommodate the different learning styles of all students, the teacher needs to incorporate integrated content instruction as part of the instructional process and use a variety of instructional approaches to tap all students into the learning objective. One approach is to engage students in prior knowledge as much as possible in order to make the learning inspirational and relevant to real life situations.

10. Maintain good rapport with all students. Quite often students perform poorly in class because of personality clashes with the teacher even without obvious evidence of dislike or antagonism. Simply put, if students do not like the teacher, they seem not to care much about the class. Keep in mind that students are human beings and they often can "read" a teacher before the teacher can "read" them. Maintaining warm relationships with students will increase students' motivation to learn.

Prospective educators should know that these are suggestions only; they are not academic panaceas and there is no guarantee any suggestion will work well with all students in all classes. However, the development of curricular approaches that help all students learn in a multicultural classroom where English is the primary language of instruction is critical to the provision of equitable, quality education for all students. However, at least, the system must let go of the hidden curriculum in order to minimize the impact of deficit ideologies based on hegemonic principles.

Summing Up

This chapter presented information that gives educators insights into the reality of the hegemonic hidden curriculum and its negative effects on the education of all students. Keep in mind that curricular approaches require tremendous effort and professional commitment in order to overcome the difficult challenges of the culturally diverse classroom. The hidden curriculum needs to be redressed formally and academically; otherwise, adherence to the status quo will continue to segregate students on the basis of race, ethnicity, religion, class, SES, gender, culture, and language. Although large-scale education reform is not possible in the short run, curricular reform is possible at any time. Without meaningful curricular approaches, the education of language-minority students will continue to lag behind and the academic achievement gap will grow even wider.

Chapter Thirteen

Multicultural Instructional Practices

> The only thing that endures over time is the law of the farm....
> I must prepare the ground, put in the seed, cultivate it, water it, and then
> gradually nurture growth and development, not full maturity....
> There is no quick fix.
>
> —Stephen Covey

Overview

Much has already been said about multicultural dimensions, cultural diversity, sociocultural factors, psychosocial environment, at-risk students, and the hidden curriculum that inhibits learning opportunities in schools. At this point, it is probably very difficult for prospective educators to think about their professional responsibilities and commitments to meet all the diverse needs and abilities of students in today's classrooms. Teaching and learning are the most critical elements in education. In addition to all the other issues educators must consider, questions may still linger in the minds of prospective teachers: How can students overcome difficult academic barriers? How can teachers reach out to them and address their special needs? What are the best ways to assess student learning?

Understanding cultural diversity will enable teachers to be more sensitive to the overall needs of students; however, designing responsive lesson plans and teaching schemes to address the needs of each student is nearly impossible in today's educational environment because of time constraints and other factors associated with the ways public schools handle academic challenges and issues in education.

This chapter explores multicultural instructional practices that involve teaching and learning contexts and multicultural applications. In multicultural settings, teachers require theoretical principles and philosophical foundations to develop meaningful humanistic approaches as well as other instructional approaches to accommodate the diverse needs and abilities of language-minority students. This chapter was written in the hope that prospective educators will incorporate and/or integrate these approaches into their daily teaching schemes and professional practice.

Areas of Competence in Teaching

Today's teachers have a full plate of huge teaching responsibilities, including teaching, lesson plan design, evaluation of student learning, classroom management, discipline, assessment, curriculum design, supervision, and professional development. According to Ryan and Cooper (2001) and Cooper (1999), areas of focus in teaching associated with professional competence are (a) professional attitudes that foster learning, (b) knowledge of subject matter, (c) theoretical knowledge about learning and human behavior, and (d) repertoire of teaching skills.

Practically, the three basic types of knowledge in which teachers should be competent are (a) disciplinary content knowledge—subject matter preparation, or the knowledge learned from coursework, (b) curriculum content knowledge—academic standards, or the knowledge associated with academic activities and content area standards, and (c) pedagogical content knowledge—teaching methodologies, or the knowledge used to combine disciplinary content and curriculum content to devise teaching methods required for instruction to meet pedagogical learning objectives and goals.

Keep in mind that teachers play many roles in education, and their leadership and ability to make good decisions are crucial to the process of teaching and learning. Their personal qualities, professionalism, and passion determine the quality of instruction they provide to all students in their classrooms.

The Process of Instructional Practice

The process of instruction requires a number of decisions from teachers each and every day. Figure 13.1 illustrates the four major stages of the instruction process: planning, implementation, evaluation, and feedback (Cooper, 1999; Ryan & Cooper, 2001). Each stage involves different elements that prospective educators need to take into consideration when assembling the whole curriculum as a teaching theme, or unit.

The planning stage consists of three basic elements:

1. Preplanning involves the gathering of ideas, resources, and academic standards.
2. Ongoing planning is action that takes place throughout instruction as the teacher adjusts to the needs of students.
3. Postplanning involves reflective practices and self-assessment.

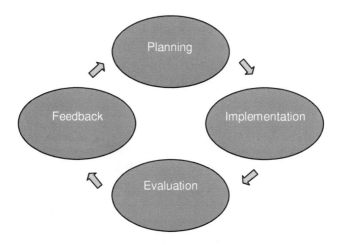

Figure. 13.1. The process of instructional practice

The implementation stage involves the delivery of instruction, and its components vary according to the delivery method. For instance, if a five-step lesson model is used, as illustrated in Table 13.1, the teacher assembles specific information for each of the five steps. In this example, implementation consists of the five steps of anticipatory set, instruction, guided practices, closure, and independent practices. In the anticipatory set, the teacher engages students and taps them into the lesson plan objective. The instruction section includes all steps the teacher takes in showing, modeling, illustrating, and demonstrating the key concepts in the lesson. The guided practices section continues the same strategies from the instruction section but includes examples of problems, trying out different ideas, calling on students to give responses, drills, and exercises for independent practice. The closure, or evaluation or assessment, section involves independent practice, group practice, cooperative learning, handout exercises, activities, quizzes or other tests, depending on the nature of the lesson. The independent practice section usually allows students to practice the concepts or ideas they have been taught on their own, beyond the lesson plan; this section could be done through individual work, group work, or homework.

The evaluation stage usually involves assessment of student learning after a unit is taught. Some teachers include this stage in every lesson plan and others do not. The teacher could design a teacher-made test to evaluate or assess student learning. Some teachers use unit tests or chapter reviews, whereas others have weekly tests on vocabulary words. The assessment method may depend on the nature of the lesson, but evaluating student learning is crucial to teaching. Without evaluation, there may be little or no connection between instruction and student learning. Similarly, some teachers use the process of a three-step lesson plan for language arts or reading: Into, Through, and Beyond.

Table 13.1. Sample Model of Five-Step Lesson Plan

Lesson Component	Sample Activities
Title of lesson plan	Choose a good title for a lesson—e.g., The Life Cycle of a Butterfly
Time	Specify time: 15, 20, 25, or 30 minutes
Subject area	Science, language arts, social studies, or math
Grade level	Choose a grade level
Content area standards	Choose specific standards and write out the standards
Objective	State a concise and clear objective; one objective per lesson plan is preferable
Materials	List all materials to be used for the lesson plan activities
Anticipatory set	List of ideas, questions, statements, or prompts to engage students and their prior knowledge to tap them into your lesson plan objective
Instructions	State teaching plan of actions and follow through in timely manner: showing, modeling, illustrating, and demonstrating
Guided practices	Samples of problems, ideas, tryouts, worksheets, individual or group activities, and independent practices
Closure (evaluation or assessment)	Testing, reviewing, pop quiz, or summarizing the key concepts covered in the lesson plan
Independent practice	Extension of lesson plan, individual or group activities, worksheet, or homework; activity beyond the classroom

The feedback stage is normally designed for teachers to reflect upon their effectiveness in promoting student learning. This stage is crucial to designing academic lesson plans appropriate for specific grade and age levels. Teachers who understand reflective teaching and self-assessment become effective and responsive practitioners who can adjust instructional practices to meet the needs of diverse learners.

Multicultural Instructional Approaches

Prospective educators may want to ask themselves about their own personal teaching styles or instructional approaches because each teacher is unique and has his or her own ways of conveying information to students. There is no single perfect way of teaching, but some methods are more effective than others. Some instructional approaches are direct instruction and differentiating instruction, scaffolding instruction and reciprocal teaching, ELD instruction and SDAIE instruction. Some teachers vary their instructional approaches to accommodate different learning styles; however, nearly 80% of teachers today use the direct instruction model, which is a one-model-fits-all approach. Most importantly, regardless of what instructional approach is used, the teacher needs to be creative in order to make the subject matter interesting, intriguing, and fun. Rigid teaching methods, such as direct instruction, are not beneficial to English language learners because most of these students do not learn by listening, but by doing, or firsthand experience. However, direct instruction is effective when time is limited.

To help prospective educators gain insight into the various instructional approaches, Table 13.2 illustrates different models of instruction. Teachers may want to vary instruction by incorporating a number of different approaches when dealing with diverse learners in the classroom.

Regardless of what instructional approach is used, the teacher is the key to effectiveness of instruction. The teacher's preparation, organization, time management, and classroom management play essential roles in teaching and learning. Prospective educators should not rule out an eclectic approach because some learners may need individualized instruction.

Furthermore, prospective educators also need to know the three-tiered pedagogical framework involving the design of effective instructional strategies, as illustrated in Figure 13.2. In this framework, instructional strategies are divided into three areas: lesson plan strategies, activity strategies, and task strategies (Doolittle, 2002).

Table 13.2. Selected Traditional and Modern Instructional Approaches

Traditional Approach	Modern Approach	Recommended Approach
Whole language	Phonics	Need both, depending on the nature of the lesson plan.
Whole group	Small group or centers	Both approaches are crucial to student learning; however, varying instruction helps teachers focus on specific learning needs.
Learners are passive in the learning process	Learners are active in the learning process	Learners should learn to be both passive and active, depending on the learning objective
Product is the most important part of learning	Process is the most important part of learning	Both are essential to learning because students need procedural knowledge as well as application to real life experiences
Part to whole is emphasized	Whole to part is emphasized	Both concepts are valuable, depending on the nature of the lesson plan.
Learning relies on sequence of skills	Learning depends on relevant, real, and prior experiences	Approaches equally important because learners need to develop both in order to compete academically.
Extrinsic motivation is best in learning	Intrinsic motivation is best in learning	Depends on the learner's personal desire to learn each subject matter; however, both approaches are critical in the development of rounded-knowledge and repertoire of learning skills.
Ability grouping	Interests, needs, or desires grouping	Depends on grade level and age of learner.
Competition stressed	Cooperation stressed	All learners need both in order to perform academically and socially.
Teacher-centered	Student-centered	Teacher-centered saves time but creative student-centered produces better learning.
Teacher as leader	Teacher as facilitator	Both roles important.
Textbook	Children's literature and portfolio	Both approaches are needed in order to broaden students' personal understanding of multicultural society and cultural diversity.

Table continues on next page

Table 13.2, continued

Traditional Approach	Modern Approach	Recommended Approach
Tests used to assess student learning	Portfolio and progress used to assess student learning	Both approaches are appropriate, depending on grade level.
Book-centered setting	Child-centered setting	Both approaches are important because learners need the right tools as well as the right attention in order to excel academically.
The child must fit to the book	The book must fit to the child	Both approaches important; however, ELLs will not be able to read difficult texts if they are not prepared academically. Appropriate reading materials necessary.
One model-fits-all	Multiple approaches to deal with diverse learners	Depending on learners' academic ability and comprehension level, teachers need to incorporate different teaching methodologies to accommodate different learning needs.

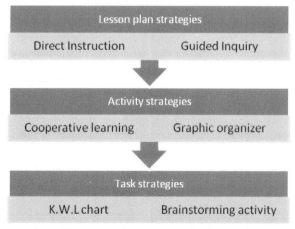

Figure 13.2. Three tiers of instructional strategies

The Nature of Teaching

Literally, teaching is a creative art. Teaching could be defined as the systematic presentation of general information, facts, ideas, skills, knowledge, principles, and techniques to an audience of students who may lack learning in the formalized process. Teaching involves human interaction, relationships, socialization, bonds, and exchange of ideas through communication. Teaching is an ongoing process of academic instruction and curricular activities that involves encoding, decoding, interaction, creation, integration, and transference of knowledge taking place in a well-established setting. Whether one believes teachers are born or made, teaching is an art that must be developed by practice.

Keep in mind that there are different methods of teaching. Teaching is not the same as preaching, lecturing is not the same as engaging in hands-on activities, and teacher-centered instruction is not the same as student-centered instruction. Consider, for example, the three questions that guide instructional strategies:

1. Philosophical approach: What should students learn in class?
2. Educational psychological approach: How should students learn the academic content?
3. Pedagogical approach: How should students be taught instructionally and academically?

Furthermore, good teaching is not about presenting answers to questions; rather it is about questioning the answers. Regardless of how one defines teaching or views it, the beauty of teaching is in its techniques, skills, knowledge, tools, creativity, and applications.

Developing Appropriate Teaching Styles

Each educator has his or her own unique teaching style, and that style will be effective with all students or with only some. Flexible teaching styles accommodate diverse learning styles, grade levels, and ages of students; however, teachers need time and energy to execute various styles effectively. A teacher's teaching styles could reflect that teacher's learning style. For instance, consider these questions: How many people read the instructions given by the manufacturer before assembling a bicycle? How many people read the instructions and assemble the bicycle at the same time? And how many people assemble the bicycle without reading all the instructions? People are individuals, and they teach and learn in their individual styles. An effective teacher allows students to perform tasks according to their ways of thinking and solving problems even if those ways differ from those of the teacher.

To help prospective educators understand differences in teaching styles, Figure 13.3 gives a broad picture of different types of approaches that are considered appropriate in multicultural classroom settings.

Approaches in the Telling, or Cognitive Undemanding, quadrant might be appropriate for K-1 classrooms, where the teacher does most of the talking and students primarily listen, repeat, recite, and memorize. Approaches in the Showing, or Some Cognitive Demanding, quadrant are appropriate for second and third grade, where the teacher expects students to learn some facts and recall key concepts in formal exercises. In the Trying, or Context-Embedded Learning, quadrant, the teacher can expect students to perform basic independent academic tasks, such as completing worksheets or doing a specific task. And in the Doing, or Context-Reduced Learning quadrant, the teacher expects a high level of comprehension and academic performance from students, such as reading to learn more information. Keep in mind that it is extremely difficult to find a teaching style that fits all students. If teachers know how to use and apply these basic styles appropriately, they can deal effectively with diverse students. Teachers may have to learn to work outside their preferred styles.

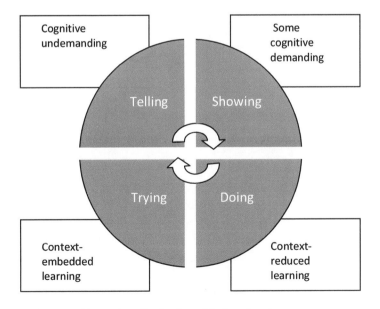

Figure 13.3. Teaching styles effective in multicultural settings

Most importantly, a good teacher should be able to function in all four quadrants and thus be competent in the entire teaching process. A teacher might need to start in the Telling quadrant and gradually progress through the other three quadrants as students advance. The teacher also needs to be able to move backward to stay at or return to the level students need. Actually, teachers could start anywhere and move around or back and forth as they need to meet the learning objective of the lesson plan. Understanding the quadrants and moving through them as appropriate keeps teaching styles flexible, accommodating, and reflective. Moreover, as Cummins (1981) pointed out, students need to experience both BICS and CALP in the learning process. When teachers use this teaching style model, most students learn BICS in the first two quadrants and CALP in the second two quadrants.

What Are Teaching Methodologies?

Teaching methodologies are sometimes called instructional approaches, teaching styles, and instructional strategies. The word *methodology* in academia refers to how to teach, not what to teach. Thus teaching methodologies are methods of instruction. The words *methodologies* and *approaches* are generally used interchangeably, and sometimes the word *strategy* is also used with the same meaning. Educators speak of instructional strategies, lesson plan strategies, activity strategies, and task strategies. These terms are even more confusing to new teachers when they are mixed with the term *pedagogical skills*, which refers to how to teach and how students learn.

Teaching methodologies, or lesson plan strategies, are types of approaches teachers use when designing lesson plans for instruction. For instance, direct instruction, group instruction, and inquiry instruction are three different methods of instruction. Advanced organizer, jigsaw, and problem-based learning are examples of activity strategies. Strategies such as K-W-L, think aloud, and think-pair-share are task strategies. Sometimes teachers mix these strategies together because of their commonalities and similarities, as illustrated in Table 13.3.

These methods of instruction are typically effective if used appropriately; however, most teachers today are expected to use only direct instruction because of time constraints and a push for instructional uniformity. Keep in mind that direct instruction is not conducive to all learning styles, and is especially ineffective for English language learners. Moreover, most teachers are not trained properly to use most of the methods listed. In theory, teachers should know all of them even if they typically use only one or two when doing actual teaching in the classroom. Despite the widespread use of direct

Table 13.3. Selected Teaching Strategies

Acronym	Actual Strategy	Example of Use
TI	Thematic instruction	Organizing or framing instruction around key areas, concepts, or ideas to make connections
CALLA	Cognitive Academic Language Learning Approach	Involve topics, academic language skills, and language acquisition
ILA	Integrated language arts	Whole language approach to learn new language
5w's + H	What, when, where, who, why, and how	Question-based instruction, inquiry instruction, or investigative approach
DI	Direct Instruction	Systematic approach, one-model-fits-all, use in all subject matter teaching
ELD	English Language Development	Transitional bilingual education programs without primary language (L1) support
ESL	English as a second language	ELD or SDAIE instruction or whole language approach
K-W-L	What I *know,* what I *want* to learn, and what I *learned*	Student-centered approach
LEA	Language experience approach	Use mostly in language arts for writing and reading based on student's experiences and prior knowledge
PQ5Rs	Preview, question, read, recite, reflect, review, and respond	Use in all subject matter teaching and with any instructional methodologies
PR	Preview and review	Engage prior knowledge and tap into lesson plan objective
CL	Cooperative learning	Groups, centers, or stations
PW	Process writing	A process of writing or POWERS: Prewrite, organize, write, edit, rewrite, and submit
RT	Reciprocal teaching	Question-based approach and use mostly in language arts for reading: 4-step process: Summary, clarification, question, and prediction
Scaffolding	Backing out or withdrawal strategies, or building skills as layers or levels	Use in all subject matter teaching, ELD, SDAIE, TESOL, ESL, SEI, and others
SDAIE	Specially designed academic instruction in English	ELD instruction with primary language support (L1)
SEI	Sheltered English instruction	ESL, TESOL, ELD, or SDAIE instruction

Table continues on next page

Table 13.3, continued

Acronym	Actual Strategy	Example of Use
TESOL	Teach English to speakers of other language	ESL, ELD, or SDAIE instruction
TNA	The natural approach	Use mostly in language arts
TPR	Total physical response	Music, dance, physical education, or body movement
GI	Guided inquiry instruction	Student-centered, investigative instruction, question-based

instruction, most children benefit more from hands-on and minds-on activities than any other methodologies. According to Howe (2002), the engagement level of students depends on the types of activities teachers employ to involve students during the instructional process (see Table 13.4).

Keep in mind that personal and professional theories will play a part in teaching, and these theories could overshadow how one teaches and expects students to learn in class. The praxis, putting theory into practice, may also influence the ways teachers view teaching methodologies required for instruction. For instance, schools may require teachers to use only direct instruction even though a teacher may believe that guided inquiry is a better method. This type of conflict is normally healthy for new teachers as they get used to and feel comfortable enough to use both methodologies.

Other Kinds of Teaching Methodologies

The methodology of co-teaching is not taught in college courses; however, it is widely and frequently used by teachers in K-6 classrooms, particularly in kindergarten, ELD class, SDAIE class, ESL class, and classes for students with special needs or learning disabilities. Co-teaching was originally designed for teaching secondary schools and special education classes. However, new teachers usually finish their student teaching practicum with a co-teaching methodology. Student teachers are often assigned to a cooperative teacher or master teacher in a classroom, who serves as a mentor. During the 14 weeks of student teaching, the mentor teacher shows and guides student teachers through planning, delivery of instruction, assessment, classroom management, and disciplinary actions. This on-the-job training is a co-teaching practice. Several models of co-teaching are available for teachers to consider while using direct instruction or other methods of teaching (McNamara, 2007; Rice & Zigmond, 2000; and Weiss & Lloyd, 2002). Some are presented in Table 13.5.

Table 13.4. Engagement Level by Activity Type

Activity Type	Engagement Level	Sample of Tasks
Minds-on activities with concrete materials	High	Writing/jotting down thoughts and reflections in journal after conducting an experiment.
Hands-on activities with concrete materials	High	Doing firsthand experience, observing an experiment, or conducting an investigation in a group.
Visiting school garden	High	Observing different plants or vegetables, picking some leaves for experiment, or harvesting some fruits.
Computer lab activities	Medium to high	Logging onto websites to find out more about a specific topic or finding answers from computer.
Guided discussions	Medium to high	Students participate in learning activities, ask questions, listen to peers, take a role in the learning process, and work responsibly. Teacher is a guide or facilitator, not the leader and controller.
Reading activities	Low to medium	Reading aloud, silent reading, or teacher reads and students listen.
Listening and watching the teacher	Low	These types of activities barely engage students or hold their interest.
Listening only	Very low	These types of activities are considered to be disengaging.
Lecturing or preaching	Very low	These types of activities are not academically appropriate for Grades K-12.

Keep in mind that regardless of what type of instruction is used, the personality, attitudes, passion, and patience of the teacher plays a significant role in all humanistic approaches. Carl Rogers (1967) noted that three qualities of the teacher make the greatest difference in student learning: (a) genuineness or realness toward students, (b) positive unconditional regard for students, and (c) professional empathy for students. Teachers with these qualities who try different approaches to lesson planning and delivery should be able to deal successfully with the diverse needs and abilities of language-minority students.

Table 13.5. Co-Teaching Models

Model	Basic Activities	Types of Lesson Plans or Classes
One teaches and one observes	One provides instruction while the other observes students for specific reasons.	Useful in any class with any lesson plan whether monitoring student progress or behavior.
One teaches and one drifts	One provides instruction for the whole class while the other moves around the class to assist students with problems or understanding.	This is a common practice in K-1 grades, where teachers work together as a team.
Team teaching	Meshing instruction by two teachers at the same time, sharing different parts of lesson plan or dividing lesson for coverage, depending on the nature of teaching.	Works well with specific subject matter, perhaps for science or math in grades 4–6 or higher. Also used in ELD/SDAIE classes where aide instructs bilingual students while the teacher is delivering whole-class instruction.
Alternate teaching	Reteaching or reflective lesson plan in a small group, also called center or individualized instruction.	Works well with group of students with similar needs, interests, and academic levels. Similar to individualized instruction.
Parallel teaching	Instruction on the same lesson plan delivered by two teachers in the same room.	Works well with all subject areas, but usually used in lower grades or large classrooms with diverse needs and abilities.
Station teaching	One or two teachers work at different locations, or centers, with different groups of students.	Typical practice in Grades K-6 where teachers group students and assign them to different stations for specific instructions.
Monolingual and bilingual teaching	Monolingual teacher and bilingual aide or teacher assistant work simultaneously in ELD class where translation is needed to help language-minority students comprehend the content in the lesson plan.	Works well with ELD lesson plans with EL adaptations or with students with special needs adaptations targeting language-minority students or students with learning disabilities.

Theoretical Principles of Teaching

Like politics and education, teaching and learning are inseparable when it comes to providing quality instruction. Over the last 100 years, many experts have researched teaching practices and developed theoretical principles to help teachers, social workers, doctors, parents, and other professionals learn about humanistic approaches to increasing their understanding of child development. To help prospective educators gain insight into the ways theories of child development have influenced teaching practice, Table 13.6 presents a brief historical overview of the beliefs expressed by some pioneers in the field.

Keep in mind that there is no perfect theory that can ultimately guide teachers to one "right" teaching approach or help students learn the "right" way. All theoretical approaches should be considered, and theoretical principles should be applied appropriately. In addition to the theories listed in Table 13.6, the critical theory recently emerged as an influence in the fields of education and child development. Quite likely, postmodern thinking about children and the ways they learn is different from the ideas of the past; however, past influences remain the foundations of educational philosophies in teaching and learning.

Philosophical Principles of Education

Philosophy is a bit different from theory, but oftentimes the two overlap in practice. A theory is used to explain or find answers to events or behaviors, and philosophy is normally used to elicit ideas and suggestions to help understand the way events or behaviors ought to be in real-life situations. In other words, philosophy tends to be a general approach to a matter and theory focuses on specific approaches.

Philosophy literally means a search or quest for wisdom or new ideas. In modern society, teachers develop personal and professional philosophies on the basis of their educational experiences as they search for wisdom for maximizing teaching and learning. In teaching, philosophical development provides different perspectives and frameworks for conceptualized thinking to guide professional practice. Thus philosophy has implications for academic curricula, teaching, and learning.

Table 13.6. Theorists Who Have Influenced Education

Theorist	Year of Impact	Theory	Theoretical Principles
Arnold Gesell	1925	Maturational theory	Personal development has biological basis; bad and good experiences; body types of endomorph, ectomorph, and mesomorph.
Sigmund Freud	1935	Psychoanalytical theory	Behavior disorders, behavioral problems, and psychodynamic models designed for children with special needs.
Jean Piaget	1952	Constructivist theory	Based on logico-mathematical knowledge, individualism, autonomy in learning.
John Dewey	1956	Learner's experience or prior knowledge approach	Learner's experience is the starting point of instruction instead of rigid and programmed curricula.
Jerome Bruner	1966	Knowledge theory	Enactive, iconic, and symbolic modes; also, the spiral curriculum approach.
Lawrence Kohlberg	1969	Constructivist theory	Preconventional stage, conventional stage, and postconventional or principled stage.
B.F. Skinner	1974	Behaviorist theory	Environment has role in individual development or behavior modification and programmed learning.
Lev Vygotsky	1978	Sociohistorical theory	Emphasis on sociohistorical context, language and literacy learning, and child's zone of proximal development.
U. Bronfenbrenner	1979	Ecological system theory	Emphasis on the influence of microsystem, mesosystem, exosystem, and macrosystem.
Howard Gardner	1983	Multiple intelligence	Eight types of intelligence: linguistic, logical/ mathematical, visual/spatial, musical, bodily kinesthetic, interpersonal, intrapersonal, and naturalist.

Four branches of philosophy impact education: epistemology, metaphysics, axiology, and logic. Epistemology is concerned with how we know what we know; metaphysics, or ontology, stresses what we know and what is real; axiology emphasizes values and ethics; and logic is concerned with processes of deriving conclusion from basic principles. In practice, prospective educators should bear in mind that these overlap the traditional philosophies: idealism, which focuses on absolute ideas and time; realism, which is concerned with natural law; pragmatism, which emphasizes experience and practical understanding; and existentialism, which focuses on freedom, responsibility, and self-awareness.

Basically, four educational philosophies underlie modern education: perenialism, which emphasizes the values of idealism and realism; essentialism, which emphasizes fundamental skills and academic subject areas (reading, writing, mathematics, social studies, and science); progressivism, which focuses on the practice of pragmatism; and postmodernism, which stresses contemporary approaches based on restructuring and constructivism.

Keep in mind that these philosophies may not shed any light on the understanding of children coming from diverse backgrounds. Today's teachers must focus on many things, such as teaching assignments, learning outcomes, philosophical implications, and education policies affecting professional practice. Not all teachers received the same college education before going into teaching credential programs. Teachers come from a variety of educational backgrounds, and some may lack specific college courses that would enhance their teaching, such as child development, multicultural education, assessment, education policy, and classroom management.

The Basics of Child Development and Education

Basically, the study of child development is concerned with the physical, intellectual, social, and emotional changes that occur from birth to adolescence. The field of child development encompasses a variety of factors that positively or negatively influence the child's life. For example, heredity, family members, peers, school environment, community, biological factors, economic factors, critical life experiences, elements outside of and within the child, and other human issues contribute to the development of the child. Studying child development provides practical guidance for teachers and childcare providers that enable them to promote and support healthy growth in the children in their care. For instance, understanding early brain development is essential to teaching and learning in the classroom, and this kind of knowledge can lead teachers to provide better learning opportunities for intellectual and cognitive development in children as well as for learning stimulation.

Lessow-Hurley (2000) described the stages of first-language development in children. Crying, babbling, and telegraphic speech stages are critical in language development. Adults can modify these stages with various inputs, such as making corrections and facilitating communication. These modifications help children learn child-directed speech or "motherese." Keep in mind that children develop at different rates and their ages play a factor in how they first learn "motherese."

Lessow-Hurley gave the typical progression of early language accomplishment as follows: (a) crying as an expression of discomfort, birth to 2 months; (b) cooing sounds as an expression of satisfaction or pleasure, 2 to 4 months; (c) babbling later changing to echolalic babbling, 4 to 9 months; (d) one-word utterances, 9 to 18 months; (e) two-word utterances or the beginning of using simple syntax, 18 months to 2 ½ years; and (f) use of expanded syntax and vocabulary or basic communication skills, 2 ½ to 4 years.

Furthermore, the eight states of personality development described by Erikson (1950) are crucial in understanding the stages of child development. According to Erikson, the stages are (a) oral-sensory, birth to 18 months; (b) muscular-anal, 18 months to 3 years; (c) locomotor, 3 to 6 years; (d) latency, 6 to 12 years; (e) adolescence, 12 to 18 years; (f) young adulthood, 19 to 40 years; (g) middle adulthood, 40 to 65 years; and (h) late adulthood, 65 years to death. During these personality development stages, children, adolescents, and adults explore and discover the world around them and make adjustments accordingly. In some cases, conflicts, crises, and unexpected events shape personality positively or negatively or both. For example, an abused child develops personality differently from a non-abused child. Also, dysfunctional family life could alter development in any of these stages.

Understanding child development helps teachers deal better with children with special needs. For instance, dealing with autistic students requires tremendous in-depth knowledge and skills. Teachers of students with emotional disorders, conduct disorders, and learning disabilities need knowledge and skills specific to the children's conditions. Otherwise, the special needs present obstacles that inhibit the students' educational opportunities. Studying child development provides teachers with information and experiences they might not have in their personal lives. The study produces self-understanding, self-awareness, self-growth, and self-fulfillment.

Not all teachers grow up in the same socioeconomic environment. Some teachers were raised with lots of books, and others grew up without books. These differences in experiences could cause teachers to assume their developmental experience is the norm. To avoid such preconceptions, teachers need to learn about cognitive and social development in children. For example, most children would naturally assume from observation that the world is flat until they are taught that the world is actually round, not flat. Children are born as blank slates; they learn their languages, cultures, and facts about the world and people around them. Formal education is part of their learning. Therefore, an understanding of child development should be integral to teaching and learning philosophies.

Dealing with Different Forms of Learning

There are different forms of human learning, such as habituation, sensitization, observation, and language learning. Learning can take place inside or outside the classroom, and it can be formal or informal. Formal learning usually takes place in school under the guidance of a well-trained professional teacher, whereas informal learning takes place through emulation, observation, experience, and listening to folktales. Most children learn how to cry, talk, speak, behave, and socialize before entering school. All human learning directly involves cognition, affection, psychomotor activity, and social process. Literally, learning simply means acquiring knowledge through formal and informal processes or developing the ability to perform tasks based on prior knowledge or new experiences. Charles and Senter (2002) explained how people learn and retain information. The correlation they made between active participation in learning and retention of information is shown in Table 13.7.

Learning is a non-stop process that continues throughout life. Learning changes life and shapes the way the learner thinks about certain things in life. Learning will affect everything people do positively or negatively. Learning could arouse traumatic or painful memories from the past. People can learn a wide range of information and behaviors, from simple concepts to complex ideas and concrete applications. Amazingly, human learning can be sparked by a single stimulus or multiple stimuli, depending on curiosity or the motivation to learn.

Table 13.7. Correlation Between Active Role in Learning and Retention

Role	Retention	Possible Explanations
Reading	10%	Students retain only what is relevant to their real-life experiences or interests.
Listening or hearing	20%	Students retain only what is interesting, amazing, and exciting.
Seeing	30%	Students retain only the highlights of scenes, actions, and episodes that they like.
Combining listening and seeing	40%	Students retain only their favorite parts of the story that are relevant to their personal life experiences and what they can remember by encoding and decoding the messages.
Engaging in discussion or saying	70%	Discourse, conversation, or discussion allows students to retain more information by engaging in critical thinking and analysis of the situation.
Experiencing, practicing, or doing hands-on activity	90%	Experiencing, doing, practicing, engaging in hands-on activity or firsthand experience enhances students' knowledge, skills, critical thinking, analysis, and logical application.

Note. Information from *Elementary Classroom Management* (3rd ed.), by C. M. Charles and G. W. Senter, 2002, Boston: Allyn and Bacon

Learning is closely related to or associated with memory in the conscious mind and the subconscious mind, both short-term and long-term memories. Young children, curious about the world around them, taste different food flavors. The taste buds located on the tongue produce immediate reactions to different flavors or medications. Children learn the difference between cold and hot by firsthand experience. Once they learn, the experiences are stored in their memories for future use.

Keep in mind that not all children learn the same way. Some take a longer time to develop specific motor skills, whereas others may learn cognitively and apply the knowledge more quickly. Many factors affect learning in children: age, motivation, prior experience, intelligence, life crises, warfare, trauma, malnutrition, and learning and developmental disorders. Understanding how children learn is essential to teaching and learning in the classroom. Table 13.8 presents the cognitive modes by which students learn as characterized by Gardner (1983) and the ways they process information critically and effectively.

Table 13.8. Multiple Intelligences

Type of Intelligence	Basic Definition	Areas of Interest	Areas of Strength	Possible Learning Styles
Linguistic	Word-smart or understand words and language easily.	Read, write, memorize, and tell stories.	Memorization and reading.	Reading, saying, hearing, or seeing words: The word player.
Logical/ mathematical	Logical-smart, number-smart, or understand logical connections among different ideas, concepts, and theories.	Do experiments, work with numbers, ask questions, explore patterns or relationships between objects, and infer results.	Math, reasoning, logic, problem solving, analogy, and details.	Categorizing, ordering, sequencing, classifying, abstracting, and explain patterns or relationship: The questioner.
Spatial/ visual	Picture-smart or understand the expressions of arts, visual images, or mental images.	Draw, build, design, look at pictures, examine objects, and create images.	Imagination, visualization, sensing, reading maze, interpret charts, and solving puzzles.	Visualizing, dreaming, mental imaging, drawing pictures, creating photographs: The visualizer.
Musical/ audio	Music-smart, sound-smart, rhythm-smart, or understand the patterns of sound system.	Sing, hum tunes, listen, play to music, write songs, respond to music, or create rhythm.	Memorization, picking sounds, understanding rhythms, or sensitivity to sounds.	Sound, rhythm, melody, music, voices, or artful: The music lover.
Bodily/ kinesthetic	Hand-smart, body-smart, sports-smart, physical fitness, agility, or understand patterns of body movement.	Move, use body language, gesture, touch and talk, or act out.	Perform physical activities, dance, sports, acting, crafts design, drafting, or hands-on.	Touching, moving, interacting, processing, sensations of body movement, or feeling the physical appearance: The mover.

Table continues on next page

Table 13.8, continued

Type of Intelligence	Basic Definition	Areas of Interest	Areas of Strength	Possible Learning Styles
Interpersonal	People-smart, friends-smart, social-smart, or understand grouping and social relationships.	Make friends, like people, talk to people, join groups, share with people, depending on, or player of team.	Sharing, understanding, socializing, leading, following, organizing, communicating, listening, mediating, showing, or manipulating.	Sharing, comparing, relating, cooperating, socializing, communicating, following, or leading: The socializer.
Intrapersonal	Self-centered, self-smart, self-propelled, or understand own ways.	Be a loner, be isolated, pursue own interests, set up personal goals, or independent.	Focusing on self, dealing with inward feelings, pursuing personal interests more, like own ways of doing things, choose own goals, or following instincts.	Being a loner, working alone, being very independent, being self-centered, having own space, creating own turf, liking individualized project, or being introvert: The individual.
Natural	Flexible, adaptable, accommodating, considerate, or understand diverse needs and differences.	Have flexible and adaptable patterns of thinking, feeling, understanding, or communicating with people.	Focusing on all forms of learning, interests, considering all things as important, adjusting to needs accordingly, or being able to manage change well.	Having the ability to adapt to different learning environment or subject matter, adjusting to needs accordingly, or controlling changes with flexibility: The flexible learner.

Note. Information from *Multiple Intelligences: The Theory in Practice,* by H. Gardner, 1993, New York: Basic Books.

Moreover, there is a difference between learning and acquisition of skills. Learning usually takes place in a formalized setting that involves a conscious process of memorizing rules, forms, and structures as a result of deliberate teaching, recitation, review, repetition, testing, and response. On the other hand, acquisition happens in any setting that engages an unconscious process of internalizing ideas and developing functional skills as a result of direct exposure, experience, and comprehensive input of information. Both learning and acquisition of skills progress according to age.

How quickly a child learns may depend on the child's IQ; however, IQ is a subject of much debate because it does not account for multiple intelligences. Consider, for example, that a child may do poorly in English class but may perform well in math, music, or physical education. Furthermore, some students are single-sided learners who pick and choose what they are interested in and apply themselves to learning those things to the exclusion of others. These differences do not mean that students cannot learn subjects that are not their strengths; however, learning those things requires more time for them. Once young children practice learning in a style with which they are comfortable, they are often open to learning different subject matter in new ways. Teachers need to disregard the claim, presented in the *Bell Curve*, that people of different races have different IQs determined by their race. Only then can teachers promote multicultural education for all students regardless of their racial and ethnic backgrounds.

How Children Learn in School

In a multicultural setting, it is crucial to consider the stages of human development from a cross-cultural perspective in order to understand how different children learn in school. Cultural factors as well as environmental factors can influence the course of development in children, and moreover, individual personality factors, cultural norms, socioeconomic status, environment, and language barriers may also influence the pace of a child's development. Some factors that can impede learning are poor physical health, poor family status, reaction to loss, unexpected life disruption, lack of a support system at home, and social stress related to the failure to meet basic human needs. Maslow (1954) believed that people are motivated by unsatisfied needs, and he established a hierarchy of human needs, from most basic to highest, as follows: physiological needs (the need for air, food, water, love, sex, and shelter), safety (the need to feel secure without being threatened), love (the need to be loved, to belong, and to be accepted), esteem (the need to feel competent and recognized by others), and self-actualization (the need for self-fulfillment or becoming an individual).

To help prospective educators gain insights into how children learn in school, Table 13.9 presents a comprehensive outline of the stages of human

Table 13.9. Stages of Human Development

Stage	Approx. Age	Basic Biological/ Physical Maturation	Basic Psychological Development	Basic Cognitive Development	Basic Social Development
Newborn period	0-4 months	Sensory capacity, reflexes, movement of head and limbs	Basic trust formation and bonding with mother	Using reflexes, crying for food, movement of limbs, sleeping patterns	Bond to mother and feel her presence or absence
Infancy period	4 months to 2 years	Rapid growth, mobility, coordination, pulling and pushing ability, roll over, crawling, walking, and control of basic body functions	Basic trust continues, use mouth for gratification, bond with mother, respond to activities, alert	Learn to use limbs, cause and effects process, playful, recognize objects, learn to speak or have basic speech development	Recognize siblings, playful, self-mobility, clumsy walking, pulling or pushing objects, learn environment
Preschool period	2 years to 4 years	Slow growth, motor skills development, coordination skills, change from infantile to juvenile body, control body functions	Learn to say no, autonomy, anal phase, understand basic needs and training	Learn to manipulate symbols, pick up words, imitate others, playful	Like friends, recognize peers, learn about siblings, like to do like others, go to school
Juvenile period	4 years to 6 years	Continue to improve motor skills and coordination, run around, playful, learn about speed and agility	In oedipal phase, learn about gender difference, have curious mind, bonding with parents continues	Recognize numbers, quantity, and time; understand basic questions (what, why, how, etc.); ask for details	Start school, make friends, learn school rules and routines, adjust to social norms, playful with friends

Table continues on next page

Table 13.9 (continued)

Stage	Approx. Age	Basic Biological/ Physical Maturation	Basic Psychological Development	Basic Cognitive Development	Basic Social Development
Latency period	7 years to 11 years	Growth slows, motor skills and coordination continue to improve, balance and mobility increase, teething slows, know personal grooming needs, increase appetite, like activities	Form strong identity for self, learn to follow rules, recognize fairness and justice, be close to friends, develop personality	Develop reasoning skills, use ideas, solve problems, understand more complex issues, apply imagination, curious about learning	Like to make friends of same age group, follow and copy others, recognize gender issues, socialize with friends
Preadolescence	11 years to 14 years	Enter another rapid growth period, reach puberty, body changes, muscular development, make transitions	Recognize self-identity, acceptance of peers, physical changes, orient toward self-actualization, develop personality and independence	Enter rapid intellectual growth, reasoning skills, recognize mental ability and brain games, ability to accept challenges, become autonomous in learning	Friends become important part of daily life, encounters with opposite sex, interests are high, hang around with peers, make independent decisions, take personal responsibility

Table continues on next page

Table 13.9 (continued)

Stage	Approx. Age	Basic Biological/ Physical Maturation	Basic Psychological Development	Basic Cognitive Development	Basic Social Development
Adoles-cence	14 years to 21 years	Physical growth slows, puberty con-tinues, hor-mone changes, body changes, cosmetic pe-riod, voice changes, grooming and personality development continue	Continue to form personal identity for self to achieve independence, attracted to opposite sex for physio-logical needs, learn to be responsible, face social and emotional struggles	Have abstract reasoning skills, engage in complex ideas, have great ability to use the mind to deal with academic learning	Center values with peers, some conflict at home, dat-ing games take place, form social class, recog-nize wealth and assets, learn societal values
Young adulthood	21 years to 35 years	Have stable growth, enter procreation and parenting stages, prepare for family values and life style	Find intimacy; have sense of competence; recognize self-worth, self-image, self-esteem, and self-concept	Learn through life experi-ence, develop learning ca-pacity, in-crease level of understanding, apply concrete details, choose learning style to meet peak performance	Recognize societal val-ues, class status, em-ployment, education, friendship, peers at work, continue to have love and intimacy for survival
Adult transition period	35 years to 40 years	Life is stable, family values continue, be parents, reach peak physical strength and prowess, women cease to conceive children	Reassess self-actualization, success, rela-tionships, intimacy, career, finan-cial stability	Have stable cognitive development, improve through train-ing and ex-perience, and continue to develop wis-dom	Reach peak life expecta-tions, make necessary changes, re-align social life, midlife adjustments, continue look-ing for quality of life

Table continues on next page

Table 13.9, continued

Stage	Approx. Age	Basic Biological/ Physical Maturation	Basic Psychological Development	Basic Cognitive Development	Basic Social Development
Middle age	40 years to 60 years	Decline in physical health in general, sexual changes, encounter more health issues, engage in less physical activities	Face identity crisis, body changes and images, deal with unhappiness or happiness in life, live alone after children leave home, learn to cope with retirement	Decline in cognitive abilities, build reasoning skills and abilities, continue to improve wisdom, retain information but lack rapid processing	Center around friends, peers, and family members for comfort; employment could be issue; involved in children's lives; become grandparents; engage in civic responsibilities
The older years	60 years and older	Face sensory loss, skeletal degeneration, more health issues, brain functions slow, aging continues	Face loss of many things, such as sensory loss, family members, and friends; explore new interests; encounter confusion and depression; face changes in life; time to relax and enjoy life	Decline in cognitive functioning and development, wisdom increases based on life experience, explore new interests, create new mastery of skills	Enter retirement, health problems, tough financial needs, neglect by family members, live in isolation, lose friends, subject to medical care facility, enjoy life with family and friends

Note. Information from *A Mutual Challenge: Training and Learning with the Indochinese in Social Work*, by Training Center for Indochinese Paraprofessionals, 1982, Boston University School of Social Work.

development in four basic areas: biological, psychological, cognitive, and social. These areas are critical for understanding children. However, as with the stages of language progression described by Lessow-Hurley (2000) and of personality development posited by Erikson (1950), these developmental milestones cannot be rigidly assigned ages or specific places in a child's development. In the table, they are given approximate age ranges, but even these should not be taken as absolute. If the developmental stages occur within the periods suggested in the table, that finding could be reassuring to teachers. If the developmental patterns are different, they may still be normal, but further assessment of learning is appropriate.

Teachers can use these stages of human development to organize teaching materials, design lesson plans, find appropriate teaching schemes, and establish responsive classroom rules and procedures to maximize teaching and learning for all students in the multicultural setting. Most importantly, these stages should help teachers focus on understanding student learning and thinking rather than on rote memorization, drill, and practice.

Designing Effective Curricula and Instruction for All Students

Today, public schools need to have a comprehensive academic framework for the design of curricula and instruction in responding to the academic needs of the diverse student population. In some areas, curricula and instruction are changing; however, most changes are in the direction of more teacher-centered than student-centered approaches. The majority of public schools use direct instruction, which is teacher-centered, the one-model-fits-all approach.

Language-minority students do not benefit from this method of instruction because they have not acquired the language skills required for this type of instruction. In California, teacher performance expectations and teacher performance assessments require new teachers to identify an English learner (EL) and a student with special needs (SN) and design a lesson plan with EL adaptations or adaptations for the student with special needs. Based on the student demographic data and background information, both adaptations must contain specific pedagogical skills, instructional strategies, student activities, and assessment plans for monitoring the student's learning and academic progress.

Practically speaking, effective curricula and instructions should serve as an academic game plan to address how children learn and how teachers teach. A curriculum is a set of organized academic activities for instruction, and instruction is merely the mode of delivery of planned action designed to make connections between teaching and learning. Vosniadou (2001) encouraged teachers to design academic learning environments that encourage students to be active listeners, to collaborate with other students, and to use meaningful tasks and authentic materials. She offered several models of curricular instructions for consideration, as shown in Table 13.10. Moreover, Howe (2002) explained that each academic lesson plan should contain either a cognitive content objective (knowing *that*) or a cognitive process objective (knowing *how*).

Designing effective curricular instruction requires consistent effort and practice. The models of instruction in Table 13.10 have not been proven successful at all grade levels; however, most of its academic game plan are appropriate in K-8 classrooms. At higher grade levels, teaching appears to more rigid and involve more disciplinary action than in lower grades. However, all forms of teaching at all levels require classroom management and logical discipline; otherwise, teaching and learning would be chaotic. Do not forget to include adaptations for ELLs and students with special needs. For instance, teachers may apply scaffolding techniques along with ELD and/or SDAIE instructions to target ELLs and K-W-L or graphic organizers as task strategies to evaluate response to instruction (RTI) of students with special needs.

The Importance of Classroom Management

To have enough time for teaching and academic engagement, the teacher needs to employ effective classroom management techniques. Among other responsibilities, classroom management is a critical element in teaching and learning because student discipline depends on the way the teacher manages the class. Kounin (1970) listed several characteristics of effective teachers that are helpful for teachers to consider when managing the classroom; these are shown in Table 13.11. Moreover, Table 13.12 presents some transitional activities that prospective educators can use to facilitate ongoing classroom management.

Table 13.10. Instructional Models with Academic Game Plan

Model	Focal Point	Examples
Active and attentive instruction	Keep students awake and academically accountable. Learning requires active, attentive, constructive, and enthusiastic involvement of the learners.	Provide hands-on and minds-on activities, such as writing, sharing, experimentation, observation, group project, and collaborative activities.
Collaborative and cooperative instruction	Interaction and communication are essential to learning since learning is primarily a social activity and participation in the social life of the school is central to learning.	Put students in groups; facilitate the process; and provide guidance, modeling, coaching, and supervision.
Multicultural instruction	Connecting experience with learning increases motivation since students learn best when they participate in activities that are perceived to be useful in real life and are culturally relevant.	Give students opportunities to share their experiences in real life situations in authentic context and prescribe activities that reflect their cultural values.
Preview and review instruction	Engage students by relating new information to prior knowledge since new knowledge is constructed on the basis of what is already understood and believed.	Preview key concepts with students to demystify false conceptions and beliefs before tapping them into the learning objective and later review with students what they have learned.
Strategic instruction	Enhancing study skills increases productivity since students learn by employing effective and flexible strategies that help them to understand, reason, memorize, extrapolate, and solve problems.	Teaching study skills, organizational strategies, coping skills, and access to resources helps students learn by developing personal strategic plan of action.
Autonomous instruction	Promoting self-management and self-regulation increases personal responsibility since students must know how to plan, organize, and monitor their learning by setting learning goals for themselves and correcting their personal mistakes.	Allow students to set learning goals; make sure they are working toward those goals in a timely manner; show how to develop effective strategies and when to use them; and promote self-management, self-confidence, and self-regulation.
Retrospective instruction	Besides preview and review, going back to basics to restructure learning is necessary since prior knowledge can stand in the way of learning new concepts and students must learn how to solve internal inconsistencies or restructure existing conceptions.	Allowing students to ask questions about any misconceptions, recognizing prior beliefs and incomplete understanding of concepts, building on existing knowledge, and prescribing meaningful hands-on and minds-on activities to validate learning.

Table continues on next page

Table 13.10, continued

Model	Focal Point	Examples
Cognitive process instruction	To minimize memorization and maximize understanding, students need to learn how to find answers since learning is better when material is organized around general principles and explanations rather than based on the memorization of isolated facts and procedures.	Teaching students how to find the answers rather than giving them the answers is critical in developing cognitive academic skills since the process is more important than the product.
Transferring instruction	Connecting learning to experience makes learning fun and enjoyable since learning becomes more meaningful when the lessons are applied to real life situations.	Help students transfer learning experience to real life situations or vice versa, such as a personal time line, family traditions, favorite food, and personal childhood story. Transference can be either implication or application, like moving from simple to complex.
Apprenticeship instruction	Spending time to practice is key to successful results since learning is a complex cognitive activity that cannot be rushed and requires considerable time and periods of practice to start building expertise in an area.	Allowing time for academic engagement increases student learning, spending time showing and modeling increases comprehension, and practicing over and over again helps student learn.
Differentiating instruction	Recognizing developmental and individual differences promotes learning in multicultural settings since students learn best when their individual differences are taken into consideration.	Using multiple approaches or differentiating instruction benefits diverse students, introducing a wide range of materials creates learning opportunities, allowing students to pursue areas of interest, and encouraging students to be who they are.
Motivational instruction	Motivating students to learn is key to successful results since learning is critically influenced by learner motivation, attitude, and personality, and modifying these behaviors can create an academic breakthrough.	Recognizing extrinsic motivation or intrinsic motivation, acknowledging accomplishment, giving praise, encouraging learning, and promoting progress and success motivate students to succeed.

Note. Information from *How Children Learn* [Educational Practice Series-7], by S. Vosniadou, 2001, Brussels, Belgium: International Academy of Education.

Table 13.11 Teacher Behavior Effective in Classroom Management

Behavior	Examples of Teacher's Actions
With-it-ness	At all times, keep alert to sights, sounds, movement, and interactions in the class.
Overlapping	Engage or attend to two or more teaching events at the same time to keep the process of the classroom functioning and moving forward optimally.
Smoothness	Prepare or preplan the lesson so that extraneous matters are taken care of beforehand.
Momentum	Plan well to keep the lesson plan moving briskly, avoid overdwelling on minor issues, and make adjustment to minimize fragmentation.
Group alerting	Plan to call on students randomly, be mobile, and apply response in unison.

Table 13.12. Selected Transitional Activities

Activity	Examples of Tasks
Poetry reading time	Ask students to put their hands on their desks, put their heads down, and just listen to the poems.
Rhyming words	Use a vocabulary word and ask students to find words that rhyme with it.
Counting by 2s, 5s, 10s, 15s, or 20s	While lining up or waiting in line, ask students to count by 2s, 5s, 10s, 15s, or 20s, depending on the grade.
ABC alphabetical order	Ask students to line up by their first names in order alphabetically.
Vocabulary building	Write down words with missing vowels on the board and ask students to add vowels to make as many new words as they can: For example, bts (bats, beets, boots, boats…), cht (chat, cheat, chute, choke, chase…
Playing adjective games	Use an adjective to describe an object or noun and ask students to use as many adjectives as possible to describe the noun. For example, red dog…
ABC challenge	Ask students to write a word that begins with each letter of the alphabet. For example, A for apple, B for bat, C for cow…
Color games	Call students by the color of their shirts, shoes, pants, or backpacks to line up.
Quietest student or group	Call on quietest student or group to line up first.
The magic bell	Train students to pay attention, listen, or freeze when they hear the bell.
Making new words from a word	Write a word on the board and ask students to write new words that begin with each letter of the word. For example, candy: cat, apple, nose, day, yellow…
Antonym or synonym games	Write a few words on the board and ask students to find the word's antonyms or synonyms.

Keep in mind that there is no perfect form of classroom management that will fit all students and all behavioral situations. Both discipline and management should be parts of the daily routine. Whereas teaching should be based on sequences of knowledge and skills, disciplinary actions should be based on logical consequences that will modify behaviors. Effective classroom management is not all about being able to control the class at all times mentally, physically, or psychologically; it is about the ability to teach effectively and allow students to engage in academic tasks adequately while managing the class academically.

There is no single definition for classroom management, and each teacher has his or her own way of defining classroom management in terms of experiences and philosophies. Classroom management has to do with the ongoing academic activities established by the teacher that involve student participation, teaching, learning, and modification of student behaviors to maximize the outcome of student learning.

To assist prospective educators gain more insight into classroom management and student discipline, Table 13.13 presents several different models that are comprehensive in their approach to dealing with misbehaviors and unexpected disruptions in the classroom.

Keep in mind that classroom disciplinary actions could be daunting to some students; however, their reactions depend on the nature of the discipline. For instance, if the teacher imposes discipline rather than teaching discipline, students could feel embarrassed by disciplinary action.

General approaches to dealing with misbehaviors should include the following: (a) ignoring the behavior; (b) taking immediate action; (c) the mobility approach; (d) whispering a message; (e) delay or postponement; (f) making correction later; (g) pulling card or putting name on the board; (h) talking to in private or public; (i) giving warning; and (j) notifying parents, sending to the office, and holding a conference. These actions could take place in any order, depending on the severity of the behavior. Teachers need to establish clear procedural guidelines for a classroom management plan. For example, Table 13.14 illustrates some classroom rules for handling misbehaviors that are appropriate at different grade levels. In addition, Table 13.15 shows some basic guidelines for dealing with rule infractions in the classroom; however, prospective educators may need to establish their own logical consequences in accordance with students' needs and the types of classes they are teaching.

Table 13.13. Classroom Management Models

Model	Basic Approaches
Beyond discipline	Looking, thinking, and going beyond current practice and believing in students to make changes and corrections.
Positive discipline	Focusing on human values, teaching manners, and addressing the overall needs with students when necessary.
Three C's school and classroom discipline	Focusing on civic values, cooperation, and conflict resolution.
Behavior modification	Using positive and negative reinforcement to modify or shape behaviors.
Teacher effectiveness training	Teaching self-discipline, using "I" messages, applying logical consequences to solve problems.
Instructional management	Using effective instruction to influence student behaviors.
Discipline with dignity	Showing human caring, establishing clear rules, and modeling good behaviors.
Consistency management and cooperative discipline	Total school approach to discipline, teaching good behaviors to students, and providing caring and loving environment for all.
Judicious discipline	Establishing procedural guidelines for dealing with student behaviors and working in a democratic setting to improve relationships.
Assertive discipline	Establishing rules and consequences for class to follow, enforcing these rules, and applying consequences as needed.

Note. Information from *Classroom Management: Models, Applications, and Cases* (2nd ed.), by L. M. Manning and K. T. Bucher, 2007, Princeton, NC: Merrill

Classroom teachers need to reexamine the effectiveness of their classroom rules periodically in order to reflect upon the needs of different students. Cultural and linguistic issues keep some students from clearly understanding the rules even if they are simple; therefore, teachers need to make sure that all rules and logical consequences are concise. Consider, for example, the RSVP model for rules: they should be reasonable, simple, valuable, and purposeful. Keep in mind that the purpose of establishing rules is to create an environment for effective teaching and learning; the purpose is not to garner personal advantage to minimize teaching responsibilities on the basis of a hegemonic philosophy and hidden curriculum mentality.

Table 13.14. Examples of Classroom Rules, by Grade

Grades K-3	Grades 4-6	Grades 7-8	Grades 9-12
• Raise hands before speak • Keep hands to self • Listen when someone speaks • Do not leave seat without permission • Follow orders to move in and out of class	• Be ready to learn • Follow directions • Keep hands and feet to self • Raise hands if need help • Be kind to others	• Be in seat before bell rings • Come to school prepared • Follow directions • Raise hands if have questions • Keep hands and feet to self • No foul language is allowed in class	• Be in seat before the bell rings • Follow directions • Be kind and responsible for personal actions • Wait for order to be dismissed • All assignments are due on time

Table 13.15. Logical Consequences for Selected Infractions

Types of Infraction	Logical Consequences
First offense	Verbal warning and teacher talks to student either privately or publicly, depending on the behavior and its severity.
Second offense	Taking away privileges and losing one recess.
Third offense	Taking away privileges and losing two recesses.
Fourth offense	Taking away privileges and losing all recesses for the day.
Fifth offense	Taking away privileges and calling parents or guardians.
Sixth offense	Taking away privileges, sending to the office, having meeting with parents, and evaluating for possible suspension.
Physical or verbal threats, severe disruption, or being rude to the teacher and classmates	Will not be tolerated; results in immediate referral to the offices of principal, assistant principal, or appropriate administrators for intervention.

Enhancing Instructional Practices Through Assessment

The most critical part of teaching is the ongoing assessment of student learning. Teachers make two basic types of assessments: informal and formal. Informal assessments are made on the basis of observation or perceived abilities. Formal assessment focuses on systematic data gathering and record keeping. Assessment results help teachers reflect upon the effectiveness of teaching and learning. Howe (2002) stated that the purpose of assessing student learning should be closely tied to daily instruction, and assessment should be an ongoing part of classroom life. Moreover, assessments should be used to lead students to understand that their academic achievements are a result of their abilities and efforts rather than luck or task difficulty. Reflective assessment should be directed toward helping students achieve the cognitive, affective, psychomotor, and social goals of instruction. Howe suggested making the following changes in common assessment practices:

1. Change from what is easily known to what is highly valued.
2. Move from assessing knowledge to assessing understanding and reasoning.
3. Instead of finding out what pupils do not know, find out what pupils do know.
4. Change from end-of-term assessment to ongoing assessment.

Howe (2002) described several types of assessments, and these are listed in Table 13.16. Keep in mind that using nonstandardized instruments to assess student learning on the lesson plan that was taught or content areas covered in the classroom is not the same as standardized assessment. Most assessments in class consist of teacher-made tests; they may be subjective tests or objective tests, depending on the nature of the assessment approach. However, standardized tests such as LAS, CELDT, CAT6, SAT9, BSM, IDEA, ITAS, MAC II, and SLEP are either norm-referenced tests or criterion-referenced tests.

Keep in mind that assessments can be adapted or modified to meet the needs of students, and both the teacher and student should play a role in assessment. Most importantly, communication of the results of student learning through assessment should be available to students, parents, and teachers on an ongoing basis. Assessment results allow teachers to reflect upon teaching effectiveness and make necessary adjustments to improve their professional practices. For instance, formative and summative assessments are designed for feedback and evaluative summary of student learning. On the other hand, quantitative assessment involves test results or scores in numerical format, and qualitative assessment describes test results or scores based on rubrics or rating scales.

Table 13.16. Types of Nonstandardized Assessments

Type	Basic Purposes
Traditional	Paper and pencil tests, multiple choice tests, true/false tests, quizzes
Authentic	Measuring accomplishment based on learned experiences with real-life situations beyond the classroom
Rubrics	A set of criteria used to measure student product
Workbook	Journal entries assessment or log of academic activities in writing
Concept map	Idea web page to connect learning activities or a map diagram designed for monitoring learning progress
Essay and open-ended questions	Allowing students to write responses to the questions based on their own understandings of learned objective(s)
Performance	Design test to assess what students can do rather than ask what they know
Behavior checklist	Informal assessment based on observational interpretation of student behaviors or SOLOM
Product	Assessing the outcome or final result that students produced
Portfolio	Assessing a collection of student works or a compilation of student records collected over a period of time
Short answers test	Paper and pencil tests, multiple choice tests, true/false test, quizzes

Furthermore, prospective educators should be aware of the difference between standardized testing and authentic assessment. As cautioned by Manning and Baruth (2009), McNamara (2007), and Lessow-Hurley (2000), often, public schools use results from both types to determine the academic progress or achievement of students. However, in best practices, this misapplication of assessment results should be avoided because it is a misleading, inaccurate, prejudicial, and biased measurement of student learning, even if the results are used to determine English proficiency in English language learners. To help prospective educators gain insight into the difference between the two types of assessment, Table 13.17 contrasts the two types of tests.

Keep in mind that these are not the only differences between standardized testing and authentic assessment. The list can be quite lengthy. Educators should take these differences into consideration when selecting assessments to measure student learning. For instance, prospective teachers can choose between discrete point tests and integrative tests. As Lessow-Hurley (2000) explained, choices among tests are sometimes made on the basis of political, theoretical, and practical considerations. Interestingly, testing is a big business in America (McNamara, 2007).

Table 13.17. Differences Between Standardized Testing and Authentic Assessment

Standardized Testing	Authentic Assessment
Reduces students' rich and complex real-life experiences to a collection of empirical scores, percentiles, or grades.	Gives teachers the opportunity to integrate or incorporate the student's unique experience as part of the learning outcome.
Creates a mythical standard or norm that requires that a certain percentage of students fail; the normal curve ideology.	Establishes a learning environment where every student has the opportunity to succeed.
Pressures teachers to narrow their curricular focus to only what is relevant to the test and what is tested on an exam.	Allows teachers to develop meaningful curricula and assess student learning within the context of what has been taught.
Discriminates against some students because of cultural backgrounds, language barriers, and learning styles.	Creates culturally fair assessment to measure student performance and gives all students equal opportunity to succeed.
Regards testing and instruction as separate activities.	Regards assessment and teaching as two sides of the same coin.
Provides empirical results that can be fully understood only by trained professionals.	Describes student performance in common sense terms that can be understood by parents, students, others.
Focuses on the right answers.	Deals with process to achieve final product.
Uses time limits that constrain students' thinking processes.	Provides student with time needed to work through processes.
Tends to place focus on student's weaknesses.	Emphasizes student's strengths.
Focuses on single set of data to make decision.	Uses multiple sources of evaluation to plan instruction

Becoming a Reflective Teacher

As they teach, educators should keep a good record of their daily teaching assignments and experiences because reflective writing is one of the ways to stimulate fruitful reflection that enables teachers to keep track of what they are doing each and every day in the classroom. Journal entries should include critical analysis of teaching and student learning. For instance, a good record of experiences helps new teachers reflect upon their teaching effectiveness, identify areas of needed improvement, and plan more effective curricular activities. Becoming a reflective teacher requires professional passion, patience, persistence, consistency, time, energy, commitment, and dedication; without these qualities, the process of reflective writing will be meaningless and discouraging to new teachers. Reflective teaching is one of the ways to help new teachers gain more insight into the practices of self-assessment and self-regulation. Thus it should be considered constructive reinforcement rather than negative criticism.

Responsive teachers usually reflect upon teaching and learning in the following areas:

- Curriculum content knowledge
- Pedagogical content knowledge
- Planning and delivery of instruction
- Lesson plan objectives
- Academic goals
- Student activities
- Instructional activities
- Guided practices
- Assessment, evaluation, testing, and closure
- Academic achievement
- Grading system
- Classroom management and disciplinary actions
- Homework assignments
- Standardized testing and results
- Parent/teacher conferences

There are two types of reflective teaching: reflection in action and reflection on action. *In action* means that the teacher reflects instantaneously and adjusts accordingly while teaching the lesson plan. *On action* means that the teacher reflects upon the overall effectiveness of a lesson plan after it is taught and uses the feedback to adjust so as to improve curricular planning for future teaching. There is always room for professional growth, and growth comes through reflective teaching.

Finally, reflective teachers will always demonstrate, engage, and inspire students to learn through the process of constructivism. Teachers can be judged only through the academic lenses that determine the quality of instruction and professional commitment to student learning outcomes.

Summing Up

This chapter presented a comprehensive overview of instructional practices that are sensible and meaningful in multicultural settings. There is no such thing as a perfect teaching model. All teaching should be adjusted according to the needs and resources of the classroom to accommodate diverse learning styles. Learning is a complex topic, and teachers may need to use multiple forms of evaluation to get an accurate view of students' progress and achievements. Using one model of instruction will not benefit all students. Teachers should use a variety of instructional practices that target the learning needs of all students. Not all students learn the same way, and not all students think, understand, feel, and process information the same way. Learning styles should shape the way teachers teach. Selecting appropriate and responsive teaching methodologies will help teachers design quality instruction. Remember, it is not *what* teachers teach that matters most; it is *how* teachers teach that matters. In the multicultural approach, the purpose of education is not to change the learners, but to empower the learners to change themselves.

PART FIVE

THE FAMILY AND SCHOOL PARTNERSHIP DOMAIN

Ways to Communicate with Diverse Parents

Those who educate children well
are more to be honored than they who produce them;
for these only gave them life,
those the art of living well.

—Aristotle

Overview

Those in the current educational system need to find ways to develop a total-school effort to promote multicultural education for all students. Whether one leans for or against multicultural education, all can agree that the process of informing and involving parents regarding their children's education needs to be changed in order to allow different voices to express their views concerning the current educational practices that are based on hegemonic leadership and actions. More children of diverse backgrounds are being left to fend for themselves, and their parents have not been informed about the school's inability to educate them.

This chapter examines communication between schools and parents, giving prospective educators insights into the roles and responsibilities of school administrators, teachers, and parents in promoting partnerships that increase parental involvement and participation in the social, emotional, and academic growth of all children.

Establishing a Link Between Home and School

Prospective educators and school administrators should think about the benefits of having a positive relationship with students' parents or guardians. It has long been said that when parents, teachers, and school administrators work together as a team, student attendance tends to improve dramatically, and in most cases, so does student achievement. Public trust is the single most important element parents look for when they consider the quality of teacher their children will have. Positive relationships increase the level of mutual trust and respect because parents who have good relationships with their children's teacher worry less about whom their children are with each and every day in the classroom. Most importantly, parents who have a congenial relationship are also less likely to believe false reports of classroom management problems and teacher's treatment of their children. When students perceive that their parents support, like, agree with, and accept the teachers and school administrators, their behaviors and attitudes seem to be more accepting of their learning responsibility.

The linkage between home and school is a bond of obligation and responsibility. For example, positive and effective communication will facilitate parent involvement in solving problems at school, parent participation in school activities, parent help with homework assignments and independent projects, and parent attendance at parent/teacher conferences. In some cases, parents are willing to help the teacher by sharing insights, information, and experiences that are essential to the teacher's understanding of the needs and wants of their children relative to their academic achievement and work productivity in the classroom. Of course, when parents, teachers, and administrators support one another's efforts to assist the learning needs of the children, everyone wins.

School Administrators' Roles in Multicultural Education

In a total-school approach to multicultural education, school administrators have the role of setting objectives and goals for the school regarding multicultural education and devising a plan of action to meet those objectives. Administrators who are serious about meeting the needs of all students in their diverse classrooms can take ten deliberate steps toward fulfilling their role.

First, school administrators must demonstrate a genuine commitment to understanding cultural diversity by recruiting, hiring, and employing personnel who reflect the student body and the community. For instance, hiring teachers who speak Spanish, Mien, Portuguese, Punjabi, and Cambodian would be appropriate in a school where the student population speaks these languages. Currently, administrators in American schools are predominantly from one culture, as Table 14.1 illustrates. This profile of U.S. educational administrators explains why most school curricula are Euro-centric.

Second, school administrators need to make sure that all students have equal opportunity to learn academically. Multicultural education supports neither watered down curricula nor second-class education; it ensures that quality instruction takes place in all classrooms. Without properly implemented multicultural education, language-minority students are often taught by paraprofessionals who do not have proper credentials to teach, and they are subjected to impoverished curricula.

Table 14.1. Ethnic Backgrounds of U.S. School Administrators

Ethnic Background	Superintendents	High School Principals	Junior High & Middle School Principals	Elementary School Principals
White	96.3%	91.4%	88.0%	83.8%
Black	1.7%	4.6%	6.0%	10.2%
Hispanic	1.0%	1.3%	4.0%	4.2%
Asian	--	1.3%	4.0%	4.2%
Native American	0.7 %	0.7%	1.0%	0.6%
Other	0.3%	0.7%	--	0.6%
Total	100%	100%	103%	103.6%

Note. Data from American National Board Journal, December 1996, as cited in *Those Who Can, Teach* (9th ed.), by K. Ryan and J. M. Cooper, 2001, New York: Houghton Mifflin. Some totals do not equal 100% because of rounding.

Third, school administrators should demonstrate a strong professional commitment to working with all learners and teachers at all levels. In other words, school administrators need to be sure that multicultural curricula are implemented across all grade levels. Currently, some schools hire bilingual aides for K-3 classrooms but not for Grades 4-6. Secondary schools have a limited number of bilingual teachers who speak the languages spoken by the language-minority students in their classrooms.

Fourth, school leaders should show a willingness to improve social relationships between the school and the community. Sometimes, the relationship is poor because there is no professional commitment to bridging the gap between home and school.

Fifth, school administrators should provide adequate professional development training to staff on how to improve the self-concept, self-image, self-esteem, and self-worth of culturally diverse students. Teachers come from different cultural and economic backgrounds, and some may not have tolerance for language-minority students. Some teachers consider the learning styles of language-minority students not only odd, but incompatible with middle-class values. In reality, these teachers need firsthand experiences with a wide variety of people in order to learn more about other cultures and learning styles.

Sixth, school administrators should see that multicultural education curricula are planned well, with appropriate procedural guidelines for implementation to ensure they meet objectives and goals. In many cases, multicultural education programs are officially developed but are not implemented as part of the operational curriculum. In many schools, for example, the master plan for LEP students calls for the hiring of BCLAD teachers to provide primary language support to ELLs during class; however, most ELLs are placed with monolingual teachers who provide no such services. Many schools do not even have bilingual education programs in place to help language-minority students.

Seventh, school administrators need to provide learners with teachers who reflect the cultural diversity of the student body and the community. For example, in some schools in Los Angeles County, the student population is 80% Hispanic and the teaching staff is 80% White. This imbalance is not only academically disastrous, but is also unacceptable in a pluralistic society.

Eighth, school administrators should demonstrate a strong commitment to providing appropriate leadership for a total-school approach to multicultural education. Leadership is the most important ingredient in successful academic programs. Strong leadership committed to multicultural education produces strong academic programs that incorporate multicultural approaches.

Ninth, school administrators should be strong advocates for cultural diversity and must be willing to combat discriminatory attitudes, racism, and prejudice in school staff. Consider, for example, the issue of direct eye contact while talking to Asian students, Hispanic students, or parents of diverse cultures. Teachers who lack cross-cultural knowledge might think a student who avoids eye contact is a troublemaker who does not respect authority. This is a simple misunderstanding of the difference in values of one culture versus another.

Finally, school administrators should be willing to involve parents and community leaders in improving services and communication. Quite often, school administrators want to stay away from educated and vocal parents and community leaders because they do not want to deal with the political pressures coming from outsiders. However, school administrators should realize that politics and education are inseparable and the best interests of the students should be their primary concern.

Teachers' Roles in Multicultural Education

Classroom teachers are in a position to identify what their students really need to help them learn. Most importantly, teachers must learn how to apply test scores to determine the needs of students rather than using the data in the tests against them. Teachers can convey their knowledge of the students' needs to administrators for support and evaluation. However, it is the teacher's responsibility to follow through with appropriate actions when the administrators have been notified of the problems. When teachers present findings about problems to administrators to obtain their assistance, they should provide input on how to resolve the problems and work closely with the administrators to follow through on solutions. In most cases, teachers have a better perspective on the problems than administrators because they are with the learners for more time. However, without adequate support from administrators in the form of financial resources, time, effort, energy, and professional commitment to perform their responsibilities, teachers come to dead ends.

As with administrators, teachers in public schools come predominantly from one culture. Table 14.2 illustrates the ethnic backgrounds of teachers in California. Although the population of the state is about 50% Hispanic and includes many other cultures, teachers are overwhelmingly White.

Table 14.2. Ethnic Backgrounds of California Teachers

Ethnic Background	Number of Teachers	Percentage of Total
American Indian	1,826	0.6
Asian	14,740	4.8
Pacific Islander	719	0.2
Filipino	3,960	1.3
Hispanic	46,830	15.2
African American	14,000	4.5
White	221,822	72.1
Multiple/no response	3,967	1.3

Note. Data from California Department of Education, Educational Demographics Office, 2005-2006, retrieved from http:// www.schoolmatters.com

Teachers in special education classrooms play an important role in advocating for students with learning disabilities. In addition to advocating for the best interests of the students protected under public laws, these teachers can play another vital role in multicultural education by making sure that cultural factors are taken into consideration when prescribing individualized education plans for students of minority cultures. Consider, for example, that testing and assessment of Hmong students with learning disabilities may require additional assistance from Hmong professionals who understand Hmong culture and languages and can explain the results to Hmong parents. The parents may also require educated personnel who understand translations of academic language and technical interpretations.

Keep in mind that students of some cultures are overrepresented in special education and students of other cultures are underrepresented. African American children are overrepresented in special education, and this is a pressing issue. On the other hand, Asian American children are underrepresented; some who perhaps should receive special education services are instead placed in special needs classes because they speak a language other than English at home. In the late 1980s to early 1990s, nearly 90% of Hmong students in grades K-3 were placed in special needs classes because they had difficulties with the English language; they did not speak English well enough when their parents enrolled them in public schools.

The Roles of Special Education Teachers

Undoubtedly, the current educational system has serious problems educating students in special education programs because there is a shortage of teachers in these programs. Many students are taught by teachers who are not properly and professionally trained to handle the needs of these students. As Manning and Baruth (2009) pointed out, "The role of special education teachers includes responding to the increasing cultural diversity among learners by using culturally appropriate assessment devices and making placement decisions that reflect an understanding of cultural differences" (p. 297).

Teachers need to pay close attention to PL 94-142 when testing and assessing students with learning disabilities. This law protects the basic right of the disabled to fair and equal protection related to evaluation, identification, and placement. According to McNamara (2007), the four components of the law are: (a) a right to an education; (b) a right to a free, appropriate education; (c) a right to a nondiscriminatory evaluation; and (4) a right to due process.

The sole purpose of this law is to make sure that assessment results are used to guide the individual education plans for such students. Special education teachers must be especially careful to interpret the results without making faulty decisions; otherwise, the test results are considered faulty and biased (Manning & Baruth, 2009). Also, special education teachers must take extra caution to test and assess students properly before placing the "special needs" label on students because some students may not have learning disabilities at all. For instance, Hmong and Hispanic students are often placed in special education classrooms because they have problems speaking English even though they have no difficulty in their primary languages.

It is vital that special education teachers separate the criteria used to evaluate learning disabilities from the criteria used to evaluate learning differences. Regardless of what tests are used, no test is bias free, and teachers must take into careful consideration the cultural insensitivity of tests; otherwise, heavily relying on test scores as the only measure of students' intelligence could lead to a misdiagnosis of learning disabilities and improper placement.

As a result of several litigations and the requirements of PL 94-142, standards have been established to help special education teachers deal with the problem of the relationship between assessment results and students' intelligence. Manning and Baruth (2009) and McNamara (2007) listed 12 standards:

1. It is inappropriate to measure LEP students' intellectual capabilities in English.
2. More than one measure of intellectual capabilities is required for mildly mentally retarded students.
3. Overrepresentation could result in test bias and unfair assessment of intellectual capabilities, and causal factors could include linguistic and cultural issues, identification and eligibility criteria, lack of proper procedures and special services, and heavy reliance on IQ test results as placement criteria.
4. Pay close attention to the criteria used or testing items that do not suffice to account for misplacement of disproportionate numbers of students from culturally different groups.
5. Student placement must be in accordance with legal requirements.
6. Students have right to due process.
7. Students have right to nondiscriminatory evaluation.
8. The specific education services to be provided and the extent to which the student will participate in regular education should be stated.

9. A description of the schedules and evaluation procedures for determining what objectives are being met should be stated.
10. Parents are entitled to a written or recorded word-for-word record of the proceedings.
11. All information presented must be shared with parents at least 5 school days before the hearing.
12. Parents will be informed of the hearing within 45 calendar days of the request.

These standards are only some of the requirements that schools and special education teachers need to adhere to when assessing students with disabilities. Other laws impose additional requirements. For example, section 504 of PL 93-112, the Rehabilitation Act of 1973, requires schools to accommodate individuals with disabilities.

Here are some exercises for teachers to use to examine their own professional attitudes and feelings about working with students and parents of diverse cultures. For each attitude, teachers can ask themselves if they have constructive or biased attitudes.

1. Recognizing personal cultural baggage or stereotypical attitudes. Intolerant teachers look at parents with thoughts such as:
   a. The parents just don't care.
   b. The parents have substance abuse problems.
   c. The father is an alcoholic.
   d. The father never lets his wife speak.
   e. Neither parent has any ambition; they are satisfied to live off welfare.
   f. The parents are lazy.
   g. There are no English speakers in the home.
   h. No one is available to translate for them.
   i. The parents are unable to read or write English.

2. Misapplying misinformation about families based on prototypical scenarios. Some teachers are judgmental when dealing with culturally and linguistically diverse parents, assuming that all parents of all families of a particular ethnic group are the same. Some teachers believe all Asian families and parents are the same, all African American families behave the same way, and all Hispanic families and parents expect the same for their children.

3. Using SES factors to inaccurately profile parents' social behaviors. Some teachers fail to consider that differences in languages, cultures, values, SES, attitudes, behaviors, beliefs, professions, social classes, lifestyles, educational levels, poverty levels, and gender roles play significant roles in the way people think, behave, communicate, and relate to professional people such as teachers, administrators, and authority figures.

4. Presuming parents of diverse SES lack ambition, motivation, expectations, and aspirations. Some teachers believe that parents of lower SES or lower classes do not want to improve their lifestyles, do not want to work, do not want to be involved in their children's schools, do not want to change their current status, and do not want to overcome family issues. These assumptions are not only wrong, but they are discriminatory and harmful.

5. Overgeneralizing cultural characteristics without regard for generational differences. Some teachers still believe that most Hmong parents are culturally alike, but in fact, younger and Americanized Hmong parents are more educated and are very different from older Hmong parents who were born in other countries and immigrated to the U.S.

6. Disbelieving the existence of conflict between individualistic and collectivistic approaches. Many teachers emphasize the value of independence or individualism over group orientation and collectivism. They do not believe that the values they share with students in class cause direct conflict between students and parents at home. In fact, many students of diverse backgrounds are confused about some of these values, such as self-reliance versus adherence to a hierarchical system based on collectivism. In other words, teachers need to consider the difference between individualistic cultures and collectivistic cultures in areas such as communication, values, roles, and responsibilities.

To help teachers gain a larger perspective in working with students and parents of diverse backgrounds, Manning and Baruth (2009) suggested that teachers examine their professional and personal perceptions by asking the following questions:

1. Are my opinions based on myths and stereotypes or on accurate and objective perceptions?
2. Do my experiences include positive, firsthand contacts with people of culturally diverse backgrounds?
3. How have I learned and employed the customs, values, traditions, beliefs, and differences of other people?
4. How do I perceive differences in family size, lifestyle, and family poverty level?
5. How do I handle personal and professional prejudices toward other people and toward myself?
6. How do I deal with stereotypes, biases, and racial epithets?
7. What do I perceive a family should be?
8. How have I learned about the strengths and weaknesses of cultural diversity?
9. How can I acquire more accurate information about a particular culture?
10. How can I professionally develop warm and close relationships with the parents of students in my class?

Keep in mind that there is no perfect way to make everyone a happy camper. However, teachers are role models, and they need to lead the way in helping students of culturally diverse backgrounds understand the values of cultural diversity through positive feelings and meaningful sharing.

Who Are the Parents of Students?

The parent is the person who provides for the child. Teachers need to keep an open-minded attitude about who the parents are when dealing with culturally and linguistically diverse families. Parents come in different forms and they have different lifestyles. A child's parent may be a mother, a father, a member of the extended family, a foster parent, a caregiver, a guardian, a godparent, a lesbian or gay couple, or someone who merely provides for the child. What has historically been considered to be a parent or parents has changed and a broader definition is now accepted. For instance, adoptive parents are legal parents, court appointed advocates are guardians, and social workers are legal protectors and care providers. In a court of law, people sometimes have to sort through the legality of parenthood. However, in schools, teachers and administrators want to know only whose custody or care the child is under; the "parent" could be an aunt, uncle, relative, brother, sister, or friend of the family so authorized by the legal parent or parents.

Parents' Roles in Multicultural Education

Multicultural education is not required by federal, state, county, or district policy; however, it is the best way a community can make sure that public schools provide the best education to all students in the community in compliance with federal, state, and local government policies. It is the best way to ensure that parental rights and students' rights are protected and that public schools serve all children fairly and equitably. Parents can play a large role in promoting multicultural education in their children's schools.

One basic element that all parents need to know is that public schools have never been honest enough to tell parents about their rights when it comes to their children's education. It is also true that public schools do not want to explain to parents that their children have the right to receive a fair, nondiscriminatory, equitable, and sound public education. Public schools list many of the education codes and school board policies in the parent/student handbook they distribute; however, most of these codes and policies are about disciplinary issues, not parental rights, students' rights, or procedural due process. Even uniform complaint procedures are often vague and ambiguous.

All parents should be concerned about multicultural education, about helping public schools become more accountable and responsible for quality teaching and learning and at the same time making sure that all children are treated equally and fairly. Multicultural education is not simply about respect, celebrating holidays, recognizing differences, and having potlucks. Rather, it is about fairness, restructuring, empowerment, prejudice reduction, equal opportunity, quality education, equity of instruction, social justice, advocacy, and constitutional rights. How many children of diverse backgrounds have been neglected and injured academically as the result of racial injustice, hidden curricula, hegemonic actions, covert discrimination, and unlawful segregation in schools? The answer is "countless numbers." Parents need to keep their eyes open and pay close attention to court decisions and litigations regarding public schools.

In fact, legal segregation takes place each and every day in schools; however, most parents are unaware of this. Many language-minority students are placed in homogeneous groups to learn basic ESL. When parents of segregated children ask school personnel, "How is my child doing in school?" 99% of the time the answer is "Fine except . . . ; otherwise, he or she is doing just like the other students." The answer is seldom clear or directed to the point of the question. Evasive responses are common. Parents have no idea that the child, in fact, is not "doing just like the other students."

When children are segregated in this way, given a completely different curriculum from that delivered to majority students, do their grades reflect the quality of education their parents think they do? Of course not. They can earn "As" in less rigorous classes, but the content and quality of instruction is inferior to that received by other students.

All parents, not only parents of minority students, should be involved in their children's education, monitoring the school curricula and how well school administrators and teachers implement the curricula. The majority of schools today gear instruction toward testing and assessment; that is, the curricula are measurement-driven. What does this mean to parents of culturally diverse backgrounds? It means that schoolteachers do not have time to teach what their children need to learn before being tested. With measurement-driven curricula, all children need to learn is how to take tests. This makes students better test takers, but not better learners or more knowledgeable or more skilled individuals. Test scores mean everything to school districts and administrators because politicians, who control funding, have set the system up that way. Every year a district's students hit the target or gain points on the standardized tests; the district makes local headlines and can brag about test scores, improvements, and claims that more ELLs are proficient in English. But when test scores are low, the poor students are blamed for not being able to perform well on tests and dragging down the scores for the district.

The fact of the matter is that test scores do not measure language proficiency in English because the tests are not designed to measure language proficiency. The way school districts explain the difference between proficient and advanced scores in English language arts and math is as follows: *Advanced* means students demonstrate a comprehensive and complex understanding of the knowledge and skills of a subject; *proficient* means students reflect a competent and adequate understanding. Test scores are generally used to place students where they belong among their classmates with the expectation of a normal curve. Norm-referenced test scores are the number one misleading measure in public education. Actually, test scores should be used only to evaluate the teaching effectiveness of teachers and to help determine academic needs of students.

All parents should play a larger role in education to make sure that all students receive the academic support they need to be successful. Most schools with LEP students receive federal monies to provide instructional assistance to help students learn transitional English; however, in most cases, LEP monies are diverted to other purposes. Sadly, schools require LEP students to continue enrollment in ELD classes in order to qualify for federal monies, but the monies are being spent on college preparatory classes and technological equipment. Therefore, parents need to serve on site councils or other parent advisory councils to monitor how schools spend money.

Lastly, parents who have children with disabilities need to pay closer attention to the way public schools handle the IEP process and whether they place their children with special education teachers who are not professionally trained. For example, the student is usually present at the IEP meeting at which the IEP team discusses the student's needs and the plan to address those needs. Sometimes the team discusses the child's life without regard for the emotional and psychological trauma this may inflict on the child. Some parents who attend these meetings, especially bilingual parents who do not speak English and rely on older children to translate for them, do not understand all that is going on. They may not know if the school violates federal laws regarding proper procedures for conducting this kind of meeting. Many critical issues are lost in translation. Few children know how to translate or interpret the words "assessment," "cognitive development," "intellectual level," and "psychological needs" to their parents. Even some paraprofessionals are unable to translate these words correctly. In Hmong languages, for example, these words have to be explained in detail; otherwise, Hmong parents have no idea what they mean.

Placement is a serious problem for students with learning disabilities and LEP students who need extra language support during class. Many mildly disabled students of diverse backgrounds are placed with severely disabled children due to the lack of teachers in special education. In some cases, LEP students are placed with mildly disabled students for no reason whatsoever. In most cases, LEP students and disabled children are left to fend for themselves in an environment that is not academically suitable for learning at all.

Therefore, all parents should consider the advantages of getting involved in the educational system. Parents of culturally diverse backgrounds, particularly, have much to gain and very little to lose. Some of the advantages are the following:

1. They learn and understand school policies, curricula, and expectations.
2. They understand changes that need to be made to comply with federal, state, and local education policies.
3. They become aware of the educational process and the academic needs of students.
4. They understand testing, assessment, placement, and special education programs.

5. They are in a position to advocate for essential and critical services that are not currently offered.
6. They expect high or better student achievement.
7. They can help recruit highly qualified teachers.
8. They learn and understand school budget and expenditures.
9. They assume leadership roles that result in improved school-community relations.
10. They become involved in parent education programs.

Parents have a responsibility to get involved in school to advocate on behalf of their children and make sure their children's constitutional rights are not violated. No child should be left behind or subject to any form of discrimination. The multicultural approach can help students and parents meet their needs by reducing any negative impact of cultural diversity and working collectively and collaboratively toward eliminating the hidden curriculum and deficit ideologies.

Resistance to Parents' Involvement in Education

Both school administrators and teachers need to understand cultural diversity in order to involve culturally diverse parents in the educational process. Even if some parents have limited involvement in school activities, many others are inhibited from getting involved in school activities because of many logistical constraints, including the following:

1. Feelings of being inferior, distrusted, or disrespected. In some cultures, parents might harbor feelings of distrust and disrespect toward people of other cultural backgrounds, and these kinds of feelings could lead them to develop negative or false beliefs about themselves and others. For instance, some Hmong parents resist going to school because they feel inferior and incompetent to meet with teacher face-to-face; they think of teachers as authority figures on the same level as government officials. Harboring such feelings and attitudes makes it hard for school personnel to work with Hmong parents effectively.

2. Cultural and language barriers. Besides being unable to speak English, many parents feel strongly about protecting the privacy of their families, and they do not want to disclose familial information about

any members of the family. They may fear shame, blame, and public humiliation.

3. Transportation problems. Many low income families may own cars, but those cars may be needed by several family members for transport to work, school, medical appointments, and other places. Other means of transportation are available, but taking a city bus to and from a child's school may take hours. And they may have children in more than one school. Minority parents who lack transportation are less likely to get involved in school activities because of personal responsibilities that may interfere with school functions.

4. Problems understanding the system. Culturally diverse parents who do not speak English well may resist attending meetings at school because they believe they would not understand the meeting anyway. Some feel they would ask too many questions about the system because they do not understand it, and that would make them look bad in the eyes of the teachers.

5. Too much respect for teachers. Immigrant Hmong parents who grew up in Asia hold onto the old feelings and beliefs that teachers are like clergymen in prestige. Asking them questions would be rude and inappropriate because teachers know how to teach and what to teach. In other words, these parents assume teachers would not listen to them regardless of what they have to say because teachers are professionals and authority figures. Challenging teachers would not do any good because they are in powerful positions.

6. Childcare problems. Minority parents who have three or more children provide their own daycare for their children at home. If one parent is employed, the other is responsible for taking care of the children at home. To get involved in school activities, they would need to make childcare arrangements, which is not a common practice. Moreover, having large families, many minority parents are reluctant to divide their time between home and school.

7. No time to devote to school activities. Working parents are not available during the day on a school day. Any spare time they have is for their families. Some parents work two jobs. Finding time to get involved in school activities is just impossible for many. In fact, most volunteer parents are either non-working or retired.

8. Conflict of interest with Western views. Involvement in schools requires not only time, energy, language skills, and personal commitment, but also paraprofessional characteristics consisting of Western values, beliefs, and expectations. These cross-cultural characteristics may be opposed to the parents' personal and traditional values and beliefs. This conflict appears in the areas of family size, childrearing, parental expectations, discipline, gender roles, individualism, egalitarianism, and social norms.

9. Education adequate to understand the educational system well. Some European American parents do not get involved in school activities because they are aware of school expectations, school culture, and community culture and are able to provide support at home for their children. So, they feel no need to volunteer or to get involved in school functions. On the contrary, some European American parents are eager to get involved in school business because they want to make sure school curricula reflect academic quality mandated by education policies. Non-European American parents seldom have the same understanding of the educational system.

10. Fear of being labeled a "helicopter parent." Some teachers label vocal, assertive, articulate, and well-informed parents who are involved in school functions "helicopter parents," implying that they hover over the teachers because they know what is done and what should be done in the classroom. School administrators and teachers tend to shun these parents as well because they are aware of their power to shape school curricula, management, and leadership.

These are some reasons parents decide not to get involved in the educational process, and there could be many others. If the communication between school and home is reasonably clear in regard to the school curricula and expectations, parents may see no need to get involved. However, the only way to make sure the system is working properly is to include responsible people in the process. The system itself could be perfect, but the people who are running it may not be.

Serving on Parent Advisory Councils

Keep in mind that politics plays a key role in public education. Public schools need to have culturally diverse parents serving on their site councils or parent advisory councils for a variety of reasons. Five good reasons are as follows:

1. The members of school committees should reflect the general student population.
2. The voices and opinions of the council should influence the overall operation of the school.
3. The school curricula, teaching, and learning should reflect the multicultural nature of the community.
4. Cultural diversity should not only be part of teaching and learning, but also be reflected in policy and practice.
5. The council sets agendas, objectives, and goals for the school.

Together, members of the council work cooperatively and collaboratively with school administrators and teachers to achieve agreed-upon objectives to reach the ultimate goals of all. However, to be culturally accommodating, the council should provide each member with clearly written guidelines for meeting procedures, roles, and responsibilities. If possible, designated members should organize informative orientation sessions to help new members learn and understand the mission and purposes of the council. Members should learn how to talk with one another, but they should not talk over one another at the meeting.

In the past, English learners advisory committees and bilingual education committees excluded language-minority parents who lacked English skills because their presence required interpreters at the meetings. Therefore, language-minority parents were not fully informed of school budgets, expenditures, voting processes, and other items that directly affected them. The meeting minutes did not reflect the content of the discussion taking place in the meetings because many language-minority parents did not vote for specific expenditures as stated in the minutes. Disputes among members should be anticipated if parents are lost in the translation process. If language is a problem, the school has the responsibility to select a representative of each language group to serve on the committee. Moreover, school administrators should explore a meaningful medium of communication that would serve all parents whose children attend school.

Ways to Communicate with Culturally Diverse Parents

The public school system is one of the biggest businesses in this nation. Each year billions of dollars are allocated for its operation of educating more than 55 million students in K-12 schools. Each state spends nearly half of its general fund on public education, and that amount represents nearly 50% of the total cost of public schooling in the state. The federal government provides at least 3% of the funding, and local taxpayers are responsible for the remaining 47%.

The single most important element in the school business is communication; the school must communicate with all its constituents, including students, parents, community leaders, and the general public. Many people do not look at education as a business enterprise, but as a social service system to which its constituents are entitled. Therefore, schools often see no need to communicate well. However, in reality, education is one of the most expensive publicly funded businesses in America. In that regard, communication is vital at every level of this business.

In the business world, communication usually takes one of three major forms as follows (Lesikar, Flatley, & Rentz, 2008):

1. Internal operational communication is the communication a business entity uses to plan, implement, and evaluate its operating system to make sure that the process is done and the product delivered in a timely manner or to ensure the means justify the ends.

2. External operational communication is the form of communication a business entity uses to connect with outsiders, such as its customers. For an educational enterprise, "outsiders" are constituents, other schools, the public, businesses, government agencies, private citizens, individuals, parents, and such.

3. Personal communication, both formal and informal, is the sharing of information that may or may not be related to the business operations but is essential to the success of the overall business.

Any public school system can engage in these forms of communication to help parents know what is going on in their children's classrooms, and school administrators or teachers do not have to wait until something happens—such as testing week, disciplinary actions, lock-downs, or school violence—to communicate with parents and other "outsiders."

It is time for school administrators and teachers in multicultural settings to think about better ways to communicate with parents; however, they must take into serious consideration the fact that people communicate differently. Some prefer oral communication, others want communication in writing.

Keep in mind that some communication behaviors and attitudes are to be culturally understood and may not fit professional expectations. For instance, Asian parents might listen to teachers attentively without looking them in the eyes, but they cannot be expected to have middle-class values concerning communicating with teachers about their concerns over the education of their children. Asian parents might ask indirect questions or use a spiral approach to solving problems instead of coming directly to the main point. Teachers who are not culturally sensitive might consider this kind of talking boring, rude, and a waste of time, but in Asian cultures, this is communicative respect. Moreover, although maintaining eye contact while talking is a middle-class value, in Asian cultures this behavior is a direct insult and a form of intimidation.

Keep in mind that American standards and expectations regarding communication may conflict with the values of other cultures. This is true of direct or indirect communication through face-to-face contact, e-mail, telephone, or writing. In direct contact, people use different types of communication to signal approval or disapproval of the messages, such as body language, verbal expressions, non-verbal cues, body posture, tone of voice, facial expression, and gestures. Some of these signals require interpretation across cultures. For instance, in Asian cultures, calling someone by motioning with all fingers or one finger facing up is considered rude. The appropriate way to call someone is to move one or all fingers facing down. Consider the American custom of using crossed fingers to signal a wish; in Vietnamese culture, this gesture means to have sexual interest.

Human communication is culturally and linguistically sensitive. Because communication is essential to human interaction, people have to learn the right ways to communicate in particular situations. Keep in mind that there is no perfect way of communicating with all people; all forms of communication have the potential for problems and misunderstandings. People have to learn the preferences and nuances of others and adjust accordingly.

Because of the cultural differences in communication and the possibility of offending people unintentionally out of ignorance, the following suggestions are offered to help prospective teachers avoid cross-cultural misunderstandings:

1. Consider the English skills levels of the speaker and listener that may inhibit effective communication. For instance, nodding or bowing is cultural and does not mean that one understands the conversation. Similarly, smiling in many cultures does not necessarily denote happiness. The word "okay" may not mean complete understanding. Also, the phrase "I don't care" is a sensitive expression in some Asian cultures.

2. Use nonverbal communication wisely to avoid insult, intimidation, or the appearance of disinterest.

3. Use gestures carefully to avoid rudeness, impoliteness, meanness, and authoritarian demeanor.

4. Use body parts (legs, arms, hands, etc.) carefully to avoid humiliation, rudeness, impoliteness, and such. For instance, putting feet on the table is rude in Asian cultures because feet are considered to be the dirtiest part of the body.

5. Explain English jargon carefully to avoid misunderstandings. Some educational terms that may need explained are assessment instrument, intelligence quotient, cognitive development, affective domain, BICS, CALP, CALLA, ELD, CST scores, and immersion.

6. Be careful in using the telephone as a means of communication; it can generate instant positive or negative reactions. Parents with limited English skills may worry about the nature of the call because they do not understand the conversation entirely; on the other hand, parents who understand may appreciate the information.

7. Use e-mail carefully to avoid complications and misunderstandings. Many bilingual parents do not know how to access e-mail, and they must depend on their children for help. The children may delete e-mails concerning themselves before their parents can see them. In some cases, children may respond to e-mails on behalf of the par-

ents. Communicating sensitive information via e-mail is not wise because e-mail is not confidential.

8. Cell phone texting is relatively new; use it carefully to avoid misunderstandings.

9. Calling parents at work should be avoided except in the case of an emergency. Instead, call the home number and leave messages for parents.

10. The wisdom of sending a note home with the child to the parents depends on what is in the note; parents may not ever see the message. However, sending notes that report positive achievements of students is encouraged.

School administrators and teachers need to take some precautions before communicating with culturally diverse parents. Keep in mind that parents are human beings and they usually understand the intent of a communication even if the method is not culturally perfect. Do not let language and cultural differences interfere with overall communication. Educators should try to address parents appropriately, convey the message with an appropriate tone of voice, discuss more positive items than negative when meeting with parents, use simple expressions that parents can understand, choose words carefully, allow parents to ask questions, paraphrase if parents seem not to understand, use professional interpreters rather than their older children, respond with genuine praise and empathy, show respect to both parents, encourage both to speak, and thank them for having their children in your class. Keep in mind that the only time communication is blocked or stalled is when both parties harbor their own cultural preferences.

Certain forms of communication are more effective for specific purposes than others. Burden and Byrd (2003) described the purposes of several different methods of communication that might be used with parents (see Table 14.3). These authors suggested that the method be carefully selected to match its purpose. For instance, teachers rarely communicate through a home visit; other forms of communication are usually sufficient unless a critical need exists for a home visit.

Most importantly, teachers need to accommodate bilingual parents who may not be able to speak, write, and read English. Monolingual teachers may have to find translators to translate some of these forms of communications for them. Some teachers like to open communication with parents at the start

Table 14.3. Purposes of Selected Methods of Communication with Parents

Method	Purposes
A greeting letter or card	Sending a greeting letter to all parents a few days just before school starts to let them know that you are expecting to see their children in your class.
Introductory letter	Formal letter, welcoming messages, basic information about the class, curricular activities, and alert parents about incoming events.
Letter about classroom management and discipline	Sharing details about the plan for classroom management and discipline and teaching and learning expectations.
A thank you note or letter	Sending a thank you note home to parents after you have received all requested information from parents to appreciate their cooperation and support.
Back-to-School Night	Preparing a package of information on teacher's profile, academic program, grading guidelines, homework policy, rules and procedures, and classroom expectations.
Information sheets	Sharing information about school curriculum, grading guidelines, expectations, services, rules and procedures, disciplinary plan, and other academic information for parents to review.
Open House	Preparing and organizing classroom for parents to visit, displaying student work, having information package ready for parents to take home, and doing formal presentation about the program and academic curricula.
Newsletters	Sharing briefly with parents about the class, special events, tests, quizzes, curriculum, projects, field trips, and student work.
Assignment sheets	Sharing weekly assignment sheet with parents to alert them about learning expectations, schedules, due dates, and the requirement of parent signature for complete tasks.
Individual notes and letters	Informing parents of a child's academic progress, achievement, or issues related to learning; asking parents to meet if they have questions about teacher's assessment of the child; and inviting parents to visit class or give suggestions for improvement.
Special events and informal contacts	Meeting or contacting parents at special events, such as sporting events, plays, games, fair, shopping, carnivals, or community events, sharing a few words about their child's progress and inviting them to come by the class.
Progress report and report cards	Sharing about their child's academic progress and performance; informing them about academic grades, grading guidelines, and assignments; and asking them to contact if they have any questions about the grades.
Home visit	Making home visit is the very last resort to share with parents about their child's academic progress, achievement, or other issues.

Table continues on next page

Table 14.3, continued

Method	Purposes
Parent-teacher conferences	Having brief formal meeting with parents to go over academic progress, performance, success, and student citizenship; preparing to share information and to answer questions; and inviting parents to make suggestions for improvement.
Phone calls	Making necessary contact with parents to discuss specific progress, achievements, or issues; requesting them to meet if necessary; and inviting them to give suggestions for improvement.

Note. Information from *Methods for Effective Teaching* (3rd ed.), by P. R. Burden and D. M. Byrd, 2003, Boston: Pearson Education.

of the academic year, some prefer to begin in the middle of the year, and others wait until the end of the year. However, teachers need to be available to parents, and thus it is a good idea to keep the lines of communication open at all times.

Use Appropriate Bilingual Interpreters and Translators

It is very important for public schools to employ appropriate paraprofessionals or professionals who are bilingual and speak the languages spoken by the students and their parents. Often, public schools do not have enough interpreters or translators, and they rely on family members for interpretation and translation. School secretaries are sometimes called on to translate or interpret for parents. One cautionary note: there is a difference between interpretation and translation. An interpreter puts verbal conversation between two or more persons into a different language; a translator puts written materials into a different language. Public schools need to have professionals who can perform both tasks in order to meet the needs of linguistically diverse students and parents.

Moreover, public schools need to stop using minor children to translate or interpret for parents because children are not properly trained in the two languages and they are often uncomfortable communicating sensitive information to their parents. Minor children generally do not know how to translate or interpret complicated vocabulary or phrases. For example, a Hmong child would not be able to interpret or translate the words "academic achievement" and "assessment" into Hmong because there is no direct interpretation or translation of these words in the Hmong language. A professional who understands Hmong languages has to interpret or translate the words into descriptive phases to explain the real meanings to Hmong parents. In many states, such as California, written materials are widely available in English and Spanish, but not in many other languages, such as Hmong, Lao, Cambodian, Tagalog, Chinese, Japanese, Korean, Punjabi, Vietnamese, Mien, Iraqi, Farsi, Portuguese, French, or Russian. Non-English-speaking parents will continue to be "lost in translation" if this pattern of practices continues.

Preparing for Parent-Teacher Conferences

One of the biggest tasks for K-6 teachers is preparation for parent-teacher conferences. Most school districts set a few days at the end of each report-card period for scheduling parent-teacher conferences. The sole purpose of these meetings is to report information the teacher has gathered about academic progress, performance, assessment results, and other items related to the student's citizenship and special needs. The process of organizing these meetings usually falls into three main phases.

Phase 1:   Preparation for the conferences requires thorough planning, organization, and coordination by the teacher. The teacher needs to be mentally and physically organized to avoid a chaotic conference. Phase 1 entails the following:

1.   Curricular planning involves assigning work to students so they have something to do during the conference times.
2.   Preparing, staging, and planning the classroom for the conference require rearrangement, organization, clean up, decoration, and displaying of student work.
3.   Student folders, records, and files must be organized to share with parents at the conference.
4.   Resources must be gathered and arrangements made for translators and interpreters to be available during conferences to help non-English-speaking parents.
5.   The teacher must keep track of appointment times and reorganize meeting times when necessary.
6.   The teacher must follow up with phone calls as necessary to confirm appointment times with parents.
7.   Teachers have to anticipate cancellations, no shows, and delays.

8. Times must be set up for working parents who cannot attend conferences during school hours.
9. Tables and chairs must be set up for the conference.
10. The room should be kept tidy, clean, and organized physically, academically, and professionally.
11. Accommodations must be made for parents who are non-English speakers.
12. Teachers must get ready to run the show.

Phase 2: This is the big one. Actually conducting the conference requires a strategic plan of action, an agenda; otherwise, the 15-minute time limit will run out quickly and the teacher will have a long line outside the door waiting to come in. Time elapses quickly. Keep in mind that some parents may require more time to deal with some issues, especially questions or disagreements with the teacher.

The basic rule for holding an effective conference is to focus on specific items on the agenda. These are generally discussion and questions about academic progress, performance, assessment, student citizenship, and specific ways to improve learning. The teacher may provide positive information to parents, obtain useful information from parents, and summarize the conference with parents. In some cases, the teacher may suggest a follow-up meeting. Any issues that are not resolved at the conference or specific questions regarding testing or assessment of language proficiency may be addressed in a subsequent meeting. It is the teacher's responsibility to carry through with any follow-up, and failure to do so will have negative consequences.

To help teachers feel confident in conducting effective and smooth conferences, Burden and Byrd (2003) suggested some technical guidelines to follow; these are shown in Table 14.4.

Phase 3: Post-conference planning is known as follow-up. This is one of the weakest areas in teaching, and many teachers neglect it. They either forget to take notes or do not give much thought to the discussions when the conferences are over. Afterward, they become busy in the classroom and have little time to reflect on the meetings. In practice, they should keep notes every time they meet with parents. Often unanswered questions and unexpected issues arise during conferences, and these need follow-up actions. However, without notes, some teachers forget, ignore, or disregard these important concerns. Keep in mind that some parents can come back to bite teachers for being irresponsible if this becomes a pattern of behavior.

To make Phase 3 the most effective, here are a few things responsible teachers should do following all conferences:

Table 14.4. Guidelines for Conducting Conferences

Approach	Examples of Discussion
Greeting parents	Show great respect to different cultures and customs while greeting parents, such as handshake, bowing, nodding, salute, hugging, kiss on the cheek, and other forms.
The purpose of the conference	Briefly explain the purpose of the conference to parents before going into the conference agenda.
Have professional manner and positive attitudes	Be professional and cordial with parents while starting to share information about their child and in subsequent discussions with them.
Starting with positive outcomes	Share positive things about the child with parents before moving to the areas that need improvement.
Encourage parents to share and suggest ideas about the child	Allow parents the opportunity to ask questions, share information, and suggest ideas as to how to help the child in school.
Apply human relations and interpersonal skills during the process	Anticipate questions, disagreements, and issues from parents; be an active listener; be flexible and reflective; accommodate different views; try to resolve issues as quickly as possible; be careful about giving advice; be willing to follow up with questions; and avoid being antagonistic.
Develop an improvement plan with parents	If necessary, list a few things upon which parents and teacher can take immediate action to minimize problems and ask parents to meet again at a different time to have a more thorough discussion on the issues.
Bring the meeting to closure with mutual consensus	End the meeting with positive and affirmative results both sides can agree upon and look forward to working with the child and parents to improve the current situation.
Prepare to give information to parents to take home	Have information sheets about classroom rules and procedures, discipline, assignments, grading guidelines, curricula, expectations, and special events ready for parents to take home.
Follow up with a thank-you note	Send a card or letter to parents to thank them for attending the conference and look forward to seeing them again next time.

Note. Information from *Methods for Effective Teaching* (3rd ed.), by P. R. Burden and D. M. Byrd, 2003, Boston: Pearson Education.

1. Send out thank-you letters to parents thanking them for coming to the conference.
2. In the letters, acknowledge positive things learned during the conference.
3. List some of the things the teacher will adjust to meet the needs of culturally diverse students so as to improve teaching and learning in the classroom.

4. Send e-mails or thank-you letters to paraprofessionals for helping translate for non-English-speaking parents.
5. Reaffirm with parents the importance of their involvement in their children's education.

This kind of open and responsive communication holds teachers professionally accountable for fulfilling their responsibilities. Parents appreciate responsive professionals who take time to tend to the details of their children's education. Most importantly, keeping relationships warm and cordial is one of the ways to make teaching and learning productive as parents trust teachers to do a good job. Harboring negative attitudes about cultural differences does not improve communication, partnership, or parent engagement in the educational process.

The Benefits of Having a Parent Engagement Center

There are different ways public schools can get parents and community leaders involved in the educational process. Creating a parent education program that helps culturally diverse parents with specific needs is a good starting place for building partnerships that promote parental involvement in the cultural, social, emotional, and academic growth of children. Whether the education program is a site-based one-size-fits-all model or another model, an effective inclusive approach should have some of the following features (Burden & Byrd, 2003; Manning & Baruth, 2009; Parette & Petch-Hogan, 2000):

- Written policies and procedures
- Administrative support and commitment
- Training programs on a variety of topics
- Partnership objectives that promote communication, collaboration, and cooperation
- Specific and measurable goals that are aimed high
- Communication between schools and homes
- Celebration and promotion of cultural diversity as part of school curricula
- A networking system and resources for targeted needs
- Encouragement of school personnel to take part in the program
- A plan for assessing program effectiveness

One approach to having a consistent parent education program for all parents in a school district is to create a parent engagement center that all parents, community leaders, administrators, and teachers can be part of. Instead of having a site-based model, establishing the center can be a total-school effort to provide broader services to the entire school community, and culturally and linguistically diverse parents are benefited along with everyone else. Many large school districts in California and elsewhere already have centers of this kind that provide free educational services to parents on a variety of issues. The centers offer consultation, translation-interpretation, trainings, workshops, classes, and community surveys (see Table 14.5).

Table 14.5. Examples of Services Provided by Parent Engagement Center

Consulting Services	Activities	Trainings and Workshops	Translation-Interpretation Services
Parental involvement and participation in educational services	Home visitation	Academic Performance Index (API)	Translating school materials into Spanish, Hmong, Lao, Cambodian, and other languages
Building community and school partnership	Parent telephone networking	Interpreting SAT9 and CAT6 scores	Title I parent meetings
Multicultural development and activities	Parent survey	U.S. education and customs	Title I annual parent meetings
Title I program services	General assistance	Title I program and services	Migrant parent meetings
Cultural awareness trainings	Referral services: Housing, counseling, and food	How to help children with homework	Cultural issues
Community curriculum resources	Rights and responsibilities	School site council	Instructional assistance
Truancy and attendance policies	Gang awareness and prevention	Uniform complaint procedures	School policies, procedures, and guidelines
High school exit exam	Barriers to parental involvement	Parent-teacher conference	Computer literacy classes/ESL classes
Healthy families enrollment	Promotion and retention	Parenting skills classes	Parent leadership

Note: Information from information folder given by Fresno Unified School District's Parent Engagement Center, 2003.

Today, educators should realize that formal and informal communication with families, parents, and community leaders is extremely important. However, public schools can do more to offer culturally and linguistically diverse parents the opportunity to learn more about child development, behaviors of children and adolescents, the cause-and-effect of relationship between cognitive development and behaviors, changes in behavioral patterns, school expectations, parents' roles and responsibilities, assessment results, curricular matters, instructional strategies, classroom management, discipline, homework, extracurricular activities, educational resources, and parental rights. Providing these services requires tremendous effort and commitment. Perhaps, this kind of approach to multicultural education could be called the bully-pulpit strategy for reforming the way public schools communicate with parents.

Summing Up

This chapter recapped the reasons multicultural education is so important in promoting equality, social justice, and equal opportunity for all students in the educational system. Of course, no child should be left behind. However, without a total-school approach that includes a multicultural curriculum, language-minority students are left behind because the tracking system traps them in a designation for years, the public schools make empty promises they cannot fulfill, the schools pay lip service to high-sounding ideals, and the cosmetic education public schools provide does not prepare them for a good future. The hidden curriculum needs to be dismantled before more children become silent prisoners in English-dominant classrooms. The No Child Left Behind legislation actually left many children behind in academic limbo.

The educational system should recognize and celebrate the tremendous cultural diversity in its classrooms. Educators should demonstrate and actively promote educational partnerships. Many may still deny and refuse to embrace cultural diversity because they lack knowledge of unique cultural backgrounds and the special needs of culturally and linguistically diverse parents and families. Everyone can contribute to the improvement of the quality of public education in our pluralistic society.

Appendix: Selected Resources

The mediocre teacher tells; the good teacher explains;
the superior teacher demonstrates; and the great teacher inspires.

—William Arthur Ward

Education Websites:

www.csustan.edu
> This is the website of the Education department of California State University, Stanislaus (CSUS).

www.csustan.edu/financialaid/data/scholarship-information/index.html
> This site offers information on applying for CSUS scholarships.

www.csustan.edu/mscp
> This is the website of the Multiple Subject Credential program at CSU, Stanislaus.

www.bb.csustan.edu
> This is the Blackboard website that gives you access to TPA documents.

www.aft.org
> The American Federation of Teachers (AFT) is an ally of the teacher's union.

www.nbpts.rog
> The National Board for Professional Teaching Standards (NBPTS) offers services to teachers to improve teaching through voluntary certification.

www.nea.org
> The National Education Association (NEA) is the nation's largest professional organization for public school teachers.

www.pta.org
> The Parent Teacher Association (PTA) is a professional organization of parents and teachers.

www.interventnioncentral.rog
> Intervention Central provides tools and handy resources for teachers for dealing with students and promoting productive classroom behaviors.

www.disciplinehlepl.com
> *You Can Help Them All* offers practical resources for teachers for dealing with common classroom misbehaviors.

www.atozteacherstuff.org
> *A to Z Teacher Stuff* offers practical instructional resources and tools for teachers for dealing with everyday life in the classroom.

www.eric.edu.gov
> *Ask ERIC* offers educational resources in the ERIC library for teachers.

www.coolessons.org
> *Cool Lessons* offers cool teaching lessons and units that help teachers improve instructional practices.

www.lessonplanspage.com
>   *Lesson Plans Page* offers thousands of lesson resources for teachers.

www.loc.gov
>   The Library of Congress offers instructional resources and tools for teachers.

www.nationalgeographic.com
>   *National Geographic* offers resources to help both students and teachers learn about and explore the world.

www.teachertube.com
>   *Teacher Tube* offers video clips and media resources to help both students and teachers.

www.teachervision.fen.com
>   *Teacher Vision* offers assessment tools to help teachers understand traditional and alternative assessments.

www.rubistar.4teachers.org or http://rubistar.4teachers.org
>   These sites offer practical rubric templates for teachers.

www.mindtools.com
>   *Mind Tools* offers survival resources for teachers for dealing with everyday life in the classroom.

www.time.management-guide.com
>   This website offers a variety of ways to help teachers save time and manage their time to maximize teaching and learning strategies.

www.ed.gov/nclb or www.ed gov/nclb/landingjhtml
>   The United States Department of Education offers in-depth information on the No Child Left Behind Act of 2001.

www.school.discoveryeducation.com or http://school.discoveryeducation.com
>   This site offers useful resources that help teachers make their classrooms attractive and conducive to learning.

www.images.google.com or http://image.google.com
>   This site offers practical ideas that help teachers set up their classrooms.

www.theteacherscorner.net
>   *The Teacher's Corner* offers practical applications and tools that help teachers decorate their rooms.

www.chadd.rog
>   Children and Adults with Attention-Deficit/Hyperactivity Disorder (CHADD) is the nation's leading non-profit organization advocating for ADD and ADHD students.

www.cec.sped.org
>   The Council for Exceptional Children (CEC) is the nation's largest organization advocating for children with special needs, exceptionalities, and disabilities.

www.rfbd.org
>   Recording for the Blind and Dyslexic offers educational resources for blind and dyslexic students.

www.eslcafe.com
>   *Dave's ESL Café* offers instructional resources for both ESL students and teachers who work with ESL students.

www.ldpride.net
>   This site offers practical resources for teachers for dealing with learning styles and disabilities.

www.csr.edu.uiuc.edu or http://csr.edu.uiuc.edu
> This site offers research and practical resources for teachers on reading practices in the classroom.

www.cde.ca.gov
> The California Department of Education provides lots of information on education policies.

www.ctc.ca.gov
> The California Commission on Teacher Credentialing offers complete information on credentialing, testing, and other requirements.

http://teachnet.com
> This site offers practical tools for busy teachers.

www.dhc.net/artgeek/index.html
> This site offers designed tools that aid teachers in a variety of ways.

www.lessonspage.com
> This site offers plenty of lessons for busy teachers.

www.lessonplanz.com
> This site offers lesson plans in language arts, social studies, math, and science.

www.educationworld.com
> This site offers plenty of instructional assistance for teachers.

www.teachingideas.co.uk/
> This site offers lots of teaching ideas for primary teachers.

www.jigsaw.org
> This site offers cooperative techniques that help teachers.

www.school.discovery.com
> This site offers instructional support for teachers.

www.conductingconduct.com
> This site provides ideas for classroom management for teachers.

www.crayola.com
> This site offers ideas to encourage teaching creativity in children.

www.teachersfirst.com
> This site offers plenty of classroom resources for teachers.

www.iteach.com
> This site offers ideas and tools for teachers.

www.teachingtips.com
> This site offers lots of teaching tips for teachers.

www.learning.network.com
> This site offers useful resources for parents, teachers, and students.

www.theteachersguide.com
> This site offers practical resources for teachers.

www.kinderart.com
> This site provides hundreds of free art lesson plans and activities for teachers.

www.creativeteachingsite.com
> This site offers practical creative teaching ideas for teachers.

www.superkids.com
> This site offers educational reviews of children's software.

Education Books:

Author(s)	Title of Book	City of Publication	Publisher	Year
Bianco, Arnie	*One-minute Discipline: Classroom Management That Works*	San Francisco, CA	Jossey-Bass	2002
Jones, Fredric H.	*Tools of Teaching*	Santa Cruz, CA	Fredric H. Jones and Associates	2000
Smith, Rick	*Conscious Classroom Management*	Fairfax, CA	Conscious Teaching Publication	2004
Burke, Jim	*Teacher's Essential Guide: Effective Instruction*	New York	Lawrence Erlbaum	2004
Danielson, Charlotte	*Enhancing Professional Practices*	Alexandria, VA	Association for Supervision and Curriculum Development	2007
Johnson, Louanne	*Teaching Outside the Box: How to Grab Your Students by Their Brains*	San Francisco, CA	Jossey-Bass	2005
Dobson, Michael S., & Susan B. Wilson	*Goal Setting: How to Create an Action Plan and Achieve Your Goals*	New York	AMACOM	2008
Springer, Steve; Brandy Alexander; Kimberly Persiani-Becker	*The Organized Teacher*	New York	McGraw-Hill	2005
Fay, Jim, & David Funk	*Teaching with Love and Logic*	Golden, CO	Love and Logic Press	2006
Mendler, Allen	*Connecting with Students*	Alexandria, VA	Association for Supervision and Curriculum Development	2001
Rief, Sandra	*How to Reach and Teach All Children in the Inclusive Classroom: Practical Strategies, Lessons, and Activities.*	San Francisco, CA	Jossey-Bass	2004
Boushey, Gail, & Joan Moser	*The Daily Five: Fostering Literacy Independence in the Elementary Grades*	Portland, ME	Stenhouse	2006

Basic Education Supplies and Documents:

A calendar

A planner

Key ring for room and cabinet
  keys

Three-ring binder

Notebook paper

Notepads

Pens and pencils

Self-sticking notes

Colored highlighters

Staplers and staples

Hole punch

File folders

Labels

Scissors

Stackable trays

Vertical and horizontal files

Calculators

Transparent tape

Masking tape

Rubber bands

Overhead pen and projector

Overhead transparencies

Big screen

Computer projector

Laptop or desktop computer

Board erasers and board markers

Chalk and dry erase markers

Tissues and paper towels

First aid kit

Storage bins

Blank paper

Construction paper

Crayons and glue

Colored pencils

Rulers

Safety pins

Note cards

Thank you notes

Stickers

Jars of candies or goodies

Paper clips

Antibacterial liquid or soap

Curriculum guides

Lesson plan book

Grade book

Professional portfolio

Student contact information files

Emergency procedures

Staff directory and contact information

Telephone

Extra tables for group or center
  instruction

Pencil sharpener

Trash can

References

Abrams, L. S., & Gibson, P. (2007). Reframing multicultural education: Teaching white privilege in the social work curriculum. *Journal of Social Work Education, 43*(1), 147–159.

Abrams, S. F. (1993). Meeting the educational and cultural needs of Soviet newcomers. *Religious Education, 88*(2), 316–324.

Alba, R. D. (1990): *Ethnic identity: The transformation of White America.* New Haven, CT: Yale University Press.

Allied Media Corporation. (2007). *100 questions about Arab Americans and cultures.* Retrieved June 14, 2009, from http://www.allied-media.com/Arab-American/100Q.htm

American Council on Education. (1994). *ACE 12th annual status report on minorities in higher education.* Washington, DC: Author.

American Institute for Research. (2006, February 21). *Five-year study of Proposition 227 finds no conclusive evidence favoring one instructional approach for English learners* (Press release). Washington, DC: Author.

American Speech-Language-Hearing Association. (1983). *Committee on Language Report, ASLHA, 25*(6).

Anderson, C. J. M., & Jones, C. (1974). *Historical linguistics.* Amsterdam: North-Holland Publishing.

Arlotto, A. (1972). *Introduction to historical linguistics.* Lanham, Maryland: University Press of America.

Association of Statisticians of American Religious Bodies (2009). *Standard Denominational Adherents Information for 2007.* Retrieved June 14, 2009, from http://www.asarb.org/statistics.html

August, D., & Hakuta, K. (1997). *Improving schooling for language-minority children: A research agenda.* Washington, DC: National Academy Press.

Axelson, J. A. (1999). *Counseling and development in a multicultural society* (2nd ed.). Monterey, CA: Brooks & Cole.

Banks, J. A. (1988). Ethnicity, class, cognitive and motivational styles: Research and teaching implications. *Journal of Negro Education, 57*(4), 453–462.

Banks, J. A. (1991). Introduction. In National Council for the Social Studies, *Curriculum guidelines for multicultural education: NCSS position statement and guidelines.* Washington, DC: Author.

Banks, J. A. (2008). *An introduction to multicultural education.* Boston: Pearson Education.

Barr, R. D., & Parrett, W.H. (1995). *Hope at last for at-risk youth.* Needham Heights, MA: Allyn and Bacon.

Batalova, J. (2006). *Spotlight on limited English proficient students in the United States.* Washington, DC: Migration Policy Institute.

Birkel, L. F. (2000). Multicultural education: It is education first of all. *Teacher Education, 36*(1), 23–27.

Birrel, J. (February, 1993). *A case study of the Influence of Ethnic Encapsulation on a Beginning Secondary School Teacher.* Paper presented at the annual meeting of the Association of Teacher Educators, Los Angeles.

Bloom, B. (1956). *Taxonomy of educational objectives: Handbook I, cognitive domain.* New York: McKay.

Boykin, A. W. (1984). Reading achievement and the social-cultural frame of reference of Afro-American children. *Journal of Negro Education, 53*, 464–471.

Bronfenbrenner, U. (1989). Ecological systems theory. In R. Vasta (Ed.), *Annals of child development* (vol.6). pp. 187–249. Greenwich, CT: JAI Press.

Brown, R. (1986). State responsibility for at-risk youth. *Metropolitan Education, 2*, 5–12.

Brunner, J. (1966). *Toward a theory of instruction.* Cambridge, MA: Harvard University Press.

Burden, P. R., & Byrd, D. M. (2003). *Methods for effective teaching* (3rd ed.). Boston: Pearson Education, Inc.

California Department of Education. (1989). *A Handbook for teaching Cantonese speaking students.* Sacramento, CA: California Department of Education.

California Department of Education. (2005–2006). Retrieved August 15, 2009, from http://www.schoolmatters.com

California Department of Education. (2006). *Schools and language minority students: A theoretical framework* (2nd ed.). Sacramento, CA: Bilingual Education Office.

California Special Education Resource Network. (1985). *Psychoeducational Model.* San Francisco: Author.

Cecil, N. L. (1990). Black dialect and academic success: A study of teacher expectations. *Reading Improvement.* January–March.

Charles, C. M., & Senter, G. W. (2002). *Elementary classroom management* (3rd ed.). Boston: Allyn and Bacon.

Cheng, L. (1999). Sociocultural adjustment of Chinese-American students. In C. C. Park & M. M. Y. Chi (Eds.), *Asian-American education: Prospects and challenges* (pp. 1–17). Westport, CT: Bergin & Garvey.

Choy, B. Y. (1979). *Koreans in America.* Chicago: Nelson-Hall.

Cooper, J. M. (1999). *The teacher as decision maker, in classroom teaching skills* (6th ed.). Boston: Houghton Mifflin.

Cooper, R. (1999). Urban school reform: Student responses to detracking in a racially mixed high school. *Journal of Education for Students Placed At-Risk, 4*(3), 259–275.

Cooper, R. (2000). Urban school reforms from a student of color perspective. *Urban Education, 4*(2), 302–345.

Costello, M.A. (1996). *Critical issue: Providing effective schooling for students at risk.* Washington, DC: North Central Regional Education Laboratory.

Crawford, J. (1989). *Bilingual education: History, politics, theory, and practice.* Trenton, NJ: Crane.

Cummins, J. (1981). The role of primary language development in promoting educational success for language minority students. In California State Department of Education, *Schooling and language minority students: A theoretical framework* (pp. 3–49). Sacramento: Office of Bilingual Education, California State Department of Education.

Darling-Hammond, L. (1995). Inequality and access to knowledge. In J. A. Banks (Ed.), *The handbook of multicultural education* (pp. 465–483). New York: Macmillan.

Dayton, C., Ruby, M., Stein, D., & Weisberg, A. (1992). The California partnership academies: Remembering the "forgotten half," *Phi Delta Kappa, 3*(2), 539–545.

Del Vecchio, A., Guerrero, M., Gustke, C., Martinez, P., Navarrete, C., Nelson, C., et al. (1994). *Whole-school bilingual education program: Approaches for sound assessment: NCBE program information guide series 18.* Washington, DC: National Clearinghouse for Bilingual Education.

de Melendez, W., & Beck, V. (2010). *Teaching young children in multicultural classrooms: Issues, concepts, and strategies* (3rd ed.) Belmont, CA: Wadsworth.

DeNavas-Walt, C., Proctor, B. D., & Smith, J. (2007). *Income, poverty, and health insurance coverage in the United States* (U.S. Census Bureau Current Population Report P60-233). Washington, DC: U.S. Government Printing Office.

DeVillar, R. A. (1994). *Cultural diversity in schools: From rhetoric to practice.* Albany: State University of New York Press.

Dewey, J. (1956). *The child and the curriculum. The school and society.* Chicago: University of Chicago Press.

Dillon, S. (2006, August 27). In schools across U.S., the melting pot overflows. *New York Times*, pp. A7, A16.

Doolittle, P. E. (2002). *How people learn. Practical Strategies for teaching and learning.* Educational psychology. Virginia Polytechnic Institute & State University: Virginia.

Dougherty, V. (1989). Youth at-risk: The need for information. In J. M. Lakebrink (Ed.), *Children at-risk* (pp. 3–17). Springfield, IL: Charles C. Thomas.

Erikson, E. (1950). *Childhood and society.* New York: Norton.

Ferris, J. (1996, January). Reading gets call to return to the basics. *Fresno Bee*, p. A4.

Flannery, M. E. (2006). Language can't be a barrier: Here are practical ways to reach students when they speak what you don't (425 first languages). *NEA Today*, p. 24.

Fort Gordon Equal Opportunity Office. (2009). *Arab American experience and Middle Eastern culture.* Retrieved June 14, 2009, from http://www.gordon.army.mil/eoo/arab.htm

Four Worlds Development Project. (1982). *The sacred tree.* Lethbridge, Alberta, Canada.

Fresno County Department of Social Services. (1993). Indochinese cultural awareness training for social work services. Fresno, CA: Author.

Fresno County Department of Social Services. (1998). Asian Pacific Islander cultural awareness training. Fresno, CA: Author.

Fresno Unified School District. (1995). *1995–2000 LEP master plan.* Fresno, CA: Author.

Fresno Unified School District's Parent Engagement Center. Fresno, CA: Author.

Freud, S. (1935). New introductory lectures on psychoanalysis. New York: Norton

Gardner, H. (1983). Frames of mind. The theory of multiple intelligences. New York: Basic Books.

Gesell, A. (1925). The mental growth of the pre-school child. New York: Macmillan.

Goldstein, B. L. (1985). *Schooling for cultural transition: Hmong girls and boys in American high schools.* Unpublished doctoral dissertation, University of Wisconsin, Madison.

Gollnick, D. M., & Chinn, P. C. (2009). *Multicultural education in a pluralistic society* (8th ed.). Upper Saddle River, NJ: Pearson Education.

Good, T. L., & Brophy, J. E. (2000). *Looking in classrooms* (8th ed.). New York: Addison-Wesley Education Publishers.

Goodman, G., & Olivares, V. (2004). Who's at risk? The chaotic world of diverse populations: Critical multicultural conversations. Cresskill, NJ: Hampton Press.

Gordon Equal Opportunity Office. (2009). *Arab American experience and Middle Eastern culture.* Retrieved June 14, 2009, from http://www.gordon.army.mil/eoo/arab.htm

Hakuta, K. (1985). Mirror of language: The debate on bilingualism. New York: Basic Books.

Harrow, A. (1972). A taxonomy of educational objectives: Handbook III, psychomotor domain. New York: McKay.

Hays, D. G., & Chang, C. Y. (2003). White privilege, oppression, and racial identity development: Implications for supervision. *Counselor Education and Supervision, 43*, 134–144.

Heacox, D. (1991). *Up from under-achievement: How teachers, students, and parents can work together to promote student success.* Minneapolis, MN: Free Spirit Publishing, Inc.

Hmong Tribune Newspaper (2008). Hmong in Census 2000. Fresno, CA.

Hoover, M. R., & Taylor, O. (1987). Bias in reading tests for Black language speakers: A sociolinguistic perspective. *Negro Educational Review, 38*(2–3), 81–98.

Horn, L., Chen, X., & Adelman, C. (1998, May). *Toward resiliency: At-risk students also make it to college.* Washington, DC: U.S. Department of Education, Office of Education Research and Improvement.

Howard, T. C. (2001). Telling their side of the story: African American students' perceptions of culturally relevant teaching. *Urban Review, 33*(2), 131–148.

Howe, A. C. (2002). *Engaging children in science* (3rd ed.). Upper Saddle River, NJ: Pearson Education.

Hubbard, L., & Mehan, H. (1999). Scaling up an untracking program: A co-constructed process. *Journal of Education for Students Placed At-Risk, 4*(1), 83–100.

Huffman, F. E., & Proum, I. (1978). *English-Khmer dictionary.* New Haven, CT: Yale University Press.

Hussar, W. J., & Gerald, D. E. (1998). *Projection of education statistics to 2008.* Washington, DC: National Center for Education Statistics.

Ichioka, Y. (1988). *The Issei: The world of the first generation Japanese Immigrants, 1885–1924.* New York: Free Press.

Jensen, A. R. (1969), How much can we boost IQ and scholastic achievement? *Harvard Educational Review, 39,* 1–122.

Kim, B. L. (1978). *The Asian-American: Changing patterns, changing needs.* Montclair, NJ: Association of Korean Christian Scholars in North America.

Kirk, S.A. (1962). *Educating exceptional children.* Boston: Houghton Mifflin.

Kitano, M. K., & Perkins, C. O. (2000). Gifted European American women. *Journal of the Education of the Gifted, 23*(3), 288–310.

Kohlberg, L. (1969). Stage and sequence: The cognitive development approach to socialization. In D.A. Goslin (ed.), *Handbook of socialization theory and research.* Chicago: Rand McNally.

Kossak, S. (1980). District court ruling on non-standard dialects needs cautious interpretation. *Phi Delta Kappan, 61*(9), 617–619.

Kounin, J. (1970). *Discipline and group management in classrooms.* New York: Holt, Rinehart, and Winston.

Krathwohl, D., Bloom, B., & Masia, B. (1964). *Taxonomy of educational objectives: Handbook II, affective domain.* New York: McKay.

Kuehn, P. A. (1996). *Assessment of academic literacy skills: Preparing minority and LEP students for postsecondary education.* Washington, DC: U.S. Department of Education.

Lange, C. M., & Lehr, C. A. (1999). At-risk students attending second chance programs: Measuring performance in desired outcome domains. *Journal of Education for Students Placed At-Risk, 4*(2), 173–192.

Lee, C. (1975). The United States immigration policy and the settlement of Koreans in America. *Korean Observers, 6*(2).

Lee-Pierce, M. L., Plowman, T. S., & Touchston, D. (1998). Starbase-Atlantis, a school without walls: A comparative study of an innovative science program for at-risk urban elementary students. *Journal of Education for Students Placed At-Risk, 3*(3) 223–235.

Lesikar, R. V., Flatley, M. E., & Rentz, K. (2008). *Business communication: Making connections in a digital world.* Boston: McGraw-Hill.

Lessow-Hurley, J. (2000). *The foundations of dual language instruction* (3rd ed.). New York: Addison Wesley Longman.

Litton, E. F. (1999). Learning in America: The Filipino-American sociocultural perspective. In C. C. Park & M. M. Y. Chi (Eds.), *Asian-American education: Prospects and challenges* (pp. 131–153). Westport, CT: Bergin & Garvey.

Llamson, T. A. (1978). *Handbook of Philippine language groups.* Quezon City, Philippines: Ateneo de Manila University Press.

Loide, M. (1994). *The CLAD and BCLAD examination book I/II.* Sacramento, CA: Praxis Publishing.

Lyu, I. Y. (1977). Korean nationalist activities in Hawaii and the continental U.S., 1900–1975: Part I: 1900–1919, *Amerasia Journal, 4*(1).

Macaranas, F. M. (1983). Socioeconomic issues affecting the education of minority groups: The case of Filipino Americans. In D. T. Nakanishi & M. Hirano-Nakanishi (Eds.), *The education of Asian and Pacific Americans: Historical perspectives and prescriptions for the future.* Phoenix, AZ: Oryx Press.

Macias, R. F., & Kelly, C. (1996). *Summary report of the survey of the states' limited English proficient students and available educational programs and services 1994–1995.* Washington, DC: National Clearinghouse for Bilingual Education.

Manning, L. M, & Baruth, L. G. (2009). *Multicultural education of children and adolescents* (5th ed.). New York: Pearson Education.

Manning, L. M., & Bucher, K. T. (2007). *Classroom management: Models, applications, and cases* (2nd ed.). Princeton, NC: Merrill.

Marx, K., & Engels, F. (1848). *The Communist Manifesto* (1955 ed.). New York: Appleton.

Maslow, A. (1954). *Motivation and personality.* New York: Harper and Row.

McLaren, P. (1998). *Life in schools: An introduction to critical pedagogy in the foundations of education.* Los Angeles, CA: Longman.

McNamara, B. E. (2007). *Learning disabilities: Bridging the gap between research and classroom practice.* Upper Saddle River, NJ: Pearson Education.

McQueen, A. (1999, September 14). Law not protecting children from inequities in learning standards, group says. *Fresno Bee,* p. A5.

Menken, K., & Look, K. (2000). Making chances for linguistically and culturally diverse students. *Education Digest,* 65(8), 14–19.

Mercer, C. D., & Pullen, P.C. (2005). *Students with learning disabilities* (6th Ed.). Upper Saddle River, New Jersey: Merrill/Prentice Hall.

Michels, R. (1962). *Political Parties.* (E. Paul & C. Paul, Trans.) New York: Free Press. (Original work published 1915).

Miller, L. (2007, July 30). American dreamers. *Newsweek,* p. 24–33.

Miller, R.A. (1967). *The Japanese language.* Chicago: University of Chicago Press.

Miranda, A., Halsell, S., & Debarone, M. (1991). *A model for interventions with low achieving minority students.* Washington, DC: National Association of School Psychologists.

Montgomery, D. (2001). Increasing Native American Indian involvement in gifted programs in rural schools. *Psychology in the Schools, 38,* 467–474.

Murry, C., & Herrnstein, R. (1994). *The bell curve: The reshaping of American life by differences in intelligence.* New York: Free Press.

National Center for Health Statistics. (2002). *Marriage and divorce statistics.* Washington, DC: U.S. Census Bureau.

356   *Educational Psychology of Methods in Multicultural Education*

National Institute for the Education of At-Risk Students. (1998). *Facts about limited English proficient students*. Washington, DC: U.S. Department of Education.

Negro Educational Review. April-July 1992.

Nel, J. (1994). Preventing school failure: The Native American child. *Clearing House, 67*, 170–173.

Newman, C., & Ralston, K. (2006). *Profiles of participants in the national school lunch program*. Washington, DC: U.S. Department of Agriculture.

Nieto, S. (1992). *Affirming diversity: The sociopolitical context of multicultural education*. White Plains, NY: Longman.

North Central Regional Educational Laboratory. (1999). *At-risk students* (technical report). Washington, DC: U.S. Department of Education.

Oakes, J. (1990). *Multiplying inequalities: The effect of race and social class and tracking on opportunities to learn mathematics and science*. Santa Monica, CA: RAND.

Oakes, J. (1992). Can tracking research inform practice? Technical, normative and political considerations. *Educational Researcher, 21*(12), 12–22.

Oakes, J., Gamoran, A., & Page, R. (1992). Curriculum differentiation: Opportunities, outcomes, and meanings. In P. Jackson (Ed.), *Handbook of research on curriculum* (pp. 583–605). New York: Macmillan.

Ogbu, J. U. (1978). Minority education and caste: *The American system in cross-cultural perspective*. New York: Academic Press.

O'Malley, J. M. (1992). Response to Jack Damico's presentation *Proceedings of the Second National Research Symposium on Limited English Proficient Student Issues*. Washington, DC: U.S. Department of Education.

Orfield, G. (1993). *The growth of segregation in American schools: Changing patterns of separation and poverty since 1968*. A report of the Harvard Project on School Desegregation to the National School Boards Association. Cambridge, MA: Harvard University.

Origins of the names of U.S. States. (1997). *World Almanac and book of facts 1998*. New York: Simon and Schuster.

Ovando, C. J., Combs, M. C., & Collier, V. P. (2006). *Bilingual and ESL classrooms: Teaching in multicultural contexts* (4th ed.). New York: McGraw-Hill.

Parette, H.P., & Petch-Hogan, B. (2000). Approaching families. *Teaching exceptional children, 33*(2), 4–9.

Park, C. C., & Chi, M. M. Y. (1999). *Asian-American education: Prospects and challenges*. Westport, CT: Bergin & Garvey.

Perkins-Gough, D. (2007). Focus on adolescent English language learners. *Educational Leadership, 64*(6), 90–91.

Piaget, J. (1952). *The child's conception of number*. London: Routledge & Kegan Paul.

Ponce, D. E. (1980). Introduction: The Philippine background. In J. F. McDermott, Jr., W. Tseng, & T. W. Maretzki (Eds.), *People and cultures of Hawaii: A psycho-cultural profile*. Honolulu: John A. Burns School of Medicine and the University Press of Hawaii.

Portman, T. A., & Herring, R. (2001). Debunking the Pocahontas paradox: The need for a humanistic perspective. *Journal of Humanistic Counseling, Education and Development, 40*, 186–198.

Posner, George J. (1995). *Analyzing the curriculum*. New York: McGraw-Hill.

Reyes, O., & Jason, L. A. (1993). Pilot study examining factors associated with academic success for Hispanic high school students. *Journal of Youth and Adolescence, 22* (12), 60–71.

Rice, D., & Zigmond, N. (2000). Co-teaching in secondary schools. *Learning Disabilities Research and Practices, 15*, 190–197.

Rogers, C. (1967). Learning to be free. In C. Rogers & B. Stevens (Eds.), *The problem of being human*. Lafayette, CA: Real Property Press.

Ryan, K., & Cooper, J. M. (2001). *Those who can, teach* (9th ed.). New York: Houghton Mifflin.

Sanders, G. (2004). Is special ed becoming a place to dump minorities? *California Educator, 8* (7).

Schofield, J. (1991). School desegregation and intergroup relations. *Review of Research in Education, 6* (17), 335–409.

Scourby, A. (1984). *The Greek Americans*. Boston: Twayne.

Sedlacek, W. E., & Kim, S. H. (1995, January). Multi-cultural assessment, *ERIC Digest*. (ERIC Document Reproduction Service No. ED 391112)

Shorr, A. A., & Horn, J. E. (1997). They said it couldn't be done: Implementing a career academy program for a diverse high school population. *Journal of Education for Students Placed At-Risk, 4*(4), 379–391.

Simmons, E. A. (1991). Ain't we never gonna study no grammar? *English Journal, 80*(8), 48–51.

Siu, S. F. (1996). *Asian-American students at-risk: A literature review*. (Report No. 8). Baltimore, MD: Center for Research on the Education of Students Placed At Risk.

Skinner, B. F. (1974). *About behaviorism*. New York: Knopf.

Slavin, R. E., Karweit, N. L., & Madden, N. A. (1989). *Effective programs for students at-risk*. Boston: Allyn & Bacon.

Sleeter, C. E. (2005). *Un-standardizing curriculum: Multicultural teaching in the standards-based classroom*. New York: Teachers College Press.

Steele, C. (1992). Race and the schooling of Black Americans. *Atlantic Monthly, 4* (4), 69–78.

Stein, L. (1995, July). Reading, writing, and phonics coming back to California schools. *Christian Science Monitor, 6*, p. 3.

Stotsky, S. (1979). Teaching the vocabulary of academic discourse. *Journal of Basic Writing, 2* (7), 15–39.

Sung, B. (1967). *The story of the Chinese in America*. New York: Collier Books.

Thomas, W. & Collier, V. (1997). *School effectiveness for language minority students*. Retrieved August 15, 2009, from Ohio Department of Education http:// www.ode.state.oh.us

Training Center for Indochinese Paraprofessionals, Boston University School of Social Work. (1982). (1982). *A mutual challenge: Training and learning with the Indochinese in social work*. Boston: Boston University School of Social Work.Tugent, A. (1986). Youth issues in prominence on national agenda. *Education Week, 6*(9), 13.

Um, K. (1999). Scars of war: Educational issues and challenges for Cambodian-America students. In C. C. Park & M. M. Y. Chi (Eds.), *Asian-American education: Prospects and challenges* (pp. 263–284). Westport: Bergin & Garvey.

U.S. Census Bureau. (1997). *International data base: The world factbook*. Washington, DC: Author.

U.S. Census Bureau. (2000a). *Census 2000 Demographic profile highlights*. Summary Files 1–4. Washington, DC: Author.

U.S. Census Bureau. (2000b). *Profile of select social characteristics*. Retrieved August 15, 2009, from http://www.census.gov

U.S. Census Bureau. (2005). *American Community Survey*. Washington, DC: Author.

U.S. Census Bureau. (2006). *Statistical abstract of the United States*. Washington, DC: U.S. Government Printing Office.

U.S. Department of Agriculture. (2006). *Characteristics of Food Stamp Households: Fiscal Year 2005* (Report FSP-06-CHAR). Washington, DC: Author.

U.S. Department of Education (1998). Richard W. Riley, "Secretary's Statement on Religious Expression" Washington, DC, retrieved from http://www.ed.gov/inits/ religionand-schools

Vang, A. T. (1999). Hmong-American students: Challenges and opportunities. In C. C. Park & M. M. Y. Chi (Eds.), *Asian-American education: Prospects and challenges* (pp. 219–236). Westport: Bergin & Garvey.

Vang, C. T. (2001). *Histories and academic profiles of successful and unsuccessful Hmong secondary students.* Unpublished doctoral dissertation, University of California, Davis and California State University, Fresno.

Vangay, J. (2004). *Unique problems and opportunities within the Southeast Asian family: Critical multicultural conversations*. Cresskill, NJ: Hampton Press.

Vincente & Associates. (1990). *Planning for diversity*. Davis, CA: University of California.

Vosniadou, S. (2001). *How children learn* [Educational Practice Series 7]. Brussels, Belgium: International Academy of Education.

Vygotsky, L. S. (1978). *Mind in society. The development of higher psychological processes*. Cambridge, MA: Harvard University Press.

Weinberg, M. (1977). A chance to learn: *A history of race and education in the United States.* New York: Cambridge University Press.

Weiss, M. P., & Lloyd, J. W. (2002). Congruence between roles and actions of secondary special educators in co-taught and special education settings. *Journal of Special Education, 36* (2), 58–68.

Wells, A., & Grain, R. (1994). Perpetuation theory and the long-term effects of school desegregation. *Review of Educational Research, 64* (13), 53–76.

Weslander, D., & Stephany, G. V. (1983). Evaluation of an English as a Second Language program for Southeast Asian students. *TESOL Quarterly, 17*, 473–480.

Williford, David (1992). A "pin" is not a "pen"; is a "pan"? Is southern pronunciation incorrect? *English Journal, 77*(6), 25–28.

Winfield, L. (1986). Teacher beliefs toward at-risk students in inner-urban schools. *The Urban Review*, 18: 253–266.

Wingfield, M., & Karaman, B. (1995). Arab stereotypes and American education. *Social Studies and Young Learners, 7*(4), 7–11.

Wojdacz, M. (2009). *What's the real status of divorce in America?* Retrieved on June 15, 2009, from http://www.legalzoom,com/legal-articles

Wong Fillmore, L. (1985). Second language learning in children: A proposed model. In R. Eshch & J. Provinzano (Eds.), *Issues in English language development* (pp. 33–41). Rosslyn, VA: National Clearinghouse for Bilingual Education.

Wright, R. (1997). *A study of the academic language of college-bound at-risk secondary students.* Unpublished doctoral dissertation, Joint Doctoral Program in Educational Leadership, University of California, Davis/California State University, Fresno.

Yamano, T. K. (1994). *Brooding silence: A cross-generational study of informal learning socialization and child rearing practices in a Japanese American family*. Doctoral dissertation, University of California, Los Angeles.

Zehr, M. A. (2000). Un dia nuevo for schools: Overview. *Education Week, 20*(10), 1.

Index

Critical Pedagogical Perspectives

Greg S. Goodman, *General Editor*

Educational Psychology: Critical Pedagogical Perspectives is a series of relevant and dynamic works by scholars and practitioners of critical pedagogy, critical constructivism, and educational psychology. Reflecting a multitude of social, political, and intellectual developments prompted by the mentor Paulo Freire, books in the series enliven the educator's process with theory and practice that promote personal agency, social justice, and academic achievement. Often countering the dominant discourse with provocative and yet practical alternatives, *Educational Psychology: Critical Pedagogical Perspectives* speaks to educators on the forefront of social change and those who champion social justice.

For further information about the series and submitting manuscripts, please contact:

Dr. Greg S. Goodman
Department of Education
Clarion University
Clarion, Pennsylvania
ggoodman@clarion.edu

To order other books in this series, please contact our Customer Service Department at:

(800) 770-LANG (within the U.S.)
(212) 647-7706 (outside the U.S.)
(212) 647-7707 FAX

Or browse online by series at:

www.peterlang.com